FREE MOVEMENT OF LEGAL IDEAS

This seminal book develops a new perspective on the debate concerning the Europeanisation of private law.

The theory is both realistic, building on existing experience, and normative as it focuses on the future. It outlines 'good' Europeanisation in which legal sources can be used across borders; hence the free movement of legal ideas. At its core, is the analysis of the legal consequences of growing societal uncertainty and increasing use of micro-politics, leading to a situation where the law develops through small narratives rather than according to a coherent master plan. The inevitable rule of law concerns around such a development, have to be addressed by transparent legal reasoning.

The author masterfully illustrates how this can be achieved in decision-making across Europe, drawing on arguments, which are both substantive and authoritative in nature. He shows how all legal actors, including decision-makers and scholars, are morally responsible for the choices made. This is a fascinating intervention in the field of European private law by one of its leading authorities.

The Future of Private Law

Series Editors

Marija Bartl, Anna Beckers, Simon Deakin, Daniel Markovits, and Hans-W Micklitz

A new wave of scholarship is remaking and invigorating private law. Legal regimes that were long understood as invisible systems of technical rules governing purely private relations are being reconsidered in their social, economic, and political context. This scholarly trend interacts with three major developments in 20th century private law. First, private law itself has undergone a series of fundamental transformation. Openly public and political values were inserted into private law regimes both before and immediately after 1945, only to be rejected in favour of a purported re-privatisation of law and society alike in the heyday of neoliberalism. Neoliberalism itself is now subject to increasingly intense critique, under the mounting pressure of multiple social and environmental crises. Second, private law has had to respond to fundamental transformations in the global economy, which have simultaneously placed inherited legal orders under economic and political pressure, and denaturalized previously unquestioned doctrinal arrangements. And, third, private law has been challenged by the call for and recognition of legal pluralism as a constitutive feature of legal systems.

Legislatures and courts, responding to these forces, have relied on private law to achieve openly moral ends, such as social justice, gender and ethnic equality, and more recently, sustainability, climate change and intergenerational justice, as well as adaptation to a digitalized economy and society. Scholars have similarly begun to observe the regulatory character of private law, its connection to public values, and even its 'constitutionalisation'. These developments blur the boundaries between what has been perceived as the 'classical' private law of the nineteenth century and the new regulatory private law of the twentieth. Along the way, they are redefining the relation between private law, societal values, and political objectives. Even 'classical', formal, or, as it is sometimes labelled, 'neutral' private law, is becoming inflected with political objectives. The possibility that the basic concepts that traditional private law scholarship deploys could themselves be related to hegemonies based on race, gender, or class, or the outcome of colonial imaginaries and interests, only reinforces the importance of unmasking the supposedly neutral or technical quality of private law. All these developments suggest that private law will in the future become even more clearly interwoven with normative objectives and societal claims. The question of which values will infuse private law therefore becomes unavoidable.

Changes in the economic regime that private law governs – both domestically and at a global scale – are reinforcing the need for new approaches. Within countries, private actors (including civil society organisations, trade and industry groups, and even individual firms) have gained the power to influence law-making and legal enforcement, and to create their own regulatory orders. Private forms of rule-making and administration have therefore become a part of private law, both by constraining the state from making effective law, and by empowering non-state actors to use law as a tool for promoting private interests. Moreover, across countries, a liberal commercial order that once purported to separate international economic law from domestic private law has been displaced by a transnational commercial regime that openly confers on private law a central role in global economic arrangements. Digital technologies, and the new forms of regulation that they enable – including in particular data- and code-driven regimes that fuse legal regulation with technical infrastructure and interfaces – further reinforce these trends. These new forms of digital governance threaten the state's traditional monopoly over legal regulation, while breaking down the legal categories through which private law has traditionally constrained state over-reach. In short: non-state actors have increasingly used private law for their own increasingly political ends, and states have sought to shape nominally private economic arrangements in order to promote national economic and geopolitical interests. Critical legal scholarship is beginning to expose the ways in which these developments within private law are not simply failing to address inequalities of resources and power, but actively perpetuating them.

Such developments are not entirely new, but they were previously confined to the borders of private law. Now, under new conditions, they appear in a vivid and insistent light. Together, these developments demand a new orientation from private law and place private law scholarship at the centre of the broader development of legal thought. The objective of this series is to publish books that answer this call.

This objective requires the series to embrace a broad understanding of private law, which combines the traditional core of private law with regulatory private law and its interaction with international economic law and legal pluralism. Substantively, the series stresses the need to think through the future of private law and to understand anew its pillars, modules, and institutions, including its most fundamental conceptions of the person, contract, tort, and property. The series will also pay close regard to legal process, by attending to interactions among the several national private law orders and between domestic and transnational law. To this end it will aim to analyse the relationships among different levels of legislation and between law, private regulation and technology. It will also pay close attention to the way private law is made to work in practice through a variety of public and private enforcement mechanisms, on the part not just of the executive and judiciary, but via non-state actors.

Methodologically, the series is committed to exploring the breadth and depth of the challenges private law is facing from the perspective of multiple disciplines. We expect the series to reflect the growing debate about exactly what doctrinal method consists of, as part of which a comparison of legal methods with those of other disciplines is becoming increasingly necessary. Thus not just the paradigms of other disciplines in the human and social sciences, but the methods they typically employ, ranging from statistical and other quantitative approaches to the ethnographies used in fieldwork and the hermeneutic techniques employed in the analysis of texts, will be of interest. Contributions from scholars engaged in critical analysis of inequalities and power relations, associated with race, gender and class among other categories, are among those we particularly welcome, as are contributions from legal researchers engaging with the data sciences across a broad range of applications, including but not limited to those associated with artificial intelligence. Our hope for the series is that it will expand the boundaries of private law scholarship as conventionally understood, while retaining the coherence necessary for private law as both discipline and practice.

Free Movement of Legal Ideas

Towards a Dynamic Europeanisation of Private Law

Thomas Wilhelmsson

•HART•

OXFORD • LONDON • NEW YORK • NEW DELHI • SYDNEY

HART PUBLISHING

Bloomsbury Publishing Plc

Kemp House, Chawley Park, Cumnor Hill, Oxford, OX2 9PH, UK

1385 Broadway, New York, NY 10018, USA

29 Earlsfort Terrace, Dublin 2, Ireland

First published in Great Britain 2024

A catalogue record for this book is available from the British Library.

A catalogue record for this book is available from the Library of Congress.

Library of Congress Control Number: 2024932810

ISBN: HB: 978-1-50997-725-3
ePDF: 978-1-50997-727-7
ePub: 978-1-50997-726-0

Typeset by Compuscript Ltd, Shannon

Preface and Acknowledgements

THIS BOOK HAS a long history. I started writing it during the first decade of the third millennium. Or rather I started writing something that I planned to be quite different from what you now have in your hands. The work started smoothly, boosted by the success we had in obtaining a position as a Centre of Excellence funded by the Academy of Finland. The Centre of Excellence in European Law and Polity led by Kaarlo Tuori (and myself as Vice Chair) was a very fruitful project and would have provided a productive environment in which this book could have been written.

Destiny made other choices, however. I became engaged in university management, and in 2008 was elected Rector and in 2013 Chancellor (in the British sense) of the University of Helsinki. For 10 years, I was engaged in university reform and had no opportunity to participate in the private law debate. I have subsequently struggled to return as an active participant in the field of European legal discourse.

The struggle related not only to the need to absorb the vast amount of new materials that were now available; it also required deeper rethinking. When I left research, the discussions concerning European legal development focused on issues such as the European Constitution and the European Civil Code. Few questioned the optimistic and forward-looking perspective of the European project: the debate only related to how far-reaching the goals should be and what means one should use to achieve those goals. When I returned to the field, I found myself in a completely different world. Brexit and, more generally, rising nationalism and populism, had resulted in an EU with a much more uncertain future that included very pessimistic alternatives. In this new societal context, I had to completely rewrite much of what I had thought and sketched before.

The underlying ethos of what I wanted to write, however, remains. I am still interested in how a legal actor in the field of private law can contribute to building an EU in a way that promotes equality and a just and sustainable society. Can the social and the European be combined in a mode of thinking that recognises the opportunity and responsibility of each legal actor to contribute to the shaping of a better world?

During my career as a legal scholar, I have continuously struggled with these kinds of questions. I have in part been able to lean on my earlier work. Some of the chapters build on ideas and sometimes even repeat some parts of my earlier publications.[1] This book, however, is not merely a collection of past ideas combined with some new

[1] See in particular Wilhelmsson (2001), (2002), (2004), (2005), (2007), (2008) and (2014).

ones. It is an attempt to build a 'theory' of a social and dynamic Europeanisation of private law that includes some of my previous thoughts. In this sense, it is a legal autobiography.

With this aim, the main contribution of the book lies in the way the different parts are tied together and in the structure of the reasoning as a whole. Many of the detailed issues in the various chapters have been analysed deeply by other thinkers. I have gathered inspiration from many quarters and from many schools of thought. In this volume, I have attempted to show how I have combined these sources of inspiration in my understanding of the development of private law in the EU today. Primarily, I have written this book for those who are interested in the debate concerning the Europeanisation of private law.

Although this book builds on past experiences, its primary perspective is the future. It presents an approach that at least in some cases has been realised in concrete legal life. The coming decades will show whether this kind of thinking can become more mainstream, or whether it was just a luxury of an era that eroded with the return of nationalism and the war in Ukraine.

I feel grateful to many institutions and scholars both in Finland and in Europe at large who have supported me in writing this book. The Faculty of Law at the University of Helsinki has provided the necessary infrastructure and a positive working environment. The discussions within our Centre of Excellence in European Law and Polity have deepened my thoughts in many ways. Many European colleagues in various groups have had a similar impact. As a list of acknowledgements could easily fill many pages, I will limit myself to a general but still heartfelt thanks. Here I will only mention those who have read my manuscript and commented on it, namely my old friends Geraint Howells, Hans-W Micklitz and Kaarlo Tuori. Both your encouraging words and your many insightful critical comments have been extremely valuable.

I was privileged to be able to complete work on the book as a visiting scholar at the European University Institute in Florence. The two months that I spent at the EUI helped to improve the quality of the manuscript in many ways. The Finnish Society of Sciences and Letters supported my stay in Florence.

I would also like to thank Docent Emeritus Mark Shackleton who has carefully and diligently checked the language of the most important chapters of this book.

Last but not least, I thank my sons, Niklas, Alex, Alvar and Elias, for their emotional support during turbulent times.

Thomas Wilhelmsson
Helsinki, May 2023.

Contents

1

Setting the Tune

THE ISSUE OF harmonisation and codification of European private law has been topical in legal policy discourses in Europe since the 1990s. Starting as a specialist discussion, mainly driven by academics working in the area of comparative law, in the present century it also attracted more attention from the European Union (EU) policymakers, and as a consequence the discourse expanded to include experts on (national) substantive areas of law as well. At present, there is an abundance of literature on the subject.[1] At the start of this century the debate predominantly related to the issue of codification. However, after the completion of the Draft Common Frame of Reference[2] and its failure to advance in the legislative process, the goals and the focus of discussion have become more modest. Both practical and theoretical winds have been blowing against the codification project.

Against this background of the debate, one could expect this book to offer yet another attempt to look at the development of the structure of and legal strategies behind an emerging European[3] private law. However, the purpose of the book is simultaneously broader and narrower than this.

The perspective is broader, as the book is intended to reach beyond the present discussions concerning techniques of harmonisation and Europeanisation of private law. My aim is to build an approach to the idea of Europeanisation of private law that is related to the special features which are characteristic of contemporary late modern society rather than to the advantages and disadvantages of various legislative techniques. This requires a both a broader and a deeper look at the needs and pressures related to private law in general in contemporary society.

On the other hand, the perspective is narrower in the sense that the goal is not to formulate a comprehensive theory of European private law. I will instead attempt to show how the fragmented character of legal change in late modern Europe broadens the opportunities for many kinds of developmental narratives that proceed in different directions, some for good and some less desirable (depending on the preconceptions of the evaluator).

[1] The 'classic' in the field is probably Hartkamp et al (2011). The first academic reactions to the intervention of the Commission are well documented in Grundmann and Stuyck (2002). I have myself written an earlier book on the issue in the 1990s: Wilhelmsson (1995).

[2] See DCFR (2009).

[3] In this volume I use 'Europe' and 'European' to refer to the Member States of the EU.

In such a perspective one cannot avoid the question what lawyers can and should do. What is the role of a good legal professional in this societal context? Answering these questions requires an analysis of the use of Europeanised private law in a field constituted by law, power and micro-politics. What tools does fragmented Europeanisation offer law to help it fulfil its mission as a counterbalance to (other) power? In what way can comparative law function as a means of legal (dogmatic) critique? Or, put more generally: How can the social and the European perspectives be fruitfully combined in today's uncertain and fragmented society?

The contemporary pace of social change makes an analysis of the societal needs and their reflection in law extremely challenging. I made a similar analysis (in Swedish) concerning late modern liability law in a Nordic setting two decades ago,[4] but European society has changed in many ways since then. These changes have required much rethinking, in an analysis based on societal diagnosis. The rethinking, however, has not meant abandoning the basic fragmentation thesis that I have defended in the past. On the contrary, the fragmentation thesis, as well as the ethical demands placed on legal professionals, may even be more on point in Europe today than two decades ago. The deeper ideological and ethical cleavages, the decline of the belief in expertise and media, and the revival of nationalism in various forms have shone a light on late modern uncertainty, an uncertainty that used to appear in more subtle forms.

The COVID-19 pandemic took the feeling of societal uncertainty to a higher level and led to the creation of many new experimental private law solutions.[5] This book could be read as a legal-theoretical comment on the pandemic and its private law consequences. 'Real life' has forcefully proven the theses of the book to be relevant. The emerging and spreading of climate change litigation, to some extent in private law form as well,[6] has also added to the topicality of the chosen perspective.

This is also a book on the opportunities for European private law after Brexit. As the reader can see, I have chosen to continue to include UK legal materials and UK actors in the narratives that I describe. This is because common law of the future will have representatives within the EU legal family and because UK law will remain in the European legal sphere, being strongly affected by European law.[7] The main suggestion of this work – a free movement of legal ideas – is not directly ruled out by Brexit, but may continue across the EU–UK border if the receiving legal actors wish to keep this door open. More generally, in a period when the idea of a European civil code sits awkwardly, and when not only Brexit, but other nationalist strategies, aim at discrediting European solutions, it is important to ask what a European-minded

[4] Wilhelmsson (2001), published in Swedish. Chs 2–4 of the present book are partially written on the basis of that volume.

[5] See eg Hondius, Santos Silva, Nicolussi, Coderch, Wendehorst and Zoll (2021); COVID-19- Consumer Law Research Group (2020); and da Rocha, Pepino and Martins (2020). See also ELI Principles for the Covid-19 Crisis (2020) and on them eg Wagner (2020), under the heading 'Corona Law'.

[6] See eg Burgers (2000).

[7] See eg Johnston (2022) and Twigg-Flesner (2022).

legal actor can and should do. What kind of moral responsibility with regard to the European project does a legal actor have?

Originally groups of researchers and journals representing substantive law, EU law and comparative law were the main engines of the debate on the Europeanisation of private law. The phenomenon of European legal integration was at first not clearly visible in the mirrors of mainstream legal theory, either because the scholars saw EC law as just another strand of substantive law that did not give rise to any fundamentally new jurisprudential questions or, on the contrary, they perceived it as so different and difficult to reconcile with prevailing theories of law that it could only be met with silence.[8] The natural addressees of this book would at that stage have been the emerging research community on the Europeanisation of private law, and it is indeed still the primary audience. However, legal theory soon realised the peculiar nature of the Europeanisation, as well as the globalisation,[9] of law, and the need to rethink traditional perspectives, like the theory of legal sources,[10] in light of new legal phenomena. Nowadays the legal-theoretical foundations for a discourse on Europeanised law have been firmly established, often in an interaction between legal theory and substantive areas of legal study.[11] This study continues such interaction by presenting a societally founded approach to European private law. It offers a particular perspective on the methodology of the Europeanisation of private law.

I. THESIS: FRAGMENTATION

In private law, the debate on European harmonisation has to a great extent focused on issues related to system-building, and more broadly, to legal culture.

One strand of the discussion concerns the level of (legal) cultural homogeneity required to make real harmonisation of law possible. Various views have been expressed, ranging from those who see the cultural differences, in particular between common law and continental law, as so deep-rooted that 'no converging' of the systems can be assumed,[12] to those who stress that private law 'is not folklore'[13] and therefore can be harmonised, despite cultural differences.

Another strand of the discussion looks at the consequences of Europeanisation for the systematic structure of private law. Here one usually finds scholars deploring the unsystematic nature of European interventions, resulting in what somewhat poetically has been called a 'hamburger-, nasigoreng- and pommes-legal culture'.[14] The solutions offered to this perceived problem of a lack of system point in two

[8] See eg Ward (1996: 94): 'European jurisprudence is "silent" because any crisis of identity and meaning, as Derrida repeatedly observes, creates a silence.'

[9] Already early: Twining (2000).

[10] See eg Nielsen (1996) and on the reasoning of the European Court of Justice, Bengoetxea (1993).

[11] See eg the very comprehensive analysis of various aspects of European legal methodology in Riesenhuber (2017).

[12] Legrand (1996).

[13] Lando (2000: 61) (concerning contract law).

[14] Schneider (1991: 1993).

directions. Some seek the right answer in less European private law, keeping the systems of the national laws as intact as possible. Others wish for more European law, of a qualitatively different nature. In the latter view, the right cure for the lack of system might be a European codification that would create a new European system of its own.

In other words, the discourse on Europeanisation and harmonisation of private law, in very broad terms, has produced two categories of answers related to the question of how one should develop the systematic structure of private law. Both the adherents to the 'not converging thesis' and many of those presenting a 'nasigoreng-critique' emphasise the need to defend national legal systematics in the face of the disintegrative force of EU law. Others, just as vehemently, defend the ideal of a common European structure that would cure both the substantive fragmentation and the territorial fragmentation of European legal space, divided as it is into greatly differing national systems. It is easy to see that both groups of answers seem to build more or less closely on the assumption that the systematic structure and internal coherence of law carry a strong positive value. The aim to develop or retain a systematic and coherent structure of private law has a very high priority in the discourse on Europeanisation.

In this book, I approach the issue of Europeanisation from a different angle. I will not deny the positive value of systematisation and coherence, but I will argue that this value is mostly grossly overemphasised. In the process of the Europeanisation of private law, one cannot and should not prioritise the systematic coherence of private law as much as many tend to do in the prevailing discourse. On the contrary, in my analysis 'fragmentation' is the keyword. I will link a fragmented Europeanisation with a general trend towards fragmentation of law. In other words, I defend a Europeanisation that acknowledges and uses the unsystematic and flexible features of law, namely an experimental European law based on a free movement of legal doctrines and solutions.[15] My approach is in line with the relatively few voices that have defended more fragmented visions within the process of harmonisation.[16]

My thesis concerning the fragmentation of European private law is both empirical and normative. As I see it, there are tendencies in late modern society in general, as well as in the EU as a late modern state-like creation in particular, which make a stronger fragmentation of law more or less inevitable. Many may agree with this as an accurate description of societal facts. However, I will take a step further in a normative direction. I do not condemn the process towards more fragmentation as something inherently and by necessity negative. Although system and coherence to some extent and in some contexts most certainly are valuable, fragmentation and freedom from rigid systematic structures have their merits as well. I will explore the positive side of the fragmentation related to Europeanisation and defend a view according to which it is important to retain a certain pluralism and fragmentation within private law.

[15] My first sketches in this direction were published in Swedish in Wilhelmsson (2001a) and in English in Wilhelmsson (2002).

[16] Early eg Smits (2002).

This goes not only for a period of change from a national to a European perspective, but also within a more permanently established European private law, if such a state is ever achieved.

In the codification discourse, the front lines were sometimes described in terms of a clash between backward-looking nationalists, who defend their national system, and future-minded European codifiers, who actively participate in shaping a new united Europe. Some participants in the debate indeed fit relatively well into this dichotomy. A language that speaks about nationalism in private law is by no means out of tune with reality.[17] Probably some of the opponents against a European codification are at least subconsciously driven by the typical lawyer's fallacy of seeing one's own law as qualitatively superior. It might even be that such a nationalist perspective on law is gradually growing stronger, as more crude forms of nationalist political ideology gain ground in various quarters of Europe.

To my mind, however, the dichotomy between nationalist opponents and European-minded supporters of European codification is false, as it excludes the possibility of choosing a European, or even a globalist approach to law, without committing oneself to the idea of comprehensive codification. In fact, the perspective on European private law that I will present escapes the dichotomy mentioned above – and I would certainly not like to be compartmentalised with the contemporary European-hostile nationalist movements just for being reluctant to applaud a European codification. I am presenting a third kind of solution which opposes strict and comprehensive legal structures, such as a European civil code, at the European level and at the same time argues for a radical lowering of the national legal borders within the EU. Even though I view the idea of a comprehensive European codification with suspicion, I am not advocating the (re)degradation of law into a nationalist *Landesjurisprudenz*,[18] but rather supporting a European legal approach that is more in line with the nature of the EU as a new kind of late modern state-like structure. I claim that it is perfectly possible to take a positive stance towards the process of deepening the integration of the EU without committing oneself to the vision of a comprehensive, harmonised and systematic European law. As an alternative to this vision I advocate a free movement of legal ideas across internal borders. If it were used to its full potential, it would amount to a radical form of Europeanisation.

Much of the debate on the harmonisation or codification of European private law is on the surface purely legal in terms of arguments and visions. Society, and the role of law in society, often becomes visible only in the form of commercial needs. From a societal point of view, the usual question is whether the differences between the legal systems of the Member States create barriers to trade and hamper the cross-border working of businesses within the Union. More basic perspectives, like the role and development of law in late modern society and their impact on harmonisation

[17] On nationalism in European private law, see eg the papers published in *European Review of Contract Law* 3/2012, as well as Comparato (2014), discussing also 'Euronationalism' (229 *et seq*). Hesselink (2021) ch 4 discusses contract law nationalism, Europeanisation and globalism in the context of various political philosophies.

[18] Paraphrasing Rudolf von Ihering's well-known complaints about developments during his time.

and codification processes, are often neglected. Some have compared the European harmonisation movement of this century to the German legal unification process in the nineteenth century and the debates between codifiers and cultivators,[19] between Thibaut and Savigny,[20] without questioning whether our society and our time really are sufficiently similar to make such comparisons convincing. The role and function of law in late modern society may be different from what it was during the period of building the modern bourgeois society and market economy. Therefore, in this book I attempt to analyse Europeanisation in relation to a diagnosis of late modern society and an analysis of the consequences of this diagnosis for the role and function of law. Through societal diagnosis I want to show that the emphasis on fragmentation is not only connected with surface-level processes of Europeanisation in the EU's present state of existence, but also with deeper changes in the role and function of law in late modern society.

A particular strand of contemporary societal diagnosis focuses on the role and nature of the EU itself. Its appearance as a new kind of 'post-modern state'[21] – or, as I would prefer to call it, a late modern state-like structure – raises the question whether this as such requires a new approach to private law. The recognition of the 'multi-level structure' of European private law[22] has indeed changed the perspective on its fundamentals in a more pluralist direction. Fragmentation may be as natural a phenomenon for the EU as codification was for (many of) the national states in the nineteenth century.

In legal theory, therefore, various pluralist visions on European law[23] offer a natural source of inspiration for this work. The fragmentation thesis has many points of contact with legal theories questioning the 'top-down' conception of law that places the state or the Union in the centre of the legal universe.[24] In these theories the radically new governing structures of Europe are reflected in new ways of understanding law and its development. The traditional strongly state-centred and hierarchic (Kelsenian) conception of law is considered untenable in a situation in which law production has become much more pluralist and multi-centred. In the present work, my focus is on legal actors, some acquiring their participatory role from the Union or from the state, others from the academic community, and some from more private sources.

As is well known, the discourse around the theme of 'law decoupled from the state' has also been intense in a broader, global perspective, one catchword being 'transnational law'.[25] As my perspective is on Europe, I will not engage in that debate, even though it has been inspirational for me.

[19] Lando (2000: 65).

[20] Lando (2000a: 359).

[21] See already eg Caporaso (1996: 44 *et seq*).

[22] See eg Brownsword, Micklitz, Niglia and Weatherill (2011), Pt III.

[23] See already eg Arnaud (1991), Delmas-Marty (2002) and Tontti (2002). See also the collections by Niglia (2013) on pluralism and European private law and Davies and Avbelj (2018) on legal pluralism and EU law in general. V Mak (2020) explores legal pluralism in European contract law.

[24] I have much liked the paper by Schäfer and Bankowski (2003).

[25] Coined already by Jessup (1956). As to contemporary discourse, see eg Maduro, Tuori and Sankari (2014) and Cotterrell and Del Mar (2016).

II. SOLUTION: (GOOD) SMALL NARRATIVES ON LEGAL CHANGE AND FREE MOVEMENT OF LEGAL IDEAS

A study of law can employ different temporal perspectives on its subject. One may, for example, picture law as a cross-section of the content of the norms in a particular area at a particular moment. The scholar presents 'the law in force' as a snapshot that is taken at some precise moment (for example, the day a scholar sent a manuscript to a publisher). Such a static picture of law may serve the needs of some legal actors perfectly well. However, it disregards the dynamic nature of law. Law is constantly changing and evolving, and it is important to acknowledge its dynamics both to be able to understand law and to use it. The perspective adopted in this book emphasises the dynamic features of law.

However, this is not to say that law is in a state of constant flux. Law needs to be static as well as dynamic. A functioning legal order is characterised by both stability and change. Legal certainty requires some kind of stability, whilst the need to adapt law to the development of society requires flexibility and an openness to change. The balancing of change and stability, of a dynamic and a static approach, of 'revolution' and 'evolution'[26] is a key challenge of law. The societal diagnosis on which the analysis is built indicates the growing importance of the dynamic aspects of this balance in contemporary law.

Emphasising the dynamic nature of law, I will picture my contribution to resolving this challenge with the help of the metaphor 'small narratives on legal change'. This metaphor illustrates how law in a certain area or concerning a certain issue moves from one position to another, often in several steps, including legislation, case law, legal writings and other legally significant activities. It pictures how periods of dynamic change in a particular area or even a particular spot of law – the narratives – alternate with more static periods when there is no story to tell. The metaphor of small narratives understood in this way is a useful tool when sketching a positive vision based on the fragmentation thesis. It helps one to see how despite general fragmentation one can find elements of system, coherence and learning in law and what opportunities this creates for the various players on the legal scene. It is an attempt to combine fragmentation with coherence and predictability in a novel way.

I have called the narratives on legal change 'small'. This does not mean that all narratives of this kind would be of legally or societally minor significance. As the example of climate change litigation, which I will return to several times, shows, sometimes legal change narratives have societally or legally an almost revolutionary dimension. I have called the narratives 'small' in order to reflect what I perceive as a lack of a 'grand narrative'. As I will show, there is little linearity in the development of law in late modern society, no great plan that the development of law might follow.

This view on law dissociates itself from the strong belief in system and structure that is typical of legal thinking, especially in its continental forms. The solution,

[26] Papers exemplifying 'revolution and evolution' in private law are published in Worthington, Robertson and Virgo (2018). 'Revolution' here seems to mean paradigmatic or important change.

however, does not imply a plea for a European private law that would develop exclusively in a way that resembles the common law type. The small narratives that I describe may, for example, contain strong elements of scholarly activity that is characteristic for the continental setting. I am focusing not only on the role of courts and case law, but on all legal actors who contribute to the narratives. The vision offered is 'Brexit-proof'.

As I will base the fragmentation thesis both on a general societal diagnosis of Western late modern societies as well as on an analysis of the role and needs of Europeanisation, the small narratives metaphor is both general and European. It is a metaphor relating to late modern law as such[27] and it is only strengthened by the specific structures brought about through the Europeanisation of law. It is not a metaphor that illustrates European private law alone, but it is certainly more convincing in the multi-level European context. In this sense, it is a part of the picture of Europeanised private law.

However, in the European perspective the issue of how the various national legal orders can interact with each other, both directly and via EU law, is a particular and prominent additional challenge. The metaphor of small narratives can also be used to illustrate the various ways of interaction in this context. The legal actors may advance the small narratives by seeking and using legal sources across national borders. To illustrate such use I will introduce yet another metaphor, the 'free movement of legal ideas'. I advocate the increase of such movement of legal ideas across the borders between the Member States. I offer the metaphor as an answer to the Europeanisation challenge that is in line with the understanding of legal development as a continuous starting and ending of small narratives on legal change. It is based on the vision of the EU as an experimental and learning community in which legal experience can easily be used across the internal borders.

The movement of legal ideas across the borders can happen in many ways. One channel is the national impact of EU law that in turn is based on national experience, another is through national legislative procedures relying on comparative knowledge. From a theoretical-methodological point of view, however, the most interesting and most radical road is the direct cross-border use of foreign materials in case law and scholarly reasoning. When exploring the 'free movement of legal ideas' I will focus in particular on such direct cross-border legal learning.

The main responsibility for using such a perspective must for practical reasons lie on legal scholars. At least in the continental setting they play an important role in promoting small narratives on legal change, and when speaking about the free movement of legal ideas their reasoning is decisive throughout Europe. When I speak about legal reasoning I will therefore include and even emphasise the reasoning found in scholarly writing. I focus on activities that are usually called 'black-letter-law' or 'legal dogmatics', or with a somewhat broader reference (including, eg, comparative law) 'scholarly writing' or 'academic writing'. I use these terms interchangeably.

[27] I have originally developed it with this general focus, but for tort law, in Wilhelmsson (2001) (in Swedish only).

My focus on academic writing also explains why I speak about the movement of legal ideas rather than of legal solutions or legal cases. The learning processes involved in scholarly thinking do not only relate to solutions of particular legal cases and issues, but also to doctrinal concepts and constructions. My vision concerning cross-border inspiration covers both forms of intellectual artefacts.

In principle, the legal phenomena created by the EU can be studied from two perspectives. On the one hand, one may continue the use of a national or domestic approach and ask what implications for national law and national legal method the European materials have or should have. On the other hand, one may place the discursive starting point in Europe, in a perceived or constructed European legal audience, and look for traces or elements of a joint European legal content and method. The perspectives of the small narratives on legal change, however, do not relate to either category only. As the very nature of the small narratives is pluralist and situation-dependent, within this metaphor the distinction between the national and the European collapses. One may tell small narratives on legal change both on the national and on the EU level, as well as by moving across these levels.

As I am particularly interested, however, in the free movement of legal ideas within the EU, I will discuss in detail how legal reasoning in domestic cases or concerning domestic legal issues may learn from legal experience across the borders. In such cases, when I speak about 'national' or 'domestic' law I refer to the law of the court or scholar who is performing the reasoning. I do not relate this national or domestic perspective to any particular Member State, unless I have indicated otherwise.

The picture of legal development as small narratives and free movement of ideas, without any grand master plan, would easily lead to a cynical attitude towards attempts to make moral assessments of legal rules. However, this is not my approach. On the contrary, in a state of uncertainty moral assessment becomes at the same time both more necessary and more difficult. One has to search for 'good small narratives' and avoid the bad ones, without having decisive general criteria for the classification. Because of the missing master plan, the assessment of a small narrative always has to be to some extent contextual.

It would be extremely naïve, however, to believe that fragmented changes would always be for the 'good' (whatever that means). If assessing the 'good' from some kind of welfarist perspective, emphasising rules on the protection of weaker and more vulnerable persons, one cannot assume that small narratives would always or most often proceed in this direction. On the contrary, one might argue that, for example, flexible litigation patterns would tend to favour stronger parties as repeat players and otherwise more resourceful actors.[28] Strict rules may protect the weaker better than an empathetic judge. My point, however, is another. I do not claim that all small narratives are good, but that all legal actors – the legislator, the courts, and, of great importance, legal scholars – have the opportunity to contribute to good narratives in a fragmented and flexible contemporary legal environment. My focus is on the opportunities to do good, and the opportunities to promote Europeanisation in this spirit.

[28] It suffices here to refer to one of the classics, Galanter (1974).

This underlines the personal responsibility of all legal actors to reflect about their moral choices and make those choices consciously, as they cannot make them based on some generally accepted societal master plan. This is a key element in the perspective of law and legal development adopted in this book. Even though one can describe much of the day-to-day legal practice in the terms of relatively formal and detached application of given legal rules in routine cases, there is always some element of moral choice present in the activity as well. The metaphor of small narratives on legal change highlights this element of choice and moral responsibility of legal actors. I will discuss the issue of 'goodness' of small narratives further in chapter three section VI and chapter four section VII.

Questions about societal 'goodness' are often at the forefront in developments pushed by various kinds of micro-political actors that have entered the legal scene. Therefore, I have found the term 'micro-politics' useful to illustrate some of the reasoning presented in this book. By using some examples concerning express micro-political actions, however, I am not signalling any intention to restrict the scope of my reasoning to such cases alone. Most small narratives on legal change are started and continued by more traditional legal and societal actors and many such 'traditional' narratives are also used here as examples.

III. DIAGNOSES OF CONTEMPORARY SOCIETY AS A STARTING POINT

My vision builds on some much-discussed interpretations of general features of contemporary society and its future development. Rather than using detailed empirical knowledge concerning limited questions, I have looked for broader perspectives on the dominant characteristics of societal development. I have taken for my starting point what one could consider a kind of diagnosis of contemporary society – what the Germans call *Zeitdiagnose*.[29] Such diagnoses attempt to look beyond quickly changing fashions and varying public opinions – and therefore also beyond phenomena that can easily be caught empirically – and discuss whether and to what extent one can find features that reflect the nature of our time on a deeper level. Obviously such diagnoses must to a considerable extent be dependent on the specific experience of the persons making them and on their values and utopias. On this level, the empirical and the normative are by necessity mixed. A societal diagnosis offers a visionary understanding that enables us to combine our experience with our empirical knowledge and our values.

In contemporary discourses, diagnoses of society have received much attention. They reflect the task of social science not only to accumulate an ever-growing body of knowledge, but also to implicitly and explicitly mirror contemporary society. Societal diagnoses from the last decades of the twentieth century that have also become well known among a legal audience are, for example, the analyses of the so-called risk society[30] as well as broader descriptions of 'reflexive modernity' and

[29] See eg Reese-Schäfer (1996) and Lichtblau (2017).
[30] Beck (1986) setting the tune.

'post-traditional society'.[31] In a productive tension in relation to these theories on risk and uncertainty, one finds other theories that emphasise the focus on controlling risk in the insurance society.[32] The diagnoses of the information society and its main features are also abundant.[33] All the various analyses of the features of so-called post-modern society contribute interesting observations to our knowledge of our present societal environment. The question concerning the alleged crisis of the welfare state and its evolution towards some form of post-welfare state has also generated an extraordinary number of texts. During the last few decades various versions of 'post-truth' societies related to the decline of democracy and the rise of nationalism and isolationism have occupied an important place in the societal debate. 'Retrotopia'[34] has dominated parts of this discourse. This turn is connected to the effects of technological advancement, to the deep disruption of all spheres of society caused by the simultaneous and interdependent processes of digitalisation and globalisation.[35] The features that dominate the debate in the twenty-first century, however, do not make the diagnoses of the end of the previous century obsolete. On the contrary, they rather affirm and deepen the claims concerning ambivalence and uncertainty in those diagnoses.

Many of those inspiring diagnoses of contemporary society refer to the specific temporal setting and to the features attributed to this setting by using the term 'post-modern'. In some previous papers, I have indeed myself used this term. However, here I have preferred to speak about 'contemporary society' or 'late modern' society, and use the terms 'post-modern' and 'post-modernity' only when referring directly to writings in which these terms are used. This choice of terminology, however, should not be understood as an attempt to dissociate myself from diagnoses of post-modern society that often appear to be rather convincing, and from their legal implications. I have decided to refrain from using the term 'post-modern' for other reasons. First, it is well known that 'post-modern' has been used to signify a large variety of phenomena in contemporary society and culture. Post-modernism obviously has at least a partially different meaning in architecture, the arts and literature and various branches of the social sciences. Sometimes it is associated with a certain method or approach, like deconstruction. Various combinations of 'post-modernisms' and 'modernisms' from different areas are also in use.[36] Those who use a label with such vague and ambiguous meaning obviously run the risk of being associated with writings to which they would not necessarily like to subscribe. Personally, I have been inspired mainly by some sociological (in a wide sense) diagnoses of post-modernity and would like to avoid discussions concerning any broader relationship. Secondly, as the term 'post-modern' seems to be loaded with emotions, it may provoke discussions

[31] Beck, Giddens and Lash (1994) provide a good discussion here.

[32] Ewald (1986) and (1989).

[33] Most attention has probably been attracted by Manuel Castells. Castells (1997), the second volume of his well-known trilogy on the information society, has been most useful in this context.

[34] Bauman (2017).

[35] See eg Downes and Nunes (2014) on big-bang disruption and business survival.

[36] *cf* Kennedy (1997), who in his large *fin de siècle* critique of adjudication calls his approach a 'mpm version of leftism': 'm' stands for cultural modernism and 'pm' for – among other things – post-modern theory (eg 346).

that are not useful in relation to my approach. Debates on 'correct' classifications – is this 'real' Marxism; is that 'typical' neo-liberalism? – that are also easily raised by terms like 'post-modern', are to my mind less interesting than exchanges on views on how convincing the substance of the analysis is. Finally, the use of the term 'post-modern' might produce an impression of a more dramatic break with the past than might be the case. Some may think that one could legitimately speak about a 'post-modern law' only if one could show that not only legal culture but also the common deep structure of modern Western law would have undergone important changes.[37] Although such a requirement for allowing the terminology is not necessarily well-founded – as post-modernity in post-modernist writing indeed has been characterised for example also as 'fully developed modernity', as 'modernity conscious of its true nature'[38] – these doubts can be avoided by speaking about 'contemporary society' or 'late modernity' instead. In a terminology mirroring the societal debates of today, one might in relation to many of the features of contemporary society that could be labelled post-modern more naturally speak about features of a globalised and digitalised society.[39]

Irrespective of how they are identified, the diagnoses of contemporary society referred to in this book have offered important building bricks for the construction of my own view on reality. Diagnoses of this kind, however, cannot alone determine the basis for the analysis. Even though they are diagnoses created by the social sciences, they do not offer knowledge that can be empirically tested in any strict sense. The diagnoses are contributions to the debates on society rather than verifiable scientific 'truths'. However, the fact that the diagnoses have emphasised certain features of contemporary society may be taken as an indication of those features being, so to speak, in the air,[40] even though they are not scientifically proven in any strict sense.

Therefore, when in this work I have used the diagnoses of contemporary society of some more or less well-known social scientists, one should interpret this neither as a blind belief in their 'truth', nor as an attempt to use them as authoritative arguments within a less prepared legal community. They should just be seen as a collection of materials which have given me a considerable measure of inspiration when developing my own understanding of society. It is clear that my own intuition and experience in the last resort have determined the choice of the perspectives. Every author's intuition and societal experience have a major influence on why for that author some diagnoses appear more credible and useful than others.

As I see it, when one discusses broad features of social and legal development there is never merely one 'correct' interpretation of reality. Every understanding is

[37] Tuori (1999) bases his criticism of the idea of a 'post-modern' law on this prerequisite. According to Tuori, as the deep structure of law has not changed one should not speak about a new post-modern law, but rather a coming of age, a final maturation of modern law.

[38] Bauman (1992: 187).

[39] On post-modernism and globalisation in legal theory, see Twining (2000: 194 *et seq*).

[40] For example, the descriptions of the growing role of micro-politics (sub-politics) by Beck, Jameson, Bauman and Castells are astonishingly similar, even though these scholars have used different concepts to describe this phenomenon as well as to make their general diagnoses of society. These diagnoses seem at least partially independent of each other, Castells (1997), for example, does not refer to the other three mentioned scholars.

determined by what features of complex social structures one wants to emphasise and what features one wishes to leave out. We cannot know today what will be called true tomorrow. In all development one is confronted both with lasting, traditional features and with new ones. In an analysis of development one can choose to lay stress either on the traditional or on the new elements. Different choices in this respect necessarily produce different diagnoses.

In this book, I have focused on diagnoses related to change, and on diagnoses that emphasise the new features of contemporary society. This provides me with the tools for analysing possible new features on the legal level. This focus of the work should be borne in mind when reading the conclusions. When I describe an interesting new feature of society and law I do not claim that all societal and legal activity is characterised by this new feature. There are many situations and areas in which traditional approaches may offer more correct descriptions and/or normatively more acceptable solutions than the notions that I put forward here.

The focus of the small narratives metaphor is on legal change. It directs our attention towards new forms of thinking and hard cases, whilst static periods and routine cases are less interesting. This choice of a dynamic perspective is based, on the one hand, on ontological reasons: the focus on change deepens our understanding of what law is and how it functions. On the other hand, the choice is also related to the diagnosis of contemporary society: as society is changing at an ever-faster pace, law has to follow suit. Mechanisms of legal change become ever-more important.

Many of the diagnoses used in this work have a global perspective. They attempt to describe the main features of a contemporary and emerging 'world society'. However, many of them are, obviously, built on Western experience, and this is probably one reason why I have found them compelling, being socialised in Western society myself. From the point of view of this work, the Western bias of the diagnoses is not, however, a problem, as I am discussing the Europeanisation of law.

This focus of the diagnoses is useful to bear in mind when discussing the particular European perspective adopted in this work. I will ask whether, and to what extent, within this Western world, one may speak about a particular 'European way of life' and particular European values. At least for some legal theories, the existence of a joint 'form of life' is a prerequisite for rational legal reasoning.[41] Again, whether a diagnosis could establish the existence or lack of such a form of life depends on the perspective chosen by the author. Looking from inside a defined group, one tends to overemphasise the differences, whilst a glimpse from outside and a comparison with others outside might lead to a focus on internal similarities. When I discuss the European 'way of life', I attempt to adopt the latter perspective. Believing in the idea of Europe, I am assuming the existence of at least some fundamental legal-cultural similarities within the EU.

At the same time, however, the particular legal way of life into which I am socialised influences my reasoning. It is obvious that one can read my Nordic legal and societal experiences at least between the lines of my theoretical edifice. The Nordic

[41] Aarnio (1987: 221 *et seq*).

countries are characterised by a high level of trust,[42] both in courts and in other legal actors, which favours an understanding of law as a tool of social engineering for the benefit of an equal society. As small societies the Nordic countries are also open to learning, innovation and change as well as to influences from across borders. It is easy to see that the metaphors of 'small narratives on legal change' and 'free movement of legal ideas' fit well into such a societal background. In addition, the structure and methodology of Nordic private law that acknowledges the continental understanding of legal sources, including the role of a system-building academia, but nevertheless lacks a civil code of the continental type, obviously leaves greater room for the flourishing of small narratives on change than a strictly codified system of law. However, despite my no-doubt Nordic bias, my aim is to discuss private law in a European perspective. Due to both societal and legal development, described in the later chapters of the book, other European legal orders seem to be developing in a more situation-oriented pragmatic and less formalist direction that brings them closer to the Nordic approach.

I have based my diagnosis of society partially on legal experience. I believe that the legal perspective is valuable as a producer of diagnoses of contemporary society and of visions of its improvement. The study of law offers a method for gaining practical knowledge that one needs to imagine new opportunities.[43] It enables one to connect visionary thinking with the realistic possibilities of contemporary society.

IV. LEGAL REASONING CONCERNING HARD ISSUES

It is self-evident for any lawyer that law is not static. The law continuously undergoes changes, both in detail and concerning broader issues. In the continental perspective, the legal dynamic is primarily created by legislation. Most lawyers know the famous phrase that three words from the legislator can turn whole libraries into maculature.[44] This, however, has not prevented the use of more static perspectives for describing 'the law in force', in particular when there is no legislative activity in the area.

Whilst acknowledging the different roles of the legislator and other legal actors in creating the dynamics of law, one should not overemphasise the differences. Even though legislators can manoeuvre more broadly, they cannot completely step outside the bounded narratives on legal change.[45] On the other hand, such legal actors who do not have as their primary task to issue new norms, like courts and legal scholars, also have a role in the narratives on legal change. I have chosen to direct the limelight predominantly on the latter actors, as I can best demonstrate my focus on the

[42] See eg Svendsen and Svendsen (2015).

[43] *cf* Unger (1996: 1), who claims that legal analysis has a potential 'to become a master tool of institutional imagination in a democratic society'.

[44] So formulated by Julius Hermann von Kirchmann (1802–84).

[45] See the description of the function of various legal actors in ch 4 section V and ch 5 sections II and IV.

dynamic nature of law by analysing the legal reasoning that they perform and should perform. The dynamics of law is best illustrated by the dynamics of legal reasoning. As will be shown later, from the perspective of Europeanisation the role and reasoning of legal scholars is particularly interesting. In this sense, this is a book on legal scholarship.

Looking at law through the lenses of legal reasoning one finds legal dynamism expressed in particular in what is often called 'hard cases'. These are, as defined by Ronald Dworkin, cases in which 'no settled rule dictates a decision either way'.[46]

The distinction between hard cases and easy or routine cases is useful as a tool for describing variations in the spectrum of legal reasoning, though this distinction should not be understood too absolutely. Routine cases are cases in which the available authoritative legal sources clearly designate the solution of the issue. From a continental perspective, the best example would obviously be a situation where the issue at hand is covered by the unambiguous wording of a statute – a situation that Kaarle Makkonen described as a case of *Isomorphie*.[47] Moreover, case law may be so well-established that new cases related to the issue can be classified as easy ones. More generally, a routine case is one in which almost all legal actors in the area would undoubtedly reach the same solution.[48]

In everyday legal life, most decision-making concerns routine cases. This is important with regard to the rule of law and predictability. As Kaarlo Tuori notes, 'Routine cases hold a key position with regard to legal certainty and predictability: if all cases were hard cases, legal certainty would be under great pressure.'[49] The vision painted here, concerning small narratives on legal change and free movement of legal ideas, is not thought of as coming to the fore in each and every situation when legal reasoning is applied, except as a dormant opportunity. The routine cases are, however, usually less interesting from the point of view of understanding the development and the dynamics of the legal order. Only the hard ones reveal how the law truly works, as embedded in its legal culture. Therefore, my focus is predominantly on hard cases or hard issues. A small narrative on legal change typically starts and evolves through hard issues, until the narrative ends and the situation stabilises in a position that is felt to be routine.

It is important to acknowledge, however, that the dichotomy of hard and easy cases is relative. Due to the particular features of the issue at hand, due to changes in societally accepted values or due to some other reason, an apparently easy case may be turned into a hard case and thereby start a small narrative on legal change. In this sense the 'indeterminacy thesis'[50] – or one should perhaps preferably speak about an 'underdeterminacy thesis'[51] – is also relevant with regard to routine cases. It rightly claims, among other things, 'that it is often possible to destabilise the settled beliefs

[46] Dworkin (1975: 1060).
[47] Makkonen (1985: 84 *et seq*).
[48] The relevance of the legal audience is emphasised by Aarnio (1987: 221 *et seq*).
[49] Tuori (2011: 166).
[50] Defended among others by American Critical Legal Studies, see eg Yablon (1985).
[51] Davis and Klare (2019: 28).

of a legal community, in which case the experience of "bindingness" or constraint imposed by the legal materials may weaken or dissolve.'[52]

The dichotomy of hard and easy cases is in other words merely a useful analytical tool. In reality, one instead finds a scale of situations, from very open-ended and particularly challenging ones that include several possible solutions, via cases with some room for manoeuvre for the decision-maker, to typical routine mass cases. The amplitude of choices available for the legal actor has many variations. In some cases there might be 'strong' arguments pointing in both directions, making the cases very difficult. In other cases, the majority of reasons may indicate one solution, but if there are some reasons that those in favour of the other solution can convincingly use by emphasising the value of that type of argument the case remains a hard one.

I have elsewhere used the term 'the legally possible' to refer to the field of choices available for the decision-maker.[53] As 'the legally possible' means what can be argued in a way that would not be unacceptable for almost all legal actors, one should include it as part of a dynamic understanding of law at any given moment. The width of the legally possible varies depending on the issue at hand. In addition, the borderlines of the field of the legally possible in each situation are also somewhat porous. New materials, such as new cases, may extend the field of the legally possible. This is in fact one of the features of a small narrative on legal change. What was not legally possible in the beginning of the narrative may become possible as a consequence of its intermediary steps.

As will be described in more detail in chapter eight, at least some established doctrines of legal sources seem unrealistic because of their inability to acknowledge the fact that from a legal point of view some cases are easier and some harder. Doctrines that enumerate legal sources in a hierarchical order usually reflect the pattern of reasoning in easy cases fairly well. However, in legally more interesting hard cases schematic doctrines tend to fail to give sufficient guidance. Hard cases appear as hard precisely because they cannot be solved with the help of a formal doctrine of sources. That is why in the following chapters I often use the term 'legal materials' interchangeably with 'legal sources'. I wish to signal that one cannot realistically order the texts that I call legal materials or sources into a schematic doctrine of legal sources. In my analysis 'legal materials' or 'legal sources' denote all kinds of materials that have some authoritative flavour, be it strong, like domestic legislation, or weak, like foreign case law.

I have here mainly used the term 'hard cases' as it is established in legal theoretical language. In my approach it would be more correct, however, to speak about 'hard issues'. My aim is not only to look at legal reasoning by the courts in particular cases, but also at the activities of other legal actors. As noted above, I am particularly interested in the reasoning of legal scholars, as they seem to occupy a key position with regard to the Europeanisation of the small narratives on legal change. Scholars discuss issues rather than cases.

[52] Davis and Klare (2019: 29).
[53] Wilhelmsson (1992: 227).

V. PRIVATE LAW – A PARTICULAR PERSPECTIVE?

Based on the societal diagnosis of contemporary Europe, I attempt to build a vision of legal reasoning in private law, which is becoming increasingly Europeanised. However, in EU law proper, the distinction between private and public law has little relevance. The societal pressures and demands of late modernity do not have any particular orientation towards private law. The borderline between private and public law is by no means clear either. So why this delimitation to private law alone? Does the metaphor of the small narratives not also apply to other fields of law?

To some extent it does. I do hope that these thoughts can also inspire other legal scholars beyond those working in the field of private law.[54] The aim of the delimitation is not to deny the possibility of similar discourses within other fields of law. It is only an indication of the typical self-restraint of a researcher. As I know private law better than other fields of law, I have taken my examples from this area, and I feel safer keeping my reasoning within these boundaries. In addition to these subjective reasons, there are also, however, some objective reasons that at least justify some cautiousness when transferring these thoughts to other areas of law.

Private law is typically focused on conflict management, and the law is often used only as a light steering mechanism. As the variety of conflict scenarios is unlimited, private law cases often appear to be more or less unique, and give the decision-makers a relatively large space within which they can find a legally possible solution. This often requires a relatively high grade of flexibility. In arbitration proceedings it is even possible to ask the arbitrators to decide the case *ex aequo et bono*. In other words, hard cases are probably more prevalent in the private law scene. Features like these are of course not typical for all private law – for example property law and family law are often more strictly regulated – but sufficiently common to make it easier within this area to defend an experimentalist conception of law.

The feeling that hard cases play a more dominant role in private law practice – this is just a feeling that I cannot validate empirically – is easy to understand as a consequence of the fact that the involved parties are usually free to decide whether to bring the legal machinery into motion. If both parties realise that a case is legally easy, there is often not much point in going to court to find a solution. The proportion of hard cases in private law adjudication is therefore probably much higher than in, for example, criminal law, as routine cases also have to be processed legally in the latter field of law.

On the other hand, if one looks in particular at commercial (contractual) cases of higher value, one can see that a large part of these cases are solved outside the domestic court system, for example through (confidential) arbitration. Therefore, many of the examples in the following are taken from areas like tort law and consumer law, which are not directly affected by this phenomenon. The widespread use of arbitration in certain commercial cases, however, does not eliminate the public role of all 'ordinary' legal actors with regard to such issues. The fact that case law might be

[54] *cf* Waldron (2005: 129), who claims that a credible theory on the use of foreign sources should be 'broad enough to explain the use of foreign law in all appropriate cases'.

more scarce does not limit the scope and influence of the activities of legal scholars. Even in this context, they can have an impact on legal development by discussing hard issues of commercial law.

The fact that the parties concerned usually are required to put the private law legal machinery into motion does not negate the role of private law as a societal steering mechanism. The focus on conflict management does not prevent private law from being an instrument for social engineering. Private law can be seen as one of the mechanisms that the state uses to regulate behaviour in the marketplace.[55] One can tell small narratives on legal change with a beneficial impact on social justice within private law as well. There are private law narratives that lead to the improvement of the position of weaker parties or to a stronger liability for those using societal power in a morally less acceptable way. When discussing micro-politics, the approach in this book emphasises the instrumental use of private law. One should bear in mind, however, that the narratives of private law justice are told in a legal context in which the legal actor ultimately has to weigh the rights of both or several parties against each other.

In contrast, in areas like criminal law and administrative law where the core relationship is between the state and the citizen, the setting is at least in principle different. The maxim *nulla poena sine lege* and the principle of legitimate expectations easily call for stricter interpretations and less experimentalism in law. A Kelsenian formal structure of norms might seem more natural for a public lawyer than for a private lawyer.[56] The different perspectives on law of private and public lawyers may lead them to somewhat different understandings of how law works.[57]

However, with sufficient recognition of such differences, I believe in a discourse across the boundaries of disciplines on the perspectives that I have analysed in this book. Discipline-related silos are becoming increasingly irrelevant anyway. The variations in appropriate legal reasoning might be more closely related to the nature of the issues under scrutiny than to the classification of the norms to be applied.

In fact, the whole approach of this book speaks against emphasising the systematic structure of law, as this can easily become an obstacle to pragmatic solutions of problems in the real world. The real challenges often transcend the borders of traditional legal classifications. Therefore, the delimitation of the scope of this work to private law should be understood only as a *caveat* concerning the limitations of the abilities of the author, and not as a plea for upholding and deepening the private law–public law divide. In line with this, when speaking about private law, I use the concept in a broad sense, including both traditional contract and tort law as well as more regulatory forms of private law.

However, as I am discussing private law as a means to counterbalance various forms of societal power, I will most often use legal materials that concern private law liability. This is why many of my examples deal with tort law in particular, but

[55] Well analysed, with regard to contract law, by Collins (1999: 56 *et seq*).

[56] In the same direction, in discussing Europeanisation, Schäfer and Bankowski (2000: 27): 'Where the public lawyer takes society as given and analyses its *structure*, the private lawyer sees its emergence out of the *action* of individuals.'

[57] See eg Tuori (2021: 2).

also with liability arising under contract or consumer law. These areas of private law also seem to be those in which the legal discourse on Europeanisation is most active. Much EU legislation in the field of private law (*sensu largo*) aimed at harmonising consumer law. Contract law again was well known as an ice-breaker with regard to the academic work on European principles, with the creation of the Principles of European Contract Law (PECL) as the starting point. With regard to tort law, such principles are contained both in the Draft Common Frame of Reference (DCFR) as well as in the competing Principles of European Tort Law (PETL).[58] In other words, these fields of law are of particular relevance with regard to both legal micro-politics and Europeanisation. Even though the DCFR covers many other areas of private law as well, and even in the field of family law some European principles have been adopted,[59] I will here keep the focus predominantly on private law liability.

VI. THE PERSPECTIVE AND THE STORYLINE

As the questions posed in this book are broad and may raise more expectations than can be fulfilled in one volume, it is important at this stage to underline the perspective of the book and note what it does not contain. I discuss the Europeanisation of private law, not European private law. This implies a predominantly domestic perspective on the issue – without choosing any particular legal order – even though a clear distinction between the domestic and the European approach collapses when looked at from the point of view of small narratives. I am particularly interested in questions like: How does national law become more European? How and to what extent should national law interact with non-domestic elements in order to support useful Europeanisation? In fact, as the story continues, my perspective becomes even narrower. For various reasons, I am interested in particular in the cross-border movement of domestic legal sources within the EU.

This perspective implies a number of important limitations. First and foremost, I am not attempting to create yet another construction of EU private law and its principles.[60] I am not theorising EU private law as such, as there are other very interesting contributions in this area.[61] Secondly, I am not discussing in detail the role of EU legal actors, the European legislature and the European courts, as vehicles for moving comparative knowledge across the borders. I only describe this well-known role relatively briefly when presenting the legal actors in Europeanised small narratives.[62] Thirdly, as I am interested in substantive Europeanisation, I pass over the role of private international law, even though Europeanisation has contributed

[58] For more on the European academic principles, see ch 5 section V.

[59] The Commission of European Family Law has issued several collections of principles concerning various aspects of family law; see ceflonline.net/principles. The creator of the principles movement, Ole Lando, enthusiastically claimed that the emergence of principles in the area of family law demonstrates that the unity of private law is possible in many other fields as well, see Lando (2006a).

[60] Comprehensively described eg by Basedow (2021).

[61] Micklitz (2018) is a modern classic.

[62] See ch 5 section II.

to a new flourishing of this field of law. Finally, the focus on Europeanisation liberates me from commenting on the broad discussion on the possible development of a transnational law, including a global commercial law – a global *lex mercatoria* – that is supposed to be developed by arbitrators and private actors.[63]

Much of the reasoning in the debate on the harmonisation and development of private law in Europe seems to have been based on a classical static perception of law. The ideal of law as a systematic structure made by consistently working law producers lies behind the weighing of many of the arguments and metaphors in the harmonisation debate. In this perspective, fragmentation appears to be something negative, to be fought against, either through re-nationalisation or through fully fledged European codification or systematisation. Here I follow a different storyline. Fragmentation and flexibility are inevitable, so what can we do? If this is the case, what are the responsibilities and power of legal actors – including academics – to work for a better society? What impact does this have and should it have on the process of Europeanisation of private law?

Societal conditions determine the working of the law. I have sought the starting-point for the analysis in a diagnosis of contemporary society. In chapter two, I describe the growing epistemic and ethical uncertainty in late modern society and its implications for the way in which the law works and should work. Epistemic and ethical uncertainty requires a fragmented and flexible law. The idea of a European civil code is outmoded.

Then, in chapter three, I discuss how societal fragmentation creates opportunities for new kinds of activism, which in its turn strengthens the fragmentation tendencies both in society and in law. Here I shine a light on new legal opportunities, on law as an instrument of micro-politics.

Based on these premises, I present a model for how one could realistically and fruitfully describe legal development in contemporary European society. First, in chapter four, I sketch a general metaphor that is applicable both to purely domestic and to Europeanised private law: 'small narratives on legal change'. The metaphor reflects the way in which an experimental law answers to the challenge of simultaneous demands for stability and change, and it acknowledges the power and moral responsibility of various kinds of legal actors.

This metaphor is then, in chapter five, applied to the issue of Europeanisation of private law. The value of experimentalism is elevated to the European level and new legal actors and new legal materials are included in the narratives, broadening the variety of possible good small narratives on legal change. As already mentioned, I am in particular discussing the opportunities of direct horizontal learning from experience of other Member States, as this is the boldest way of using the European laboratory. To picture this, I introduce the metaphor of 'free movement of legal ideas' across the borders.

The metaphor of small narratives indicates the lack of a grand narrative that would steer legal development. However, even though contemporary society necessitates processes of fragmentation and flexibilisation, there may be more

[63] See eg the comprehensive analysis by Berger (2010).

profound parameters that determine some direction for the small narratives. The issue whether one can construe such a grand narrative on European private law is analysed in chapter six. Here I find it more accurate, however, to speak about several, partially conflicting narratives related to Europeanisation, the European societal model and fundamental rights. As the European narrative is based on the acceptance and even cherishing of diversity, a general European narrative does not solve the challenges related to legal fragmentation and flexibilisation, but rather includes them as a natural part of European legal identity.

Finally, the concluding chapters of this volume are devoted to testing the vision of a free movement of legal ideas in a legal perspective. How do the small narratives and free movement of legal ideas survive an encounter with the perceived and real needs related to the rule of law? In chapter seven I test the fragmentation thesis against the basic legal values of coherence, predictability and equality. My basic message is that the ideal of coherence appears to be overvalued.

This does not solve, however, the challenge of how a legal actor can develop law both domestically and by learning across the borders without resorting to pure arbitrariness. Can legal learning processes in this complex environment be controlled and if so, with what kind of legal-methodological tools? The basic solution, offered in chapter eight, is increased transparency of legal reasoning.

With regard to the free movement of legal ideas, this means a requirement concerning a transparent justification of the use of materials across the borders. This issue is analysed in chapter nine. A typology of arguments that one might use to justify the use of foreign authority is presented, and the necessary interplay between authoritative and substantive reasoning is analysed. Even though the typology of arguments does not offer any decisive formula for when and how foreign sources may be used, it illustrates the kind of reasoning that is possible and needed to diminish the risk of arbitrariness.

The picture of the possibilities of a Europeanised private law that emerges through these chapters brings the processes of development to the fore. As contemporary society, above all, is characterised by an ever-increasing pace of change, it is consequently a moving picture that focuses on dynamics rather than static features. In other words, this is a book on how law and lawyers in Europe can cope with change. The cure underlines the importance of an eagerness to learn from and be open towards experiences from others and a willingness to engage in a discursive practice that reaches across national borders.

The reasoning emphasises the moral responsibility of all legal actors involved in creating small narratives on legal change. Ultimately, therefore, this is a book about how legal actors can fulfil their responsibility to work for a better society.

2

Societal Uncertainty and Private Law

LEGAL DECISION-MAKING IS a particular form of societal decision-making. At least partially it faces the same pressures as other decision-making. Without denying the obvious fact that legal decision-making also has specific features, it is important when analysing the contemporary role and preconditions of legal decision-making to look at the conditions for societal decision-making in general. In this chapter, I will argue that these conditions have undergone changes in late modern society that also affect the structure and functioning of law.[1] During the present century, technological and societal development has in fact strengthened the effect of the changes.

My argument is based on the insight, repeated by many social scientists, that societal decision-making in late modernity is characterised by growing uncertainty. Uncertainty is prominent in two respects. First, epistemic uncertainty relates to the difficulties in gaining sufficient knowledge and understanding about complex causality chains in an increasingly complex society. Secondly, a growing ethical ambivalence is due to the loss of belief in common ethical systems and the loss of reliance on common traditions. In this chapter, I will discuss the epistemic and ethical uncertainty in contemporary society and their impact on private law decision-making. The analysis offers a private law perspective on what has been called the 'Liquid Society and Its Law'.[2]

The challenges facing private law decision-making have an impact on how one should understand the ambitions and structure of private law. The keywords here are 'flexibility' and 'fragmentation'. As such, these concepts are not new in legal and jurisprudential discourse. Numerous scholars have described these tendencies, often deploring them as well. In domestic settings the 'flight into general clauses'[3] has been a long-standing target of criticism. As to fragmentation an almost paradigmatic example is the development of consumer law in the 1970s and 1980s which in many countries led to a discussion concerning the compatibility of the new elements with the inherited system of private law. The fragmentation of national legal systems caused by EU law is, as mentioned in the introduction, a presently recurring object of worry, fuelling the debate concerning harmonisation and systematic structure of

[1] This chapter as well as the following one are based on and broaden the perspective of my book on late modern liability law, Wilhelmsson (2001), published in Swedish only.
[2] Přibáň (2007) – a collection of papers inspired by Baumanian societal analysis.
[3] The well-known title by Hedemann (1933).

European private law. The particular contribution of this work is not the recognition of flexibility and fragmentation as such, but the adoption of a less negative approach to these phenomena, as I see them as being both unavoidable and to some extent even useful.

Naturally, in cases in which one can see flexibility and fragmentation as a result of poor drafting procedures, one should not defend the development. In my perspective, however, the increasing flexibility and fragmentation of private law to some extent appear as a necessary consequence of the conditions of societal decision-making in contemporary society. In the following, I will argue that from the point of view of an efficient legal policy under contemporary societal conditions one should welcome some flexibility and fragmentation. This insight offers the general societal basis for the theory of European private law that I am proposing in this book.

Here I have used the two F-words – 'flexibility' and 'fragmentation' – jointly as a characteristic of the effects of contemporary societal uncertainty on private law. However, it is important to note here that the terms relate to different features that do not necessarily walk hand-in-hand. I will analyse the relationship between fragmentation and flexibility more in depth in chapter 4 (II).

I. THE PARADOXES OF SOCIETAL DECISION-MAKING UNDER CONDITIONS OF EPISTEMIC UNCERTAINTY

One possible inroad into the issue of the epistemic uncertainty of late modern society can be chosen in the already fairly 'old', but still thought-provoking discussions concerning decision-making in what Ulrich Beck called the 'risk society'.[4] Societal decision-making here encounters 'the paradox of the risk society' that has interesting implications for legal decision-making as well.[5]

Social theory has suggested various interpretations of the concept of risk society. Originally, the focus was rather on various catastrophe scenarios.[6] The continuing risk discourse, however, does not cover only large, technologically induced risks, but also risks of a smaller magnitude, even those only facing individual persons. In addition, the concept of risk has been broadened to cover also various kinds of institutional risks.[7] Such risks appear for example in the stock exchange and the globalised financial markets. In this context, one should also not forget the other side of the risk society: it does not only create new risks, but offers new opportunities and chances as well. The epistemic uncertainty relates to losses as well as to gains.

The risk discourse does not only reflect an actual increase of risks in contemporary society. The focus on risks does not arise only from changes in reality, but also from how we look at reality, from a growing awareness of risks.[8] To put it more

[4] Beck (1986).

[5] I have published some parts of this text before in English in Wilhelmsson (2007), here revised and considerably expanded.

[6] Beck (1986: 254 *et seq*).

[7] See especially Giddens (1990).

[8] Luhmann (1991). Steele (2004: 10) speaks about a greater sensitivity to risks.

bluntly, irrational responsiveness to temporary fears might steer regulatory behaviour more than sensible calculation of risk.[9] In other words, in late modernity risks exist in technology, in society and in our minds.[10] For the purposes of this analysis, it is not necessary to discuss how much is real and how much perceived. It is sufficient to note that contemporary culture understands risks as a key challenge. The precise meaning of risk varies in the discourse, but the important message is the acknowledgement of the profound changes in society that have been caused by growing risks and a growing perception of risks.

The culture of the risk society generates what one could call a paradox of decision-making. One side of this paradox is a growing demand for decisions, an increasing interest in decision-making and decision-makers. This follows not only from growing risks, but also from the interpretation of what previously were considered natural dangers as risks that are related to decision-making. In the risk society, such numerous dangers to life, health and property that always have plagued humankind are understood as risks connected with human acts or omissions. Almost everything that threatens us is at least partially understood to be a consequence of human decisions.[11] As most dangers, at least in theory, can be averted or their consequences can be diminished by appropriate measures, lack of action is also treated as a form of decision-making.

The other side of the paradox relates to the growing uncertainty prevailing in the risk society. Even though the importance of decision-making is emphasised, there is a feeling that ever more decisions are made under conditions of uncertainty. This means that 'the risk issues necessitate, or, more cautiously, appeal for, the "recognition of ambivalence"'.[12] More generally, chaos and ambivalence are presented as characteristic features of society.[13] The problems are complex and, therefore, one should not under 'the cloud of decision-making' attempt to solve them by rules that are too rigid, as every consistent model soon leads to paradoxical results.[14] Societal diagnoses highlight a 'new obscurity' – a lack of an understandable general picture of society – related to the death of grand narratives and the decline of the welfare state.[15] The state of society has been summarised in the acronym 'VUCA': volatility, uncertainty, complexity and ambiguity.[16]

The recognition of the cloud of uncertainty affects the understanding of the role of expertise. The lack of experience concerning new risks means that 'experts' cannot claim a monopoly on knowledge. The scepticism of expertise is not cured even when the risk in a concrete situation may be calculated quite accurately. What in the eyes of an expert looks like a calculated risk, may be experienced as an uncontrolled danger by those affected by it. The attempts of a decision-maker to minimise a risk through risk calculations and risk strategies are experienced as failures by those who fear the

[9] See eg Sunstein (2002).
[10] So Hviid Nielsen (1996: 77).
[11] Bechmann (1991: 217).
[12] Beck (1994: 10).
[13] Bauman (1991).
[14] Foucault (1983: 60).
[15] Habermas (1985): '*Die neue Unübersichtlichkeit*'.
[16] en.wikipedia.org/wiki/Volatility,_uncertainty,_complexity_and_ambiguity.

remaining risk.[17] The relativisation of expert knowledge is further enhanced by the fact that other factors than the probability of damage can be decisive for the decision, for example the distribution of the risk within a given population.[18] The line between acceptable and unacceptable risks is a cultural, political and moral question,[19] mixing epistemic and ethical uncertainty. Suspicion of expertise pushes decision-making to become more experimental, towards a mode of learning-by-doing.

The diagnosis that I have presented so far was developed and related to the conditions of the late twentieth century. Societal development during the present century has not made its message concerning ambivalence and uncertainty as characteristics of contemporary society obsolete. On the contrary, these features are even more topical now than during the last century. As the High Commissioner of the EU Josep Borrell in a 2022 speech emphasised, we live in 'a world of radical uncertainty'.[20] Today the focus on risk has grown to a continuous tension between a yearning for control and a lack of ability to master the world.[21]

Since the heydays of risk society discourse, society has changed at an even faster pace than one could anticipate. The concept pairing that now dominates the diagnoses of contemporary society – digitalisation and globalisation – signals thorough changes of the human condition. Some have spoken about a 'digital risk society' in which the risks are flowing into the digital reality with surprising consequences.[22] The development of Internet of Things and Services and a broader introduction of what is, often somewhat misleadingly, called artificial intelligence into increasing numbers of societal and technological processes have even inspired talk about a fourth industrial revolution,[23] already following the third one which was related to 'simple' digitalisation. Changes are fast and they are often, on good grounds, labelled as 'disruptive'. 'The age of constant innovation' is said to imply 'big bang disruption'.[24]

The disruption is not only technological, but in a deep sense societal. Many branches of business and other activity are undergoing radical changes. The well-known culprits, Uber and Airbnb, are paradigmatic examples. The platform economy creates completely new structures and normative relationships that challenge established patterns. The digitalised globalisation makes the world a playground on which risks and opportunities are multiplied. Social media change the settings for networking and societal dialogue as well as for the distribution of information. Some fear that human capacities, like the capacity to choose, are gradually being lost in the pressure of efficient and immoral use of new addictive technology.[25]

Such societal changes bring the difficulties related to societal decision-making in contemporary society very clearly to the fore. The complexity of a digitalised and

[17] Bechmann (1991: 227).
[18] Ogus (1997: 144 *et seq*) analyses this very interestingly.
[19] A good example (the extinction of certain spiders) is provided by Godard (1997: 52).
[20] www.eeas.europa.eu/eeas/eu-ambassadors-annual-conference-2022-opening-speech-high-representative-josep-borrell_en.
[21] Eloquently analysed by Rosa (2018): *Verfügbarkeit* (availability) v *Unverfügbarkeit*.
[22] Korpiola and Poutanen (2021: 50).
[23] Schwab (2017).
[24] Downes and Nunes (2014).
[25] See eg Alter (2017).

globalised society deepens the paradox of decision-making. The demand for decisions made under conditions of uncertainty is growing. In addition, new important nuances are included in the picture.

In the era of social media, climate change and 'fake news', distrust in expertise and in 'certain' answers grows. The complex character of the risks that humankind is confronting and the high expectations on society make the task of decision-makers increasingly difficult:

> There is a yawning gap between what *needs* to, and what *can*, be done; between what matters and what counts to the makers; between what happens and what is desirable; between the size of the problems humanity faces and the reach and capacity of the tools available to manage them.[26]

A complex problem is so unique, or represents such a unique combination of elements, that there always remains a considerable degree of uncertainty as to the outcome.[27] The more complex the challenges become, the more experimentalism is necessary in decision-making. As examples of higher levels of complexity, one might refer to catastrophic risks related, for example, to climate change, loss of biodiversity, the plastic waste problem and other environmental challenges. Decision-making reaching for 'susformation', the attempt to combine sustainability with transformation, is almost by definition complex. The increasing complexity, however, does not relate to this level of urgency alone. On the contrary, experimental learning processes are required also in relation to challenges with much narrower impact. New technology constantly defies established patterns of risk assessment, brings about new societal structures and practices that require new regulative responses and re-orders social relationships in a way that brings new protective needs on the agenda.

The pace in which changes appear is exacerbating the challenges.[28] In the original phase of computerisation, the so-called Moore's law was an often used symbol of the rapidity of change. A similar development has taken place in genetics: the first sequencing of the human genome by the Human Genome Project, finished in 2003, took close to 15 years and costed billions, whilst now everybody can have their genome mapped for a few hundred dollars. Presently artificial intelligence and learning machines develop at the same pace. The increasingly rapid convergence between different techno-scientific fields adds to the complexity.[29] These are just examples. In all areas of technology and society ever faster change has become the new normal. In leadership manuals, one of the dominating catchwords is 'agility'. Coping with change, and using and initiating change, have become the hallmark of good decision-making.

The same pace of change also relates to the production and availability of information. The abundance of data and pieces of information, the thorough restructuring of the media sector and the advent of social media are fragmenting societal discourses.

[26] Bauman (2017: 159).

[27] See eg Glouberman and Zimmerman (2002) and Snyder (2013).

[28] Rosa (2013) has demonstrated the acceleration of technological change, social change and change in the pace of life.

[29] An interesting legal analysis by Guerra (2018).

The public sphere becomes increasingly pluralised, polarised and fragmented.[30] The multiplying offers of information and its increasingly uncertain nature tend to steer discourse and thinking from systematic and fundamental issues towards concrete real-life issues. Conceptual and analytical reasoning gives way to narrative approaches that look at the concrete in its emotional and symbolical settings. The 'age of the narratives' in many ways affects the conduct of legal reasoning too.[31]

The increasing complexity of the challenges and the pace of change that aggravates the uncertainty require a decision-making that can adapt to changes and take into account new experience. Decision-making becomes a kind of a learning process. As the pace of change grows faster, the time for learning shrinks and the place for experimentalism grows. Managing the growing complexity of society requires an increasingly experimental culture.

A prime example is the reactions to the COVID-19 pandemic. As the problem was extremely complex, involving not only medical aspects, but also a large variety of economic and societal issues, and the original knowledge basis was very thin, more or less every decision made to combat the consequences of the disease was experimental. Only by trial and error could one determine the effects of various lockdowns, border closures, obligatory use of face masks and other measures. It is not surprising that more or less every country developed its own combination of measures and flexibly changed them when the situation so required. This also made it possible to learn from the experiments of others across the borders.

However, the pandemic did not represent a peak of global uncertainty, even in late modern society. The war in Ukraine pushed the feeling of uncertainty, in particular in Europe, to a new level. It required much decision-making under conditions of extreme uncertainty, both nationally and within the EU. The recurrent sanction packages on Russia were to a large degree experimental, as one could not really foresee their effects.

If one word summarises contemporary society from the point of view of societal decision-making, it might be 'experimentalism'. The quickly increasing complexity of contemporary society and the need to cope with ever more rapid changes make experimentalism a central feature of decision-making in the society of today.

II. EPISTEMIC UNCERTAINTY AND PRIVATE LAW

The paradox of decision-making and the need for an experimental culture are also relevant with regard to the understanding of legal decision-making. A legal approach according to which one can map and understand societal relations in advance is increasingly challenged. A complex and experimental society needs an experimental law.[32]

[30] Well analysed in relation to Habermas's *Strukturwandel der Öffentlichkeit* in several contributions in Seeliger and Sevignani (2021), summarised at 461–63.

[31] See eg on the use of 'real-life language' in legal reasoning below ch 8 section V.

[32] Douzinas (2019: 233): 'the law starts resembling an experimental machine'.

The security demands related to the welfare state are also pushing legal decision-making towards experimentalism.[33] Hugh Collins describes how the reorientation of legal discourse 'towards the instrumental reasoning of welfarist regulation' tends to promote a law that is open to learn from societal experience:

> The trajectory of legal evolution alters from the private law discourse of seeking the better coherence for its scheme of principles to one of learning about the need for fresh regulation by observations of the consequences of present regulation. Information about the world, especially market practices, has to be gathered and reconstituted in a form which enables the legal discourse to adjust its own internal operations and regulatory outcomes.[34]

The paradox of decision-making in contemporary society broadens the cleavage between the expectations on decision-making and its results. In the legal sphere, the paradox signals an increasing cleavage between regulatory expectations and the performance of actual regulation. The public security expectations are continuously rising and the legislative machinery cannot cope with the expectations. The situation is confusing. There is a constant demand for regulatory measures related to new risks, but the trust in such measures is diminishing, as the results are not convincing. The cooperation between policy-relevant expertise and political and administrative decision-makers also raises concerns with regard to the position of democratic decision-making.[35]

The growing scepticism against an expertise that is not able to foresee all consequences of regulation – measures to minimise uncertainty in one area can easily increase uncertainty elsewhere[36] – may lead to demands for the abolishment of regulation. In addition, ideologically founded deregulatory tendencies connected with the privatisation and marketisation of society may support such proposals. In other words, there are conflicting expectations on regulation, expressed in simultaneous demands for regulation, deregulation, re-regulation, more regulation, less regulation, and regulation with a new approach. The need for rapid responses increases the uncertainty of the outcomes. As under such circumstances law obviously will make mistakes (whatever that means), it has to be able to learn from the mistakes. Society needs a law that can adapt to new experiences – an experimental and learning law.

This is not a new discovery. Many others have underlined both the need for more experimentalism and the fact that the law indeed 'becomes more markedly experimental in character'.[37] Karl-Heinz Ladeur even proposes a new concept of 'serial law', a law 'that is generated from a "series" of experimental search processes in conditions of uncertainty'.[38] Looking at experimentalism from another perspective and in another linguistic genre one can say that society needs a law that is

[33] See also Domurath (2017: 9), who sees the complexity of the concept of vulnerability requiring a flexible contract law.
[34] Collins (1999: 8).
[35] See eg the analysis of regulating risk in the EU from this perspective: Weimer and de Ruijter (2017).
[36] Hutchinson (1997: 28).
[37] Ladeur (2020: 316–17).
[38] Ladeur (2020: 299).

continuously open for legal innovation.[39] The value of experimentalism is emphasised in particular in connection with Europeanisation, as will be shown later in chapter five.

The demand for a law that is experimental and can learn and innovate has various implications for private law.

First, there is a stronger call for private law mechanisms to deal with the consequences of uncertainty. Although the American approach of using private liability proceedings as an important regulatory instrument has obvious drawbacks,[40] the need to increase the weight of such mechanisms is repeatedly debated in Europe.[41] In the private law discourse related to the diagnosis of the risk society, some scholars underlined a new role of tort and liability law. Risk regulation through liability was the catchword.[42] According to this view, tort law offered some answers to the challenges in coping with uncertainty.[43] It could function as a device for catching the problems that were not caught by the public security net. As public law could not remove uncertainty to an acceptable extent, private law procedures could play the role of the last resort for those seeking legal protection.[44]

The discussion concerning tort law as a device for judicial risk regulation has continued and been deepened during the twenty-first century.[45] In the debate, many well-known examples from case law in various countries have been mentioned, such as liability for drug risks, liabilities in the foodstuff sector as well as private law judge-made regulation of risks related to health and environment.[46] A paradigmatic example is tobacco litigation in various parts of the world, with profound impact on the perception of risks relating to tobacco. This is a very clear-cut example of what one could call 'regulation by litigation'.[47]

The call for private law mechanisms does not relate to tort law alone. Consumer law also contributes many illustrations. A much-discussed example is the reaction of various courts to the effects of financial crises on consumers. The clashes between different German courts in the aftermath of the crisis in the 1990s have been well analysed in the context of the theory of the risk society.[48] After the 2008 financial crisis the activism of the CJEU based on the Unfair Contract Terms Directive[49] is an example of how this court has sought new legal answers, recognising 'the macroeconomic dimension of household debt in our economies.'[50]

One topical theme of contemporary private law discourse is the capacity of private law to cope with new challenges posed by digitalisation and the platform

[39] Möslein (2010), on legal innovation in European contract law.
[40] See the comparison between European and American approaches in Howells and Wilhelmsson (1998).
[41] See for example already the interesting paper of Steele (1999).
[42] Nicklisch (1995).
[43] Brüggemeier (1997: 63 *et seq*).
[44] Damm (1996: 136) speaks about '*das Zivilgericht als letzte Auffangsstation des Rechtsschutzsuchenden*'.
[45] See in particular Dyson (2018) and de Jong (2018) with references. Steele (2004) and (2018) has a more general perspective, but she uses much materials from tort and liability law.
[46] Dyson (2018) contains chapters inter alia on these examples.
[47] See Howells (2011), in particular 81 *et seq*.
[48] Kiesow (2005).
[49] See Micklitz and Reich (2014).
[50] Micklitz (2015: 233).

economy. As the emerging legal relationships often are particularly difficult to squeeze into the established legal-conceptual structures, it easily feels natural to demand the creation of flexible and differentiated private law control mechanisms.[51] More generally, one may expect private law responses to various issues relating to new technologies, such as artificial intelligence, block-chain and digitalisation.[52] The development of artificial intelligence has even inspired discourse on the need for rethinking the approach to private law legal personhood and the applicable liability regimes.[53]

One can also hear the call for private law mechanisms (as part of the regulatory mix) from the most pressing issue of our time: climate change. As this is a field in which there is much micro-political legal activism I will return to the issue in the next chapter. Here I will just make a few remarks on the other global issue that the law has been forced to tamper with during the last years, namely the COVID-19 pandemic. As it clearly has brought the experimentalism in societal decision-making in general to a higher level, it has obviously done so in the field of private law decision-making as well.

The exceptional times of the pandemic have affected the legal orders of the world in various ways. In some countries human rights issues have been at the fore, whilst the focus in others has been on detailed practical issues. Examples from many countries show that the pandemic has caused pressure also on private law. Already during the first half year of the pandemic numerous laws related to the consequences of the pandemic were passed. In some countries moratoria postponed credit payment obligations and/or protected tenants from eviction, interest rates were regulated, contract durations were prolonged, and foreclosure proceedings and evictions were prevented. With regard to consumers, the cancelling of travel and events led to the creation of many new rules. Legal scholars have discussed the application of rules on changed circumstances and social *force majeure*.[54] Using comparative materials, scholars have analysed product liability issues related to medical products developed to tackle the pandemic.[55] Courts can be expected to play a significant role when determining emerging liability issues and recovery measures.[56] The European Law Institute has adopted a collection of principles, the ELI Principles for the Covid-19 Crisis,[57] to help develop the law, including private law principles on moratoria, *force majeure* and hardship, as well as on exemption of liability.[58] The list of examples could be made much longer.[59] My point is not, however, to discuss the substance of these measures, but to note how the pandemic managed to increase the experimentalism of private

[51] Schweitzer (2019: 12).
[52] See eg Durovic and Tridimas (2021).
[53] See eg Beckers and Teubner (2021).
[54] The examples in the text are all from COVID-19-Consumer Law Research Group (2020). On exemption of liability according to CISG, see Janssen and Wahnschaffe (2020).
[55] Fairgrieve, Feldschreiber, Howells and Pilgerstorfer (2020).
[56] Cafaggi and Iamiceli (2021).
[57] www.europeanlawinstitute.eu/fileadmin/user_upload/p_eli/Publications/ELI_Principles_for_the_COVID-19_Crisis.pdf.
[58] Principles 12–14. The critique by Wagner (2020) reflects the difficulties related to such experimentalism.
[59] For a comprehensive European account, see Hondius, Santos Silva, Nicolussi, Coderch, Wendehorst and Zoll (2021) and globally (with strong focus on labour law) da Rocha, Pepino and Martins (2020).

law quite radically. So far it is impossible to predict how many of these experiments will survive and in what form. On the level of legal culture, however, I believe that the experiences have contributed to a deepening of the experimental culture that is also evolving within private law. The pandemic at least has a potential for causing 'disruption' within private law.[60]

The subsequent global catastrophe – the war in Ukraine – has also created pressure on more private law experimentalism. Europe has so far seen only a small fraction of the private law issues created both by the war as such and by the extensive sanctions against Russia and its oligarchs. For example, sanctions against named individuals involve many new legal questions that are open for experimentalism and cross-border learning by relevant courts and arbitral tribunals.

Secondly, the management of uncertainty by judicial means must in some respects function differently than by administrative means. The lack of experience of a new risk that makes a regulation in advance difficult is in a private law case replaced by the concrete experience of the case. As private law proceedings are usually resorted to when damage has actually occurred, there is more knowledge available about the risk than there was before the case. The knowledge basis of the courts may even be broader if there are series of cases that throw light on different aspects of the risks. In this sense, case law can function as a learning-by-doing mechanism. Gert Brüggemeier has called contemporary liability law a process of learning and communication in which both courts and legal science as well as representatives of various interests, the media, public bodies and semi-private regulatory bodies take part.[61] A learning liability law can offer one of the mechanisms by which society can process complex risks. In German doctrine this was termed in the 1980s as '*Entdeckungsverfahren Praxis*'.[62]

Risk assessments that are made by the courts must in other words differ from those of public authorities. Anthony Ogus sums up:

> Of course, judges undertake this task in a broad, impressionistic manner; there is no expectation that they will quantify the costs and benefits. Further, although the adjudication of private law claims enables the victim to have a direct input into the decision-making process, the adversarial setting also means that judges will be almost wholly reliant on the parties for the data. Also, they are likely to possess neither expertise on the scientific or technical dimensions of the case nor experience of cost-benefit analysis. At the same time, these very facts may enable them to take a more 'rounded' approach to the issues than is likely within a bureaucratic context. To some extent, that approach should reflect public attitudes to risk. Judicial independence of government should mean that short-term political considerations are not taken into account.[63]

Courts can also contribute to a legitimate use of expert knowledge in decision-making when contested by unfounded suspicions. Scientific knowledge can reach the courts in various ways, through expert witnesses in the case at hand, but also by

[60] Twigg-Flesner (2021).

[61] Brüggemeier (1999: 31).

[62] Joerges (1983: 64 *et seq*). He has also used the concept '*Entdeckungsverfahren Rechtsprechung*' (judicial discovery) in the context of Europeanisation; see Joerges (2003).

[63] Ogus (1997: 141).

the use of public, half-private or private self-regulatory and standard-setting bodies that are increasingly used in various branches of business. It is important to see, however, that the available expert knowledge is only one part of the material that the court uses to make its decision; it is often not homogeneous and it appears in relation to other arguments in the process.[64] Within science and technology studies, some have doubted the ability of judges to make choices between diverging views of different experts.[65] 'Judges should remain judges' and not become amateur scientists; they should rather function as a kind of 'informational catalysts'.[66] In contemporary conditions of uncertainty, expert knowledge does not have absolute primacy, but the court must take into account other views, like the prevailing attitudes towards various risks. The court also has to weigh scientific and technical expert knowledge against 'softer' arguments of various kinds. Such weighing and balancing of various types of arguments against each other is precisely what courts are used to doing.

In particular, when dealing with vicious problems, such as loss of biodiversity and other negative aspects of the Anthropocene, it is important to acknowledge that scientific insights are continuously changing. Therefore, one may here again repeat the need for an experimentalist approach, calling for 'legal regimes that are flexible, capable of learning and adaptation, and responsive to ecosystemic changes and the resulting changes in the scientific understanding of ecosystem dynamics.'[67]

So, thirdly, private law can use accumulated experience to generate new norms only if it is sufficiently flexible. Anthony Ogus has presented his analysis of court-based risk management under the heading 'Judicial Interpretation of General Standards'.[68] Comparative studies illustrate the tension between the high complexity of late-modern society and traditional expectations of legal certainty.[69] Experimentalism walks hand-in-hand with flexibility.

In most countries, the basic structure of tort law makes it well suited to respond to the demand for sufficiently flexible rules. The assessment of negligence allows consideration of various types of arguments, the risk of damage often being one of the central elements in the reasoning. For example, the Principles of European Tort Law defines the required standard of conduct as 'that of the reasonable person in the circumstances', enumerating a large variety of factors that should be taken into account in the assessment, including 'the dangerousness of the activity'.[70] In addition to the flexibility offered by the principle of negligence, in many jurisdictions courts might also have the opportunity to create instances of strict liability when they feel such decisions needed. Often this option is directly related to an assessment of risk. For example, this is the approach of the Principles of European Tort Law,

[64] See eg Edmond and Mercer (2004).
[65] See eg Rees and White (2023) with references; the authors themselves, however, find that legal actors do have some tools for assessing expertise.
[66] Vos (2013: 163–64).
[67] Ellis (2020: 191).
[68] Ogus (1997: 140). Similarly Steele (1999: 486), requiring 'large elements of flexibility'.
[69] Fenwick, Siems and Wrbka (2017).
[70] PETL Art 4:102 as available 18 January 2019 at civil.udg.edu/php/biblioteca/items/283/PETL.pdf.

according to which a 'person who carries on an abnormally dangerous activity is strictly liable for damage characteristic to the risk presented by the activity and resulting from it.'[71]

It is therefore easy to understand that much of the discussion concerning risk regulation through judicial means relates to tort law, as it offers the required flexibility and is based on assessments in which risk plays an important role. This does not mean, however, that other areas of private law are of no interest in this context. In particular, in new fields with strong regulative aspirations, such as consumer law and environmental law, the private law parts are often based on relatively broad general clauses that expressly give the courts opportunities to contribute to the development of the required standards. Even in such a predictability-driven field as contract law, one can find much flexibility not only in the familiar issues concerning unfair contract terms and change of circumstances, but also in central rules concerning contractual liability. One may encounter, for example, an oscillation between fault-related solutions and stricter liability, including the compromise solution of the United Nations Convention on Contracts for the International Sale of Goods (CISG) that ties liability to 'control': a party is not liable if he or she proves that their failure was due to an impediment beyond their control.[72] In this assessment, there is an obvious bridge between 'control' and 'risk'.

Fourthly, the development affects the relationship between public law regulation and private law. Emerging private law solutions do not silence the demands for more regulation. On the contrary, every private law case may be understood as a failure of public law regulation that may fuel demands for new regulation. Stated in the language of a learning law: by subjecting new forms of risk behaviour to legal sanctions, private law 'discovers' possible targets of administrative action.[73]

I stress this point because I want to avoid the impression that private law would provide the only adequate means of coping with the uncertainty of contemporary society. Often detailed regulatory public law norms are more efficient steering mechanisms than general clauses backed up by a few cases. In addition, nothing guarantees that the courts will learn from experience and from the expert knowledge at their disposal in an optimal way. They may be too slow in their learning processes. As private law courts are accustomed to apply 'bipolar reasoning' dealing with the allocation of risks and errors between the parties to the case, they might have difficulties in relating to 'multipolar considerations', that is (regulatory) effects that transcend the case at hand.[74]

There is also a danger that courts, using 'the floodgate argument', are reluctant to decide for the plaintiff in such practically important cases in which the occurrence to be assessed has resulted in or may be expected to result in damage to many persons. Such a reluctance in front of the floodgates may constitute another paradox of legal decision-making: the ability of private law to respond to the challenges of uncertainty and risk might be at its poorest in cases where it would be needed the most.

[71] PETL Art 5:101(1).
[72] CISG Art 79(1).
[73] Brüggemeier (1999: 23).
[74] So de Jong (2018).

In short: even though private law needs to focus more on experimentalism and learning, it cannot replace public law regulation. A learning private law is an ideal. It can emerge in some good narratives, but one can hardly regard private law as a sufficient instrument for pervasive management of uncertainty. In addition to the 'hard cases' in which the prevailing standards of coping with uncertainty are challenged – and which are in the focus of this work[75] – there needs to be a bulk of 'routine cases' that implements the rules in a day-to-day manner, perhaps by administrative means.

In other words, what one finds in a society that struggles to find quick answers to growing uncertainty is an increasingly pluralist set of simultaneous legal steering mechanisms. One might speak of a policy mix that transcends the boundaries between the legal disciplines and makes use of the possibilities offered by contract law, tort law and public law.[76] In this mix, private law and public law fulfil different functions and their roles may vary depending on the actual challenges.

There is a complex relationship between the private law and the public law elements of the risk management mix. On the one hand, as mentioned above, efficient private law learning processes can result in new administrative regulation. Similarly, the administrative regulatory mechanisms are often reflected in decisions concerning private liability. On the other hand, it is also important that both areas retain a considerable degree of autonomy in relation to each other. A truly learning private law must be able to assess liability without being bound too tightly to the standards defined by administrative law.[77] Private law can function as an *avant garde* in the management of uncertainty only if it is free to make other demands than public law.

In other words, in the relationship between private law and public law the required flexibility results in a mix of various regulatory methods that appear as autonomous but interconnected. The flexible mix is a consequence of the need both of quick reactions to problematic situations and of continuous and effective implementation of the learning processes.

Finally, the flexibility and ability to make rapid changes relate to another feature that often encounters more criticism, namely the fragmentation of private law. Law does not only have to be increasingly flexible; it also becomes increasingly fragmented.

Private law can often best fulfil its role as a learning mechanism by focusing on concrete expressions of real-life challenges rather than abstract legal categories. Both legislatures and courts should have room for realistic and adequate responses to new situations. This means a private law that is able adequately to respond to the concrete needs within different spheres of life, within particular branches of trade and within particular markets. The flexibility of private law has to be situation-oriented, contextual. This means that the legal mechanisms of experimental learning-by-doing

[75] See ch 1 section IV.
[76] As recommended by Hart (1991: 376).
[77] But, of course, not completely independently; Damm (1996: 126) uses the telling expression '*differenzierte Feinabstimmung*'.

should not be tightly bound to an established conceptual system that reflects only past experience.

The focus on situations rather than on general (legal) categories tends to mitigate the effects of any effort to develop a coherent system of rules and principles. Societal complexity is difficult to combine with a general and formal legal structure.[78] A classical model of systematisation 'does not fit with the complexity of our contemporary societies'.[79] An instrumentalist private law, which is more open to experimentalism, cannot be based on the ideal of coherence in the traditional private law sense; some may even claim that 'an instrumentalist codification – or even a mere instrumentalist coherent Community instrument – is quite inconceivable.'[80] Contextuality means fragmentation when looked at from a traditional systematic private law perspective.

III. WHAT ABOUT STABILITY AND CALCULABILITY?

The need for experimental flexible legal decision-making in contemporary society seems to be at odds with standard legal narratives, according to which rule of law requires predictability. Businesses fear legal uncertainty and demand clear-cut rules that facilitate strategical planning. One has to find a place for the need for stability in the picture of a flexible learning private law.

The focus on risk in contemporary society does not only emphasise uncertainty and the need for experimentation. On the contrary, new methods for collecting experience and calculating risks have fostered rational ways of managing risks that perhaps even affect our world view. François Ewald's theory of the insurance society[81] offers one perspective on this. In his terminology, the heading of this section could be reformulated: The insurance society and its need for clear-cut rules.

Ewald's analysis runs parallel to the diagnosis of the risk society, as the insurance society is also based on risk. However, here, risk is primarily a danger which is rationalised and mathematised and can be calculated.[82] At first sight, this emphasis on calculability and insurance as a way of controlling uncertainty seems to be in sharp contrast to the idea that uncertainty in the risk society is inherently uncontrollable. Indeed, Ulrich Beck has explicitly dissociated himself from Ewald: 'Industrialism in its advanced stage in the second half of the twentieth century is increasingly producing effects that can no longer be encompassed or covered by the calculus of risk and insurance.'[83]

[78] Brüggemeier (1997a: 672): '*Gesellschaftliche Hochdifferenzierung und Generalität und Formalität des Rechts schliessen sich aus.*' *cf*, however, Brüggemeier (2013: 957), who compares the present scattered rules on strict liability with the chaos of Augeas's stables.

[79] Van Hoecke and Ost (1998: 209).

[80] Michaels (2011: 143) and 147 (experimentalism). Michaels (at 152–53) sees 'statute' as the expression of instrumentalist rationality, and 'code' as the expression of juridical rationality.

[81] Ewald (1986) and, in German, Ewald (1989).

[82] Ewald (1989: 390).

[83] Beck (1994a: 181–82).

The cleavage between these diagnoses, however, is perhaps not as deep as one at first sight might imagine. The starting point – the understanding of dangers as risks that are related to human activity – is the same; also Ewald emphasises the possibilities of man to control his life.[84] Some of the differences may follow from the nature of the risks that the authors are discussing. While Beck's diagnosis of society emphasises new catastrophic risks out of reach of rational calculability, Ewald's approach takes into account changes in thought structures that already occurred before the emergence of many of these catastrophic risks. The diagnosis that relates to calculable risks is still of interest in areas in which a broader experience of the risks is being accumulated. In a comprehensive diagnosis, one may combine the two approaches. Depending on the nature of the risk, one could rather see an interesting oscillation between the uncertainty of the risk society and the calculability of the insurance society.

The increasing complexity and the quicker pace of change in contemporary society probably decreases the instances of calculability. This, however, does not profoundly change the basic picture. Even though a growing number of issues are brought out of reach of calculability because of their complex and rapidly changing character, the advances of artificial intelligence in combination with growing availability of relevant data may on the other hand bring ever more complicated situations back to the reign of calculus.

The notion of the insurance society does not only focus on the development of institutions like private and public insurance. It goes deeper, assuming that a certain way of thinking permeates society as a whole. It implies the adoption of a type of rationality that is formalised in a probability calculus that is collective, as risks can be calculated only within a population.[85] The rationality of the insurance society rests on calculability and collectivity.

This comprehensive rationality, in other words, also inspires areas of law other than insurance law and social security law. The impact of the rationality of the insurance society on tort law is well known. The development towards stricter forms of liability is often justified with reference to the possibilities of insuring the liability. The application of insurance rationality in private law, however, may be seen in less self-evident examples as well. For example, in the area of consumer law, both product liability and strict rules on the liability of the seller can be justified by insurance reasoning: the seller may include the costs in the price of the goods. The argument presupposes both calculability of the costs and the existence of a consumer collective that ultimately bears the expenses associated with the risk. The liability of businesses is a method to bring about the formalised solidarity of the insurance society between consumers in situations covered by the liability.

Geraint Howells has argued that in the credit sector the impact of various risks on interest rates can be seen as a form of insurance, thus supporting the placing of certain risks on the creditor rather than on the debtor.[86] I believe that even a socially

[84] Ewald (1989: 387).
[85] Ewald (1989: 390).
[86] Howells (1999).

geared development of the protection of debtors hit by unemployment or illness (*social force majeure*[87]) can be explained in these terms. More generally, Iain Ramsay has expressed similar thoughts concerning credit and risk in an analysis of the legislation on consumer bankruptcy as a form of protection against the uncertainties of life.[88]

The functioning of liability rules as an insurance-like scheme in which the risk can be calculated and spread over a collective requires a subject of liability that either has a large enough risk portfolio or a sufficient interest to spread the risk through liability insurance. Various kinds of private and public organisations fulfil the criteria, but most typically such a risk-spreader is a business. It is therefore not surprising that that the liability of businesses has been a focal area in the development of private law in the insurance society.

The rationality of the insurance society seems to push development in a different direction than the pressures towards a flexible private law in the risk society. The demand for calculability requires clear rules. With regard to mass transactions, efficiency also requires rules that are sufficiently clear to be followed as such. For example, modern private law regulation to protect consumers often contains much precise rules.

In other words, even in the risk perspective one must combine the requirement of a flexible private law with its opposite, precise and calculable rules. The need for a learning and experimental law may push this combination into a recurrent oscillation between flexibility and preciseness. As long as there is insufficient experience concerning a risk, law needs to be flexible in order to cope with new situations. Once there is sufficient experience, it is possible to make more precise rules, either through legislation or through case law. The growth of instances of strict liability in tort law in many countries is a paradigmatic example of such a development. However, the learning process towards more precise rules is not a one-way street. During the process, new risks that require flexible rules appear. In the light of new experience, it may also be necessary to reassess already established precise rules on the basis of more general flexible principles. The continuous oscillation between flexibility and islands of precision is an unavoidable expression of the uncertainty of late modern society.

As to the fragmentation thesis, the need for more precise rules rather confirms it. Contemporary clear-cut rules are often only detailed normative interventions concerning particular issues with limited spheres of application. They are additional ingredients in the complex risk-management mix of the risk society. The oscillation between flexibility and precise rules underlines the fragmentation of law.

The oscillating learning processes are not only based on collection of experience: the outcome of the process is also related to social values. The degree of solidarity produced by any form of insurance or insurance-like regulation depends on the definition of the insured collective or, in the language of insurance, how the risk classification is made. Referring to this, in a discussion of insurance law, Nick Huls

[87] On this concept, see Wilhelmsson (1992: 180 *et seq*).
[88] Ramsay (1999).

speaks of a development 'From class struggle to classification'.[89] In consumer law, strict rules on liability have been defended as devices which create the same liability towards all groups of consumers and thereby counteract less advantageous markets for underprivileged consumers.[90] Behind the seemingly technical language of insurance rationality one often finds questions of justice. Insurance rationality does not relieve a decision-maker of the burden of ethical uncertainty in decision-making.

Arguably an oscillation between flexibility and stability is not a new feature of contemporary law.[91] It has been claimed that legal evolution constantly faces the same dilemma: on the one hand, there is a need for stability and operational closure; on the other hand, there is a need for adaptation to a changing society and of cognitive openness. Stability is needed to protect the legal order against sudden political and other changes, but law must also have a capacity to develop, sufficiently taking into account societal feedback mechanisms.[92] This is hard to deny. The features of contemporary law that I have described above do not amount to something completely new, applicable only to late modernity. It is rather a question of emphasis and relative weight. As the need for flexibility in contemporary law grows, the constant oscillation between flexibility and islands of stability becomes more apparent.[93]

The balance between flexibility and stability is not the same within different fields of private law. As noted before, tort law traditionally contains much flexibility in its structures, which makes it well adapted to the idea of a learning law. Other fields in which it is easy to pinpoint a need for experimental and learning legal practices, with fast-changing technology and patterns of behaviour, are consumer law[94] and environmental law. On the other hand, it is easy to understand that areas like property law and the law of secured credit have to be quite stable to fulfil their functions. However, even such areas encounter societal pressure for change. As mentioned above, both the CJEU and the German courts offer good examples in their reactions to the effects on individuals of the financial crisis. Also in these fields, law needs learning mechanisms, but perhaps working at a slower pace.

IV. ETHICAL AMBIVALENCE ADDING TO THE UNCERTAINTY

The uncertainty of late modern society is not only epistemic, but also ethical. The late modern ambivalence also relates to value issues. Having presented the need for an experimental and learning law related to societal complexity, I will here address a similar need for a law that is able to 'learn' contextual moral assessments.[95]

[89] Huls (1993: 155).

[90] This function of consumer protection is emphasised eg by Reifner and Volkmer (1988: 21 *et seq*).

[91] Earlier accounts of law also see it as a 'human laboratory constantly seeking improvement', Dagan (2015: 1898).

[92] Heidelbach and Evald-Schelde (2018), analysing legal evolution in the light of evolution biology and system theory.

[93] The growing need for balancing 'legal certainty' and 'adaptability' or 'flexibility' is a core theme of Fenwick, Siems and Wrbka (2017: eg 25–26).

[94] On 'learning' consumer law, see eg Höland (1997: 213–18).

[95] I have published some of these thoughts before in English in Wilhelmsson (2005).

The two forms of late modern ambivalence, the epistemic and the ethical uncertainty, are often intermingled. Even though, for example, finding proper societal reactions to the COVID-19 pandemic at first appeared to be an epistemic problem, increasingly manageable when our knowledge about the virus and its effects increased, this was only partially true. When the death toll grew and the negative economic consequences of the pandemic accumulated, decision-making concerning appropriate measures appeared increasingly value-laden. Should the measures primarily save lives (mainly of old people) or the economy? The question was usually not formulated so crudely, but it shows the importance of ethical deliberation in the seemingly medico-technical decision-making concerning the pandemic. One could of course add numerous other examples of how epistemic and ethical uncertainty are intermingled in societal and legal decision-making. This is not necessary. It is just worth noting that such a combination of perspectives often deepens the complexity faced by decision-makers. Looking for the impact of late modern uncertainty on private law, one does not necessarily need to distinguish between the two perspectives, as I have done in this chapter for analytical reasons.

The diagnoses of late modern society usually emphasise rising ethical ambivalence. The fragmentation of late modern society includes a dissolution of traditional value structures under the pressure of globalisation, a displacement of shared national and local normative beliefs by a marketplace of understandings. Globalisation puts local and national traditions in competition with other ways of thinking and acting.[96] Traditions survive only as long as they seem justified in comparison with alternative patterns of behaviour.[97] Even scholars who continue emphasising the role of tradition admit that 'there is a gradual decline in the traditional grounding of action and in the role of traditional authority – that is, in the normative and the legitimation aspects of tradition'.[98]

Tradition and ethical authority walk together. The late modern non-traditional culture decreases the homogenising effects of authoritative sources such as religion, philosophy and ideology. Key institutions, such as political parties, trade unions and even nations, lose much of their historical legitimacy.[99] There is an unregulated market for ideologies and philosophies.

The grand societal narratives are among the discredited ideologies. Socialism lost much of its force after the collapse of what was used to be called 'real socialism'. The excesses of capitalism, on the other hand, have led researchers to ask whether capitalism can be saved[100] or how it will end.[101] The belief in the universal benefits of the market does not carry such a general credibility that it could convince those who are not already believers. The European middle ground, the belief in the welfare state has also received its blows. However, as will be analysed in chapter six, this ideology might still be something most Europeans adhere to, but in a diluted form and without much legitimising authority.

[96] Giddens (1994: 95 *et seq*).
[97] Giddens (1994: 105).
[98] Thompson (1996: 93).
[99] Beck (1994a: 178), Castells (1997: 354–55).
[100] Reich (2015): 'Saving Capitalism: For the Many, Not the Few'.
[101] Streeck (2014).

In other words, diagnoses of late modern society speak about an age without ethics.[102] There is no longer a generally accepted code for how one should behave. There is no agreement on what institutions or what persons one could acknowledge as ethical experts.

This does not mean that nobody tells grand narratives of an ideological nature any longer. On the contrary, even in Europe the longing for totalising ideologies seems to be on the rise again. Growing groups in society are strongly committed to religious beliefs and patterns of action. Another popular narrative is nationalism or 'tribalism',[103] efficiently exploited by various kinds of populist movements. In combination with a revival of history, as it is imagined to have been (a retrotopia),[104] it has become a legitimising narrative that appeals to many:

> What might, however, strike the viewer most, is the Angel changing direction – the Angel of History caught in the midst of a U-turn: his face turning from the past to the future, his wings being pushed backwards by the storm blowing this time from the imagined, anticipated and feared in advance Hell of the future towards the Paradise of the past (as, probably, it is restrospectively imagined after it has been lost and fallen into ruins).[105]

However, the nostalgic U-turn to nationalism, tribalism and religion does not alter the basic picture of the present as a period without credible ethical authority. Whatever -isms are emerging and convincing some, there are usually anti-isms fiercely opposing them. Globalists and those believing in the European project are contesting nationalism and tribalism, whilst secularists are confronting religious ideologies. There seems to be no hope for a consensus, at least on the level of principle.

This is not to say that the situation has not changed at all. The advent of social media, and the increasing personalisation of media consumption in general, has promoted a development of a society of discursive communities – 'social media bubbles' – within which the adopted belief system has strong credibility, as it is not confronted with opposing ideologies. The communicative middle ground has shrunken and the preparedness to cross-ideological discourse has decreased. This emphasises the fragmented character of contemporary ethics, and the need for promoting discourse across the fragments.

The decline of the belief in universal ethical systems and in ethical expertise does not necessarily imply that society has moved into an age characterised by a lack of morality. The absence of a universal value system does not imply that values would lack importance. One just has to adopt another perspective on moral behaviour when the area of joint value structures is shrinking.

Some indeed assess the 'liberation' from ethical systems rather optimistically. Zygmunt Bauman, one of the leading advocates of a new kind of moral responsibility, claims that there is at least an opportunity for a deeper morality. According to him, the end of the 'ethical era' may be seen as a gate to an 'era of morality'.[106] As the authoritative ethical guidance that would remove the individual responsibility

[102] I have found the analyses by Bauman (1993), as well as Bauman (1995: 10 *et seq*), quite convincing.
[103] Bauman (2017: 49 *et seq*).
[104] Bauman (2017).
[105] Bauman (2017: 2).
[106] Bauman (1995: 42).

for moral decisions declines, the development returns to people the opportunity of moral choice and moral responsibility. One cannot renounce this responsibility by a reference to established ethical systems and experts. For Bauman, this is the ethical paradox of post-modernity: at the same time as people are constantly reminded of the relativity of all ethical codes they receive full moral choice and responsibility.[107] They are forced to encounter moral issues 'point blank, in all their naked truth', when the ethical clouds that have obscured personal responsibility have vanished.[108]

The connection between the decline of ethical systems and the emphasis on moral responsibility is not self-evident. However, as the legitimacy of universally accepted ethical authority is decreasing, it is at least one way forward to insist on a growing personal responsibility for everyone concerning moral choices. In a normative context, the emphasis on individual moral responsibility offers a constructive perspective.

The freedom from universal ethical authority forces people to make more personal choices: 'In post-traditional contexts, we have no choice but to choose how to be and how to act.'[109] As it is no longer self-evident to build behaviour on local tradition and on the normative patterns that prevail in the respective society, social class or group, the individual is forced to an increasing extent to make his or her own decisions regarding both their way of life and actions. This freedom from ethical authority implies a moral responsibility for those decisions. Bauman's 'era of morality' is an era during which everybody accepts to be responsible for their own responsibility.[110] As a normative hope, this focus on the individual responsibility for moral behaviour is one of the starting points of the present book – at the same time reflecting the moral choice of the author (or the ethical bubble within which the author lives).

A decision-maker who cannot hide his or her personal choices and decisions behind a predetermined ethical system is forced to develop a pragmatic approach assessing moral issues in the actual decision-making situation. As one cannot make decisions based on abstract ethical norms alone, they have to be justified also with reference to the context. A moral decision-making requires seeing and listening to the concrete persons affected by the decision. Moral decisions have to be made on practical grounds, without philosophical assurances.[111] Most people are anyway deciding moral issues based on habit and common sense rather than with reference to some universal code.[112] Moral roads are not made with the help of any pre-existing map, but we make the roads by walking them.[113]

The map metaphor is useful, as it shows how an individual and pragmatic morality can be distinguished from a total value relativism. Everybody does not choose a road of her own. On the contrary, as the roads are made by walking them, common

[107] Bauman (1992: xxii).
[108] Bauman (1995: 43).
[109] Giddens (1994: 75).
[110] Bauman, interview in the Finnish philosophical journal *niin & näin* 3/1997 at 46.
[111] Bauman (1992: xxiii).
[112] Bauman (1995: 11–12).
[113] Bauman (1995: 17).

paths and roads emerge. Even old roads (tradition) are retained, if somebody is walking them. Morality must be societal, something that one shares with others. The fact that the joint belief in a grand ethical system has vanished does not prevent people from reaching moral consensus on how particular types of human conflicts can be solved.

In other words, the community in moral questions in late modernity grows from below, from practical experience, through recurrent contextual learning processes without definite answers. The moral issues continuously have to be reassessed when confronted with new experience.

A model like this requires a continuing moral dialogue. Morality is to be found 'in the processes of moral communication rather than in specifically moral institutions'.[114] Social interaction and communication become the source for moral assessments, as the similarity of views 'needs to be cautiously negotiated in specific communicative processes between the parties to a social encounter'.[115] Moral communication becomes the instrument for performing ethical learning processes.

Social media have dramatically changed the preconditions for pragmatic moral communication. Twitter-storms and Facebook-campaigns based on moral conviction are daily occurrences. They demonstrate the fact that moral is social, and that there is a readiness to walk the same moral paths within a group on social media, but they also show how fragmented and polarised the reactions to moral issues might be. In the timeframe of a social media discourse there is little opportunity for deeper moral analysis that would go beyond quick emotional reactions. The situation is paradoxical: at the same time as moral communication has become technically extremely easy, it is substantively increasingly difficult. The need for more deeply looking *fora* for moral communication seems rather to have increased. There is a societal call for moral discourse and communication in a slower pace, such as that of law.

Ethically sensitive decision-making in late modern society has to be based on contextual moral reasoning and communication. The ethical uncertainty of late modernity supports the emphasis on a contextual perspective that above was related to epistemic uncertainty. In the following section I will discuss what role private law can play as a vehicle for contextual moral communication and learning.

V. ETHICAL UNCERTAINTY AND PRIVATE LAW

The implications of ethical uncertainty for private law run parallel to those of epistemic uncertainty. The need for contextual moral communication and learning processes calls for a law that can respond to the demand for such processes:

> As social norms become weaker a kind of moral vacuum arises … law has a tendency in our society to move into this vacuum.[116]

[114] Luckmann (1996: 76).
[115] Luckmann (1996: 81).
[116] Glendon (1991: 102).

Some may ask, however, to what extent the task of moral communication and moral learning is relevant with regard to private law, as this field of law is sometimes alleged to be relatively 'technical' and only loosely connected with ethics. Obviously, ethical sensitivity varies between areas of private law and between different types of issues within those areas.

For example, the close connection between tort law and ethics has been broadly acknowledged.[117] In theoretically inclined legal literature, analyses of the moral basis of tort law are abundant.[118] Tort law is said to contain both applied morals and applied politics[119] and to offer moral philosophy much common sense-based insight.[120] Even if one does not go so far in openness as the Dutch civil code, according to which liability can arise if a person is 'answerable according to common opinion',[121] the definition of the basis of liability (negligence) is so vague that it constitutes a broad field for practical moral discourse. In the discussions on the philosophy of tort law, however, there is a cleavage between those emphasising the autonomy and moral responsibility of the subject as the basis of liability and those downplaying the direct moral link by referring to efficient allocation of resources and losses. Tort law relates both to moral behaviour and to allocation of losses,[122] and the choice between the approaches as well as between various principles for allocation is at least partially a moral choice too. Ethical and epistemological uncertainty are interlinked in tort law decision-making.

Tort law is a particularly useful area for moral discourse and communication because it often deals with acts and activities that are easy to relate to common sense morality. Tort law offers 'More than any other area of law … examples of how people should and should not treat each other'.[123] Everybody who has taught private law to first- and second-year students knows how much easier it is to engage them in a debate on the moral tenability of tort law decisions than to achieve similar discussions on complicated property or company law issues, as student can relate much of tort law to their everyday life and grassroot experience.

Ethical controversy is not absent, however, in other areas of private law, such as contract law. This is not only the case in rare situations in which a moral issue appears as the main question, for example the question of how to apply contract law to sexual services.[124] On the contrary, such controversy permeates even the general dividing lines concerning the possible development of contract law. For example, in the debate concerning the harmonisation of private law in the EU, various approaches to the ethics of private law have led to well-known discussions on the politics of private law[125]

[117] See eg the historical introduction by Owen (1995: 1 *et seq*).

[118] As just two examples, see the collections Owen (1995), as well as Postema (2001), aiming to contribute to the articulation of 'an explanatory account of tort law' (2001: 1).

[119] Stapleton (1999: 520).

[120] Williams (1995: in particular 493 *et seq*).

[121] Art 6:162 para 3 and 6.75 (contractual liability), mentioned by Hartkamp (1992: 11).

[122] Englard (1993) defends a 'complementary vision of tort law'.

[123] Owen (1995: 27).

[124] See eg Tjon Soei Len (2015).

[125] Hesselink (2006).

and even to a much-cited Manifesto on social justice in European contract law.[126] This reflects one of the basic themes of the contract law discourse over many decades, namely the confrontation of 'traditional' or 'liberalist' contract law with something that could be described as the 'Social Side of Contract Law'[127] or 'welfarism in contract law'.[128] In fact, the situation is even more complicated than these relatively obvious dichotomies suggest. Within the 'social' or 'welfarist' paradigm new ethical cleavages appear. I will discuss these cleavages further in chapter six below.

The ethical cleavages and the need for contextual ethical assessment do not relate to the 'social side' of contract law alone. Also within the commercial sphere proper, one finds various 'sub-cultures' with different understandings of morally acceptable behaviour. National cultures are differing, some valuing competition and self-interest and others cooperation and loyalty. Special branches of business – like the IT sector – may also produce their own views on good behaviour that affect the contextual assessments of what a good law should contain.

The presentation of the contract law discourses in a language of dichotomies is analytically illuminating. This does not mean that one could convincingly describe existing legal materials in an 'either-or' language. The variety of ethical approaches appears in different combinations in national contract laws in Europe and in the *acquis* as well. The ethical starting points are too debatable to be carved in stone, under prevailing societal conditions of ethical uncertainty. Also in contract law, there is a scope for contextual moral reasoning, both for the legislatures and the courts.

Private law can offer one of the arenas for moral discourse and communication that are needed in contemporary society. Moral assessments can be made on several levels. The issue at hand may relate to the individual moral and care that is expected in day-to-day activities. It can also mean an assessment of the tenability of decision-making with broader societal impact. Such broader moral assessments may appear as political questions that should be discussed in a democratic context rather than in a legal one. An increasing engagement of law in such issues reflects a legitimacy crisis of politics: law is called to fill the demand for transparent moral assessments that politics does not offer.[129] By answering this call, it also lays the ground for an increasing use of law as an instrument of micro-politics, analysed more closely in the next chapter.

The judicial process is a hotspot for a contextual and pragmatic moral communication and encounter. When speaking about law as an arena for moral communication, not only the result of the process matters. Sometimes the moral communication in various relationships – both between the parties and the judge and in relation to the mass media and the population as a whole – may be more important than the actual

[126] Reprinted in Hesselink (2006: 171–95).
[127] Lurger (2011). Many examples can be found in the collection of essays on critical contract law edited by Wilhelmsson (1993).
[128] Brownsword, Howells and Wilhelmsson (1994).
[129] Nelken (1996: xiii).

solution of the problem.[130] Law can offer a context in which one discursively can address moral issues:

> Legal communication and legal identity may be interpreted as constructions to *make possible* a dialogue between different views of life, different conceptions of the good life, different language games and, perhaps, different expert cultures.[131]

The role of law as an instrument for moral communication is not limited to the encounters in concrete cases alone. More generally, one can describe legal practices as law-related communicative practices in which various actors take part. Kaarlo Tuori includes in a broad definition of legal practices 'all social communication whose theme is the application, interpretation or amendment of the legal order', including not only the interventions of legal actors, but also public discussions on the need to amend the law and on celebrated cases.[132] In all these quarters, law offers an arena for moral communication and learning.

The moral-building learning processes affect the involved actors in various ways. Through discursive analysis of a case, the parties and the court deepen their insights in the moral challenges involved, whilst other stakeholders and the society at large are alerted about the moral issues at hand and about possible ways to confront them. Some are learning through participation in the discourse, whilst others act as passive receivers of knowledge. The learning may happen during various timeframes. For example, a row of noticed cases on environmental issues may slowly contribute to build an environmentally conscious moral among consumers. In such a situation, one could even speak about 'law as education' rather than 'law as communication'.

The question to what extent and in what way a legal procedure can function as an arena for moral communication cannot have one answer. Moral communication in a case based on detailed regulation looks more like 'law as education', whilst other, less densely regulated areas are more amenable to productive moral communication, opening new legal-moral roads. The question relates to the qualities of the legal material at hand: what kind of private law is most susceptible to becoming a device for moral communication and decision-making? What does this function mean with regard to the structure and concepts of private law?

In very general terms, such a role requires a law that is sufficiently open towards moral assessments. A flexible law is more prone to recognise the responsibility to make moral choices of those that use and apply the law.

A general clause explicitly acknowledges the role of courts to make moral assessments. It is well known that contemporary legislation in many countries, including the EU, to an increasing extent uses general clauses that require the courts to decide whether a contract or a marketing measure is deemed to be reasonable, fair or in accordance with good morals.[133] It is a conscious choice to underline the role of

[130] Raes (1996) emphasises the communicative side of the legal procedure.
[131] Raes (1996: 38).
[132] Tuori (2002: 132).
[133] See from a comparative perspective eg Grundmann and Mazeaud (2006).

courts as moral antennas that can absorb moral views from the surrounding society into the legal order.

In addition, one may create sufficient flexibility by using more subtle means than explicitly moral-related general clauses. Many legal concepts contain an element of a moral assessment in their application. As noted above, tort law offers broad opportunities for moral assessment through the morally-sensitive concept of negligence. Even in thoroughly regulated areas, moral issues may occasionally pop up like a Jack-in-the-Box in front of an astonished legal auditorium. There is always a possibility that a routine case turns into a hard case when the 'routine outcome' appears to be morally not acceptable.

In contemporary legal discourse, references to fundamental rights is one way of strengthening the connections between law and moral reasoning. The 'Euroconstitutionalism' coined by Oliver Gerstenberg expressly relies on courts as fora for creating case-by-case fundamental rights-related debates on changing social values.[134] The fundamental rights discourse in other words increases the opportunities for moral communication and decision-making also within private law.[135] In addition, other basic principles can also function as devices to turn the procedure into a forum for moral communication. For example, the increasingly important precautionary principle, often referred to in environmental and health-related contexts, functions as 'a concrete tool to take into account ethical and social values.'[136]

Flexibility is needed to provide law with a sufficient amount of contextuality. Moral reasoning without systematic ethical assurance has to be contextual: moral roads are made by walking in concrete contexts. A private law that engages in moral communication has to formulate its arguments closer to real life than in an abstract legal conceptuality. Legal language has to be demystified in order to make moral communication within law possible. Communication requires a dismantling of such concepts and theories that function as walls between law and moral and behind which legal actors may comfortably hide their moral intuition.

This does not mean, however, that one should abandon legal conceptuality as such. In the same way as other traditions, legal conceptual traditions have to be continuously discursively scrutinised and amended. Instead of depreciating legal conceptuality, one should rather seek new concepts that are closer to the real-life grassroot reality in which late modern moral communication thrives. Legal concepts should be developed in a way that does not destroy moral discourse but rather offers it new opportunities. In chapter eight I will discuss how reasoning in real-life language promotes transparency of decision-making.

The connection to legal conceptuality anchors legal reasoning in long traditions of thought. This is important to underline in the era of social media: well-founded moral discourse is not the same as X (Twitter)- or Facebook-fed moral panic. Law is needed as a forum for moral communication precisely because the slow pace of law

[134] Gerstenberg (2018: 109).
[135] I will return to this issue in ch 6.
[136] Guerra (2018: 600).

can function as a counterweight to the fast and often draconic judgments uttered in a social media storm.

Legal tradition is facing a constant challenge from pragmatically justified contextual solutions that do not fit the system. In other words, contextuality and flexibility imply fragmentation. A private law that reflects the occasional and pragmatic character of contemporary moral is less tied to general and 'eternal' ethical principles and to rigid conceptual structures. It is a private law that gives legal actors more opportunities to make the roads while walking them.

VI. THE EUROPEAN DIMENSION

The societal diagnoses of contemporary society that have inspired the above analysis are not limited to some particular national or legal environment. On the contrary, much of the uncertainty stems from the fact that the challenges are global, and the risks cannot be contained within one national system alone.[137] The complexity of a globalised society is said to require a legal approach that is based on fuzzy logic.[138] Decisions are made in global networks with shrinking anchorage in a particular national order. In Europe, the EU, its institutions and EU-related actors have taken an important role as a decision-making structure between the national and the global level.

As argued above, societal uncertainty requires a law that is able to constantly learn how to deal with new challenges. As risks and other challenges are increasingly transnational, one may learn the lessons from across national borders as well. Efficient learning processes require a sufficient amount of legal practice. When a legal decision-maker faces a new issue, answers to similar issues in other countries may be consulted. A dynamic private law acknowledges the importance of an international outlook as one of the instruments for dealing with uncertainty.[139]

At first sight, cross-border learning seems to differ in principle from domestic learning processes. Whilst purely domestic legal actors confronted with challenges from real life have to rely on expertise and on participants in the activities that are assessed, cross-border legal learning appears as more 'purely legal' as legal actors here seem to be learning from other, foreign legal actors. To some extent this might be true, but only on a surface level. When deciding what to learn from foreign legal experience, the legal decision-maker has to evaluate the foreign experience in the light of domestic societal knowledge. After all, successful learning requires the understanding of the societal conditions and consequences of the solution. I will discuss this more closely in chapter five.

It is not only epistemic uncertainty that calls for a greater readiness to learn from experiences across the borders: ethical ambivalence requires cross-border learning as well. The function of law as a device for communicating and facilitating moral

[137] Beck (2007) sketches a *Weltrisikogesellschaft*.

[138] Delmas-Marty (2020: 197).

[139] Also Andenas and Fairgrieve (2015a: 9) claim that the increasing use of comparative law is a consequence inter alia of the complexity of contemporary decision-making.

discourse is relevant not only nationally, but also in a European and globalised context. It may even become particularly important for the moral discourse across the borders that is necessary in the era of globalisation. To what extent can the international legal community make legal roads by walking them?

Examples of the use of law as a way to establish an internationalised moral discourse are abundant. A radical version is the establishment of institutions like international war crimes tribunals. The cross-border moral-building function of the law, however, also appears in more mundane private law contexts. For example, understanding the law as a medium for moral communication adds a dimension to our comprehension of the development of an international *lex mercatoria*. Its rules on international business transactions reflect a pragmatic morality, based on the expectations of the participants in the transactions. It has grown out of a discursive confrontation of various views on acceptable behaviour in business. This does not mean that the discourses have resulted in one joint highway. They might produce only smaller roads that are accepted in certain communities or lines of business. As national commercial cultures are different they may produce different expectations on good moral behaviour.[140]

In principle, both epistemic and ethical learning across borders may occur globally. In particular, in globalised fields related to, for example, transportation or digitalisation, it happens that legal experience is collected globally. Obviously, however, conditions for successful legal learning are more favourable if the countries involved share basic legal, cultural and societal features. The EU is supposed to share some legal cultural values and practices that are partially different than those of the rest of the world, including the US.[141] One could claim that the EU, with strong national legal traditions on the one hand and relatively similar societal conditions on the other hand, offers a good breeding ground for cross-border legal learning. The main proposal of this work – the appeal for a free movement of legal ideas across European borders – builds on such a vision.

During the present century, however, the openness towards cooperation and learning across the EU is increasingly challenged by various kinds of 'tribalism'[142] (nationalism and provincialism). The force of this movement is considerable, as it has its roots in real tensions between a globalised economy and shrinking local social cohesion, 'a swelling abyss between the free-floating global elite and locals fixed to the ground'.[143] Perhaps surprisingly, the nationalist movements often also have legal visions demanding a re-nationalisation of law and legal institutions. The importance of 'own courts' and 'own laws' – the content of which those who make the claims often possess very vague knowledge – may even become an identity issue. The stance of the UK on the possible role of the CJEU in the arrangements related to Brexit illustrates this well. The independence of the British courts was, to cite a public statement

[140] *cf* the various attitudes towards pre-contractual information duties, see eg Brownsword, Hird and Howells (1999).

[141] Helleringer and Purnhagen (2014: vi).

[142] Bauman (2017: 49 *et seq*).

[143] Bauman (2017: 70).

by Theresa May, 'non-negotiable'[144] – and this stance did not require any explanations on whether or why one could expect substantively better solutions from the British Supreme Court. It was just a question of national pride and identity to have the courts freed from relations to the EU.

Again, in this tension between Europeanisation on the one hand and the longing for a return to the national and local on the other hand, law should provide a forum for a slower and more thoughtful discourse. It is the responsibility of legal actors to fall neither for sirens of national purity and isolation when such nationalism cannot be founded on good reasons, nor for temptations of Europeanisation if it appears as unfounded in the context. Legal professionals should consistently insist on good ethical and epistemic reasoning when looking across borders.

It is self-evident that a law that has left its safe harbour in the tight alignment with the national state must be much more complex and chaotic than pure and isolated national law. As William Twining notes, 'a global jurisprudence needs to depict the phenomena of law in the modern world as to a large extent disorderly, unsystematic and serendipitous.'[145] Already the tension between the aim to decrease the differences between nations and a perceived need to protect the unique and local is bound to produce fragmentation as a result. The increasing volume of cross-border legal discourses strengthens the fragmentation tendencies related to late modern uncertainty.

That this is the case in particular within the EU is too well-known to demand a lengthy justification. The multi-level governance structure of the EU is bound to produce fragmentation if measured in comparison with a traditional private law structure. The clash between the internal market logic of European private law and traditional private law structures means that contemporary European private law 'can only be un-systemic'.[146] Much of the private law debate confronting a perceived need for a European civil code with a demand on the EU not to dive deeply into central private law is driven by the worry of traditional private lawyers that the private law system is breaking down as a consequence of European interventions. In this chapter, however, I have tried to show that one does not have to see the fragmenting effect of EU law as a deficiency only, but as a natural answer to the need for a learning law in late modern uncertainty.

The code-words 'contextuality', 'flexibility' and 'fragmentation' are as topical in the cross-border context as in the domestic one. Europeanisation also adds to the pressures towards developing legal concepts that reflect real life more closely. The fact that one in a cross-border learning setting often encounters concepts with different meanings on each side of the relevant border underlines the particular importance of this issue in the cross-border context.

Much EU secondary legislation seems to be in line with the real-life-oriented conceptual demands of late modern society. The European rules are often developed

[144] Interview BBC, citation repeated several times on BBC World, spring 2019.
[145] Twining (2000: 62). See also Culver and Giudice (2016), who argue that it is not useful to discuss contemporary transnational legality based on the idea of law as a system.
[146] Micklitz (2014: 86).

in relation to specific factual situations without taking into account the different conceptual structures of the national legal systems. In building the *acquis* 'modern phenomena and new legal problems could be looked at more directly, without the impediment of legal tradition.'[147] Directives are related to real commercial situations, such as distance-selling or time-sharing, whilst traditional domestic private law is based on more general, and in this sense more abstract, legal concepts.[148]

The pressure on traditional legal concepts does not stem from EU law alone. Learning that originates in other domestic jurisdictions may have the same effect when it impinges on national systematic edifices:

> The realisation that foreign legal systems are able to cope with certain factual problems without a highly sophisticated dogmatic legal framework may lead the judge to realize that the systemisation of the law in his own country is not so much done in a concern for the functioning of the legal system but merely 'out of a tendency to suffer theoretical controversies'.[149]

VII. A FRAGMENTED LAW INSTEAD OF A EUROPEAN CIVIL CODE

In this chapter, the increasing flexibility and fragmentation of law have been pictured as natural and needed adaptations to an experimental societal reality. This does not only put pressure on the traditional systematics of national laws: it also has implications for the discourse on the harmonisation of European private law. The vision of a European civil code looks less feasible against this background. As the vision seems in any case to have lost its appeal, as shown by the very limited impact of the Draft Common Frame of Reference (DCFR), I will not add yet another long analysis of the issue to those already existing. Only a few additional comments linking the issue to the present work are required.

In the analysis of the need for a European civil code, it is important to recognise the prevailing societal conditions. When academic lawyers draw parallels to the situation when the great European codes, the French *Code Civil* and the German *Bürgerliches Gesetzbuch* (*BGB*), were adopted – as symbols of the French Revolution and the unification of Germany – they often devote too little attention to the changes in the societal basis since the adoption of the codes. The *BGB* was made for a bourgeois society and for an original market capitalism and could therefore reflect a fairly homogeneous world view. Its strong foundations in a market-liberalist vision of society made it possible to erect it as a relatively coherent edifice.[150] Those parts that did not fit into this structure were left to special legislation (*Sonderprivatrecht*) and societal visions that conflicted with the basic credo were neglected.[151]

[147] Grundmann (2004: 701).

[148] A recent example is the Digital Content Directive, which focuses on digital content and not on formal contract types and thereby can pose implementation problems for Member States, which legally systematise remedies related to contract types, see Sein and Spindler (2019: 391).

[149] Berger (2001: 890).

[150] Wieacker (1974: in particular 9 *et seq*).

[151] Well known is the contemporary critique by Menger (1904).

In addition, the mechanisms of market society were probably understood in a relatively simple manner. Today such an ethically and politically homogeneous approach, combined with an epistemically simple understanding of society, is not convincing. The complex structure and ethical pluralism of late modern society are not easy to reconcile with grand system-building of the traditional type. Contextual morality and flexible learning are difficult to combine with a rigid systematic structure of private law.

Contemporary society does not only need another content of law, but also another form of law than the nineteenth-century German and French societies. The need for a private law more open towards processes of constant learning and reassessment seems difficult to fulfil in an optimal manner within the reign of a general civil code. This is the case at least if the concept of a code is understood as a collection of norms that should meet strong demands of systematic coherence and be relatively immune against quick changes. Such a code does not offer sufficient space for creating the roads by walking them. The codifications rather act as 'prison cells' of private law.[152] An instrumentalist codification is said to be impossible to conceive.[153] In the words of Jan Smits: 'The Idea of a Binding Codification seems to be Contrary to the Spirit of the Times'.[154]

There is an obvious counterclaim to the allegation that large-scale codification is an outmoded form of regulation: there has relatively recently been a 'successful enactment of new civil codes', for example in the Netherlands and in a variety of post-socialist countries.[155] As other countries have also amended their codes, one could even describe the situation as a 'new wave of codifications'.[156] The Dutch code was prepared for a long time, more than half a century, whilst the post-socialist enactments were the result of thorough societal upheavals. However, the contextual morality and need for continuing learning processes generate pressures for changes in a shorter timeframe and within more stable general social structures. The jury is still out on the question how new codes are able to respond to such learning demands.

The required dynamic of a learning law relates both to case law and to the capacity of the legislature to create contextual responses to new challenges. The existence of a civil code tends to strengthen the static elements of law in both respects.

It is generally recognised that the threshold for amending and reforming a civil code is higher than for developing specialised freestanding legislation. A civil code is often relatively immune both against market-oriented pressures for amendments raising from changes in commercial reality and against democratically founded demands for more regulation of the welfarist type. Some codes have indeed 'proved quite resistant to large scale revision'.[157] Even when limited amendments are made

[152] Jansen (2010: 160).
[153] Michaels (2011: 143).
[154] Smits (2002: 29).
[155] Basedow (2001: 40 *et seq*).
[156] Discussed in detail in Schulze and Zoll (2013).
[157] Mattei, Ruskola and Gidi (2009: 428). See on amendments made in various codes ibid at 428 *et seq*.

and auxiliary statutes are used, the fundamental edifice remains. The structure and concepts of the code may remain as obstacles to contextual learning.

Some assess the static nature of a code as a virtue rather than a disadvantage. In such a perspective, the dignity of a civil code lies precisely in the fact that 'it is not so freely amended like some statute for consumer or tenant protection'.[158] In an approach that emphasises the need for an experimental law, however, it is hard to accept that main parts of the legislation are frozen in this way. Legislation is always experimental, as one can assess its results only when it is tested in practice, but the system (the code) is not experimental if it cannot be contested.

Despite the static nature of a code, its existence does not make it impossible for courts and scholars to engage in developing the law in an experimental fashion. Codifications have not prevented academic scholars and courts from developing and changing the law.[159] Even the traditional codes have experienced a declining authority, sometimes described as a process of de-codification.[160] A modern code, like the Dutch one, may support the required experimentalism by expressly providing the courts 'with so much freedom that they essentially determine what the law is'.[161]

Whatever one thinks about the capacity of various national codes to respond sufficiently to the risk of making law too static for an experimentalist society, the drawbacks would be even more obvious in connection with a possible European civil code. If a national code appears difficult to amend, it is easy to imagine how high the threshold for amending a European code would be when all Member States with differing interests should have their say. Even early in the debate many expressed fears that a European civil code would lead to stagnation.[162]

What might be even more problematic is the fact that a European civil code would restrict the opportunities of other actors, like national legislators and courts, to participate in experimental learning processes. A binding and exclusive code would bring large parts of private law outside the scope of national rule-making. Even if the code would be adopted only as an optional European alternative (a 28th order), in practice it would certainly grossly hamper the willingness of national legislators to produce new experimental solutions. The particular strength of the present European legal order – its capacity to promote experimentalism[163] – would be lost or diminished in a private law dominated by a European civil code.

The weight of the critique of a European civil code depends on what kind of code one is discussing. The critique is certainly strongest in relation to a code of traditional type with a relatively abstract systematical structure, crowned by a 'general part', including detailed rules and being expressed in a legal language that is relatively distanced from the language of real life.[164] Another type of code that would

[158] von Bar (2000: 333).
[159] Jansen (2010: 154).
[160] Niglia (2015: eg 4–6).
[161] Smits (2002: 30).
[162] See eg Hahn (2002: 273) with references.
[163] See more closely ch 5.
[164] *cf* the criticism of the DCFR, below ch 5 section V.

only contain a few flexible principles would better fit into the required flexibility paradigm.[165] The critique of a detailed codification does also not rule out concrete European regulation of more limited parts of the private law edifice. The lack of belief in a grand all-compassing European private law does not preclude the possibility or even desirability of systematical part structures for example concerning certain contract types. Such partial legislative interventions of the EU do not risk becoming 'sacred texts' comparable to the status of a European civil code.

VIII. IN OTHER WORDS

Societal diagnoses stress the increasing uncertainty of decision-making. This has an impact on the structure of law and legal reasoning. Fragmentation and flexibility, related to an increasing contextuality, become key catchwords when describing late modern private law.

The growing epistemic uncertainty in the risk society requires an experimental approach to legal development that tends to result in fragmented legal solutions. Simultaneously ethical uncertainty and the retreat of generally recognised ethical authority increase the difficulty to uphold the idea of law as a coherent systematical structure. Moral communication becomes more contextual also in the legal sphere.

Parallel to fragmentation runs a growing flexibility. The epistemic uncertainty requires flexible rules to cope with unforeseen challenges, and contextual moral reasoning seeks a flexible legal basis as well. On the other hand, there are continuous attempts to diminish uncertainty with the help of detailed and precise regulation (catchword: 'insurance society'). As new instances of uncertainty continue to appear this cannot, however, be but a partial solution that has to be continuously re-examined in the light of new experience. Instead of a linear growth of precise rules, one therefore encounters an oscillation between areas of preciseness and flexibility that as such underlines the fragmented character of late modern law.

In this picture, flexibility and fragmentation are not understood only as unwanted consequences of certain features of late modernity. They are also analysed as valuable features of a law that attempts to cope with contemporary societal conditions. A learning law that is capable of adequate reactions to new situations without being bound too strongly by a given systematical structure is seen as an adequate response to epistemic and ethical uncertainty.

The need for continuous legal learning implies a turn towards a more contextual legal reasoning. Both epistemic and ethical learning requires a legal language that is able to describe the relevant problems with reference to the features of factual situations. The societal processes therefore tend to produce legal categories that are closer to 'real life'. Law has to be able to communicate with the language of real life, the language of both the commercial world and the citizen's world.

[165] Hesselink (2022) has recently suggested the adoption of such a code. See more closely ch 6 section III. See also earlier in the same vein Mattei (2002).

The need for flexibility and fragmentation explains why the idea of a general and coherent European civil code seems to be contrary to the spirit of the times. A sceptical attitude towards the idea of a European civil code does not imply the same degree of scepticism concerning Europeanisation of private law as such. The legal learning processes should also allow for adequate learning across borders. One should only look at Europeanisation of private law through different lenses than those of a codifier. This is the perspective of the present book.

3

Private Law as an Instrument of Micro-politics

LEGAL DISCOURSE CREATING moral roads in a complex society does not take place in a space void of power and politics. Self-evidently, politics is present in the arena in which law develops. However, the actors on the legal-political scene and the ways in which politics affects law do not remain constant.

Politicians continue to make enacted law as they have traditionally done, and probably at an increasing speed. The various actors that form 'the legislator' are relevant participants in contemporary narratives on legal change. In this chapter, however, I focus on other types of actors that have become more important on the political scene. Various kinds of groups, networks, organisations and even individual persons have brought political issues out from their parliamentary home ground into the public sphere. They may use law, including private law, as a tool for supporting their aims. This is what I have in mind when I refer to 'private law as an instrument of micro-politics'.

I call this politics 'micro', because it is not part of a structured comprehensive political agenda and is not performed through the regular legal-political structures. The issues that micro-political actors bring forward may be even very 'macro', such as climate change. I will here discuss the increasing impact of both small and large legal micro-political activities on the narratives of private law. The activities entail new inroads for critical legal practice and critical legal research.

Some have explained the rise of micro-politics by a crisis of traditional politics. They have suggested that politics seems to have lost its meaning, as the traditional divide between left and right no longer reflects the real cleavages of contemporary society, and governments are seen as managing effects of globalisation rather than leading the development of their societies. This was a strong narrative among political analysts at least until a partially new political landscape emerged after the 2008 financial crisis. The rise of populism and strong right-wing movements activated politically passive layers of the population, and at the same time inspired and strengthened parties that feared a conservative backlash, such as the green parties. Climate change also activated young voters. In this sense, interest in traditional forms of politics has returned with partially new actors. This, however, does not seem to have decreased the importance of new forms of micro-politics. Rather, the working modes of new political actors and the effect of social media have broadened the scope of micro-political activities, and the activities have become increasingly intertwined with traditional forms of politics. The growth of micro-politics seems to be rooted in deeper structural layers of society than the surface-level political system.

I. THE GROWTH OF MICRO-POLITICS

In the societal diagnoses of the late twentieth century micro-political activity has an important place. One did not get a true picture of politics by looking only at institutional politics, without noting the emergence and growth of what was called 'sub-politics'[1] or 'micro-politics'.[2] 'Micro-politics' means that a variety of actors outside the political system (in a narrow meaning) is active on the scene where society is developed. Ulrich Beck mentions as examples 'professional and occupational groups, the technical intelligentsia in plants, research institutions and management, skilled workers, citizens' initiatives, the public sphere and so on'.[3] Not only various kinds of post-traditional movements, such as peace activists, feminists, gender and sexual rights groups and environmentalists, but also many other kinds of groups and individuals could participate in micro-political activism.

This kind of politics did not affect society from above, but was growing from the grassroots level. Small-group micro-politics seemed like a more efficient way to express oppositional politics, as dissatisfaction in consumer society was mostly fragmented[4] and did not lend itself to the creation of mass movements, except in particular cases.

Micro-politics does not require established institutional or organisational settings. However, some of the activities of established organisations, like trade unions, and of public authorities, like the UK Office of Fair Trading (in 2014 replaced by the Competition and Markets Authority), and the Nordic Consumer Ombudsmen, can also be described as a kind of micro-politics. The potential subjects of micro-political activism are varying and, for the purpose of this work, there is no need to use a narrow definition of the phenomenon.

In micro-political activism, the focus is on one issue at a time, often related to some particular interest or value. Micro-politics is openly fragmented politics. It is fragmented both as to content – expressing the decline of coherent ideologies and ethical systems – and as to the structure of political actors. The epistemic and ethical uncertainty of late modernity is seasoned with a dimension of uncertainty concerning possible actors.

One may have different opinions concerning the importance of micro-politics as a part of the societal power structures. Its influence varies from society to society. It is hard to deny, however, that many topical contemporary societal issues have been put on the political agenda by various kinds of small groups and movements:

> [T]he themes of the future, which are now on everyone's lips, have not originated from the farsightedness of the rulers or from the struggle in parliament – and certainly not from the

[1] Beck (1994: 16 *et seq*).
[2] Jameson (1991: 318 *et seq*).
[3] Beck (1994: 22).
[4] Stutterheim (1993: 357) illustrates very well the lack of solidarity between consumers.

> cathedrals of power in business, science and the state. They have been put on the social agenda against the concentrated resistance of this institutionalized ignorance by entangled, moralizing groups and splinter groups fighting each other over the proper way, split and plagued by doubts. Sub-politics has won a quite improbable thematic victory.[5]

The theoretician of the network society, Manuel Castells, has presented an optimistic account of the opportunities related to micro-political action, emphasising new forms of grassroots activism as one of the most central characteristics of contemporary society. Castells related his analysis to the power of identities.[6] He noted the crisis of the legitimising identity caused by the dissolution of industrial civil society and the retreat of the national state, and showed how identity-building became related to the emergence of powerful resistance identities. The emergence of such project identities may 'be the main potential source of social change in the network society.'[7]

Presently, and for good reasons, micro-political activity related to climate change is a paradigmatic expression of both the need and power of such activity. Addressing the most pressing contemporary issue it appears both in global and in local forms; in activities started by individuals like Greta Thunberg and in more organised actions; and using both legal and illegal means. The results are not yet convincing, but without the micro-political activity, the situation would probably be even worse. As the micro-political actors have also used legal means, in a creative manner, I will return to climate change activism later in this chapter.

Some relate the death of ideologies in late modern society to the emergence of the consumer society.[8] A society that focuses on consumption, however, also offers new opportunities for micro-political activism. The growing awareness of consumers has created space for consumer activism, in the form of boycotts,[9] 'buycotts'[10] and similar activities. The consumer movement has broadened its perspective, and terms like green consumerism and ethical consumerism have emerged as labels for new forms of micro-politics.[11] The consumer role has been enlarged, moving 'from consumer to citizen'.[12] One may of course question how genuine the bottom-up processes of consumer influence are, and some have called the account of the force of empowered citizens exaggerated.[13] In the digital society, however, the advent of social media has armed consumers with new and strong weapons for micro-political activities. Consumer assessments on the web have become increasingly important with regard to the marketing of consumer products and services. Through social media, campaigns against unwanted business behaviour can be launched with almost immediate effects.

[5] Beck (1994: 19).
[6] Castells (1997: 354 *et seq*).
[7] Castells (1997: 67). Ferguson (2017) in his historical account of the interaction between hierarchies and networks shows that the period since the 1970s is characterised by the importance of networks.
[8] Jameson (1991: 398).
[9] A comprehensive analysis of different forms of consumer boycotts is presented by Friedman (1999).
[10] The term is used by Friedman (1996), meaning organised favouring of businesses following certain ethical standards. See also Friedman (1999) ch 9.
[11] Gabriel and Lang (1995) analyse inter alia 'The Consumer as Rebel' (ch 8) and 'The Consumer as Activist' (ch 9).
[12] See eg Hutchinson (1997).
[13] See such criticism eg by Burgess (2001: 104–05).

In the tool-kit of micro-political activism, an active relationship to publicity and the public sphere is important. As contemporary society, in the words of Zygmunt Bauman, is based on imagined communities that are kept together only by the belief in their presence, public attention becomes an important good. Political struggle concerns the production and distribution of public attention because 'reality' as well as the authority of the imagined communities are related to the level of attention.[14] The central focus of most micro-political strategies is the attraction of public attention. The 'new movements' are actively using publicity as a means to promote and maintain their activities.[15]

Analyses of late modernity usually stressed the central position of what today would be called 'traditional mass media', and the rule of journalism was proclaimed.[16] Media controlled the public agenda and functioned as gate-keepers with regard to the access to the public.[17] Politics had become a publicity play[18] in which the actors attempted to open the media channels. In this arena, the actors of micro-politics developed various means, including legal ones, to reach the desired publicity.

The advent of social media changed this setting. Traditional mass media still play a central role in bringing issues on the public agenda, but they have lost their monopoly with regard to agenda-setting and their gate-keeping is increasingly porous. One has to recognise 'the profundity and enormous effects of the transformation of the public arena', so deep that we are not only actually but also metaphorically placed in a different century.[19] The struggle for public attention is still there, but there are many more instruments at the disposal of micro-political actors. The advent of social media relativises the impact and relevance of other micro-political instruments, as it offers new channels for promoting the micro-political cause at hand.

As noted in the previous chapter, the role of social media increases the uncertainty of contemporary society. Not only do the issues of societal discourse arise at a much faster pace than previously, but the new media environment also increases uncertainty related to the power of various actors. The growing activity of ad hoc groups and societal movements driving particular issues has become even more characteristic than before in the society shaped by social media. Fluidity, temporary character and absence of organisational structure are appropriate catchwords in this context:

> In practice, this means that the 'reference group' deployed as a yardstick of suffered discrimination no longer needs to be coherently composed. In most cases, it is indeed heterogeneous, disjointed and all in all logically flawed and unsustainable. Nor does it need to aspire to durability, or legitimize itself by the presumption of constancy and staying power – the most common tendency being to compose and decompose such groups, ad hoc.[20]

[14] Bauman (1992: xx and 200).
[15] Siisiäinen (1998: 228) sees this as the greatest concrete change in the selection of means used by societal movements.
[16] Bourdieu (1998: 97 *et seq*).
[17] Moring and Himmelstein (1993: 157 *et seq*).
[18] The term is used eg by Uimonen (1992) and Moring and Himmelstein (1993: 23 *et seq*).
[19] Bauman (2017: 28–29).
[20] Bauman (2017: 101).

The chaotic character of micro-political activism creates greater opportunities for a diversity of societal values and agendas to reach the public agenda. With regard to politically sensitive issues, this seems to support a tendency to push the standpoints in more extreme directions, nurtured by the social media 'bubbles' in which the discussants exchange views with equally minded participants. The nature of public discourse changes, and the goals and methods of micro-political activity follow suit. This makes the question of 'good' versus 'bad' micro-politics acute; some aspects of this issue are analysed later in this chapter.

II. MICRO-POLITICS AND LEGAL ACTIVISM

Law offers one instrument for micro-political activism. Socio-legal research has directed increasing attention to the issue of law and social movements.[21] It illustrates a part of the huge variety of activities that one can describe as expressions of legally oriented micro-politics. As mentioned above, I define micro-political actors more broadly, including not only social movements, but also both occasional groups and more institutionalised actors when performing a micro-political agenda.

The 'size' of the goal of micro-political activism may vary from fundamental issues affecting the future of humankind to small problems of daily life. Legal micro-politics covers spectacular cases concerning climate change and human rights, but also mundane day-to-day problems. Micro-politics is both 'macro-politics' and 'nano-politics'. I have deliberately chosen the main example below, concerning the customer service of Finnish banks, to illustrate that the concept of micro-politics should not only be used with regard to politically sensitive, societally important activities.

In some cases, micro-politics are made legal from a defendant position. Micro-political actors may advance their case through civil disobedience and raise their issues as part of the defence when sued for the disobedience. Climate change protests might also lead to this kind of litigation.[22] I will here focus on the active use of private law.

I have mentioned climate change several times above. As a reaction to slow political processes, micro-political activity in this area has been strong, also producing legal cases. Micro-political legal activism concerning climate change is astonishingly broad and visible, taking into account the creativity needed in order to translate climate goals into concrete actionable legal issues. According to the United Nations Global Climate Litigation Report there were, as of 1 July 2020, at least 1,550 climate cases filed in 38 countries (of which about 1,200 in the US).[23] The comprehensive Climate Change Litigation Databases run by the Sabin Center for Climate Change Law at Columbia University in the beginning of 2023 listed 1,522 US cases and

[21] See eg the collection of essays on law and social movements in McCann (2016). In the collection actors like 'movements for rights of minority racial groups, rights of indigenous peoples, various women's rights issues, gay and lesbian rights, rights of the disabled and environmental causes' are representative for social movements, McCann (2016: xvii).

[22] Burgers (2020a: 66) compares civil disobedience and climate lawsuits.

[23] Global Climate Litigation Report (2021: 4).

659 cases from elsewhere.[24] Most of the cases are not based on private law, but as I will note later, there are important such cases as well. There are already sufficiently many to give rise to interesting discussions on the legitimacy of private law judicial law-making in this area.[25]

Turning now from the 'macro' cases on climate change to my 'nano' example, in 1999 a local consumer organisation in Finland[26] organised a campaign to push banks to do something about the deteriorating service and growing queues in the bank offices. It did this partially by legal means. The association distributed invoice forms and called on customers to hand in an invoice for lost working hours or lost leisure time if they had to queue more than 15 minutes. The suggested basis of liability was breach of contract by the bank. The campaign received much publicity and several hundred consumers handed in invoices to their banks.[27] Some went so far as to bring their claims to the Consumer Complaint Board for legal scrutiny. The Board found that banks had committed breach of contract if the customer had been forced to queue for more than half an hour, but it did not recommend any compensation, as the consumer had not shown any economic loss in the cases that had reached the Board.[28]

This example is already outdated. Digitalisation has made queuing in banks an unnecessary activity for most consumers in most cases. For consumers lacking digital literacy the problem is probably today even more acute, but it would be difficult to create a similar mass movement on their behalf. However, the example still offers a good illustration of several features of micro-political legal activism.

First, the example illustrates the need to distinguish between the micro-political actor and the legal actor. The subject who organises the activity is not necessarily the same as the plaintiff in the legal case that is used as an instrument to reach the goal of the activity. The consumer association was the driving actor, whilst the consumers bringing their cases to the Consumer Complaints Board with the support of the organisation acted as plaintiffs. Similar examples can be found among the tobacco cases. In Finland an organisation called The Social Responsibility of Doctors[29] chose a suitable cancer patient to act as plaintiff and they financed and organised the plaintiff's proceedings.[30] Within the health and environmental sector, there are other prominent examples, like *Reay and Hope v British Nuclear Funds*,[31] in which lawyers had contacted cancer patients living close to the nuclear facility in Sellafield in order to arrange litigation discrediting the facility. In the US poverty law discourse, some stress that a poverty lawyer also has to be an organiser;[32] sometimes the empowerment

[24] climatecasechart.com.

[25] Burgers (2020), under the exciting heading 'Justitia, the People's Power and Mother Earth'.

[26] Kuluttajat-Konsumenterna.

[27] According to the newspaper *Helsingin Sanomat* (11 October 1999), the Association had after about a half year of campaigning distributed 73,000 forms around the country and about 750 consumers had informed them that they had invoiced their bank.

[28] Finnish Consumer Complaint Board cases 99/39/2077, 2133, 2384 and 2385.

[29] Lääkärin sosiaalinen vastuu.

[30] The case is widely discussed and commented by Aurejärvi (2004) (working for the plaintiff, as the title indicates: 'The Anatomy of a Murder').

[31] (1994) 5 *Medical Law Review* 1.

[32] Wexler (1970: 1054).

of the poor related to the organising around a legal action is even considered more important than the result of the action.[33]

In cases of general interest, one may have to invent plaintiffs to pursue the interest. Climate cases are paradigmatic examples of such a situation. As climate actions 'are on behalf of us all, and behalf of future generations and the environment', it is necessary to reframe the ways in which these issues are dealt with.[34]

The digital world has increased considerably the variety of possible actors that may organise micro-political action. Inspiration and resources for bringing legal action may be gathered through social media. This activity may even become professional. New 'mass dispute entrepreneurs' have entered the scene, using online platforms and other digital tools in order to create the opportunity to produce mass claims.[35] This may be done for a commercial purpose, but micro-political ambitions may also be involved. For example, a coalition of legal service providers, US law firms and European consumer organisations that developed the legal fight against Volkswagen, concerning fraudulent programming related to emissions testing of diesel-engine cars in the so-called Dieselgate,[36] does not only fight for their and the consumers' compensation, but also strives to have a broader impact on the discourse on sustainability and the societal responsibility of businesses.

Secondly, the Finnish bank service example illustrates how the goal of micro-political action is often to achieve a change of society and of the behaviour of societal actors rather than to safeguard the rights of the individual plaintiff(s). It did not matter much whether the bank customers really got some compensation for their queuing; the goal was to force the banks to change their behaviour and improve their customer service. The package was created to direct as much public attention to the problem as possible, and the individual consumer claims were constructed to support reaching this goal. Similarly, in the above-mentioned Finnish tobacco case, the aim of the organisation of medical doctors was to create more public debate concerning the health risks connected with smoking rather than to receive damages for the plaintiff. In fact, he died before the final decision. American 'poverty lawyers' have brought cases concerning the right of homeless people to have a home to courts primarily in order to receive public attention for the problem of homelessness.[37] Some claim that the primary purpose of litigation by poverty lawyers should be to support the collective self-assertion of the poor,[38] to 'enable poor people to become more politically effective in their own lives'.[39]

Litigation is indeed one way to score in the struggle for public attention. Some have compared the functions of law to the functions of news: Both legal actors and journalists work 'in terms of an event orientation, conflict resolution, individualization

[33] Gearey (2018: 121). For a critical reflection on the 'law and organizing' movement, see Cummins and Eagly (2001).

[34] Graver (2020: 905); on 'Judging for Utopia'.

[35] Biard and Kramer (2019: 254–56). With regard to mass tort claims, some even speak about 'the tort law industry', Kortmann (2009).

[36] See eg Rehder and van Elten (2019).

[37] See eg Harris (1999: 916 *et seq*).

[38] Gearey (2018: 178).

[39] White (1987: 539–40).

and personalization of problems, and realism' and there are parallels 'in how they rely on precedent, and in their use of sources.'[40] Public trials offer a way to place moral issues on the public agenda, to be used for example by various kinds of small groups and imagined communities. In the struggle concerning the public agenda, it may not be the most central goal to win the case, but to use the case in order to receive the desired-for attention. From a micro-political perspective, it would be tempting to add to the traditional pair of concepts 'law in books' and 'law in action' a third concept related to these more subtle effects of law: 'law in media'.

In fact, a micro-political action that is lost may even lead to stronger pressure towards legal change through new legislation if it is skilfully combined with indignant publicity and political activity. This has been called 'the paradox of defeat'.[41] For similar reasons a legal victory may passivate the legislator and the public debate, leading to a 'paradox of victory'.[42]

To be clear, even though micro-political legal action may have societal rather than legal goals and strive at influencing the public agenda rather than safeguarding some concrete legal rights, the legal goals are not irrelevant. The legal outcome is not always playing a secondary role. The main aim of a micro-political action may be to help the plaintiffs to have their rights established and confirmed, or to reach a precedent that develops law in a wished-for direction. There is a potential of 'judicial activism' embedded in the court system[43] and if micro-political activism succeeds in meeting the minds of judges with such activist inclination, legal change may indeed occur. The ambitions concerning the level of change may even be higher than just reaching an advantageous decision concerning a limited problem. The ultimate goal may be a larger change in prevailing legal doctrine.[44] Strategically working micro-political actors may play important parts in the narratives on legal change.

Thirdly, the example shows how legal measures may be part of a broader campaign in which other instruments are used as well. One may combine legal action with other measures to influence decision-making and public opinion. The usefulness of private law as an instrument of micro-politics has to be assessed with regard to its role in the whole package of instruments used to achieve the set goal.

The goal of the legal activity in the example case was to bring the issue on the public agenda through traditional media coverage. Today digitalisation and social media have considerably changed the content of the package of instruments at the disposal of micro-political actors. This has an impact on the need to use legal means to attract public attention. A twitter storm or a Facebook campaign may prove to be cheaper and more fruitful than legal action. Experience tells us, however, that legal means still have a place in the process of setting the public agenda. In addition, if micro-political legal action is successful it can permanently change the world in a way that a pure social media campaign, quickly arising, but soon forgotten, is perhaps not able to achieve. Social media may make legal action less important as an

[40] Ericson (1996: 196–97).
[41] Lindblom (2006: 306).
[42] Andersson (2016: 63).
[43] See eg Spier (2010).
[44] See Boulanger (2020: 1376) with references.

instrument for pushing micro-political aims, but they cannot make it superfluous. On the contrary, sometimes the combination of activity on social media and legal action may even increase the relevance of legal micro-politics. Social media campaigns may both support and be inspired by legal action in a way that enhances the impact of the legal measures.

Finally, often some creativity is required to make the issue suitable for legal dispute and litigation. For example, one may have to invent implied contract terms, as was done in the example case. In private law, tort law can more easily be used as an instrument of a legal strategy, as the tobacco cases demonstrate.[45] The general duty of care and the negligence principle are handy tools in almost any situation, at least as long as the plaintiff has suffered some recoverable loss. Many of the examples presented in this book are taken from tort law.

III. WHY PRIVATE LAW?

Useful tools for supporting micro-political activity can be found in various corners of the legal order. At first sight, one may contest the usefulness of private law in the micro-political toolbox as compared with strongly value-laden areas like constitutional law. Indeed, fundamental rights litigation seems to allow a more direct focus on the societal issue to be resolved. A considerable part of the micro-political climate litigation is based on the application of constitutional and human rights.[46]

However, even in such cases private law can provide the organisational setting for the constitutional issue. The 'constitutionalisation of private law', which I will look at more closely in chapter six, can to some extent be described as an increasing use of constitutional arguments in private law litigation. Also other important societal goals, like sustainability[47] and corporate social responsibility,[48] can be supported by private law means. The adding of private law means to the constitutional and administrative law toolbox of activists has meant a kind of 'socialisation' of private law.[49] There are in fact good reasons why bringing a case in a private law framework can suit a micro-political strategy.

The path-breaking Dutch *Urgenda* case[50] – brought by a micro-political actor, an organisation[51] representing 886 Dutch citizens – illustrates how creatively one can use private law to enforce human rights based climate responsibilities. In this case the courts established that the Dutch Government was in breach of its obligations under the European Convention on Human Rights by not taking sufficient steps to reduce greenhouse gas emissions. The case was argued before civil courts in a private law procedure. The breach of the human rights obligation gave the Supreme Court

[45] See on this issue eg Howells (2011).
[46] Global Climate Litigation Report (2021: 41–42). On private law cases, see Global Climate Litigation Report (2021: 42–43) and Burgers (2020).
[47] As an example: Eftestøl-Wilhelmsson (2015).
[48] See eg Rühmkorf (2015).
[49] Kennedy (2020: 102).
[50] www.urgenda.nl/en/themas/climate-case. See eg Stein and Castermans (2017).
[51] Its name Urgenda coming from 'urgent agenda'.

a basis for ordering the Dutch Government to reduce emissions by a fixed percentage (at least 25 per cent compared to 1990). In the following case, *Friends of the Earth Netherlands v Royal Dutch Shell*,[52] a Dutch court found that a construction of obligations based on a combination of private law and human rights law also could succeed against a private party. Applying the provision in the Dutch Civil Code[53] according to which tortious behaviour extends to 'what according to unwritten law is contrary to what is required in societal interrelations' the court issued an injunction ordering Royal Dutch Shell to reduce its emissions with a certain percentage.

Private law has one self-evident advantage when searching for suitable instruments: it is at the disposal of private actors. The claimant can pursue a private law claim without involvement of any public authority and has the power to decide what issues are brought forward for legal scrutiny. It is easier for the citizen to bring the legal machinery in motion than to move other powers. Before the court, everyone can have a voice.[54] A micro-political subject can choose whether to launch a procedure and how to pursue it.

Some even consider private law action as the most promising tool for achieving societal change. With a bottom-up approach individuals and lawyers can create a 'new ecological private law' that reconnects private law to distributive justice and can 'reverse the sequence Commons-Private Law-Capital into Capital-Private Law-Commons'.[55] Others may assess the potential of private law to cause large-scale societal change more modestly. Be it as it may, experience shows that private law at least occasionally has offered useful tools for bottom-up legal micro-politics.

Private law, however, is not always easily available for a micro-political legal strategy. There are legal hurdles, related to the focus of private law on the rights of individual legal subjects. The hurdles are both procedural, related to the question of standing, and substantive, concerning possible private law remedies. There seems to be a pressure, however, towards more liberal interpretations of these hurdles against opening the doors more widely for micro-political legal activity.

As mentioned before, the real subjects of micro-politics are not necessarily the same as those whose rights are at stake in the procedure. The more or less organised associations and groups that can be the main micro-political actors do not have automatic standing to represent individual claimants. In practice, this competence problem may be solved either by choosing to back up individual claimants or by collecting powers of attorney from the claimants. Self-evidently the spread of class action and similar collective instruments to Europe[56] increases the possibility of micro-political action by associations and other groups,[57] and shortens the distance

[52] ECLI:NL:RBDHA:2021:5339. A good analysis in the blog Burgers (2021).

[53] Article 6:162.

[54] Lindblom (1997: 620). More generally, and in English, on 'progressive procedure' see Lindblom (2017).

[55] Mattei and Quarta (2018), citations at 6 and 148.

[56] See eg among many, Fairgrieve and Howells (2009), Nagy (2019). The EU legislator has entered this scene: see Directive (EU) 2020/1828 of the European Parliament and of the Council of 25 November 2020 on representative actions for the protection of the collective interests of consumers and repealing Directive 2009/22/EC.

[57] The above-mentioned Directive 2020/1828 requires that 'qualified entities' – which may include both consumer organisations and public bodies – shall be able to bring representative actions (Art 4).

between the micro-political subject and the legal subject(s). The development of new opportunities for class actions indicates an aspiration to strengthen the role of micro-political actors and private law in resolving societal issues, even though the public policy function of class actions has been played down in Europe as compared to the US.[58] As long as there are individuals, who have a claim recognised by private law, the question of standing is a challenge that can be solved by practical means.

The real difficulties lie elsewhere. There is an inherent limit to the usefulness of private law for micro-political activism related to its requirement of self-interest as a basis for action. Traditional private law is designed to protect private or individual rights, whilst it does not care about public or collective rights.[59] In the words of a common lawyer: 'Wherever the goal pursued by legal action is wider than the orthodox self interest of the plaintiff, it will be beyond compensation through damages.'[60]

The need for a broader approach is widely recognised, for example in relation to ecological damage and to human rights violations.[61] With regard to ecological damage, there is a need for an opportunity to grant damages for a 'victimless harm'.[62] Such widening of the perspectives of private law brings back the issue of standing on the agenda. This issue has been addressed repeatedly for example in climate litigation in various countries.[63]

A well-known counter-argument questions the practical value of such an expansion of private law remedies. Claimants cannot be expected to initiate procedures if they do not have any self-interest in the outcome of the decision. Travel contract law, for example, would not be a useful instrument for solving ecological problems caused by tourism, as neither party to the contract has any (short-term) interest in fighting the externalised harm.[64] In the contemporary societal and legal landscape, however, this counter-argument is not fully convincing, as altruistic forms of behaviour, in particular in relation to sustainability issues, occur quite frequently. In the era of micro-politics, when various organisations and groups become legal actors, one should look at the connection between private law and self-interest in a new light. The growth of more or less organised collective activities makes it more realistic to foresee processes in which the plaintiff side is primarily motivated by an idealistic concern for what is seen as a general good. The involvement of new subjects of micro-politics enhances the practical relevance of increasing opportunities to transgress the traditional limits of private law and standing.

The pressure in this direction seems obvious. Without diving deeper into this issue of legal substance, I will illustrate the issue, and the potential of Nordic private law to transgress conceptual limits, by mentioning a much-discussed Swedish case concerning the killing of two wolverines. The wolverines were protected. The person who

[58] Nagy (2019: 113).
[59] Wetterstein (1997: 30).
[60] Wightman (1999: 268). See also eg Collins (1997: 412): private law analysis 'commences with the unit of the individual and the interests of that individual which deserve protection.'
[61] On the latter, see eg Tjon Soei Len (2017).
[62] Steele (1999: 488) uses this concept.
[63] Global Climate Litigation Report (2021: 37–39).
[64] Tonner (1992: 18).

had killed them was sentenced to pay damages to the state, even though the animals did not have any economic value.[65] This case has been considered a turning point towards a new ecological tort law,[66] as it reassesses the individually oriented conceptuality of tort law.[67]

Another important flaw with regard to environmental hazard is the retrospective and reparative nature of private law. Typical tort law, as known today, regulates damages that have occurred, and has preventive effects only indirectly through the examples set by reparative decisions. For actions that directly aim at hindering something from happening in the future, tort law proper is not the right basis if injunctive relief is not a part of its remedies.[68] In legal literature, therefore, some have suggested that one should give actors defending ecological interests a right to claim damages for costs incurred through reasonable measures for supervising and averting of the risk even before any direct ecological damage occurs.[69] In certain situations, it might also be possible to argue that the increased risk as such could be understood as a compensable loss.

Creative climate change litigation has found various ways to circumvent these drawbacks of an individualistic private law. The above-mentioned Dutch climate cases, *Urgenda* and *Royal Dutch Shell*, show how private law injunctions can be used as a means to promote desirable future behaviour. In both cases, the backward-looking character of private law was eliminated by turning provisions on responsibility into bases of injunctive relief.

Not only is private law readily available for private actors to pursue their claims. Private law has other advantages from the point of view of micro-political actors as well. It is a good instrument for reaching media attention. The element of conflict in a private law case makes it interesting for the media.

Media narratives on law often focus on court cases and other legal practice, as such narratives are easier to make engaging. They are more suitable to present in visual media than, for example, relatively abstract and textual processes of legislation. In the media, the growing focus on entertainment and the mixing of information and entertainment into a culture of 'infotainment'[70] supports a case-based perspective on law: court cases may be both entertaining, informative and cheap to cover. Cases on tort and other private responsibility are particularly good tools in media-directed strategies, as the news criteria that steer the selection of material by the media[71] fit these cases very well. A tort case features a high level of human interest, as it deals with misfortune and unwanted behaviour. The case typically includes an element of surprise, of an occurrence that is new in some way. Many cases are also relatively easy to visualise. The important element of conflict that is present in all litigation may be relatively strong in tort cases, as the injured party often is emotionally engaged in the case.

[65] Swedish Supreme Court, NJA 1995 p 249.
[66] Kleineman (1995–96: 106).
[67] Sandvik (1996–97: 402).
[68] Mattei and Quarta (2018: 143) demand *ex ante* access to courts as part of tort law.
[69] Pöyhönen (1999: 356).
[70] See eg the interesting analysis of American media culture in McManus (1994).
[71] McManus (1994: 119–20) enumerates 10 news criteria for TV news, among them the criteria mentioned in the text.

A tort case is particularly attractive for media coverage when it can be pictured as a conflict between the good, the innocent injured party, and the bad, the tortfeasor. In an empirical study concerning automotive product liability judgments in the US the authors showed that judgments that contained an element of punitive damages attracted more interest among the media.[72] Punitive damages are awarded when the respondent has been guilty of a behaviour that can be strongly morally condemned. In such cases, the opportunity to picture the conflict in terms of a struggle between the good and the bad is obvious.

Tort law as based on a general principle of negligence is usually sufficiently flexible to be used as an arena for legal struggle. This is not to say, however, that areas with more detailed and relatively inflexible regulation would be immune against micro-political strategies. There may exist pathways around the most inflexible regulation, and the aim of a micro-political action may be precisely to find or to create such pathways. A general principle like the principle of negligence, however, offers a more straightforward tool for achieving the legal twist on a micro-political cause.

For the media it is important that one can picture the case in a real-life language instead of using legal-technical words. It is difficult to reach public attention for a cause that only lawyers understand. It is usually relatively easy to make a negligence-based tort case intellectually accessible for laypersons as well.

IV. CROSS-BORDER ACTIVISM AND PRIVATE LAW

Contemporary micro-politics is not confined by the limits of the national states. Micro-political campaigns, such as consumer boycotts, are often international. The globalisation of micro-politics is an important part of contemporary globalisation processes. Many 'new movements' have an internationalised consciousness. Some have even suggested, perhaps exaggerating the role of the movements, that 'NGOs, like Greenpeace or the Red Cross, are more credible candidates to be genuine transnational actors than are companies.'[73] The number of non-governmental organisations that are active in several countries has risen dramatically. Also outside large organisations activists increasingly cooperate with and take inspiration from activists in other countries. One could speak about a 'globalization from below' or a 'counter-hegemonic globalization'.[74]

The development of information technology has rapidly increased the opportunities for micro-political activity across borders. A leading information society analyst, Manuel Castells, underlined this aspect at the end of the 1990s. He noted how the Internet was used by grassroots movements as an instrument for information, communication and organisation.[75] The information society therefore offered a fruitful soil for internationalised forms of micro-politics. This is much more the case today, as social media have become central tools of micro-political action. Their scope is not limited by national borders; their outreach is (almost) global.

[72] Garber and Bower (1999: 120–21).
[73] Hirst (1997: 12).
[74] de Sousa Santos and Rodrígues-Garavito (2005).
[75] Castells (1997: eg 2 and 352).

As micro-politics transcends national borders, its legal strategies may do so as well. Private law is a useful tool for transnational legal micro-politics. For example in tort law, there are many examples of cross-fertilisation across the national borders, to such an extent that the development already decades ago was said to turn tort law into a 'transnational case jurisprudence'.[76] Globalisation of consumption in turn makes transnational campaigns in the field of consumer law quite natural. Consumer law has from its beginning focused more on comparative experience than many other areas of law.

The growth of transnational legal activism led by transnational groupings creates opportunities for micro-political legal strategies that consciously take into account the international perspective. Playing 'double-strategies', combining the national and the international, legal actors may achieve 'relatively significant social and political changes … which would often be politically unachievable on the purely national level where formalised politics and institutional frameworks constrain such strategies.'[77]

Legal activism in one country may support similar activities in other countries. By coordinating activities in different places, micro-political actors might both strengthen the resources to create legally convincing actions and increase the opportunities to succeed in the struggle to attain public attention. They may even use international diversity strategically to promote their cause. They may first seek 'good' results from countries where the claim seems most likely to succeed and then use the result in other countries as a normatively compelling example. Or they may use a 'double-strategy' that combines the advantages of proceeding at EU level and making use of EU law on the one hand, and making national advances on the other.[78] In all cases, the opportunities for exchange of legal information and building international legal strategies have increased immensely in the world of internet and social media.

In particular, when dealing with transnational risks, micro-political efforts may gain much from joining forces across the borders. The recurring example, climate change litigation, is topical in this context. No doubt, the success in the *Urgenda* case gives inspiration to climate activists all over the world. Climate change is a transnational problem, and therefore it is natural for private parties, the micro-political activists, to 'communicate across the boundaries of nation states and legal systems.'[79] The success of climate activists in the Dutch cases may inspire courts elsewhere to take a stand on the claims, instead of refraining from doing so for example with reference to the political character of the issue.[80] As Pau de Vilchez Moragues concludes, almost poetically:

> [J]udges around the world can be deterred or inspired by the decisions made by their colleagues in foreign courts, thousands of kilometres away. Albeit incipient, this global

[76] Brüggemeier (1997a).
[77] Madsen (2006: 32).
[78] Madsen (2006: 31).
[79] Burgers, van Duin and Mak (2020: 871).
[80] This has been one way for courts to avoid taking a stand in climate cases, see eg Weller and Tran (2021: 603).

> conversation is already starting to shape the evolution of environmental and human rights standards and, therefore, judges around the world are joining scientists, politicians, activists, entrepreneurs, and ordinary people in the collective efforts that are needed if we are to tackle global warming.[81]

Legal scholars also participate in the global conversation on climate change, creating new transnational concepts and systematisations. A recent example is Benoit Mayer's classification of cases in holistic ones, focusing on compliance with general mitigation obligations and establishing their requisite levels, and atomistic ones, related to particular substantive or procedural measures.[82] Using this global systematisation, expressly disregarding national variations in the applicable legal material,[83] the author attempts to show why holistic approaches, like the relatively exceptional *Urgenda* case, usually have been less successful than more concrete atomistic ones.

Micro-political activism may enhance cross-border learning also in cases where the risk is not really transnational but the problem to be addressed is the same across borders. Tobacco litigation, another recurring example, offers a good illustration. Trials on the liability of tobacco companies have been started in many countries, and the exchange of experiences across borders has been active. There has been co-operation not only on the claimant side, between the subjects of micro-politics, but also between the defendants, the tobacco industry. This may help to understand why American tobacco companies used huge amounts of money (measured from a Finnish perspective) to help the defendants in the Finnish tobacco case mentioned earlier. The Finnish case was one episode in a larger international narrative on strategies and counterstrategies. The tobacco companies considered it important not to risk losing a case anywhere in the world as such a case could be used even globally as a tempting example in the legal strategies of the micro-political actors in their fight against tobacco. The investments of the tobacco companies were not in vein. They won the Finnish litigation.[84]

Another example of cross-border learning is the litigation related to the above-mentioned so-called Dieselgate. This is not a case on product liability, nor a typical case on sales law, as most of the cases have been brought against the manufacturer of the cars. Claims in tort against a manufacturer might encounter various kinds of challenges in different domestic settings. It is therefore understandable that possible actors in other countries look at the tens of thousands of German court decisions on this issue with great interest.[85] Dieselgate is also an interesting example of how both domestic and European courts can be involved in the legal aftermath of an international scandal.[86]

[81] de Vilchez Moragues (2022: 36–37).
[82] Mayer (2023).
[83] Mayer (2023: 236).
[84] Finnish Supreme Court: KKO 2001:58.
[85] Klauberg and Lebro (2022: 277). The authors are discussing Finnish and Estonian law based on German experience.
[86] The CJEU on 14 July 2022 handed down three decisions on 'defeat devices' with an impact on private law liability for guarantee: Case C-128/20, *GSMB Invest GmbH & Co. KG v Auto Krainer GesmbH*; Case C-134/20, *IR v Volkswagen AG*; and Case C-145/20, *DS v Porsche Inter Auto GmbH & Co. KG, Volkswagen AG*, discussed eg by Arbour (2022).

Transnational micro-politics might be required also when the counter-party is a multi-national actor or network. The growing importance of decisions concerning, for example, broad environmental risks enhances the need for action against the instances by which the decisions in reality are taken. This might require a possibility to cross national borders. It should, for example, be possible to take action against companies whose subsidiaries dump hazardous products or in other ways endanger the environment in other countries. In a micro-political strategy that seeks public attention, it is crucial to direct the action against the real decision-maker in the country where the decision-maker is situated. A media covered process in the country of a mother company feels more pressing than cases against subsidiaries or smaller actors in 'remote' countries. I will briefly return to this issue later in this chapter. Here it suffices to note that such internationalised micro-political litigation strategies are fertile grounds for cross-border legal learning as well.

From the perspective of Europeanisation of private law both EU legislation and the European Convention on Human Rights offer a good breeding ground for European micro-politics. Various organisations have contributed in many ways to the establishment of the European legal space. The European consumer organisation Bureau Européen des Unions de Consommateurs (BEUC) has played a considerable role in the development of European consumer law. Other lobbying organisations in Brussels have played similar roles. In many ways these are established parts of the EU law drafting machinery and perhaps no longer appear as genuine 'grassroots' actors. The same goes for public micro-political actors like the Consumer Ombudsmen and other consumer law enforcement organisations whose intense cooperation in Europe[87] has contributed to the development of an increasingly joint European understanding of consumer law. In this field, there are even structures for learning across the borders on a global level, within the International Consumer Protection and Enforcement Network (ICPEN).

Real 'grassroots' actors can be assumed to contribute to Europeanisation as well, even though a European civil society that could support genuinely European level micro-politics is still not well developed. Europe does not have a joint media landscape and a joint public space that could incentivise micro-political actors to use legal means for setting a European public agenda. However, as far as politics becomes more Europeanised, micro-politics will probably follow suit.

Anyway, even without a joint European public space the rise of transnational micro-political activism that uses private law as a tool has obvious implications for the Europeanisation of private law. As analysed in chapter two, both the epistemic uncertainty and the ethical ambivalence of contemporary society increase the need for legal learning processes across national borders. Transnational legal activism contributes and adds some nuances to the learning processes. It brings in a variety of new actors on the legal scene that can have an impact on the cross-border movement of legal ideas. The Europeanisation of law from below may bring in more 'counter-hegemonic' perspectives in the transnational learning processes.

[87] A formal European consumer protection framework is now set up by Consumer Protection Cooperation Regulation (EC) 2006/2004 (CPC Regulation).

V. MICRO-POLITICS AND FRAGMENTATION OF PRIVATE LAW

Micro-politics obviously contributes to the processes of fragmentation and contextualisation of private law. Legal micro-politics and legal system-building do not fit well together.

The actors of micro-politics are not participants in a grand societal strategy. The goal of micro-political activity is to have impact on a particular societal issue. The publicity given by the media is capricious and does not have a coherent societal goal. The results of micro-political activity are punctual and varying. Legal development induced by such activity easily appears as fragmented and less compatible with the idea of a systematic development of law.

The rise of micro-politics in other words boosts the processes of increasing fragmentation of law that were analysed in the previous chapter. This effect probably grows stronger in the present century. As deepening societal cleavages, both in socio-economic and in ideological-ethical sense, broadens the variety of directions in which micro-political actors may attempt to use legal means, the fragmentation effects of micro-politics increase. In the deeply divided era of social media bubbles and populism, one may foresee an increasing pressure towards more fragmentation of law.

Micro-politics is often associated with 'critical' or 'alternative' approaches to law. Insofar as such alternative approaches are successful, they create ruptures in the mainstream understanding of law. As the aim of a critical approach may be the turning of what appears as a routine issue into a hard one, success means a crack in the mainstream routines. Analysing the traditions of poverty law and legal activism, Adam Gearey mentions the thought that 'praxis "unfreezes" dead routines and ways of being'.[88]

As law becomes increasingly experimental in late modern society, critical legal approaches need to be so as well. In a complex world it is not easy to find the right balance between measures to improve the situation of the weak and the vulnerable, to defend human rights and to fight climate change and loss of biodiversity, and a critical scholar (as other scholars) must be able to change course if experience so demands. One continuously has to learn what works to the benefit of the cherished values in various contextual settings. Hence, critical tradition often refers to a politics of experience and experimentalism,[89] to 'an exercise of learning by doing'.[90]

Micro-political activity is strongly publicity-driven. As has been noted above, the struggle for publicity generally strengthens an emphasis on cases rather than systematic legal and administrative structures. A case based picture of law, in which the facts come to the fore and the general rules appear as less interesting, challenges the vision of a systematic legal order.

The adaptation of law to the demands of media and the public affects the conceptual structure of legal reasoning. The success of micro-political action may require reasoning in a way that can be understood by the general public (= the journalists). This can contribute to the suppression of arguments of a legal systematic nature,

[88] Gearey (2018: 168).
[89] See eg Gearey (2018: 44, 146, 159, 163).
[90] Mattei and Nicola (2007: 40).

as such arguments for a non-lawyer may appear as technical or even as purely fictitious. The struggle for media attention promotes contextualism, both as to content as well as to legal language. As noted above, late modern law is pushed towards formulating its arguments in a language closer to real life rather than in abstract legal categories. Media-oriented micro-politics is not interested in describing issues in a distant legal expert-terminology, but rather in words that appeal to the media and other relevant players.

Sometimes it might even be the main goal of a micro-political action to have the actual problem redefined in new terms. It may be important how a social problem is defined and law has a constructive power concerning problem-definitions.[91] A micro-political legal strategy may focus on the opportunities to redefine a societal issue through the use of law.

The legally non-systematic character of micro-political activism is even more obvious when the activism is conducted in cross-border networks. The fragmentation of law is connected with globalisation and Europeanisation and the emergence of cross-border legal micro-politics is one feature of this development. The more the law loses its ties to a national systematic structure, the greater are the possibilities for cross-border legal strategies. And vice versa: a micro-politically induced flow of private law across the borders contributes to the hollowing out of the established domestic systems of law.

Here I wish to repeat my starting point that one should not only deplore increased legal fragmentation. There is another side of the coin as well. As far as one sees micro-politics as a desirable engine of societal development, it should have legal tools that are useful for that function. A law that is less strictly tied to rigid systematical structures might be more responsive to changes demanded through processes of micro-politics. Fragmentation may be 'good', as far as the goals pursued by micro-politics are considered to be 'good'.

VI. 'GOOD' OR 'BAD' MICRO-POLITICS: PRIVATE LAW AND SOCIETAL POWER

In narratives on micro-politics, the micro-political actors usually represent 'the good', the power that has affected societal development in a healthy way. Even for an optimistic believer in micro-politics, however, the picture is not that straightforward. One cannot automatically assume that micro-politics only promotes values that one would regard as 'good', not to speak of what the democratic majority of the population would classify as positive.

As Ulrich Beck rightly notes, 'Sub-politics is always available to the opposite side or the opposing party for their opposing goals.'[92] Also, those in power may make use of legal proceedings, including private law ones, to carry out their agenda.[93]

[91] Niemi (2018).
[92] Beck (1994: 20).
[93] Ericson (1996: 204): 'Through its [the news media] law stories, it offers a pervasive and persuasive means by which authorities can seek wider consent for their moral preferences.'

For example, the targets of micro-political campaigns and boycotts may use tort claims against responsible organisations and individuals as preventive or reparative counterstrikes. A well-known example is the so-called '*McLibel*' case – a lawsuit filed by McDonald's against two activists concerning a critical factsheet.[94] Cases of this kind can be found in many countries. They often involve a difficult balancing between the legitimate interests of both parties, which easily leads to contextual and fragmented solutions.[95]

Micro-politics can become an activity in which the actor promotes its own limited group interests rather than strives to carry a broader moral responsibility, based on, for example, solidarity with the poor, suppressed and vulnerable. In the digital environment micro-political activity can be organised by a small elite and among the symbolic personalities appearing in this context one can most certainly find both 'good' and 'bad' prophets.[96]

Micro-politics usually is targeted against somebody, whose behaviour the activists strive to influence. It may have as its goal to compel a societal actor to refrain from harmful behaviour or to act positively to cure a problem. Typically, the targeted actor is a person or body of power. Much micro-politics, in other words, relates to the power structures of society. Startling micro-political activity targets macro-power. In this chapter, I will look at the power aspect of micro-politics and its consequences for private law. In chapter four I will return to the more general question on how to define a 'good' narrative on legal change.

With regard to societal power, law has been allotted a particular role. An important function of law is the control of societal power. Ever since Montesquieu law is supposed to limit political and administrative power, and a fair law should also counterbalance economic power. Respect for democracy and human rights demands that societal power should be constrained by law.[97] The principle of rule of law requires law to provide a bulwark against arbitrary use of societal power. 'Good' narratives on micro-political legal activism often relate to this role of law.

Not only public law, but also private law affects societal power. Private law both confers power, for example through the recognition of contractual liability, and restricts power, through a variety of protective rules.[98] The latter are designed to counterbalance and control the use of societal power. Some even see the 'counter-hegemonic interpretation' of private law as a part of a 'counter-hegemonic project' that can change the power structures in society profoundly.[99] Probably more realistically, one can at least claim that private law occasionally can help representatives of suppressed interests to challenge more powerful societal actors.

Private law offers instruments to tackle various forms of societal power. As private law is traditionally understood as a body of norms that regulates relations

[94] *McDonald's Corporation v Steel & Morris* [1997] EWHC QB 366.
[95] Like in the leading case in Finnish law, Supreme Court decision KKO 1983 II 187, where the result was based on two very vague concepts: 'particularly important reasons' and 'good morals'.
[96] Castells (1997: 361).
[97] Tuori (2021: 22).
[98] On private law and power, see eg Barker, Degeling, Fairweather and Grantham (2017).
[99] Mattei and Quarta (2018).

between private parties, it is natural first to look at private law as a device for controlling economic power. Probably the preponderant part of micro-political actions relates to the responsibility of businesses, and both contract and tort law as well as more specialised disciplines like consumer law, environmental law and labour law are used to support such actions. As much power is vested in the media industry, including the industry that provides digital infrastructures and social media, issues related to media power and digital power are worth mentioning separately. These are probably issues concerning which many micro-political battles will be fought in the future.

As mentioned before, tort law, and more broadly the law of private liability, is a useful instrument for controlling societal power. Gert Brüggemeier has even claimed that tort law 'has been transformed into state control of personal and corporate conduct through private law'.[100] Other scholars also emphasise the importance of tort law as such a progressive instrument. Ugo Mattei and Alessandra Quarta go as far as claiming that 'There is perhaps no area of private law that shows more potential for transformative power than tort law'.[101] This is perhaps no news for an American audience, as punitive damages and class actions have made such litigation a visible tool for development, but one also meets similar tendencies in Europe. Therefore, I will make a few comments on what one can require of tort law if developing it as an instrument for controlling societal power.

I pass over the challenge that the use of tort law as a micro-political tool might be as source of joy and earnings of well-paid lawyers, making it difficult to see whether the primary goal of a micro-political action is the 'good' or the profitable. The Dieselgate case mentioned above is a good example.

In most countries, one can find good examples on how micro-political actors have used negligence-based tort law rules against problematic behaviour of economic players. As discussed in chapter two, however, tort law in a risk and insurance society typically displays an oscillation between the flexible principle of negligence and scattered islands of strict liability. In continental Europe in particular, the areas of strict liability have been growing for a century already, both through special legislation and through case law related to particularly dangerous activities.[102] The preponderant part of the rules on strict liability relates to enterprise liability.[103] This seems like a step forward from the point of view of a law that aims at taming economic power. Indeed, it is not difficult to find examples where micro-political activism has resulted in rules on strict liability for some particular business activity.

Some have related the development of strict liability to a principled discourse on the role of businesses in a capitalist society. In Norway, for example, the highly influential professor Fredrik Stang a century ago laid the foundation for an unusually broad use of strict liability by claiming that the negligence principle was not sufficient to handle the risks of an industrialised society and by emphasising that the masses

[100] Brüggemeier (1997: 59).
[101] Mattei and Quarta (2018: 121).
[102] Short overview: Brüggemeier (2009: 297–99), and more extensively Werro and Palmer (2004).
[103] Brüggemeier (2009: 299–300).

should be protected against individuals.[104] However, even though clear and strict rules are well founded when dealing with particular economic activities that feature high risk levels, a vision of a strict liability that would more broadly cover large areas of entrepreneurial activity could also have drawbacks with regard to the control of economic power.

Such a broad rule would not leave sufficient scope for the late modern need for an open moral discourse. The growth of strict liability may reduce the opportunity for micro-political actors to use tort law as a device to bring societal problems on the public agenda. A thinning of the feeling of moral responsibility may occur, in particular when tort liability in practice is replaced by an insurance mechanism. When a collective pharmaceutical insurance covers damages caused by the use of drugs, which is the case in Finland and Sweden, the company producing the drug avoids being individually accused. The use of such collective means breaks the connection between responsibility and damage, but strict liability tends also more generally to untie the legal responsibility from the moral discourse.

A fragmented development, in which elements of strict liability are introduced for particularly dangerous activities, is perhaps less prone to separate the issue of liability from the moral perspective. Arguments related to the dangerous character of an activity often include a moral element, and the openness of the basis of liability invites reasoning concerning distributive justice as well, as a fair distribution of risk is an important part of the agenda in late modern society. A relatively open-ended general clause-like provision, which broadly defines possible instances of strict liability referring, for example, to the dangerous nature of the activity, keeps the door open for moral assessment, as it expressly gives courts the power to create and develop new instances of strict liability.[105]

Another issue of importance with regard to the use of tort law for micro-political purposes is the question of the subject against which one may bring legal action. It concerns the choice of defendant in tort law litigation and touches on deeper legal-cultural questions like the definition of private law personhood.

In a globalised economy that tends to move environmentally or socially problematic activities to less affluent countries, the opportunities to take action against mother companies of multi-nationals are of great importance. One should be able to direct the legal action against the real decision-maker – the parent company – rather than the subsidiary, in which the formal decision-makers perhaps only 'followed orders'. Liability rules can best contribute to a functioning control of economic power if the legal liability catches those by which the actual decisions are made.

The narrative concerning the liability of a mother company for the activities of its daughters has been told under different headings, like 'disregarding the legal entity', 'lifting or piercing the corporate veil' or '*Durchgriffshaftung*', with various

[104] Stang (1919: 43–45).

[105] In Europe the Principles of Tort Law (European Group of Tort Law: Principles of European Tort Law (PETL), available at www.egtl.org), 5:101(1) has chosen this approach: 'A person who carries on an abnormally dangerous activity is strictly liable for damage characteristic to the risk presented by the activity and resulting from it.' For a similar approach in the USA, see Restatement (Second) of Torts § 520, Restatement (Third) of Torts § 20(b).

results in different countries. It is not necessary to dive deeper into the details of this well-known discussion. It suffices to note the importance of the issue:

> [T]here are numerous such situations where procedures to deal with environmental or health issues in the state of the activity are inadequate or simply not available – and thus cannot be used by members of the public who are at risk of suffering harm. In these cases increasing procedural opportunities outside the state of the cause (activity) may be instrumental for justice.[106]

The opportunities of increasing the focus on real decision-makers have gone further than seemed to be possible within the framework of the traditional theme 'piercing the corporate veil'. Actions against real decision-makers abroad do not necessarily require the existence of a corporate group structure. Claims against those actually responsible for the decision may nowadays be based, for example, on the existence of contractual networks. The rise of the discussion concerning global value chains, placing responsibilities on the lead firms, indicates the direction of the development.[107] The development of the legal liability of corporations for their own corporate codes is another step towards broader liability.[108] Specific corporate social responsibility legislation extending corporate responsibility to cover behaviour of dependent businesses, like the French *Loi de vigilance*,[109] pushes private law in this direction and the EU is active as well.[110] The perceived 'regulatory tsunami' with regard to environmental, social and corporate governance (ESG)[111] increases the responsibility of companies for human rights and environmental abuses by their suppliers. Private law theory can contribute to the development by creating new conceptual structures, for example by developing a distinct form of 'network liability'.[112]

The narrative on parent company liability can be a starting point for further narratives. For example, if one accepts the idea that liability can follow from influence or dominance, the natural next step is to ask what liability a credit institution may have for the activities that it finances. In the last century, there was considerable debate on lender liability towards interests damaged by the debtor under headings like 'environmental liability for banks'.[113] Today, when the idea of responsible and sustainable lending has become mainstream, there may be openings for further narratives in this direction. Again, this is not the place for diving deeper into the issue, but it is an example of developments that may be pushed forward by micro-political

[106] Ebbesson (2009: 290).

[107] On global value chains, see eg the Special Issue of European Review of Contract Law 1/2020, introduced by Eller and Salminen (2020), and the issue European Journal of Risk Regulation 4/2022, introduced by Verbruggen (2022). Regarding product liability in global supply chains, see Salminen (2017) and (2018).

[108] See the narrative presented by Beckers (2015).

[109] Loi no 2017-399 du 27 Mars 2017 relative au devoir de vigilance des sociétés mères et des entreprises donneuses d'ordre. On this law and climate change litigation, see eg Weller and Tran (2021: 587–88).

[110] See Proposal for a Directive of the European Parliament and of the Council on Corporate Sustainability Due Diligence and amending Directive (EU) 2019/1937, COM(2022) 71 final.

[111] Renner (2022) uses this metaphor.

[112] Condon (2022: 208–16) proposes a new kind of 'network liability' as a reflection of the network society, applicable to value chains and explaining some of the climate cases.

[113] Norton, Auerbach and Gaba (1995).

legal strategies. Financial institutions are convenient targets for micro-political media activism.

Private law micro-politics can also target other powers than economic power. Tort law may be used to address political and bureaucratic decision-making, including failure to make decisions. The target of micro-political action may also be the use of legal power itself when considered unjust. There are, however, considerable variations in European national laws on the liability related to the use of public power. In some countries, like France, there are different rules and different administrative courts dealing with these kinds of issues, whilst for example in English law most torts apply equally to private and public subjects.[114]

Insofar as tort law is applicable, much of what has been said above on the oscillation between negligence and strict liability applies to the liability of public actors as well. In many countries, one can find examples of islands of fragmented strict liability related to activities of public authorities.[115] Even a question that resembles the 'piercing of the corporate veil' may turn up in relation to public actors. In particular in the context of privatisation of public authority, the question of the liability of the state as 'parent' for the activity of the 'subsidiary', to whom public functions are entrusted, might become relevant.

In the context of public sector liability, the issue of liability for omissions is particularly interesting, as it can be a forceful tool to reach political goals. Claims for a 'better welfare state' can be turned into claims for compensation under private law, for example by referring to constitutional provisions on the availability of social and health services. In a Finnish Supreme Court decision[116] a municipality was found liable in tort, as the plaintiff was not offered a child daycare place over the the course of 10 days, even though the municipality argued that it had taken extensive measures to remedy the lack of a sufficient number of daycare places. According to the legislation on daycare services, the service was a public task, but the Appellate Court in its decision also underlined a provision of the Finnish constitution, according to which the public sector was obliged to guarantee everyone sufficient social and health services.

A state may even face liability for bad or lacking legislation. Even though this at a first glance seems like private law overstepping its boundaries, in Europe there are well-known and practically functioning examples of such kind of liability. For a European lawyer the liability of EU Member States for wrong or omitted implementation of EU legislation, with its roots in the famous *Francovich* case, is a part of the generally acknowledged legal infrastructure.[117] Another example of state liability for bad legislation is the sanction mechanism related to the European Convention on Human Rights, even though formally this is not considered a private law liability.

[114] See eg van Gerven, Lever and Larouche (2000: 388–89).

[115] See eg for Germany and France van Gerven, Lever and Larouche (2000: 392–94). In Nordic case law municipal liability for water and heating pipes and state liability for mass vaccinations, and in special legislation liability for various kinds of public registers, are made strict, see more closely Wilhelmsson (2019).

[116] KKO 2001:93.

[117] On the already then abundant *Stand der Lehre*, see eg Aalto (2010: 29–31). For an analysis of 20 and 25 years of *Francovich*, see eg Haba (2015) and Granger (2017).

One may debate, whether and to what extent these European constructions can influence the law of private liability more generally. In some countries, standard textbooks on tort law more or less ignore the *Francovich* liability, while other scholars speak positively about a possible spillover-effect on national law.[118] Nationally, private law claims for damages caused by poor legislation could be based on constitutional law and fundamental rights. Some of the climate-related cases indicate that micro-political strategies against legislative omissions of the state might find constitutional support.

To what extent is this 'good'? A private law action with a relatively narrow perspective is not necessary an optimal method for decision-making concerning the distribution of public resources. It is possible that resourceful societal groups would be better equipped to enjoy the use of liability procedures. Even though the fruits of actions of societally stronger groups may benefit the whole society, one cannot assume that these groups would have much interest in taking action in areas that are of particular importance to the weakest, like the homeless and the unemployed. The critical potential then lies in the existence of action groups, organisations or 'poverty lawyers', who are prepared to take such action on behalf of and together with the weak. In other words, the assessment of goodness of public liability is often difficult.

More generally, even if one looks at private law as a device through which economic, political, media, digital and legal power may be controlled, this does not solve the question of the 'goodness' of micro-politics. Every action against an entity of power is not societally desirable: all power is not bad as such. A micro-political victory against one power may strengthen the position of another power. A limitation of public power, for example, may imply broader room to manoeuvre for economic power. In discussing this aspect, one should bear in mind that in Europe, and in particular in Northern Europe, the state and the public administration are not considered to be intrinsically bad, as may be the case in some other countries. As all micro-political action against an instance of societal power is not self-evidently good, its goodness has to be assessed in the actual context.

The focus on private law as a power-controlling mechanism does not relieve us from the basic question: What is 'good'? I will return to this issue at the end of the next chapter.

VII. IN OTHER WORDS

In contemporary society, traditional politics is increasingly challenged by micro-political activism outside the political system. A large variety of actors can be involved in micro-political struggles, ranging from informal groups, networks and engaged individuals to traditional organisations and even some public authorities. The themes of micro-political activism varies from 'nano issues', like the extent of queueing time in a bank, to 'macro issues', like climate change. Social media have hugely increased the opportunities to arrange micro-political activity.

[118] eg Arrowsmith (1992: 41–42) and Craig (1998: 83 *et seq*).

Micro-political activism may use law as an instrument, often in combination with other ways of promoting its cause. The goal of a micro-political legal action is not always the correction of a societal wrong by winning the case. It may be to bring the issue on the public agenda even when the chances to win the case are small.

Private law and in particular tort law offer useful instruments for legal micro-political action. This field of law has the advantage that it is at the disposal of private actors who may pursue their cases without the involvement of any public officials. The adversarial setting of a private law dispute may also attract media attention, as the litigation can be portrayed as a struggle between good and bad. The focus of private law on the protection of the self-interest of the parties, however, may pose problems for an altruistic micro-political strategy. There are obvious pressures on private law to overcome these problems, illustrated for example by creative decisions in climate change cases.

The raise of legal micro-politics contributes to the pressures towards fragmentation of private law. It adds to the contextualism of legal reasoning by supporting medially useful formulations of the issues at stake, in a language closer to real life. In addition, micro-politics does not only contribute to substantive fragmentation, it also brings in a variety of additional actors on the legal scene.

Micro-political campaigns are not bound by national borders. Legal micro-politics may productively use the opportunities for cross-border legal learning. Internationally networked micro-political activities contribute to the movement of legal ideas across the borders.

The fact that micro-political legal activity often targets instances of societal power (economic, political, media, digital and legal power) does not make it 'good' as such. As there are no ready-made criteria for good choices, the development underlines the responsibility of legal actors for making their own moral assessments.

4

A Law Learning Through Small Narratives

IN THE PREVIOUS chapters, I described some of the societal pressures that have contributed to shaping the law of Europe in the twenty-first century. Increasing societal complexity and growing ethical pluralism require an experimental law sufficiently open to contextual pragmatism. Micro-political legal actions related to particular societal issues add to the pressures.

In such a societal situation, an understanding of law as a static system that at any given point of time can be pictured as a more or less coherent body of norms is increasingly less realistic. Many monographs, commentaries and textbooks, however, do precisely this. They present the law in force as a fixed and systematic whole, and the possibility of legal change only appears occasionally in the reasoning (and through the need to constantly make new editions of the works). Saying this, my intention is not to deny the usefulness of such works with regard to legal practice: as I will note later in the chapter, legal scholars doing black-letter law play an important role in the narratives on legal change, both initiating new narratives and ending narratives by stabilising the situation. However, it is important to underline that an understanding of contemporary law also requires a dynamic approach, recognising legal change and adaptation (legal learning) as key elements of a law.

In this chapter, I will draw a sketch of such an approach from a national perspective.[1] In the following chapter, I will use this as a foundation for building my view on the Europeanisation of private law.

Focusing on a learning law in which individual cases may play an important role might seem like a *plaidoyer* for adopting a methodology of common law. It is therefore important to stress the differences between my analysis and a purely common law approach. My analysis is based on a recognition of the fact that a multitude of legal actors contribute to the narratives on legal change: not only courts and legislature, but also scholars and other legal actors, are included in the cast. To understand the dynamic processes of legal change, one has to see how all the legal actors can participate in the processes of legal learning.

[1] In principle from the domestic perspective of any Member State.

I. A CONTEXTUALLY LEARNING PRAGMATIC LAW

What seems to be needed is a law that is able to learn from new experience; a law that is not too constrained by legal-conceptual ties with the past. This involves a more pragmatic legal logic as opposed to a formalistic and dogmatic one. A search for societally good solutions should be more important than a search for solutions that fit the traditional conceptual order best (even though the latter should not be completely ignored).

I am here using 'pragmatism' in a relatively general meaning, underlining the need to focus on the assessment of the societal consequences of legal acts and decisions, and to search for societally good solutions. There is no need in this context to tie my notion of pragmatism firmly to any philosophy of pragmatism, even though it is easy to claim that emphasis on contextual problem-solving, practical consequences and change are features that are shared with pragmatist philosophy.[2] For my purpose, it is sufficient to use a relatively vague concept of pragmatism to illustrate the need to revise the perspective in comparison with a formalist approach. In other words, the dichotomy of pragmatism and formalism that I use is close to the legal-theoretical discussion on substance against form.[3] A similar dichotomy is the one between instrumentalist and juridical rationality,[4] but the term 'instrumental' may give an impression of closer ties between law and current political and societal goals than the acknowledgement of a pragmatic legal approach indicates.[5]

Speaking of pragmatic approaches in law is no novelty. As is well known, American law is usually described in terms of pragmatism, even to the extent that one might speak about what Richard Rorty calls 'the banality of pragmatism', meaning that the approach has been 'absorbed into American common sense'.[6] Nordic law, as a consequence of Scandinavian legal realism, also claims to be pragmatic. From my personal background in Nordic law, it is obviously not legal-culturally difficult to embrace the claim that contemporary law needs to be pragmatically focused.

The pressure towards more pragmatism is not unfamiliar in the rest of Europe either. In his interesting analysis of what he called the new European legal culture, Martijn Hesselink claimed that it was in the middle of a radical change. He saw the turn towards a more pragmatic approach that paid 'more attention to the consequences of rules and legal decisions':[7]

> Unlike a century ago, in Europe legal culture is undergoing a radical change (at least as far as private law is concerned). The instrumentalist and impressionist approach of directives, the pragmatic style of the ECJ, the subversive role of comparative law with its functional

[2] For an eloquent plea for the relevance of philosophical pragmatism to law, see Taekema (2006).

[3] On this, see eg Atiyah and Summers (1987), and applied to the law of obligations, Robertson and Goudkamp (2019).

[4] eg Michaels (2011: 144–49) and V Mak (2020: 96–97) on instrumental European law. The 'instrumentalist logic of European law' is also discussed by Schmid (2006). *cf* Bacharis and Osmola (2022), who attempt to show that the particular 'instrumentalism' of European private law is overstated.

[5] *cf* Taekema (2017: 120), who (in the context of legal pluralism) instead argues for a broader understanding of instrumentalism.

[6] Rorty (1990: 1813).

[7] Hesselink (2001: 73).

> method, the external economic, cultural and political perspectives given by academics, the success of soft law which is based on substantive authority rather than on formal enactment, and the depositivation of legal education as a result of the implementation of the Bologna Declaration together contribute to a new European legal culture that is significantly less formal, dogmatic and positivistic than national legal cultures in Europe have been.[8]

Later, Hesselink spotted a turning back to a more classical dogmatic approach to private law, claiming that the neo-formalist tendencies have become stronger since he wrote his first analysis.[9] However, two of his main arguments are the growing support of a European Civil Code of a traditional kind and the distinctly formal approach of the Draft Common Frame of Reference (DCFR), as compared to the more informal style of, for example, the Principles of European Contract Law. As is generally known, the DCFR – probably precisely because of its very traditional approach – and the project concerning the European Civil Code have not met with great enthusiasm in more recent European discourses and their practical impact has been limited. So one might safely say that the jury is still out on the question whether and to what extent a turn towards neo-formalism really is visible. A full turn in this direction is hardly conceivable in view of the societal pressures towards an experimental and learning law in contemporary society, but development is seldom linear and small moves in various directions are easy to imagine.

Some even consider that the pragmatic turn has spread into the codifications themselves. Reinhard Zimmermann notes that the 'modern German style of legal drafting is not what it was one hundred years ago',[10] but he speaks of this as an improvement:

> [A] building site bristling with the cheery voices of craftsmen and artisans may be a more appropriate metaphor for a modern code of private law than a museum in which only the weary murmurs of the occasional tourist group can be heard.[11]

In Nordic legal-theoretical research, Sverre Blandhol has attempted to define the elements of so-called Nordic legal pragmatism. The emphasis on reasoning concerning societal consequences also plays a central role in his analysis. This is reflected in the criteria he finds when attempting to define Nordic legal pragmatism. His criteria are: anti-fundamentalism, anti-formalism, a rhetorical understanding of language, problem-orientation, a focus on experience and consequences, moderate skepticism, pluralism, contextualism and style.[12] Many of these features are also recognisable in the pages of this book.

The emphasis on societal consequences does not imply a distancing from legal rules as a basis of legal decision-making. Rule of law and democratic legitimacy of law are important values in a democratic society, and decision-making that does not honour these values would not have beneficial societal consequences. Democratically

[8] Hesselink (2001: 72).

[9] Hesselink (2014).

[10] Zimmermann (2005: 487). The approach was already then met by the well-known critique of von Gierke (1889, published in English 2018), who condemned abstract dogma, the strict separation of private and public law and the lack of protection of the vulnerable.

[11] Zimmermann (2005: 489).

[12] Blandhol (2008).

legitimate legal reasoning has to take into account the consequences with regard to the value of the rule of law. I touched upon this need to balance flexible experimentalism and a respect for established rules above in chapter two when discussing the contextual oscillation between instances of flexibility and periods of stability.

In other words, the question of pragmatism and formalism in legal reasoning is not an either-or issue.[13] In the legal field, both types of reasoning are required, but, as the discussions on form and substance and the European pragmatist turn mentioned above show, the weight of the poles may vary. What is said here relates to the shifting of weight in the pragmatic direction, it does not mean abandoning systematic legal thinking. Such a new balancing implies a greater readiness to look at the societal consequences of a decision and change the established direction if its societal consequences do not appear to be acceptable.

The societal consequences are usually related to a specific context. To be able to learn from concrete experience in a complicated world, the law has to be sufficiently contextual. A contextual law analyses issues not only as expressions of legal-dogmatic case descriptions, but also as concrete societal problems. This implies the use of a legal language that recognises real-life descriptions of the situations at hand. The role and breadth of legal concepts changes. Pragmatic and contextual reasoning require narrower concepts, more directly tied to the concrete societal situation to be assessed. In chapter 8 section V I will discuss the pressure on legal language in more detail.

Finally, learning requires communication. The whole idea of a learning law rests on the ability of legal actors to learn through pragmatic discourse and contextual moral reasoning. Open and transparent reasoning is a prerequisite for a well-functioning law. This is particularly important in the contemporary societal environment. The cohabitation of experimentalism and flexible search for good solutions with the rule of law enhances the demand for transparent reasoning. Only under conditions of strong transparency is it possible to control flexible decision-making in a way that satisfies the principle of rule of law. I will return to the transparency requisite in chapter eight.

II. FLEXIBILITY AND FRAGMENTATION

Contextual and real-life-oriented legal pragmatism requires a capacity to use flexible solutions. The decline of importance of formal legal systematics means increasing fragmentation.

In the analysis of contemporary law, one should distinguish between these two aspects, flexibility and fragmentation. They are interrelated, but they are also partially based on different reasons and have different consequences for the systematisation of private law. In principle, law can be flexible, but less fragmented, or fragmented, but less flexible. I will first sketch a picture of each of these qualities, before discussing their interrelation.

[13] For a general critique of binary thinking in and about law, see Tuori (2021: 9–22).

First, by flexibility I refer to the capacity of law to integrate into legal decision-making various and even new arguments related to individual cases. The opposite of a flexible law would be a law that is determined by more precise norms.

This contrast between flexibility and strictly following rules looks similar to a dichotomy that has been much discussed in legal theory during the twentieth century, namely the distinction between principles and rules.[14] Even though the term 'principle' in legal language has been used to refer to many different qualities of a norm, in contemporary legal-theoretical discourse scholars have mainly focused on the different roles these norms play in legal decision-making. In this understanding of the dichotomy a principle is a norm which has a 'dimension of weight'.[15] It is a kind of optimisation command[16] that is applied through a process of weighing, whilst rules are applied in an either-or fashion. In such an understanding of norms principles represent the element of flexibility in law.

The understanding of how fundamental the distinction between rules and principles is varies. For some it may be only a question of degree, whilst others, like Ronald Dworkin, see it rather as a real dichotomy and emphasise the clearly different character of the categories:

> Only rules dictate results, come what may. When a contrary result has been reached, the rule has been abandoned or changed. Principles do not work that way; they incline a decision one way, though not conclusively, and they survive intact when they do not prevail.[17]

I find a strict categorisation difficult to use when describing the flexibility needs of contemporary law. As I see it, in practice many norms contain both elements that usually have to be strictly applied and elements that require more flexible weighing in their application. A good illustration are rules that require a party to give notice concerning breach of contract, within a reasonable time. Whilst the prerequisites and legal effects of such a provision might be very rule-like, the often decisive determination of reasonable time requires the weighing up of a variety of elements. Increasing flexibility may in other words mean the introduction of more elements of weighing in the application of a rule that at the outset appears strict. Occasionally a rule may even be reinterpreted as a principle. On the other hand, sometimes a flexible principle, based on the weighing of reasons, becomes in practice so stabilised for certain situations that it appears to be more rule-like, at least for a while. So when speaking about the need for increasing flexibility in contemporary law, I understand the issue to be a question of degree only. One should speak about more or less flexible norms rather than about an either-or dichotomy between flexible and inflexible norms. Strict binary distinctions are usually not very useful if one attempts to convey a realistic picture of law.

The understanding of flexibility as a concept of degree serves the purpose of my analysis. A more clear-cut classification of norms may be valuable for other analytical

[14] See eg Dworkin (1978: 22 *et seq*) and Alexy (1985: 19 *et seq*). For the Nordic countries, see Eckhoff and Sundby (1976) (rules and guidelines) and Pöyhönen (1988: 13 *et seq*).

[15] Dworkin (1978: 26).

[16] Alexy (1985).

[17] Dworkin (1978: 35).

purposes. This is not the right place, however, to dive deeper into the discourse of rules and principles. Here it suffices to note the discussion. Perhaps one might even understand the discussion as such as a symptom of the flexibilisation of private law in contemporary society.

In legal discourse, general clauses are the paradigmatic examples of flexible legislative measures. Even though the flight into general clauses was already deplored a century ago,[18] such devices seem to have become a standard instrument in the toolbox of the contemporary legislator. In the EU, one may as examples refer to the important place in private law discourse occupied by the Unfair Contract Terms Directive[19] and the Unfair Commercial Practices Directive.[20] The legal literature concerning these two directives alone is immense.

Flexibility, however, is not based on general clauses alone. As already noted, legal norms often contain some more flexible parts. When assessing the flexibility of law it is probably more important to look at the methods of interpretation and application of law within a legal culture than at the number of general clauses existing in that culture. The level of flexibility is related to the legal-cultural views on acceptable legal reasoning, on the balance between pragmatism and formalism and between substance and form. My claim that law is and needs to be increasingly flexible in contemporary society not only relates to the wording and structure of individual norms, but to the spirit of the legal culture as a whole.

Secondly, another consequence of societal pressures on contemporary law is the fragmentation of law. When I discuss fragmentation, I do not refer to the latitude given to the court for decision-making in an individual case, but rather to law as a systematic structure of thought. The more fragmented that law is, the more difficult it is to present it as a coherent system. The opposite of a fragmented law is a coherent law. As coherence of law may mean many things, this is a rather vague definition of fragmentation, but it suffices for the present purpose of distinguishing flexibility from fragmentation. I will discuss fragmentation and coherence in more depth in chapter seven.

In the same vein as flexibility I regard fragmentation as a concept of degree. Law is not fragmented or coherent, law is more or less fragmented. In contemporary law there is a pressure towards more fragmentation and less coherence, but it does not mean that the value of coherence would lack relevance altogether.

There is no self-evident correlation between flexibility and the fragmentation of law, even though pressures towards both flexibility and fragmentation are discernible in contemporary law. The discussion of principles and rules above may already generate doubts with regard to the necessary coexistence of these features. There 'principles' were described as flexible norms, whilst in the context of fragmentation the term 'principle' – albeit with a somewhat different meaning – instead leads our thoughts in the direction of a more coherent law. However, as both flexibility and fragmentation seem to be required to a greater degree in late modern society, one may assume that these features at least to some extent support each other.

[18] Hedemann (1933).
[19] Directive 93/13/EEC.
[20] Directive 2005/29/EC.

On the one hand, obviously strong flexibility tends to lead to increasing fragmentation. As flexible and contextual decisions have to be made with less emphasis on the needs of the system and its conceptual structure, the hurdle to adopt solutions that appear fragmented in relation to the system is lowered. The contextual and pragmatic pressure towards a more flexible law therefore easily leads to a more fragmented law.

A learning law is a flexible law. But learning also implies the achievement of something, advancement towards a better understanding of something. A law that is characterised by unlimited flexibility would not be a learning law; it would in fact be difficult to define it as a law at all. If law really has internalised some new learning, these insights should also be followed in future cases. Furthermore, the legitimacy of law requires a visible degree of continuation in its practices. As mentioned earlier, flexibility needs to be counterbalanced by stability. The stability achieved, however, is easily a fragmented stability. This tension explains, for example, some features of the development of modern tort law: a flexible principle on strict liability for dangerous activities may lead to a fragmented set of rules on strict liability concerning particular clearly defined lines of business. In this sense, fragmented but precise rules may appear to be a consequence of the overall flexibility of the system. The law appears as a sea of flexibility with a variety of islands (and perhaps even continents) of precise rules.

On the other hand, one can assume that a fragmented law often offers the decision-maker more leeway for flexible decisions because of its internal tensions and contradictions. The temptation to resort to formalism is smaller when the area of law from which the guidance for decision-making is sought appears to be fragmented.

As flexibility and fragmentation relate to each other in this way, but do not coincide, an analysis of flexibility and fragmentation in relation to stability and coherence requires a 2×2 matrix rather than a dichotomy. Looking at the structures of legal development one could in other words distinguish four categories:

	Flexibility	**Stability**
Fragmentation	Real-life-oriented case law	Precise rules on limited issues
Coherence	Principle-based law	System-oriented law

In contemporary society, the weight of the flexible and fragmented side becomes stronger in the two scales. There is pressure towards a flexible private law capable of learning and adapting to new situations, and the value of stability and coherence declines, but it does not vanish. Societal pressure pushes law towards the corner here named 'real-life oriented case law', but as stability continues to be valuable in legal reasoning, one will probably also find an increasing number of precise rules on limited issues, as the often used tort law example indicates. In addition, as coherence has not totally lost its appeal in the eyes of legal actors, a way to compensate for the decline of pure system-oriented law is to support the idea of a more principle-based law in which coherence and flexibility are combined in new ways. A good example is the vivid discussion on the role of human rights and fundamental rights as a structuring element of private law. This discourse, found both in national and European doctrine, illustrates the desire to find new value-laden and principle-based elements to structure private law. I will comment in more detail on this perspective in chapter six.

Societal pressure towards a more flexible and fragmented private law appears in many combinations. The challenge is to formulate a narrative that pictures the complicated interaction between flexibility, fragmentation, stability and coherence in a way that reflects the requirements and practices of contemporary law.

III. A DYNAMIC PERSPECTIVE ON LAW

The extent of the tension between the need for new learning and respect for tradition varies with regard to time and issue. Sometimes there seems to be little need for new approaches at least concerning some issues, and the legal situation appears to be relatively stable. At the same time, other issues may generate strong pressures for change and new learning. This may be due to general societal or ethical changes, but legal-political pressures may also arise from particular cases that have attracted public interest or from deliberate legal micro-political action. Therefore, a considerable degree of uncertainty is always involved when classifying the law concerning some specific issue to be in a stable or a more fluctuating state. There is continuous movement back and forth between flexibility and stability.

Legal scholars often downplay this oscillation. The content of law is portrayed as a static photograph lacking movement, showing 'the valid law' or 'the law in force' at a certain moment of time. If processes of change are noted – acknowledging that the law concerning some particular issue is in flux – these processes are often pictured as deficiencies that will be cured in due course.

In a dynamic conception of law, more attention should be paid to the processes of change. As an alternative to a snapshot, one should strive to show a moving object, a video that reflects the constant changes that a law undergoes. Through such a dynamic perspective, one is better equipped to catch, within the legal material, opportunities for legal and societal change that are waiting to be used.

In this work, I have adopted a dynamic view on change that includes such a positive element in the assessment of the situation. As I see it, fragmentation is not necessarily only an evil. Therefore one should not seek the solution in renewed attempts to build grand systems. In my writings, I have rather preferred to speak about small narratives on change. The fragmentation of private law generates opportunities to create small narratives that push the law in a desirable direction.

When I speak about a narrative on change I have in mind a narrative about how some part of law, sometimes even an issue of detail, is moved from a relatively stable position to a new relatively stable position, through the intervention of various relevant legal actors. The term 'narrative', in other words, refers to a broader development than just the solution of a particular legal case. Occasionally, a narrative on change may focus on a singular case, as just that case alone may have realised the change, but often the narrative includes many steps, involving both practice, academic writing and legislation, before it ends by the law being temporarily stabilised in a new set of rules.

The reader might have already caught a glimpse of some such narratives, above. For example, when I discussed issues related to the range of responsibilities of companies in chapter three section VI, I mentioned emerging rules on the increasing liability of mother companies through a piercing of the corporate veil, new attempts to make dominant companies liable for what is done within their global value chains, as well as the liability for financial institutions for operations financed by them. Obviously, these developments support each other and could ideally figure as steps in a narrative that concerns increasing the responsibilities of companies for other businesses dependent on them. The example also demonstrates how various legal actors can participate in a narrative: the ongoing narrative on value chains includes input both of courts, creatively deciding new issues, legislators, extending corporate social responsibility, and legal scholars, developing new concepts such as network liability[21] and a company's liability as a regulator.[22]

I will here add two examples from Nordic law to illustrate what I mean by a narrative on change. The examples indicate the large variety of small narratives. The first, on *social force majeure* in Finland, starts from a case and an enactment, proceeds through academic concept-building to end in a broader legislative pattern. The other, on Nordic law on strict liability in tort, has its starting point in academic writing, proceeds through case law and ends in different ways in the different Nordic countries. The first narrative spans merely a couple of years, the second almost a century.

I have told the story about *social force majeure* many times before.[23] I like it because it illustrates the possibilities of law to respond in an empathic fashion to the needs of the weak and vulnerable, such as the ill or unemployed, even though the response conflicts with a basic rule of the established traditional private law system. In private law, it is a generally accepted starting point that a person is held responsible for his or her ability to pay, regardless of the circumstances that may affect this ability: 'you've got to have money'.[24] Inspired by the reasoning in some decisions of the Swedish Market Court, however, Finnish legislation introduced as a detail in a new Act on Interest of 1982[25] a rule according to which the courts could adjust the interest on delayed payment to be paid by consumers if the delay was caused by payment difficulties which the consumer had encountered mainly through no fault of his or her own in consequence of illness, unemployment, or some other similar reason. Some academics, in the beginning, treated this rule as an exemption, which should be interpreted narrowly. Others, however, saw it as an indication of an emerging principle, and the principle was conceptualised by being given a name, in English '*social force majeure*'. As a result of this conceptualisation, law-drafters could then introduce similar rules in other enactments concerning insurance contracts and consumer sales, mitigating the sanctions for breach of contract by the consumer in case of *social force majeure*. The narrative that started by the inclusion of a small rule in a particular act on interest had after 20 years ended in a broader rule that in theoretically important

[21] eg Condon (2022).
[22] Suggested by Beckers (2015: 375) in relation to the liability for corporate codes.
[23] eg Wilhelmsson (1992: 180–216).
[24] Medicus (1988): '*Geld muss man haben*'.
[25] Korkolaki (Räntelag) 20.8.1982/633.

ways limited the previously prevailing starting point of private law. The narrative had changed, to some extent, a basic assumption of private law.

The story of Nordic law on strict liability is also one that I have told before.[26] The starting point of the narrative is easy to pinpoint. Everyone seems to agree that the 1914 monograph by the Danish scholar Henry Ussing on liability for dangerous activities[27] was very influential. It triggered a discourse in all the Nordic countries, which led to much of the initial development of the narrative. However, the narrative did not develop in the same direction in the different countries. From the same starting point, four at least partially different narratives emerged.

The Norwegian narrative led to the broadest adoption of strict liability. This might be due to another influential scholar, the Norwegian professor Fredrik Stang, who, echoing Henry Ussing in 1919, claimed that the negligence principle was not sufficient to handle the risks of an industrialised society, in particular with regard to dangerous activities.[28] Inspired by these scholars, the Norwegian courts have developed strict liability through extensive case law, acknowledging that activities causing more or less continuous risks for others should bear the economic consequences when the risk materialises. This has made it possible for both courts and scholars to discuss the issue in a generalising way, analysing the relevant elements of the assessment rather than focusing only on concrete situations. There is a broad use of strict liability related to so-called extraordinary, typical and continuous risks. This case law goes further than what is accepted in the other Nordic countries.[29] The Norwegian narrative, in other words, has so far ended in a legal situation in which strict liability is broadly used in a flexible and principled manner.

The Finnish narrative is closest to the Norwegian. However, there are considerably fewer Finnish Supreme Court cases on this issue and also less scholarly discussion concerning the general criteria for assessing dangerous activities. Scholars tend only to list the concrete situations in which the courts have constituted strict liability, such as liability for damage caused by the use of explosives and ammunition, liability of the organiser of a car race for injury to a spectator and liability for damage caused by burst water pipes.[30] However, even though scholars often describe the prevailing situation simply by enumeration, it is generally accepted that courts may expand the list.[31] The end of the Finnish narrative is open, however, as the Finnish Supreme Court seems to be turning towards a more generalising mode, for example by expressly stating that strict liability is also possible with regard to an activity that is not as such deemed dangerous, but to which is linked an element of danger that is not completely controllable.[32]

In the Swedish narrative, the principle of liability for damage caused by dangerous activity was adopted in the 1920s. There have been few cases, however, and Swedish scholars have been content to note that the Swedish courts have not developed the

[26] Wilhelmsson (2019). See also above, ch 3 section VI.
[27] Ussing (1914).
[28] eg Stang (1919: 43–45).
[29] And perhaps even generally in foreign jurisdictions, so Hagstrøm and Stenvik (2015: 147).
[30] Ståhlberg and Karhu (2014: 167–76).
[31] Ståhlberg and Karhu (2014: 174).
[32] Finnish Supreme Court 2000:72.

law towards a wider use of strict liability.[33] For a period, one could have seen that as the end of the Swedish narrative. However, due to new case law, critical doctrine has recently been able to proclaim the 'return of strict liability' in Swedish case law.[34]

Finally, paradoxically in the Danish narrative strict liability has been established without support from legislation in only a few cases. Even though the narrative started from the Danish scholar Henry Ussing, at least some Danish scholars claim it to be obvious that Ussing's proposal has not become living law.[35] The Danish narrative was shorter than those of the other Nordic countries. However, nothing prevents a new narrative from starting. It cannot be ruled out that the Danish courts might in the future become more active promoters of strict liability.[36]

In the dynamic perspective, it is interesting to discover how similar countries with similar starting points end up with different narratives, sometimes touching each other, sometimes proceeding in different directions. The example thus illustrates the partial unpredictability of the content of a narrative and the influence particular actors in the legal field can have on the development. This is why I wanted to include this example, despite its long time span.

The actors in the narratives were influential scholars and courts. If legislation had also been analysed, the picture that emerged would have been even more complex. All the Nordic countries have relatively many particular laws on strict liability, in the areas, for example, of transportation, energy and the environment. In this mass, one cannot easily find a coherent approach even in each national setting, not to speak about the Nordic countries as a whole. There is no need to describe these enactments in this context. It suffices to note that the legislative development of strict liability for particular situations in Nordic law, like in the laws of many other countries, offers a paradigmatic example of the fragmentation of private law: it may even go as far as it does in Swedish law prescribing strict liability for damage caused by dogs, but not by cats.[37]

The time span of the tort law narratives was very long, close to a century. In contemporary society the pace of societal change is much faster, and legal change follows suit. This is also well illustrated by many of the special enactments on strict liability for specific situations. These can be understood as small and short narratives in themselves, starting from an unclear general situation, perhaps inspired by some particular occasion or case, and ending in detailed and stable legislative rules for the activity at stake.

IV. GOOD SMALL NARRATIVES ON LEGAL CHANGE

The examples show how the development of law can be described in the form of narratives. I have in previous works used the metaphor 'good small narratives on legal

[33] Hellner (1995: 178).
[34] Andersson (2013: 313).
[35] von Eyben and Isager (2015: 205).
[36] This is discussed by von Eyben and Isager (2015: 206–07).
[37] Lagen om tillsyn över hundar och katter (2007:1150) Sec. 19. About the historical background, see Hellner (1995: 180–81).

change' to describe the dynamic and continuous development of private law.[38] The metaphor is illustrative in many ways.

The metaphor is both descriptive and normative. On the one hand, I believe it offers a good picture of how law works in contemporary societies. The metaphor reflects the way in which law both changes and remains unchanged in a society of present complexity. On the other hand, the metaphor also contains a normative proposal about how the law through its fragmented structure should be open to new ideas, reflecting the needs of contemporary society. As politics in contemporary society has moved from the realisation of large societal utopias, such as the welfare state, towards smaller steps in a complex societal environment, one cannot, convincingly, keep law immune against this societal trend, and one should not do so either. The metaphor attempts to illustrate both law as it is and as it should be under contemporary societal conditions. In this sense, it comes close to how Karl-Heinz Ladeur has sketched the future of law as 'serial law', generated from a 'series' of 'experimental search processes in conditions of uncertainty'.[39]

The metaphor 'small narratives' has both epistemological and ontological implications. Epistemologically it focuses legal research on dynamic processes of change rather than on the creation of static snapshots of private law. A deeper understanding of law requires an understanding of the ways in which legal change occurs and legal actors are involved. Ontologically, the narrative metaphor implies a possibility of choice in each junction of the narrative, in each knot that brings the narrative forward. This also goes for the starting and ending points of a narrative; even in a situation that appears to be stable there is usually some choice as to the start of a new narrative on legal change, and the ending of a narrative in stability also contains a choice. This implies a recognition that there is not only one direction in which the narrative can be developed, but there are other possible directions as well. The concept of law should therefore contain not only one likely solution, but all the alternatives that can be described as legally possible.

As the examples indicate, many actors can play a role in a small narrative on legal change. It may begin in an interesting case that is able to shake the perceived stability of the legal situation with regard to the issue. This case may be commented upon by legal scholars, and it may be followed by new cases. This may lead to a more general acceptance of a new rule or a new concept that stabilises the law in a new position and ends the narrative. Some narratives may also have a happy end through the enactment of new legislation. But all these endings are more or less temporary. One cannot completely foresee when a new narrative on change starts nor what direction it will take.

In ethical terms, the small narrative could be described as a link between the need for stability in law and the flexibility required by moral discourse. A small narrative on legal change is another way of expressing the moral metaphor of Zygmunt Bauman, according to which moral roads in contemporary society are created by

[38] Presented in detail in the area of tort and liability law in Swedish in my book *Senmodern ansvarsrätt* (Late Modern Liability Law, Private Law as Instrument for Micro-politics) (2001).

[39] Ladeur (2020: 299). His focus, though, is on administration rather than courts and scholars.

walking them.[40] A new path that has been opened through moral discourse on the legal arena – as a result of a legal learning process – can grow into a road that at least for a while stabilises the situation on and around this road.

The examples referred to above, as well as the examples on narratives on tort law and power in the previous chapter, are not particularly surprising. That law is developing in a piecemeal way, involving various legal actors, is a familiar observation for most lawyers from most jurisdictions. As this is the case, it is legitimate to ask what additional value it brings to use the metaphor of good small narratives. There are several reasons why I find the metaphor useful. It includes and illustrates a couple of features of contemporary private law that are important, in particular when private law is looked at from a micro-political perspective.

First, a small narrative illustrates the continuous tension and necessary interplay between flexibility and stability in contemporary law. Change and adaptation require flexibility, but the effects of change stop halfway if the new approach is not stabilised in a new rule. A small narrative illustrates a journey – the narrative – from a relatively stable situation, the beginning of the narrative, to another but different relatively stable situation, the end of the narrative. It pictures how law is constantly oscillating between periods of calm and stability and periods of dynamic development in relation to each issue and each field of law. Like in any narrative, there is no fixed point in which the narrative on change begins, and no self-evident point when it ends in stability, leaving lawyers living happily ever after.

The description in chapter two of how the uncertainty of the risk society and the requirement of calculability of the insurance society are reflected in law offers one perspective on the required dynamic between stability and change. Just as the risk society requires flexible rules, with whose help law can learn to cope with new risks, the insurance society demands clear rules. When the societal and legal experiences of a particular risk and its moral assessment increase, it becomes possible to establish more stable norms for this particular type of cases. It is also possible that detailed public law regulation is introduced in areas in which sufficient experiences have been gathered. However, the totality of the rules still tends to retain its flexibility, as new more stable rules appear to be fragmented solutions related to certain risks rather than parts of a consistent system. Therefore, it is also possible to question even these stable parts if a new experience demands it. There is always an opportunity for starting a new small narrative on change.

The much-used distinction between hard and easy (routine) cases, described in chapter one section IV, illustrates from another perspective the tension between flexibility and stability caught by the small narratives metaphor. Easy cases are usually related to a legal environment that looks stable, whilst the hard cases in some way are involved in a process of legal change. In an easy case the decision-maker is supposed to directly apply a legal rule that is clearly expressed in a convincing and stable legal source, whilst the hard case is the scene for legal learning and choosing the direction of the narrative on change. The distinction between hard and easy cases, however, is simply a heuristic tool, and not a clear-cut dichotomy. A case that at the outset

[40] Bauman (1995: 17).

appears to be easy may also in various ways and for various reasons, for example because of a change in societal conditions or because the case is particularly repulsive in moral terms, be turned into a hard one, starting a new narrative on change.

Secondly, the 'smallness' of the narrative illustrates the lack of a strong master plan for the narratives. In late modern society, characterised by uncertainty and ambivalence, there is no grand scheme for changes, no objectives given a priori. Law changes through continuous small learning processes rather than by following one great vision – if there are great visions there are usually several of them. Law has been described as 'the unplanned outcome of a large number of separate decisions' instead of a deliberately designed system.[41]

The lack of a coherent vision or master plan that would streamline the various narratives on change is what I refer to by speaking of 'small' narratives. The reference to 'small' narratives in other words does not imply anything about the societal or legal size of the narrative. A narrative may relate to a grand challenge of utmost weight, like the climate cases, and it might sometimes lead to legal changes that may be called 'revolutionary'.[42]

The lack of a master plan allows narratives within different fields of law or concerning different situations to proceed in different directions. This does not mean complete chaos. There may be periods in which a certain vision is dominant and there may be fields of law that for a period develop in a coherent way. In the absence of a general plan, however, the various pieces of coherence do not necessarily run parallel and there is also always the possibility for a change of direction with regard to some particular field or issue.

In other words, when one narrative has stabilised in a regulation, this does not prevent the next narrative from proceeding in the direction of deregulation. Continuous oscillation between regulation, deregulation and reregulation is typical for late modern risk society. Moreover, in a period of ethical uncertainty, one narrative may picture a change in a welfarist direction, whilst the following narrative returns the law to a more traditional liberalist position.

In a complex environment, it is often not even possible to designate, for example, the best 'welfarist' solution to a problem. In a tort law setting some may advocate a solution based on some form of commutative justice, whilst another prefers an approach guided by perceptions of distributive justice. The former may emphasise the need to establish guidelines for moral action, whilst the latter may focus on the fair distribution of risks between different groups in society. The impact of different understandings of welfarism is discussed further in chapter six. Here it suffices to note that there is no welfarist master plan for private law, but the traditional liberalist master plan has also lost its appeal.

The lack of master plans, however, does not mean that there is no deeper guidance limiting the directions of the development. Applying Kaarlo Tuori's distinction between the legal surface and the deeper levels of law, the legal culture and the deep

[41] Friedman (2000: 4). I would not, however, describe law as a 'spontaneous order', *cf* Smits (2012a: 48 *et seq*), as the individual steps of the narratives may be very conscious, and the result is not an 'order'.

[42] See eg Worthington, Robertson and Virgo (2018).

structure of law,[43] one may locate a considerable part of the small narratives on legal change on the surface level of law, with visits on the legal-cultural conceptual level as well. The basic elements of the deep structure of modern law, such as the principle of the rule of law and human rights,[44] are less prone to changes, at least in the European conception of law.[45] In addition, even some elements of legal culture may have such a strong position that they will not easily be affected by small narratives on legal change. I will later, in chapter six, explore the possibility of some such larger narratives in Europe. These larger narratives may limit the area of what is considered legally possible, but they do not eliminate the opportunities to develop legal narratives on change in various directions. Deep structure and some parts of legal culture simply form a broad frame within which a large variety of legal micro-political activities are possible.

Thirdly, like a narrative, legal change is always both bound and unpredictable. Therefore, the narrative metaphor illustrates the relationship between the actual and the possible in the work of a legal actor. A narrative is bound to its previous stages, but its continuation is open to alternatives. Every step in the narrative, every new legal element that adds to the narrative, opens up new options for the next steps and at the same time shuts the door to other previously available options.

Others have also used the narrative metaphor to describe the development of law. Most well-known is probably the metaphor of a chain novel used by Ronald Dworkin.[46] He uses this metaphor to underline 'the dimension of fit', namely how new elements of the novel fit together with the previous ones. Just as a new chapter in a chain novel has to build on the chapters already written, new cases have to relate to cases that have already been decided. However, this requirement of 'fit' is understood rather as a limitation than as an opportunity to create something new. Even though new opportunities are not ruled out, as the previous material may be given new interpretations, the focus is clearly on the limitations. The judge, according to Dworkin,

> would rarely need to decide whether some interpretation barely survives or barely fails, because a bare survivor, no matter how ambitious or interesting it claimed the text to be, would almost certainly fail in the overall comparison with other interpretations whose fit was evident.[47]

In this respect, my approach is somewhat different. Without denying the limiting effects of the previous stages of the narrative, in the micro-political perspective one should also stress the new opportunities opened up at each step in the narrative. In a narrative on change the most interesting steps are those that create new opportunities for the next steps to be taken. Even though stabilising steps are also important parts of a narrative, in a developmental perspective it is often more interesting to look at steps that have enlarged or may enlarge the area of what is deemed to be legally possible.

[43] Tuori (2002: 147 *et seq*).
[44] Tuori (2002: 190).
[45] I pass by the developments in Hungary and Poland that can hopefully be seen as less representative of the EU.
[46] Dworkin (1986: 228 *et seq*).
[47] Dworkin (1986: 231).

The fourth advantage of the metaphor on good small narratives on legal change, in other words, relates to the opportunities of positive development that are present in each narrative. The metaphor elucidates the utopian opportunities offered to the legal actor participating in a narrative.

An approach that stresses opportunities rather than limitations understands that each step in a narrative changes the possible future in both ways, but focuses on the changes that add something to the opportunities that were present before this step. Even though one can clearly see that a step from point A to point C lies outside the sphere of what could be considered legally possible, the narrative may proceed from A to B, from which point it suddenly seems much more possible to reach C. Often many more steps may be needed in order to finish the narrative. The result may then appear to be a profound renewal of the legal situation, even though one cannot precisely define at what stage of the narrative the decisive step across the border was taken. 'The landmark case' may be a case that started the narrative, but it may also be a case that finishes the narrative and brings it into a new stable state.

I use the concept 'legally possible' to signal that the opportunities created by the advancement of a small narrative are not unlimited. On the contrary, even though the decision in a particular case is often less determinate than one would imagine, there are limits to what society and lawyers could accept as decisions that would still be considered by legal professionals to fall within the realm of law. As mentioned in chapter one, law is not indeterminate but 'underdeterminate'.[48] Going beyond these limits in legal decision-making would have negative societal consequences, undermining societal trust in the rule of law. Looking at narratives from this point of view, a small narrative appears to be a story about how the legal situation at each turning point of the narrative is being reshaped and concretised in a way that can simultaneously enlarge the area of what is deemed 'legally possible' in the next step.

In other words, understanding legal development as a series of small narratives in which various legal actors participate, broadens the perspective of what in a given context may be termed legally possible. Even though one may understand that the favoured legal solution at a particular moment is impossible to defend legally, one may realise that one can in a legally acceptable way take other steps that in their turn open up paths towards the previously impossible solution. From the point of view of micro-political actors that seek profound changes it is therefore often of utmost importance to find suitable examples, suitable cases, to start a narrative. In this sense, one could describe legal development as a struggle concerning the right examples.

An illustrative example of how profound changes can be achieved through smaller legal steps is the regulation of the legal status of relationships between persons of the same sex. In most countries, a direct step from not recognising or even penalising such relationships to the recognition of same-sex marriages and the right for such couples to adopt would have been too great, but a narrative proceeding from acceptance to registration, then to marriage, and finally to adoption rights – often with additional steps in between – has been successful in many countries. In most places, this narrative has been a narrative on legislative action, but courts, other legal decision-makers

[48] Davis and Klare (2019: 28).

and scholars may also have contributed to the narrative, for example using fundamental rights reasoning.

This brings me to the fifth advantage of the small narratives metaphor. A narrative can include a variety of actors. It recognises the activity not only of the legislator and the courts, but of all kinds of legal professionals – and sometimes even others – that have an impact on the outcome of the narrative. I will in the following section look more closely at the variety of legal actors that may be involved in a narrative on change.

A narrative requires somebody to tell it. There are no narratives without narrators. In this sense, legal actors play dual roles in building narratives. In principle, all legal actors tell their own narrative when confronted with a legal issue. At the same time, they are actors in the narrative, developing it further. This double role is particularly pronounced with regard to legal scholars. They are both important legal actors in small narratives and the primary narrators of the narratives – my focus was on legal research when I noted above the epistemological implications of the small narratives metaphor. This metaphor, in other words, emphasises the scholarly perspective on legal development. I will direct particular attention to this perspective on several occasions in what follows.

V. VARIOUS LEGAL ACTORS PARTICIPATING IN THE STORY-TELLING

There is no monopoly for particular legal actors with regard to participation in small narratives on legal change. In addition to the obvious change-maker, the legislator, courts and legal research also contribute to change. Sometimes other actors like public servants, or practising lawyers involved in a landmark case, play a decisive role. Looking behind 'the legislator' one may find the strong influence of, for example, the public servants who prepare enactments and draft Parliament bills. The fact that several different legal actors can be involved in a narrative on change offers micro-political actors a variety of targets when attempting to start or change the course of a narrative. There are many possible 'Actors of Utopian law'.[49]

The role of different participating actors varies, depending on the legal culture of the jurisdiction.[50] The legal heroes of a common lawyer are often famous judges, whilst a German lawyer instead seeks for the 'big names' of law among scholars – but it is not impossible to find opposite examples.[51] Public servants writing *travaux préparatoires* seem to have more influence in the Nordic countries than in other jurisdictions.[52] These and other national variations are well known. However, even though the casting may vary, the differences do not affect the accurateness of the small narratives metaphor, illustrating legal change as a product of the action of several sorts of players on the legal scene. I will in this context look somewhat more closely at the

[49] Graver (2020: 888).
[50] A classic text is van Caenegem (1987) on 'judges, legislators and professors'.
[51] Worthington (2018: 4–5, 9) notes the crucial role of scholars in common law revolutions.
[52] See eg Lando et al (2016: 15).

actors in a purely domestic scene, whilst the additional cast in a Europeanised narrative will be discussed in the following chapter.

The textual outcome of the activities of the actors is traditionally called sources of law: legislation, cases and *travaux préparatoires*. Why do I prefer to describe the development in terms of the actors, rather than the sources? First, I avoid emphasising 'legal sources', as it would easily bring to mind traditional relatively formal theories on the value and hierarchical status of legal sources. As will be shown in chapter eight, however, in practice law seldom functions that formally and hierarchically, but 'sources' are used much more actively in an argumentative process in which the content of the source, its hierarchical status and other available sources and arguments are weighed together. Both the users and the producers of sources play a much more active role in the narrative than a formal theory of legal sources indicates, and they therefore deserve to be looked at as actors. Secondly, focusing on the actors brings more clearly to the fore the moral responsibility of each actor in the development of a narrative. This emphasis on the moral responsibility of all legal decision-makers is one of the key messages of this work.

The recognition of a multitude of various possible ways of telling small narratives, with a variety of actors involved, seems to result in a fairly chaotic picture of legal development. In legal discourse, one finds many attempts to search for a clearer division of labour between different legal roles.[53] This is often done through binary questions such as: should the legislator or the courts be responsible for developing the law? Such an either-or approach does not correspond, however, to legal reality. Moreover, one does not have to understand the presence of several different actors on the scene as something negative. On the contrary, the different actors have partially different roles to play in the narrative. It is an important message of this section that all the roles are important and valuable. In what follows I will show why the input of a variety of actors can be required for a narrative to develop in a good and legitimate way.

Sometimes the roles of the actors are so far apart that one could realistically understand the content of the law in a relative way, depending on the actor who is dealing with the issue at hand. A proper account of legal practice may require a recognition of the law becoming 'polycentric'.[54] In a situation of extreme polycentrism, different legal actors tell different small narratives that do not meet each other. Normally, however, the practices of the various actors are interconnected.[55] The activity of various actors do combine in many ways into an at least partially joint narrative. It is a feature of our legal culture that legal actors recognise what other legitimate legal actors do. The development of law is a collaborative task in which participants are expected to respect each other's contributions.[56]

Occasionally, actors on the legal scene may expressly rely on the role of other actors. It can happen that in new legislation some issues are expressly left open, 'to be

[53] For an impressive analysis of how various political philosophies relate to the division of labour between legal actors in developing private law, see Hesselink (2021) ch 3.

[54] Zahle (1995: 198).

[55] Tuori (2021: 107).

[56] See eg the theoretical analysis of the collaboration between legislature and courts by Kyritsis (2015).

resolved by case law'. The legislator in such a case acknowledges that the particular professional ability of courts to solve conflicts and decide issues in learning processes based on factual real-life situations is required to reach a fair end to the narrative. The growing use of broad general clauses is also an example of such an express transfer of decision-making powers by the legislator to the courts. In other situations, courts may send issues to be solved by the legislator. The court may, for example, say that a certain solution to a problem would be preferable, but that such a solution cannot be reached by the court and requires new legislation. The court, in other words, doubts its own legitimacy to reach a solution it would like to adopt, as it deems it to fall outside what it defines as legally possible, and asks for the democratic legitimation of legislative decision-making to solve the problem in the future.

These brief examples illustrate the different functions of the various legal actors. Generally the three main legal actors – the legislator, the courts and legal science – have different assets to add to a successful narrative. Their roles, however, are not completely different. Some of the steps of a narrative may be taken by anyone of them, depending on the situation at hand.

In the continental perception of law, 'the legislator' is the prime producer of legal rules. The legislator is needed in legal narratives with regard to the maintenance of the legitimacy of law. As democracy is the recognised basis of legitimacy of societal governance in contemporary Europe, the legitimacy of law requires that at least some of its basic elements are created by a democratically elected legislative body.

In private law expert quarters, however, private law is occasionally described as a body of normative expert knowledge, the basis of which should lie in the theories of private law recognised by this expertise. Democratic legitimation of private law would hence be less important and a demand for such legitimation could even be regarded as artificial.[57] Historically, there has indeed been little democratic political influence on the development of private law.[58] Some might consider traditional 'juridical rationality' in private law to be in less need for democratic legitimacy than contemporary more instrumentalist private law.[59] In contemporary discourse, the value of democratic legitimacy is therefore usually not denied, even though the discussions concerning a European Civil Code have brought back the tension between expertise-made law and democratically made law on the agenda. In this context, some even claim that legitimacy could be rendered only by a democratic process, not through 'essentialist private law theories, which are essentially a-democratic, anti-democratic, or post-democratic theories of private law'.[60] A civil code has its politics.[61] However, when understanding legal development as a collection of many and various small narratives a total either-or approach to the dichotomy of expertise versus democracy seems too absolute, as the legitimacy of the narrative may be collected in many steps. With this reservation, it is easy to agree that the legislator has an important role

[57] eg Jansen (2010: 154).
[58] See eg Micklitz (2015a).
[59] Michaels (2011: 155–56).
[60] Hesselink (2015: 84).
[61] Hesselink (2006).

to play in filling at least the basic narratives with a sufficient degree of democratic legitimacy.

Some consider the weight of democratic legitimacy created by the legislator to be dependent on how actively the legislative body takes part in the decision-making. 'Real' democratic legitimation would not be created by a more or less formal acceptance of a text that basically has been produced by legal experts.[62] An often-described but probably relatively unique way of attempting to increase the democratic legitimacy of the outcome is the approach taken by the Dutch when drafting a new civil code a few years after the Second World War. At the start of this process, the Dutch Government submitted a list of questions to the Dutch Parliament that, according to the minister in charge, would require a political decision, and the drafting of the code commenced after Parliament had discussed and given answers to these questions.[63] In most countries, however, law drafting proceeds to a large extent under the auspices of civil servants, and the political input during the stage of drafting is limited – in particular if the law to be enacted does not relate to a politically sensitive and publicly debated issue. This does not remove, however, the formal demand for democratic legitimacy that a parliament can offer. From the perspective of democratic legitimacy one may, for example, criticise the 2016 French contract law reform for having been adopted by presidential decree and only later ratified by Parliament.[64]

In addition, legislation functions as a channel for importing the experience and values of actors outside the law into the legal discourse. Law is not a closed part of society that can only be developed with the help of legal experts. It is also a political instrument for developing society. National legislation is a dynamic element in the development of law that can introduce new ideas and new experience and quickly respond to societal and commercial needs. Legislation is also a means to react to various kinds of media-observed scandals in real life.[65] The most interesting legal experiments are often introduced by the legislator. For example, a remarkable part of the welfarist elements of private law that relate to consumer law and labour law have been brought into the legal sphere through legislation. These are precisely such instrumentalist features of private law that also require clear democratic legitimacy.

The legislator is often understood to play a very different role than other actors in a legal narrative, as the legislator is supposed to be free to develop the law as it wishes, whilst other actors are forced to make decisions within the vaguely defined realm of what here is termed 'legally possible'. To some extent this is true, as the legislator is not limited by the same boundaries of the legally possible as other legal actors and can move these boundaries quite freely. This does not mean, however, that there are no boundaries at all for what can be considered legally possible for a legislator. Basic limits are established by human rights, fundamental rights and the implications of the rule of law. Within the EU, national legislators find themselves increasingly restrained by primary and secondary EU law.

[62] This question is posed by Hesselink (2021: 70 *et seq*).
[63] See eg Hesselink (2006: 160–63).
[64] Hesselink (2021: 70–71, 107–08).
[65] The development of many parts of consumer law illustrates this well, Micklitz, Sibony and Esposito (2018: 2).

In addition, other elements of the deep structure of law and of legal culture may be of such a character that lawyers would at least prima facie find that even legislators cannot override them without overstepping the limits of the legally possible. The legislator is to some extent bound by existing experience and cannot make 'a fresh start on a clean slate'.[66] A narrative on change concerning more fundamental issues may require more steps than just a dash of the legislator's pen.

In particular, when the legal-cultural elements have frozen into recognised legal concepts, they may limit the field of options that a legislator considers possible to choose. Even though consumers certainly have experienced problems before the idea of consumer protection emerged in the 1960s and 1970s in various countries,[67] it would at that stage have been relatively unthinkable to introduce rules that protected only consumers but did not cover other similar market participants. Earlier insurance legislation, for example, usually protected (to some extent) all insured, regardless of whether they acted as consumers or not. Only the creation of the concept of a consumer as a legal concept made the present development possible. In other words, the new concept increased the legislative options. Even though a legislator can operate within a larger framework of possibilities than other legal actors, the legislator is still part of and inspired by the interaction between all the actors.

Here I have so far spoken about the 'legislator' as one actor in the legal game. This is a very imprecise way of describing the actors participating in the use of legislative power. Even though the end product – the enactment – is one text, many persons in different roles participate in creating the narrative. From the perspective adopted here, focusing on the various actors in the small narratives on legal change, it is important not to forget the variety of real actors involved in the legislative process.

At least three layers of decision-makers or influencers are involved. The final decisions are usually taken within the political sphere by the parliament (and perhaps also the head of state) after the responsible minister and the cabinet have decided to send the legislative bill to the parliament. The details of the process vary, but democratic legitimacy requires such political involvement in some form. The preparation of the bill, however, may be done in a procedure dominated by civil servants or hired experts. Their input is often much more important, at least with regard to the legal details, than that of the political sector. Finally, in the preparation of the bill, representatives of stakeholders and civil society often have a say, sometimes even as members of preparatory committees or at least as referral bodies.

From a Nordic perspective, the relationship between law drafting by civil servants and political decisions on the enactment looks particularly important, as the position of *travaux prèparatoires* here is considered to be an important source of law.[68] Such preparatory comments are usually written by civil servants, and are often not thoroughly scrutinised during the political process, even though in principle the minister and the cabinet may require changes and the parliament can comment on them as

[66] Hesselink (2008: 24).

[67] See eg Micklitz, Hondius, van Mierlo and Roethe (2019).

[68] Lando et al (2016: 15). This is recognised even by the European Court of Justice, accepting Swedish implementation of an indicative list through *travaux prèparatoires*, *Commission v Sweden*, Case C-478/99 ECLI:EU:C:2002:66, [2002] ECR I-4147, [22].

well. With regard to narratives on less politically tense issues, this gives the civil servants preparing legislation considerable power of influence.

It is not necessary here to discuss the varieties of legislative processes within the Member States. It suffices to note the multitude of various actors who may have an influence on the emerging legislation and its details. Sometimes even the intervention of a particular actor during some stage of the procedure might change the course considerably. It is an empirical issue to reflect on where such breakthroughs might have occurred in a particular narrative. Here it is simply important not to forget that behind the legislator as a collective concept there is a multitude of actors, each carrying a personal moral responsibility for his or her activity.

The norms set by law, by legislation or otherwise, are enforced and given life by the courts and other legal decision-making bodies. Their important role in small narratives on legal change is underlined by contemporary societal pressures towards a law that is more flexible and open to constant learning processes. It is the regular task of the courts to solve the challenges and the conflicts related to the enforcement of law. This enables them to bring particular added value into the small narratives. Their input might vary, depending on the type of court. A supreme court may, for example, be more inclined to protect the legal-cultural foundations of law than a lower court, only focusing on the case at hand.[69]

Professionals in problem-solving courts and practising lawyers can accumulate particular normative learning by being in direct contact with legally formulated concrete problems, conflicts and challenges in society. They are continuously engaged in learning processes based on the encounter with real-life situations in which the law directly confronts individual citizens. The sought-for flexibility of late modern law means a recognition of the important role of courts that can use their problem-solving professionalism to learn to cope with new risks and walk new moral roads in an ethically unchartered landscape.

Some even see this opportunity for courts to be directly exposed to new situations and societal needs as a reason to emphasise the particular role of courts as drivers of change in contemporary law. Courts that face new situations are forced to consider novel approaches. When dealing with new issues, for example by being exposed to cases that present new kinds of network problems, courts are expected to develop the necessary principles.[70]

If courts do proceed in a conspicuous way in cases of notable public interest, some call it 'judicial activism'.[71] Courts may indeed occasionally function as societal forerunners, making societally important decisions when political actors fail to do so. Climate change litigation is a good example of a situation in which some courts, like the Dutch ones, have concretised required measures more than politicians have dared to do.[72] Even though the democratic legitimacy of such decisions may be and has been questioned,[73] in at least some climate change cases there is an obvious rationality

[69] Tuori (2021: 24).
[70] Mitchell (2017: 234).
[71] eg Holland (1991), Dickson (2007), Spier (2010) and Dawson, De Witte and Muir (2013).
[72] See eg Burgers, van Duin and Mak (2020: 879–880).
[73] A deep analysis (with a positive perspective) is presented by Burgers (2020).

behind the division of labour between courts and legislative actors. In these cases, the state has recognised and accepted certain goals, thereby giving them democratic legitimacy. However, as political actors have not managed to adopt sufficient measures to reach these goals, this task has been overtaken by the courts.

In particular, in complex matters one may question the ability of courts to make good innovative decisions, as the facts on which the decisions are made may be qualitatively poorer and more limited than the facts that are typically available to those preparing legislation. This is not, however, self-evidently the case, and the deficit may sometimes be counterbalanced by the practical experience of complex decision-making acquired by the courts. One should also underline that innovative judicial decision-making and legislation do not exclude each other. Micro-political litigation can be a means to push for new legislation. The courts and the legislature are participants in the same narratives.

There is no fixed balance between the measure of democratic legitimation and court creativity required in various situations. Obviously, with regard to politically sensitive issues and issues with great societal impact, like climate change cases, the question of the democratic legitimacy of innovative case law comes much more to the fore than when courts develop 'traditional' private law rules. As mentioned above, in the latter cases the role of legal expertise has usually been considered to be important. I will return to the issue of the rule of law in legal decision-making – another perspective on the issue of democratic legitimacy – in chapter eight.

In addition to the prime legal actors, various quasi-legal and non-legal actors may also affect the content and direction of narratives. Private law (in particular contract law and tort law) has been described as an open system that is 'interactional' – that is, it depends on moral norms in social practices.[74] Through various inlets, decisions of many kinds of organisations and institutions may find a way into the legal narratives on change. They bring into the small narrative concrete experience concerning the line of business and the type of activity to be assessed.

A good example that has been much discussed in recent years is the role of standard-setting organisations in developing the normative landscape. Business organisations may also affect the normative sphere in other ways, for example by creating standards of conduct that may directly affect legal assessments of unfairness and negligence. 'Private standards of fairness' clearly have a role to play.[75] Even individual companies adopting corporate social responsibility codes can have an influence on the legal reasoning concerning their responsibilities.[76] As the 'openings' for such materials are often some relatively vague legal concepts, like unfairness and negligence, these quasi-legal and non-legal actors do not affect the legal narratives on the national level in isolation from more purely legal actors, but rather in an interplay with them. Their role in the narrative is therefore ambivalent, as they sometimes only play the part of producing factual evidence on customs and acceptable behaviour for

[74] Taekema (2014).

[75] Pavillon (2014).

[76] Beckers (2015) has developed a narrative on the increasing legal enforceability of such codes. See also Beckers (2017) on how the directives on unfair commercial practices and unfair contract terms can create such a binding effect.

a concrete application of the law, without aspiring to enter the realm of legal change, whilst in other cases their input may be so normatively forceful that it affects legal reasoning beyond the case at hand and thereby becomes a step in the legal narrative. In other words, in an open private law, there is no clear dividing line between law and non-law,[77] and therefore the class of actors that can participate in a small narrative on legal change is not clearly delimited either.

This is not the place to delve further into the issue of the growing role of standardisation organisations and other private organisational actors. That has been successfully done by others.[78] It suffices to note how broad and fuzzy the group of private actors is that in various ways can contribute to small narratives on legal change. The increasing flexibility and fragmentation of contemporary private law is connected to the growth of this group both as cause and consequence. The increasing flexibility broadens the gates into the core realm of law for materials produced by private actors. On the other hand, it seems obvious that the expansion of the group of private actors that may have an influence on legal change as such contributes to the growing fragmentation of private law.

Finally, picturing legal development as an interplay between several legal actors also means describing it as an interplay between theory and practice. Legal scholars are able to conceptualise narratives and thereby connect them to other parts of the legal order.[79] They can both push the narrative to continue through creating new concepts that picture changes as legally possible and stabilise the situation by conceptualising the development that has already taken place. In addition, a teacher of law may also stabilise a narrative by making its result part of the teaching of new generations of lawyers. This is the final stage of a small narrative, or rather a part of its aftercare. In this stage, a narrative that perhaps has ended in relative stability years ago may finally sink into the level of legal culture, thereby becoming less prone to (but not immune to) being challenged by a new small narrative. As I am particularly interested in what challenges and opportunities contemporary society poses for legal research, and as the role of legal scholars is often essential in both starting and closing small narratives, I will discuss the position of scholarly writing in small narratives in more detail in the following section of this chapter.

Picturing legal development as a collection of small narratives in which a variety of legal actors participate shows how different actors bring different assets to the narratives. The legislator brings democratic legitimation and input from societal aspirations, the courts supply law with experience related to concrete cases, private actors bring in experience from a line of business, whilst scholars add conceptual thinking to the palette. In a world that requires an experimental attitude this variety of input obviously must be a strength.

The focus on legal actors also highlights the moral responsibility of all actors involved in legal decision-making. As legal discourse in contemporary society

[77] Taekema (2014: 148).
[78] For contract law, see eg Brownsword, van Gestel and Micklitz (2017) and Grundmann and Grochowski (2021), Pt IV. On the role of European standardisation in the Europeanised narratives, see ch 5 below.
[79] In some countries other actors, eg advocate-generals, are also said to contribute to the development of doctrine; see Van Hoecke and Ost (1998: 204). I will focus here on academic doctrine.

becomes more open and transparent, actors' moral responsibility for the direction of the narratives becomes societally more visible. Instead of trusting only in the ethics of a system-building monolithic legislator, one can demand that all legal decision-makers should bear their moral responsibility and as far as possible make use of their ability to promote just choices in the development of law. All legal professionals can sometimes and to some extent participate in the creation of good small narratives on legal change.

VI. CONCEPTUALISATION AS A KEY POINT OF A NARRATIVE: THE ROLE OF DOCTRINE

Legal scholars are an important group of actors. The metaphor of small narratives implies scepticism about the force of grand legal systems, but it does not imply refraining from systematic legal thinking. Legal concepts and principles are and ought to be an essential part of legal discourse. Law develops in continuous interaction between legal concepts and particular cases and issues. Scholars creating doctrine, therefore, are and should be active participants in small narratives. A narrative may start through, be supported by or finished as a consequence of a creative conceptual contribution by a legal scholar.

Saying this, I am focusing mainly on such legal research that falls under a broad definition of what is usually called 'legal dogmatics', namely research that explicitly aims at supporting the working and development of the legal order by creating authoritative statements about the law and its structure. This is not to say, however, that other forms of legal scholarship, such as societally geared research or comparative research, would not have any impact on small narratives. On the contrary, such research may influence development to a considerable extent, and later I will note how, for example, comparative law has played and must play a central role in the processes of Europeanisation.

The role of scholars is not the same in all European jurisdictions. Underlining scholarship is more in line with the continental legal tradition than with the perception of common lawyers. My impression is, however, that this is rather a difference of grade than a completely different understanding. In common law, eminent scholars have indeed exerted a considerable influence on the development of private law.[80] Whilst mostly only 'eminent' scholars can impress common law judges so much that their advice is taken seriously, in the continental setting the status of academic research and the approach to law as a kind of 'scientific' system tend to allow the influence also of other scholars than the 'big names' – even though the 'stars' even here are often treated with greater respect by the courts than other scholars.[81] '*Stand der Lehre*', the prevailing view in legal doctrine, is a recognised part of the established doctrine of legal sources. In Germany, the status of commentaries to legislative texts is important, whilst this may be less the case in some other jurisdictions.[82]

[80] On leading scholars on tort law in the common law world, see eg Goudkamp and Nolen (2019).
[81] For Sweden, see the examples mentioned by Mossberg (2020: 203, fn 770).
[82] See the comparative analysis of the role of commentaries in Kästle-Lamparter, Jansen and Zimmermann (2020).

The reluctance of common law to recognise scholarly input in small narratives is not equally strong in US law. Here the tradition of Restatements made by scholars has underlined the importance of at least this kind of scholarly work. In the Restatements, the scholarly community involved has done the same type of exercise as continental systematising academics, analysing case law in order to increase clarity and coherence. In the newest draft Restatement of Consumer Contracts, the drafters have even added a layer of transparency above the traditional analysis of leading cases from the highest state courts by supporting the results with quantitative analyses of the entire body of consumer contract law decisions in the US court system.[83] In this way, both dogmatic and empirical scholarship is involved in developing the law.

In the Nordic countries, the role of scholars may be even stronger than elsewhere, as the task of creating concepts and principles here is to a considerable extent entrusted to the legal academia. On the one hand, Nordic law lacks a comprehensive civil code that in its general part would to some extent determine the general private law structure. That leaves the field more open for scholarly interventions. On the other hand, Nordic law, belonging as it is to the continental tradition, tends to emphasise the systematic-scientific character of law more than a common lawyer would. In addition, as law from the Nordic perspective is understood as a tool for societal engineering that the legislator can use relatively unrestrained by the internal systematics of law, and as case law has not taken over the role as a system builder, the responsibility for the systematic features of law lies very heavily on legal scholars.

Even though there are national variations, in general, legal scholars can be regarded as important participants in the development of law. They may contribute on various levels of abstraction, from discussing concrete legal problems to developing legal concepts and principles. Obviously the latter task – the systematisation and conceptualisation of law – is the one in which the contribution of scholarship cannot be contested. Academic legal doctrine is needed to structure legal discourse. I will therefore here focus mainly on the task of scholars to systematise law, and only briefly mention their other task: the task of interpretation. Needless to say, scholarly contributions to interpretation may also have an impact on small narratives on legal change, inspiring courts and other actors in their decision-making.

Contemporary societal pressures towards fragmentation of law do not remove the need for conceptual doctrinal work. Even though fragmentation seems to push general legal concepts into a less prominent position, fragmentation also gives rise to new reasons for discussing systematic issues. New concepts and principles are needed to help one to understand the increasingly wide and dispersed mass of norms. Perhaps conceptual analysis is needed more than ever in critically assessing and developing the systematic side of law. Small narratives on legal change may in other words also be about how new legal concepts and principles are created. Scholars still have an important role to play in small narratives as creators of conceptual structures, but contemporary structure-building, when it reflects the fragmentation of law, tends to an increasing extent to work with narrower concepts that relate to more limited fields

[83] Bar-Gill, Ben-Shahar and Marotta-Wurgler (2019: 97). The whole issue of *European Review of Contract Law* 2/2019 is devoted to the ALI Restatement on Consumer Contract Law.

and to problems described in a real-life language. Such system fragments cannot be squeezed together into one ossified system, and the systematisations made by legal scholars can always be reconsidered in new narratives.

Scholarly conceptual work may have an impact on a small narrative on legal change in all stages of the narrative. Sometimes the narrative on change is started by an academic critique of the status quo. In other cases, the doctrinal input supports the continuation and deepening of the narrative by conceptualising some developments in case law or legislation. Finally, such conceptual work may stabilise the situation in a way that means the end of the narrative on change. In all these stages, the role of legal doctrine may be quite significant with regard to the development of the narrative. Academic conceptualisation often appears to be decisive, as it makes the change both visible and stable. As a small narrative on legal change may, using the terminology of Kaarlo Tuori,[84] include elements that relate both to the surface level and to the legal-cultural level of law, a scholarly input that stabilises the narrative may contribute to shape new conceptual sediments in the legal culture.

Performing this conceptual task, legal scholars may, like academics in other disciplines, introduce innovative and border-crossing thinking. In the fragmented and learning legal environment, scholars may produce new conceptual tools by transgressing legal borderlines, and import fruitful concepts and principles from other areas of law. This leads to the apparent paradox that contemporary private law doctrine seems to favour both broad principles and narrow situation-related approaches. On the one hand, new broad systematic connections are built, for example by diluting the borderlines between private law and public law; on the other hand, there is the fragmenting move away from grand legal systematisations. The paradox is dissolved, however, in the small narrative in which doctrinal border crossings are introduced in the situational real-life problem that the small narrative is often focused on.

A topical example of how scholars may in this way break through traditional conceptual walls and create new opportunities for small narratives is the recurrent discourse on the relevance and impact of the borderline between contract law and tort law. Without going into detail, it is easy to note how the traditionally often relatively strict differentiation between these two forms of private liability has for a long time faced growing doctrinal confrontation in many legal orders. Some have proclaimed the 'death of contract', implying that tort is pushing contract aside, ultimately leading to a 'theory of civil obligation'.[85] Others have offered brand new categories of liability that are crossing the traditional categories of contract and delict.[86] Contract law should be open to productive learning by taking the complementarity between tort and contract seriously.[87] Such critiques obviously stem from the recognition that the traditional dichotomy is dysfunctional when confronted with contemporary complex societal experience. Another way to renew the conceptual structure, making it possible to take into account such experience, is to reconstruct the concept pair from being

[84] Tuori (2002: 147 *et seq*), and on sedimentation (2002: 200 *et seq*).
[85] Gilmore (1974: 89 *et seq*).
[86] Atiyah (1979: 778–79). Another example is Köndgen (1981).
[87] Condon (2017), advocating an approach in which tort and equity could be invoked within the contractual matrix (188).

a sharp dichotomy to seeing the concepts as more vaguely delimited. Outside the core areas of the concepts, various modifications and combinations of both liability forms would be possible. In such a conceptual setting, one could focus primarily on the attributes of various real-life situations when assessing liability.[88] In this way, a broad doctrinal reconceptualisation, transgressing the borderline between contract law and tort law, simultaneously would fuel the opportunity to develop small narratives on a variety of real-life situations.

Flexible and fragmented contemporary law offers interesting opportunities for scholars to create new concepts and principles, for example based on the experiences generated by micro-politics. Scholarly concepts and principles are not only more stable elements in the interplay between flexibility and stability, they can also have a destabilising effect. They can open up paths for new narratives. Through producing alternative concepts and principles, scholars may offer tools for a judge who strives to create new morally valuable legal practice. In the interplay between theory and practice, the work of this judge may in turn fuel further dogmatic work. The more actors that participate in the narrative, the more 'true' it becomes. In the good small narrative the utopian and the actual in the work of a legal scholar are naturally connected.

Many versions of what has been called 'critical' or 'alternative' legal dogmatics are good examples of such attempts to connect the actual and the utopian in concrete scholarly work.[89] Such authors can seek to broaden the sphere of the legally possible by finding and conceptualising weak signals of new and preferred approaches in the concrete legal material. As the above-mentioned story concerning *social force majeure* illustrates, new concepts can make the invisible more visible in legal discourse and thereby broaden the understanding of what can be considered legally possible. As the development of law can be described as an eternal struggle between main rules and exceptions, conceptual focus on an exception may, if considered desirable, contribute to expanding the sphere of application of the exception and make it increasingly main rule-like.

Without discussing further the various methodological patterns that have been advanced under the headings of 'critical' or 'alternative', some of them even wanting to turn theorists from 'spectators' into participating 'activists',[90] it is easy to claim that one should see some form of critical approach as an important part of scholarly activity. As legal scholars are citizens of both the legal community and the academic community,[91] they should respect the basic principles guiding both communities. One of the basic values of the academic community is a critical attitude. In some form, this can be found in most value-statements of universities and other academic institutions. Being the main builders of the conceptual framework of law, legal scholars should therefore adopt at least a questioning attitude to the conceptual structures that tradition offers.

[88] In Finnish doctrine such an approach has been suggested by Hemmo (1998).

[89] My main favourites in this respect were Unger (1983) and Reifner (1979). The list of references from different countries could, of course, be expanded almost infinitely.

[90] Gearey (2018: 172).

[91] Tuori (2002: 144).

The recognition of the role of legal scholars as players in narratives on legal change implies that such scholars cannot escape the moral responsibility that all legal actors bear concerning the development of law. Legal scholars cannot simply hide behind a system (made by other scholars). They are responsible for choosing how to move in the recurring games on main rules and exceptions. As the contribution of scholars may be decisive with regard to the start, direction and ending of a small narrative, it is obvious that such scholars in the same vein as other participants in the narrative bear a moral responsibility for the result of the narrative. The shield of science cannot protect scholars from moral criticism regarding their contribution to the narrative.

VII. 'GOOD' NARRATIVES: THE RESPONSIBILITY OF LEGAL PROFESSIONALS

Even though I have used the metaphor of small narratives primarily in a descriptive mode, claiming that it illustrates how law is actually developing in contemporary society, there is also a normative element in the picture. I have attempted to communicate this positive undertone by occasionally speaking about 'good' narratives on legal change. What does this mean?

I have mentioned climate cases, and there are also many other issues for which legal and societal change is obviously needed. There is an urgent feeling with regard to many societal challenges that something also has to be done by legal actors. The idea of good small narratives can be characterised as a vision that attempts to show how legal actors can do 'good' without abandoning their role as lawyers.

However, not all narratives on change are necessarily good. Sometimes one feels that, for example, a court decision 'is so down-right odd that it deserves to be locked into a secure container, plunged into the icy waters of a deep lake and forgotten about.'[92] This may lead the narrative into a blind alley. A criticised decision may indeed eventually be forgotten, but a decision or a legislative act may also lead to a narrative that continues in a direction considered unfortunate by many spectators.

It might sometimes be the case that a 'good' decision is the one that does not proceed with a narrative on change, but instead sticks firmly to tradition. It should be noted, however, that such a decision is also one for which the decision-maker bears a moral responsibility, as far as there are other alternatives available within the margins of the legally possible (as there often are).

If there is no grand narrative, no predefined plan for legal development at large, how is it then possible to speak about 'good' and 'bad' narratives? In chapter two, the claim was made that the force of grand ethical systems has vanished, and moral roads can be made just by walking them. So if there are no preset ethical systems to rely on, how can one recognise a 'good' narrative on change?

Distinguishing good narratives from others based on the content and result of those narratives would require, in principle, some form of key for defining the substantive criteria for goodness. Without a commonly shared grand narrative, such

[92] Weatherill (2014: 167), in a well-founded critique of the decision CJEU Case C-426/11 *Mark Alemo-Herron and Others v Parkwood Leisure Ltd*, ECLI:EU:C:2013:521.

a key is obviously not available. Having admitted this, it is still tempting to search for at least some guidelines. Above, in chapter three, the spotlight was put on the relationship between law and power. In this light 'good micro-politics' would use law as a device for counterbalancing and controlling the use of societal power. All power, however, is not illegitimate or 'bad'. It is easy to imagine 'bad narratives' that aim, for example, at restricting welfarist advances promoted by democratic political power. In other words, understanding law as a counterbalance to societal power at most offers a possible indication of goodness, but it does not give a decisive criterion for designating a small narrative as a good one.

Other candidates in the search for criteria determining 'goodness' are, for example, both European and domestic constitutional values. The increasing importance of fundamental rights in contemporary legal reasoning requires looking more closely at this input, and this will be done in chapter six. As will be shown there, these rights might both delimit and expand the area of the legally possible, but not determine what is good or bad within these boundaries.

The list of possible goodness keys could be prolonged in many directions. The world is overflowing with value catalogues that could be used in determining the goodness of small narratives. From a global perspective, a good candidate is The United Nations Sustainable Development Goals, as the document expresses goals for the development of global society that are accepted by representatives of all humankind.[93] Designated to fight poverty and hunger, promoting health, education and equality and supporting sustainability and climate action, these goals offer a good synthesis of the direction in which humankind should proceed. The UN collection of goals has become a relatively common reference point even in value statements of sustainable investors and others who want to underline the sustainable character of their business. From a global perspective, the goals are important, and it is conceivable that one could analyse law with reference to such goals in order to indicate features of goodness. The general wording, internal tensions and global character of the UN goals, however, make it difficult to use them as determining criteria regarding the goodness of small narratives on legal change. In what direction should one proceed, for example, if the (short-term) interests of the poor and vulnerable are in conflict with the climate goals or with biodiversity-related sustainability goals in a concrete situation?

In other words, there are no ready-made answers to the moral issues confronting a contemporary legal professional. The possible grand narratives of European private law, discussed in chapter six, do not offer sufficient guidance. As judges, legal scholars, and other legal actors meet the moral issues point blank, without the protection of a generally accepted ethical system, they must themselves create the criteria for goodness. These criteria can and should be discussed in a pragmatic and transparent fashion, like other moral discourses in contemporary society. In such a pragmatic moral discourse, one might reach more unanimity on good and evil than one would expect. All legal actors do not walk along different roads, they take the paths that they have found good in more general use. However, as these paths are emerging on the

[93] www.un.org/sustainabledevelopment.

basis of pragmatic legal discourses, the discursive approaches tend to be contextual rather than principled. The 'goodness' lies in the quality of the contextual pragmatic discourse.

Not even if one chooses to take the starting point in some ostensibly clear substantive values and goals, for example related to welfarism, can one reach generally accepted concrete operationalisations of the values in the contemporary conditions of societal complexity. Even if there was agreement that legal actors should participate in walking the paths and roads of law in directions that support the weak and the vulnerable – which as such is a utopian supposition – one would still not necessarily have any determining guidance as to the best decision in a particular situation.[94] In the US, many critical scholars have struggled with issues relating to poverty and law, but they 'were not finally able to pull together their insights into a coherent ethics of poverty law.'[95] The right way, according to Adam Gearey, is to be sought by working alongside the poor: poverty law is 'good work'.[96] In other words, the assessment of goodness even with such a shared welfarist starting point is finally contextual and related to the situation at hand.

It is worth repeating that not only the criteria for goodness must constantly be renegotiated in the pragmatic moral discourse. Also in cases in which there is unanimity on the moral criteria it is often in the complex structure of contemporary society impossible to foresee whether a solution will lead to the desired societal consequences. To mention a traditional example: the decision-maker cannot, even with the help of social sciences, be sure what effect on the supply of housing the regulation of the level of rents would have and how it would affect the most vulnerable in society. In a similar vein: the decision-maker cannot make a relatively certain prediction whether the acceptance of a doctrine of *social force majeure* might make it more difficult for the potentially unemployed to get credit. A small narrative may lead to a result that is not as societally good as the decision-maker had hoped for. The narrative was not so good after all. New narratives will need to be started. In this sense, small narratives have to be experimental.

In other words, as small narratives may proceed in various directions, sometimes in directions that some regard as good and others as bad, and as the consequences of decisions are not always easy to predict, the discussion of the goodness of the small narratives cannot be based on substantive criteria alone, but also on the quality of the pragmatic moral discourse. As moral roads are made by constantly walking them, one should look at the quality of behaviour of the legal professionals who are able to exert influence over the direction of the narratives. As has been noted here, many legal actors are participating in a narrative: what kind of outlook and attitudes can and should one expect from those involved?

The traditional role of the legal professional is the role of an expert. The legal decision-makers are expected to be initiated into the secrets of legal conceptuality and to make use of this knowledge when making decisions. However, the ideal judge

[94] See ch 6 section III below on the various understandings of welfarism.
[95] Gearey (2018: 56).
[96] Gearey (2018: 178).

has always been seen to have another source of authority as well. A good judge is a person who can act as an experienced professional in making commonsense-based moral assessments. In contemporary conditions of epistemic and ethical uncertainty, the latter element in the role of the legal actor tends to gain greater weight. The legal actor, who cannot comfortably remain behind a closed conceptuality of law, has to be to a growing extent a multidisciplinary intellectual with a good ability to formulate and discuss pragmatic moral issues. As Koen Raes has pointed out, the authority of judges in the modern state is not so much based on 'theoretical expertise' but on 'practical authority'.[97] Like many other professionals in late modernity, judges can no longer hide behind their systems of knowledge, but have to encounter moral issues naked, face to face in practical situations.

In contemporary society, legal actors have to be prepared to assess and make use of a multitude of approaches. Increasing fragmentation and flexibility of law in an epistemologically and ethically uncertain environment require new talent in addition to traditional qualifications. The Danish legal philosopher Jørgen Dalberg-Larsen is very much to the point in his description of the role of a good 'postmodern jurist':

> The other (and from a postmodern point of view a better) possibility is to try to combine (the best) parts of these three roles: 1) from the classical jurist role: respect for the individual and his/her liberty; 2) from the role of the welfare State jurist: efforts to further general social aims and values; and 3) from the postmodern role: the idea of basing one's work on the realities of contemporary life and its legal affairs, and on one's own choice.[98]

What is not explicitly noted in this attempt to picture the ideal legal decision-maker is the role of the emotional element in decision-making. In late modernity, one strand of critique of the supposedly rational decision-maker implies a recognition of a greater role of intuition and emotions. As judges have to make more decisions without sufficient support from legal, ethical and epistemological systems, the relevance of intuition and emotions is bound to grow. It is not surprising that the interest in emotions as a part of legal discourse seems to have risen.[99] Whether one likes it or not, it is important to acknowledge this state of affairs. By recognising the possible role of intuition and emotions, legal actors are better equipped to bear the moral responsibility for their decision-making, but also for avoiding and fighting against a misuse of emotionally grounded standpoints.

The tension between rationality and emotions is not new in our legal culture. Our understanding of the good judge contains both features. On the one hand, a judge is supposed to act as a blindfolded emotionless and rational machine, on the other hand it is not uncommon to say that a good judge has to be empathetic and understand humans emotionally.[100] In the late modern world of uncertainty, the blindfold does not always fit well. As late modern morality develops in meetings and communication between people, a legal decision-maker has to recognise and understand those

[97] Raes (1996: 35).
[98] Dalberg-Larsen (1999: 112–13).
[99] Even giving rise to a particular law and emotions scholarship and a law and emotions discipline, see eg Conway and Stannard (2016).
[100] On this discourse, see eg Maroney (2016: 262–70).

whose acts are being assessed. A moral way of meeting the other requires at least some empathy. In critical legal practice, an empathetic legal actor sees and takes into account the particular needs of the weak and the vulnerable.

At the same time, however, it is important to underline that an empathetic decision-maker is not necessarily always able to play the role of the hero in a welfarist legal narrative. The cold letter of legislation and established practice is often better in protecting the weak groups than an empathetic judge acting *in casu*. Both for the weak groups and for society as a whole, the rule of law is an important value. Therefore, the empathetic judge also has to respect the requirements of rational decision-making.

In the flexible and fragmented landscape of contemporary law these requirements, however, are not always as tight as they once might have been. The porous limits of what I have called the 'legally possible' might give room for more empathetic decision-making and the small narratives, when they proceed, might expand the options further. This does not relieve, however, the legal decision-maker from respecting the basic value of the rule of law and the confines of the 'legally possible'. The legitimacy and authority of law presuppose a sufficient respect for generally recognised elements of formal legal reasoning; legal research methods that do not sufficiently address formal doctrine are considered to be less persuasive in the legal discourse.[101] As I will argue in detail later, the rule of law under present conditions requires transparent legal reasoning that as openly as possible accounts for all the arguments used in reaching a decision or a standpoint. Self-evidently, for example, soft emotional *ad hoc* arguments are not convincing. The integrity of the law presupposes a focus on less personal reasoning.

Some may argue, on apparently good grounds, that the rule of law is an endangered species in today's world and that the good narrative would therefore always be the one that as much as possible shrinks the area of the legally possible. The rule of law retreats in many parts of the world in front of increasing authoritarianism, and this threat is not unknown within the EU. Indeed, for this reason I believe that it is important also for critically minded legal actors to respect the boundaries of the legally possible and the rationality of legal reasoning. Acknowledging this, however, does not remove the societal pressures towards a more flexible and fragmented law. These pressures necessarily opens up more leeway for both good and bad decision-making, and a stricter theory on legal decision-making hardly offers a defence against bad judges.[102] Therefore, rather than denying the legal possibilities at hand, it is essential that a decision-maker who strives to contribute to a good legal narrative, transparently argues how the limits of the legally possible are drawn and weighed in the decision.

In other words, in my understanding the transparency of legal reasoning is the sought-for 'procedural' element in decision-making that makes it possible pragmatically to discuss its 'goodness' and to defend the value of rule of law under conditions of fragmentation and flexibility. The role of argumentative transparency as an element in retaining the trust in the rule of law is further analysed in chapter eight.

[101] See eg Eckes (2022).
[102] Rorty (1990: 1818), defending pragmatism.

VIII. IN OTHER WORDS

In previous chapters I have attempted to show how late-modern epistemic and ethical uncertainty, fuelled by micro-political legal activity, pushes law in a flexible and fragmented direction. Carrying this analysis further, I claim that contemporary society needs a law that is better able to learn from experience and more inclined to confront societal issues in real-life language rather than in the formal legal conceptuality of the past. Increasing pragmatism is a useful catchword.

Instead of a static snapshot approach to picturing the law, a more dynamic conception of law appears to be more realistic. The dynamics of flexibility versus stability and fragmentation versus coherence tends to bring law from a more comprehensive system-oriented position towards not only the production of more real-life-oriented case law, but also towards more precise fragmented rules on limited issues, and towards a more principle-based flexible law.

I have suggested picturing the development of private law today with the help of a metaphor that I have called '(good) small narratives on legal change'. A small narrative on change conveys a dynamic picture of law. It is a story of legal change in which the legislator, courts and scholars, as well as other legal actors, may participate in various combinations. Like other narratives it has a beginning, in the activity and decision-making of some legal actor, it may proceed in various steps and it ends, at least for a while, in a new relatively stable legal situation. The 'smallness' of the narrative indicates that the narrative is not bound by any grand societal master plan, but may proceed in various directions. Societally, however, it may be of considerable size, as for example the ongoing narratives on climate responsibility show.

The metaphor is illustrative in several ways. It illustrates the continuous interplay between flexibility when the narrative is active, and the stability of law when the narrative has come to an end. It conveys the idea that small changes can proceed in several directions without a pre-set general goal. The narrative is both bound and unpredictable, like a chain novel, and it shows how law is continuously open to change. It expressly recognises the opportunities of development inherent in the narratives.

The narratives include various legal actors in different roles. The legislator introduces both democratic legitimacy and societal experience, the courts as professionals in problem-solving contribute to the learning through real-life experience, and legal scholars can play an important role in starting, influencing and ending small narratives by conceptualising the development.

By noting the potential role of various actors in bringing the narrative forward, the metaphor exposes the moral responsibility of all legal actors, including legal scholars. Carrying this responsibility is not an easy task, as there are no generally accepted substantive criteria for the 'goodness' of a narrative. Moral roads have to be made by walking them. In contemporary society, a good legal actor should display openness, common sense and empathy, and be prepared to present legal reasoning that is as transparent as possible.

5

Small Narratives in the European Context: Free Movement of Legal Ideas

IN CHAPTERS TWO and three, I demonstrated how increasing epistemological and ethical uncertainty in late modern society requires a more flexible and fragmented law, and how such a legal environment offers tools for micro-political legal activism. I have condensed the picture of legal development in contemporary society in the metaphor of small narratives on legal change, which illustrates the fragmented oscillation between dynamic renewal and static tradition and brings to the fore the contribution of various legal actors.

The perspective so far has been predominantly domestic. In this chapter, I add a European dimension to the analysis. I will discuss how the processes of Europeanisation fits into the picture, both descriptively and normatively. How does the addition of a European layer change the actors and the structure of the narratives on legal change?

As the processes of fragmentation are to some extent explained by legislative and judicial interventions within the EU, the European dimension can be expected to fit well with the metaphor of fragmented small narratives on legal change. It simply adds a layer to the range of activities that may affect the course of the narratives. One may even claim that Europeanisation strengthens the appositeness of the metaphor. As EU private law, as a response to a higher level of complexity, is 'in a constant state of flux' and 'in an almost constant state of development',[1] it continuously initiates small narratives on change. In the fluid European legal context the work of a judge has been compared to navigating on the high seas, being exposed to forces one cannot control. In such a setting, judicial activism (as some call it) appears in many contexts, as part of the art of keeping the ship afloat.[2] The possibility that EU law in a concrete situation may enter the scene quite surprisingly, like a Jack-in-the-Box,[3] broadens the range of possible new starts or surprising new turns of small narratives on legal change.

Not only does the realism of the metaphor increase when one adds the European layer to the picture; the normative reasons for accepting a fragmented approach are

[1] Cafaggi and Law (2017: 1, 3).

[2] Graver (2006: 215).

[3] Decades ago, as a consciously exaggerated metaphor in a *liber amicorum*, I presented a 'Jack-in-the-Box theory' of European Community law; see Wilhelmsson (1997).

also becoming more powerful. The European perspective offers new materials for improved learning processes within law. One can understand Europe as a huge experimental legal field, where fruitful learning can be supported by the use of experiences across the borders. This positive perspective is one of the points of departure of this chapter.

The metaphor of small narratives on legal change underlines the role of the various legal actors who bring the narrative forward. The European perspective changes the scene in several respects. Europe brings in several new actors on the legal scene and they all have their parts to play in the legal game. Europeanisation, moreover, affects the working modes of national actors and the relationships between them.

In this chapter, I pay particular attention to changes in the ways in which domestic legal actors react and should react to Europeanisation. In an experimental European private law, learning may occur vertically, mediated by what European law has learnt from Member State experience, but also horizontally, directly across national borders. To me, this is not only a possible future, but also a desirable future for Europeanised private law. Consequently, I will discuss such horizontal learning at length both here and in several of the following chapters. By doing this, I am not striving to deny or undervalue the importance of vertical European law-making. On the contrary, I am certainly aware that the movement of ideas vertically between national and European actors today is more intense than the direct horizontal movement of legal ideas between Member States.[4] I am directing my main focus on the horizontal opportunity because it seems theoretically more challenging as it implies a methodological rethinking on deeper levels of legal culture. The horizontal perspective is implied in the notion of 'free movement' found in the heading of this chapter and in the title of the book.

I have presented the free movement of legal ideas metaphor on various occasions and in various forms many years ago.[5] I partially share this notion with Jan Smits, who has spoken about a free movement of legal 'rules'.[6] By speaking about 'ideas' rather than 'rules', I wished to emphasise that it is not only the rules and solutions as such but also the arguments upholding the rules that should be involved in the movement. In addition, doctrinal constructions and concepts are an essential part of learning that can move across the borders.

In such a situation in which cross-border learning occurs through citing particular sources, like cases or scholarly statements, one could also use the phrase 'free movement of legal sources'. As most theories on legal sources, however, appear to be more formal and hierarchical than the way in which arguments are used in real legal reasoning,[7] it often seems more accurate to speak about the movement of legal arguments or of legal material. In any case, even when I use the familiar term 'legal sources', I am not committing myself to any formal doctrine of legal sources.

[4] The vertical movement has been extensively described and discussed and I will refer to some of the results below. As Micklitz and Kas (2014) have shown, at that time the CJEU alone had produced more than 100 consumer contract law decisions.

[5] See Wilhelmsson (2002b: 354).

[6] See Smits (2002: 63).

[7] See ch 8.

Picturing private law in Europe as narratives that can move both vertically between domestic and European levels and horizontally between Member States creates the impression of legal actors operating on a joint playing field. One could picture the European private law scene as one system instead of 27+1, as some have proposed.[8] The question of the number of 'legal systems' in the EU (one or 27+1?) primarily seems to be a question of definition of the concept of a legal system rather than a matter of substance. Be this as it may, the understanding of law as a collection of outcomes of small narratives relativises the question. Some narratives are simply more European than others. Regarding some issues, European actors are dormant and do not need to be consulted – if they do not suddenly surprise the domestic participants by appearing as a Jack-in-the-Box – whilst in other cases they play a decisive role. One should not draw sharp delineations between the domestic and the European: even though the actors mostly belong to either sphere, substantive small narratives move flexibly back and forth across any borders.

I. AN EXPERIMENTAL LEGAL EUROPE

Across the social sciences, scholars have described the processes related to European integration as experimental. At the turn of the century, Brigid Laffan, Rory O'Donnell and Michael Smith, under the heading 'Europe's Experimental Union', pictured a European model of economic and political internationalisation that was developed 'in an incremental, pragmatic and experimental manner',[9] using metaphors such as 'Europe as a learning machine' and the Union as 'always in the process of becoming'.[10] In a much-cited analysis, Charles Sabel and Jonathan Zeitlin later showed how the governance mechanisms of the EU have developed into an experimental architecture.[11]

Whilst their perspective was on governance functions and polity instruments, others have discussed European experimentalism with a direct focus on law. Scholars have in various ways described Europe as a 'legal laboratory'[12] that offers Europeans the possibility of experimental legal development. In constitutional law, Oliver Gerstenberg's analysis of what he calls 'democratic experimentalism' is well known.[13] Comparatists such as Basil Markesinis advocated 'Learning from Europe and Learning in Europe'.[14] From an expressly critical perspective, Giacomo Tagiuri emphasises that 'democratic experimentalism' has led EU law to produce 'progressive strings of a new code'.[15]

Some underline the role of concrete legal actors in the experimental laboratory. Hans Micklitz and Carla Sieburgh designate the European Court of Justice as

[8] See Hesselink (2013).
[9] Laffan, O'Donnell and Smith (2000: 218).
[10] Laffan, O'Donnell and Smith (2000: 194, 193).
[11] Sabel and Zeitlin (2010).
[12] Eloquently, Delmas-Marty (2002).
[13] Gerstenberg (2018: 36 *et seq*).
[14] The title of an article by Markesinis (1994).
[15] Tagiuri (2022: 396, 399).

a 'laboratory' – like others who have called the European Courts 'laboratories of comparative law'[16] – but they broaden this experimental function to other European actors:

> The unstable structure of the EU and the inconsistency of the political sediment enable and promote experimentalism: experimentalism in law-making and enforcement by the executive, experimentalism in the substance of the law, experimentalism even of the judiciary. Experimentalism is inbuilt into a laboratory. Each new experiment should help to improve the procedure and the substance of European private law.[17]

The understanding of Europe as an experimental legal laboratory has been used in various concrete contexts. Yane Svetiev published a thorough analysis of experimentalism in EU competition law. According to him, this law is evolving into 'an experimentalist tool of market regulation',[18] making possible both a synthesis of alternative views on the regulation and a local contextualisation of decision-making. Interestingly, the author does not only analyse the development in an experimentalist direction, but underlines that this mode of governance is normatively desirable as well.[19]

Discussing private law in particular, Europe has been said to offer 'a unique laboratory' in which, for example, one can test the consequences of various divergent tort rules.[20] This laboratory can explore the advantages and disadvantages of using private law and public law grammars in various contexts.[21] Regarding contract law a methodology that includes the experience of all Member States is recommended to be used in legal teaching, research and decision-making.[22]

It has been claimed that such a learning approach is an active and efficient use of developmental resources.[23] National legislators are well suited as innovation laboratories, as the test of new solutions 'at a lower level mitigates the risk and affects fewer people.'[24] Experimentalism is not, however, restricted to domestic laboratories alone. Instrumentalist EU private law is considered to be more open to experimentalism than traditional private law.[25] In more general terms, the process of Europeanisation of private law has been described as a process of innovation and learning.[26]

The language varies, but the message is the same. Self-evidently, those speaking about 'experimentalism' in a 'laboratory' are using these words in a metaphorical sense. It is not a question of making controlled experiments in a scientific meaning,

[16] See eg Lenaerts (2003: 876).

[17] Micklitz and Sieburgh (2017: 8). See also Micklitz (2017: 308) and Micklitz (2018: 37).

[18] Svetiev (2020: 6). See also Svetiev (2016: 663), where he demonstrates a similar experimentalist approach in the reforms of the regulated networked service sector, calling the law 'problem-solving' and 'error-correcting'.

[19] Svetiev (2020: 25).

[20] van den Bergh and Visscher (2006: 517).

[21] Cherednychenko (2020: 46).

[22] Gordley (2005).

[23] Kerber (2008: 90) in an economic analysis of European private law regards '[d]ecentralised experimentation and mutual learning' to be 'a powerful institutional device used to ensure long-term innovation'. Collins (2008a: 275) agrees.

[24] Möslein (2010: 192).

[25] Michaels (2011: 147).

[26] See eg Joerges (2004), who also mentions the 'legal laboratory' metaphor (2004: 152).

but of creative processes of learning, of understanding the experience of others as useful test beds of new legal ideas. The focus and balance of the experimentalist features may also differ. Some primarily discuss how EU law can be developed in an experimentalist manner, whilst others also include those who develop domestic laws as users of the European laboratory. In this work, my approach to experimentalism is a broad one. My point of view could be described as 'taking experimentalism seriously'.

European legal actors, both the CJEU and the European legislative actors, frequently rely on legal experience from Member States when developing EU law. A legal activity aiming at creating an integrated market must take as one of its starting points the existing regulation in the Member States. The value of European experimentalism is not limited, however, to such obvious examples. Legal actors that acknowledge legal diversity within the EU as a collection of legal experience waiting to be taken into account, may more generally make use of that asset in a productive way. Learning processes enabled by diversity can be useful on all levels of legal activity, including the interpretation of private law concepts such as the fault standard, as various interpretations of such concepts 'may provide important information about the performance of the legal rule in real-life cases'.[27] A diversity-based trial-and-error mechanism might indeed be productive, as the economic effects of the adoption of a rule are often uncertain. Also other societal consequences of new rules are hard to predict, but can be analysed with reference to experimental experience from abroad. Full use of the experimental value of diversity requires a readiness to accept and utilise a movement of legal ideas throughout the field of legal activities.

In such a broad approach to experimental learning also legal subjects like contracting parties and their organisations may have some influence on the learning processes. Choice of law gives the parties an opportunity to assess, within certain frames, what law they find best suited to their needs – at least in principle. Drafters of widely used standard terms also have a direct impact on law in action in the fields in which the terms are used. In their learning processes, experience moving across borders certainly plays a role, and these actors should accordingly be included in the picture. This is, however, just one group among many groups of actors that contribute to the Europeanised small narratives. When Jan Smits[28] (calling the States 'experimenting laboratories') offers a plea for a competitive system in which the need for unification is 'primarily determined by legal practice itself'[29] and recommends a spontaneous development of law in which the role of the parties is central he seems to go too far in emphasising the position of private actors. Even though Smits acknowledges the 'race to the bottom' argument, and offers some minimum harmonisation rules as a remedy, the approach clearly downplays the goal of social justice in the learning paradigm, calling it 'paternalistic'.[30] As I attempted to show in earlier chapters, however, late modern uncertainty requires both epistemological and ethical learning processes, and

[27] van den Bergh and Visscher (2006: 517).

[28] Influenced by Friedrich Hayek, Smits (2006: 85). For a critique of his Hayekian approach, see Hesselink (2010).

[29] Smits (2006: 75, 78).

[30] Smits (2006: 85).

in these processes both law drafters and those applying the law have important roles to play. A general 'paternalism argument' does not fit well into the discussion of the European model.

I have consciously used the metaphor of '*Europe* as a laboratory'. Speaking about a geographically defined laboratory underlines the specific role of European experience in the small narratives on change. Of course, law should not refrain from learning from experience outside the EU and one should not build epistemological fences between 'us' and 'them'.[31] Learning from experience could indeed cover the whole world.[32] Speaking about a laboratory that might produce directly useful ideas even for a domestic discourse, however, there are good reasons to look in particular at European experience. Due to the relative similarities between the Member States both legally, societally and culturally, the use of experience from other Member States when contemplating the introduction of new legal ideas encounters fewer hurdles than the use of materials from a legally and societally more distant environment. Even though legal-cultural diversity is certainly found within the EU, a joint European legal deep structure facilitates a real cross-border dialogue.[33] As will be discussed in chapter six, both the societal ethos of a welfarist market economy and the legal ethos of fundamental rights are shared within the Union. Therefore, comparison within Europe is a kind of intra-cultural comparison as opposed to what could be called a cross-cultural comparison.[34] In addition, this sense of learning from an internal perspective is supported by the joint legal infrastructure shaped by EU law. The growing body of European law has brought the laws of the Member States both substantively, conceptually and methodically closer to each other. One may even claim that European lawyers today belong to an 'interpretative community'.[35] Experience from within the EU therefore often better corresponds to the real conditions in the society that aspires to use the experience. Without denying the importance of sharing an understanding across the globe, I am here looking at the cross-border movement of legal ideas within the EU. After all, the Union is a unique legal and societal construction that can be expected to produce at least partially peculiar forms of legal narratives.

The recognition of the value of experience from other Member States does not require any stand on the well-known and recurrent discussion in comparative law quarters on the possibility of 'legal transplants'. Alan Watson, who has used this metaphor to illustrate the moving of a rule or a system of rules from one country to another, has argued that most legal changes are based on such a transplantation,[36] as 'borrowing is usually the major factor in legal change'.[37] Others, like Pierre Legrand, have equally eloquently claimed that legal transplants are impossible, as

[31] See eg the critique by Husa (2006) of the deprivation of the European mind through such fencing. The critique by Frankenberg (2016) of, inter alia, the ethnocentrism of comparative law is well known.

[32] The continuing discourse on 'transnational law', starting from Jessup (1956), is not limited to a regional perspective. On the possibility of a global (new) *lex mercatoria*, see eg Berger (2010).

[33] Tuori (2018: 55); Tuori (2021: 255, 266).

[34] Van Hoecke and Warrington (1998: 509).

[35] Sirena (2018: 859): '*Auslegungsgemeinschaft*'.

[36] Watson (1993) (1st edn 1974).

[37] Watson (2000: 12) (reaffirming his position, and claiming that Legrand's criticism has misrepresented him).

one cannot genuinely understand legal thinking from other legal cultures.[38] Gunter Teubner in turn has shown how the metaphor easily becomes misleading and the question to be debated wrongly posed. He has introduced an alternative concept, 'the legal irritant', recognising that when 'a foreign rule is imposed on a domestic culture … It is not transplanted into another organism, rather it works as a fundamental irritation which triggers a whole series of new and unexpected events'.[39] Looking at the issue from the perspective of an experimental and learning law, the opposing views concerning the success of 'transplantation' or 'transposition'[40] indeed easily seem to lead the thoughts in a false direction. This is the case if one emphasises the importance of retaining the identity and detail of the 'transplanted' part in order to recognise it as a real transplantation – though Alan Watson and the defenders of this concept, however, usually do not claim this.[41] A real learning process in my understanding requires both a sufficient understanding of the context of the legal experience and a sufficient sense concerning how that experience would work in the environment into which it is moved. Experimental learning means gathering the legal and societal knowledge concerning the working of a legal idea in a particular national context in order to make use of that idea in another national context, as far as and in a way that it fits that context. There is evidence that the effectiveness of transplants is strongly related to their local adaptation.[42] Moving knowledge from a 'laboratory' to the 'real world' always requires an adjustment of the laboratory results to the conditions of the real context in which they will be used. It is a matter of taste whether such context-related movement should be called a 'transplant'. I prefer speaking about contextual learning from the experience of others.

As to the question whether a legal actor can understand the conditions of the legal system from which learning is sought, I am convinced that in particular within the EU one can reach a sufficient level of understanding. As has been said, identity of meaning is not required because 'partial understandings are all that is necessary to create a community'.[43]

The possible difficulties in this respect may even shrink after Brexit, as this unfortunately means a somewhat reduced input from common law in the European discourse. As is well known, Pierre Legrand has built his criticism of the idea of European legal convergence on the split between common law and civil law.[44] However, believing that Legrand exaggerates the difficulties in reaching a sufficient understanding across this border,[45] I rather hope that the common law that is left in the Union, as well as UK law, can retain a role as a fruitful part of the European laboratory. Some rightly

[38] Legrand (1997). For a new analysis in the same vein, see Carvalho (2019).

[39] Teubner (1998: 12).

[40] This term is used eg by Örücü (2002).

[41] eg Fuglinszky (2020: 275), analysing legal transplants in Hungary, points at the need to make 'a compatibility check' related to the receiving legal system.

[42] Torpman and Jörgensen (2005: 530).

[43] Schäfer and Bankowski (2003: 499).

[44] Legrand (1996).

[45] For a critique of Legrand's thesis, see eg Van Hoecke (2000).

fear that the level of private law innovation in the EU would be reduced because of Brexit.[46]

The need for cross-border learning may appear in various situations. The obvious case is when new problems require a legal reaction. When, for example, issues related to climate change, the COVID-19 pandemic, or the platform economy arise, it is natural to look at how the law of other Member States has responded to similar issues. The reason for looking at the experience of others may also be ethical. If one experiences a sense of injustice in front of the traditional approach of domestic law, foreign experience may offer a way to reach a better solution. In some cases, again, the nature of the problem as such is international, or internal market-related, making it natural to look for a harmonised solution. It should be emphasised, however, that the opportunities of experimental learning are not limited to such relatively obvious cases. On the contrary, the legal laboratory of the EU can be useful in many contexts. As examples below will show, learning across the borders can occur wherever such learning is needed.

Fitting the learning obtained from others into one's own national settings requires an adjustment of the experience to the new environment, and the impact of the transplanted ideas might be different than in their original setting.[47] The level of concreteness of the transfer may of course vary. Sometimes only some parts of the reasoning survive the move, whilst in other cases one may find a concretely formulated rule being 'transplanted' as such. One may also have to acknowledge the need for changing other domestic rules as a consequence of the adoption of a foreign solution. The result may be the creation of 'legal hybrids' that combine features from both the giving and the receiving system.[48] The consequences of learning from others, using the European laboratory, can in other words vary from directly using some solution concerning a specific concrete issue, to changing the patterns of legal reasoning or reconfiguring some larger field of law.

In other words, learning across the borders can occur in many ways and to a varying degree. From my perspective, it is sufficient to note that experience from across the Union can be seen as a welcome addition to the knowledge base for building small narratives on legal change. There is no ready-made model for how this knowledge should be introduced into the narratives. The 'European laboratory' offers useful materials for various processes of development of a law that under contemporary conditions of epistemic and ethical uncertainty has to be able to learn from experience.

II. THE ACTORS IN THE EUROPEANISED LEGAL NARRATIVES AND THEIR ROLES

The metaphor of small narratives on legal change focuses the attention on the legal actors that contribute to these narratives. The Europeanisation of private law has a

[46] See Eidenmüller (2018).

[47] Also according to Watson (2000: 2), a 'transplant' is different in its new environment than in the context from which it is borrowed.

[48] Janssen and Schulze (2011: 253). Solinas (2014), analysing the law of shares transfer, finds the notion of 'hybridity' to be an excellent conceptual tool in the transplantation discussion.

profound impact on the cast of actors in the narratives. It both adds new European actors to the narratives and changes the roles and opportunities of the national actors.

The actors in the Europeanised narratives partially perform the same roles as they are expected to do in any small narrative. Legislators bring in societal experience and offer democratic legitimacy to the narratives, courts contribute with the perspective of professionals in problem-solving, whilst scholars act as academic system-builders and conceptualisers. These and other roles in the national settings are analysed in more detail in chapter four, and what I have said there generally applies also to European legal actors. Here I will focus only on those particular features of the roles that relate to the idea of the EU as a laboratory for European learning concerning substantive private law. I will not deal, for example, with legal governance issues, such as the legal-structural fact that EU law and EU legal actors are almost completely dependent on national actors with regard to the implementation and execution of EU decision-making.

From my perspective, two questions come to the fore. The first one relates to the actual opportunities of each actor to make use of the European laboratory by participating in moving legal experience across the borders. To what extent has the actor traditionally made use of European experience and what opportunities to expand such cross-border learning does it have in the future? The second question focuses on the useful impact that each type of actor may have in the process of Europeanised learning. In what way may each actor contribute to the effectiveness, usefulness and legitimacy of the adoption of new ideas? Various legal actors can contribute to these goals in different ways. Several cooks may manage to make a better broth.

The EU has brought in several important actors on the European legal scene. With regard to the European norm production, the EU legislator in its various forms has an impressive track record. Of the many thousands of pages of existing European legislation, an increasing part affects private law relationships.[49] When these rules have been prepared, learning from European experience has certainly played an important role. Often the legislator has used a comparative analysis of Member State laws as a basis for the measure. In addition, such learning is impliedly brought into the legislative procedure both through the domestic experience of the persons participating in the drafting procedure and by the representatives of the Member States at the stage of adoption. For the European legislator it is both self-evident and practically possible to make extensive use of European experience.

A good example of the use of existing experience is the development of EU consumer law. This field of law started to develop in a mode of 'national experimentalism'[50] and when the centre of gravity of legislation shifted to the EU, comparative analysis was widely used to legitimise solutions.[51] The Unfair Contract Terms Directive made obvious use of German experiences of unfair contract terms regulation, whilst the original Consumer Sales Directive was clearly inspired by the United Nations Convention on Contracts for the International Sale of Goods (CISG).[52]

[49] See eg Leczykiewicz and Weatherill (2013) and Hartkamp (2016).
[50] Micklitz, Sibony and Esposito (2018: 5).
[51] ibid (11).
[52] Having participated in the first working group preparing the Directive I can confirm that this was a conscious choice.

A good example of how particular legal details may migrate with the help of the EU legislator is the rule on third-party liability for advertising statements in the original Consumer Sales Directive,[53] which had a background in Dutch and Nordic law, and as a consequence of the Directive was introduced elsewhere, such as in German law.[54] From fields of law other than consumer law, one could mention the almost paradigmatic example of the Commercial Agents Directive that was so clearly influenced by German law that the Commission later recommended that German law should be consulted when interpreting certain provisions of the Directive.[55]

The EU legislator is a necessary actor for the creation of the internal market and the regulation of other areas in which harmonisation of law is required. This does not mean, however, that the input of the European legislator is limited to the harmonising of rules on the basis of the experiences of national laws. The European legislator has played and can play a much more creative role in shaping the European legal landscape.[56] Its role is not only to legitimise European enactments defining an existing average standard within the EU, but also to create new solutions for contemporary challenges. This is, of course, not a sharp dichotomy: sometimes new solutions may be based on good practices found in some Member State(s) whilst in other cases the European solution may be even more innovative.

The expectation that European legislation could play a significant role in modernising private law is reflected, for example, in demands for a more social approach in EU private law. The much-cited Manifesto on Social Justice in European Contract Law, prepared by a group of critical academic lawyers, expressed such an expectation in its 'call on the Commission, the Council of Ministers, and the European Parliament … to recognize its responsibility to steer the process of constructing European private law in ways that will secure the legitimacy of its scheme of social justice.'[57] Indeed, at least in comparison with some Member States, the European legislator has introduced rules that in some ways may appear to be 'more social' than traditional rules. The best example is the use of EU law to initiate the development of principles of non-discrimination in the private laws of the Member States.[58] In consumer law, EU legislation has led to better consumer protection in several Member States, even though one can on good grounds criticise EU law for not being ambitious enough in protecting consumers.[59] The fact that in the academic processes of elaborating a draft European private law, a particular Research Group on the existing EC private law (the Acquis Group) was established reflected an understanding that in this material one could find expressions of modernised contract law thinking that could not be found in most traditional national private laws.[60] It is illustrative that Brigitta Lurger, when presenting her 'New Principle of Regard and Fairness' as the expression of the

[53] Directive 99/44/EC, Art 2(2)(d).
[54] Janssen and Schulze (2011: 243).
[55] COM(96) 364 final 10 (cited below in ch 9 section IV). See Eftestøl-Wilhelmsson (2005: 52).
[56] The innovativeness of European legislation is emphasised eg by Schulze (2007: 11) and Schulze and Zoll (2021) ch 8.
[57] Study Group on Social Justice in European Private Law (2004: 674).
[58] See eg Schiek (1999).
[59] One of the basic messages of our book; Howells, Twigg-Flesner and Wilhelmsson (2018).
[60] See eg Schulte-Nölke (2008: 28).

'social' side of European contract law, starts by describing many EU directives that she considers to reflect such a principle.[61]

The European legislator has a restricted scope of competence, derived from the Treaty, and the competence of the EU in the field of private law has been the subject of many intense discussions,[62] whilst national legislators can move right across the legal field. However, the European legislator has one advantage in comparison with national legislators with regard to the opportunities of promoting legal change. As national legislators are in practice to some extent bound to honour the legal tradition, domestic conceptual and systemic considerations may form an effective obstacle against legal innovations. These kinds of challenges affect the European legislator to a lesser extent, even though national representatives in the legislative process probably keep them in mind. There are few aspects of purely EU legal culture that would conceptually or systematically hamper the development of modern solutions. The whole ethos of EU law is pragmatic: the European legislator is supposed to find practical working solutions, whilst the task of fitting in these solutions into the domestic legal culture is left to national legal actors.

The European legislator, therefore, can have a particular role to play as an actor that can support the modernisation of traditional national laws. It can be an engine for changes that a domestic legislator could not have made alone. It forces 'national legislators to engage in debates and make choices that were once the prerogative of civil courts with their piecemeal adjudication.'[63] Perhaps outdated, but culturally strongly rooted conceptual structures may be broken up through the intervention of the European legislator. As a good example one may mention the German reform of its law of obligations in the civil code (*Schuldrechtsreform*), which was pushed forward, perhaps even made possible, by the growing amount of EU enactments that needed implementation.[64] The reform even went further than the EU legislator required. As a 'spillover' the solutions of the Consumer Sales Directive were introduced in the *Bürgerliches Gesetzbuch* for a much broader range of contracts than for consumer sales alone.[65] 'Spillovers' from EU law may appear in a context that as such is not covered by or is not even within the competences of the European legislator.[66]

The important role of national legislators to infuse the law with a necessary degree of democratic legitimacy is probably less important with regard to the EU legislator. Despite the strengthening of the role of the European Parliament, it has not (yet?) reached a level of legitimacy that would correspond to that of the national legislators (and the other actors participating in European legislation, the Commission and the Council, carry even less democratic legitimacy). The mathematical, cultural and geographical distance between the European Parliament and its electorate, and the lack of a joint discursive public sphere in Europe, make it difficult for the Parliament to reach such a position. Therefore, the legitimacy requirement

[61] Lurger (2011: 353–57).
[62] For just one example, see Weatherill (2005).
[63] Caruso (1997: 29).
[64] See eg the discussion and proposals in Schulze and Schulte-Nölke (2001).
[65] Janssen and Schulze (2011: 243).
[66] On such 'spillovers', see eg Johnston (2013).

supports a division of labour between the European legislator and national legislators. The democratic legitimacy of law still to a considerable extent rests on the latter. The European narrative has to be a mixed narrative.

The need for a mixed approach that acknowledges the roles of both European and national legislators does not follow from the requirements of legitimacy alone. In substantive terms, national legislators are closer to the societal challenges and are therefore often better equipped to find the best solutions. Sometimes the domestic legislative apparatus might function better than the European in importing experience of actors outside the law into the legal discourse. The experimentalism hailed as a strength of European law requires a balance between European and domestic actors.

A useful tool for safeguarding a blend between European legislative harmonisation and sufficient scope for national experimentation is the minimum directive. In consumer law, this instrument has traditionally been widely and wisely used. The European legislator has been able to target the internal market goals strived for by harmonisation measures, whilst the minimum character of the legislation has allowed a productive national search for innovations above the minimum standard.[67] The turn in recent years towards a broader use of full harmonisation instruments is problematic in this sense.[68] However, to some extent the static consequences of full harmonisation is ameliorated by the use of broad general clauses that allow much flexibility in the system,[69] or by limiting the issues concerning which full harmonisation is prescribed. For example, the new Consumer Sales Directive that formally turns a minimum directive into a full harmonisation directive in its heading acknowledges that it only covers 'certain aspects concerning contracts for the sale of goods', and uses a considerable part of the Preamble to describe the wide array of questions that are still retained within the power of national legislators.[70] Even though the Directive in form is a measure of maximum harmonisation, in substance it leaves much room for national diversity.[71] Also in this Directive, the balance between harmonisation and diversity has remained a key issue for the European legislator.

The European legislator may also use flexible concepts to leave the more concrete application of a EU law to the national experience of both legislators and courts. The CJEU has to some extent recognised the need for nationally anchored decision-making,[72] leaving an opening for continuous national experimentation in the field. Increased flexibility can be a means to combine required diversity with interests related to integration.[73]

[67] Weatherill (2021: 225, 230, 241).

[68] We published our critique in Howells, Twigg-Flesner and Wilhelmsson (2018).

[69] See in particular the Unfair Commercial Practices Directive (Directive 2005/29/EC).

[70] Directive (EU) 2019/771, Preamble items 18, 19, 20, 21, 22, 23, 38, 41, 42, 43, 44, 46, 54, 56, 60, 61, 62 and 63.

[71] Weatherill (2021: 239).

[72] See eg below on the reasoning in Case C-237/02 *Freiburger Kommunalbauten GmbH Baugesellschaft & Co. KG v Ludger Hofstetter and Ulrike Hofstetter*, ECLI:EU:C:2004:209.

[73] Flexibility as a means to resist disintegration is analysed in De Witte, Ott and Vos (2017). The perspectives of the various contributions are mainly organisational and/or policy-oriented and do not relate directly to the substance of private law.

As noted in the previous chapter the word 'legislator' is a collective concept, comprising many actors in various roles. On the European level the process of legislation involves even more actors,[74] often and perhaps rightly characterised as part of an internationalised elite.[75] The actors are both European, such as the Commission itself as well as the legal advisers of both the Commission, the Council and the Parliament,[76] quasi-Europeans (elected nationally) in the Parliament, and national actors in the Council, guided in various ways by domestic civil servants and political bodies. In addition, in this complicated structure external experts,[77] stakeholders and lobbyists have opportunities to influence legislation at many stages of preparation.[78] The legislative narrative displays, in addition to the formal political actors, an 'interwoven, networked governance … of private interest groups, non-state actors, and institutionalised advisory bodies that are active both on community and state level.'[79] In such a complicated legislative process, personal responsibilities become more blurred than in national legislation. However, the fact that it is difficult in this complex environment to locate the precise time and place in which decisions concerning particular details are actually made, it is even more important to underline the personal moral responsibility of each participant in the less transparent Europeanised narratives.

To complicate the picture further, one could mention that in addition to 'hard' legislation, there are also softer forms of normative guidance. In private law the Commission, based on surveys of Member State practice, has made recommendations on how some European legislation should be interpreted and applied. I have already mentioned the rules on commercial agency as an example. In the area of consumer law the Commission has published notices, giving non-binding guidance based mainly on the case law of the CJEU (but with some references to national examples as well) on how the Unfair Contract Terms Directive, the Consumer Rights Directive and the Unfair Commercial Practices Directive should be interpreted and applied.[80] European learning processes continue after the adoption of European legislation, and the Commission can in this way function as one of the facilitators of the movement of experience concerning the application of the legislation.

Europe has also brought new actors into the field of judicial decision-making. The most important are the European Court of Human Rights and the Court of Justice of the European Union. I will here look only at the CJEU. As to the ECHR, I will discuss the role of human rights in private law narratives below in chapter six. Increasingly,

[74] The role of various internal and external actors are analysed in Korkea-aho and Leino-Sandberg (2022).

[75] See the Bourdieuan analysis by Madsen (2006).

[76] Leino-Sandberg (2021) has demonstrated the less visible, but influential role of legal advisers.

[77] An increasingly influential expert organisation in the area of the Europeanisation of law is the European Law Institute (ELI), see www.europeanlawinstitute.eu.

[78] See eg the interesting studies on EU lobbying by Coen and Richardson (2009), Coen (2007), Wetendorff Nørgaard, Nedergaard and Blom-Hansen (2014) and Klüver, Braun and Beyers (2015). On legal lobbying in the EU, see eg Korkea-aho (2021).

[79] Curtin (2010: 36), describing the complicated preparatory process leading to the first Consumer Sales Directive.

[80] Commission Notice 2019/C 323/04, Commission Notice 2021/C 525/01 and Commission Notice 2021/C 526/01.

the narratives that activate the European courts are intertwined, and there is a relation of influence between the Courts, in both directions.

The role of the CJEU in the field of private law has been constantly growing.[81] Relying on both the Treaty itself and the rapidly expanding European legislation relevant to private law, the CJEU has gradually been able to establish itself as an important actor also in this field of law. The CJEU has not been afraid to address even central issues of private law. When discussing the Europeanisation of private law one should properly acknowledge the relevance of this actor.

The European courts are an important channel for the infusion of comparative learning into both European and domestic private law. In developing their case law, they have often used comparative learning from the Member States as guidance. As a witness from within the CJEU, Koen Lenaerts has described the comparative approach as a 'quasi-compelling' method of interpreting Community law.[82] This reflects the trust of the Court in the force of the experimental knowledge accumulated within the Member States. The CJEU aspires 'to find through the examination of other legal orders the solution which best suits the objectives of the Community'.[83] In addition, the use of comparative knowledge increases the national acceptability of EU law. This is important as the legal and political legitimacy of landmark decisions of the CJEU might easily be challenged on the national level.[84] It is worth noting that the use of comparative material by the CJEU is not limited to finding good solutions to concrete issues; it may also contribute to the import into EU law of broader legal ideas, such as concepts and principles. The express references to national practice by the CJEU in fact seem to be more common in cases where the Court creates and develops legal principles.[85] For example, the principles of proportionality and of the protection of legitimate expectations are based on German legal experience.[86] The CJEU mediates movement of legal ideas at all levels of legal concreteness.

Not everyone has embraced the ways in which the CJEU has used comparative knowledge. In particular there are claims that the CJEU relies too strongly on certain legal cultures, like French, German and English law. The worry that this would affect the legitimacy of the rulings has been given as a reason why comparative material is often used more extensively by the Advocate General than by the Court itself.[87] The lack of explicit reference to comparative law in the decision of the Court in other words does not exclude the possibility that comparative deliberations played a role in the decision-making.[88]

The reliance on comparative law does not mean that the CJEU would not dare to choose a solution that might be against even the strong opinion of the

[81] Comprehensively analysed eg in the collection of papers in European Review of Private Law 3/2010, in particular Basedow (2010).

[82] Lenaerts (2003: 878). See also Lenaerts and Gutman (2015: 176), calling the comparative method a crucial tool for the Union courts.

[83] Lenaerts (2003: 879).

[84] See eg the impressive analysis by Micklitz (2005), the issue of legitimacy is described on (2005: 17–27).

[85] See eg Timmermans (2017: 42).

[86] Lenaerts (2003: 894).

[87] Schiek (2011: 429).

[88] Timmermans (2017: 43).

Member States.[89] The learning process is creative and related to the context of EU law. Advocate General Poiares Maduro has argued that although the CJEU 'must be guided by the most characteristic provisions of the systems of domestic law, it must above all ensure that it adopts a solution appropriate to the needs and specific features of the Community legal system'.[90] Where it has found it to be appropriate, the CJEU has developed its views radically further than what has been previously accepted in most national laws. The case law concerning the Unfair Contract Terms Directive over the last two decades is a good illustration of this. In order to safeguard the effective implementation of the Directive the CJEU has used it as a basis for far-reaching interventions in national procedural laws, despite the principle of the procedural autonomy of the Member States.[91] National courts on their own would probably not have found such legal consequences to be within the reach of the Directive. The active role of the CJEU in removing and reshaping procedural constraints has led to national narratives on the revision of existing procedural legislation.[92] On the European level this case law has started new narratives as well: within European legal discourse the relatively high level of procedural protection of consumers with regard to unfair terms has also inspired a narrative on broadening it to cover other issues of consumer law.[93]

Like other courts, the CJEU is an inroad for such normative learning that professionals in problem-solving can offer, even though its perspective is more horizontal: it has to look at how the decision suits all the Member States, whilst national courts can search more directly for a solution to their domestic problems.[94] In addition to Union-wide problem-solving, the CJEU seems to respond to a similar need as EU legislation, that is to support and advance such problem-based modernising of private law that can be difficult to bring about in a purely national setting. Often this function means ensuring that national practices are in conformity with EU legislation by offering necessary interpretations of that legislation. In other cases, like some of those related to unfair contract terms, EU legislation seems to give the CJEU a springboard to create and add more novel ideas to private law narratives. The dialogue between the CJEU and national courts 'has been a powerful instrument of legal change in EPL [European Private Law] and has emerged as a driver of innovation'.[95]

The CJEU not only affects the legal narratives by creating new case law. The connection between the European and national judicial actors in a particular narrative may even be much closer. The cooperation between the CJEU and national courts based on the preliminary reference procedure means a direct judicial dialogue between European and domestic actors.[96] In this dialogue, the division of labour

[89] Lenaerts (2017: 307 *et seq*). See eg Case C-34/09 *Gerardo Ruiz Zambrano v Office national d'emploi*, ECLI:EU:C:2011:124, described as an example of this by Muir, Dawson and de Witte (2013: 3).
[90] Opinion of the Advocate General in Joined Cases C-120/06P and C-121/06P *FIAMM*, ECLI:EU:C:2008:98, [55].
[91] See eg Howells, Twigg-Flesner & Wilhelmsson (2018: 154–162) and Beka (2018).
[92] Beka (2018) ch 6.
[93] Suggested by Kas and Micklitz (2018: 181).
[94] Interestingly analysed by Micklitz (2005: 41).
[95] Cafaggi and Law (2017: 12).
[96] See eg Cafaggi and Law (2017).

between the CJEU and national courts is constantly developed. As to the reality of the dialogue, however, the picture is not completely straightforward. Domestic courts do not always feel it to be a real cooperative dialogue.[97] The relationship, moreover, does not mean that national courts always follow what the CJEU orders. The national courts not only act as allies of the CJEU; they also use various means of resistance and restraint towards the CJEU,[98] constantly adding their own flavour to the narratives in their local context. The judges of national courts in different Member States also respond 'with highly variable degrees of receptivity to the invocation of EU law by litigants'.[99] In the dialogue between the CJEU and national courts, the European Court can vertically exert some influence over the extent to which national courts can contribute to the domestic narratives on legal change. As will be noted in chapter 9 section IV, the CJEU has also actively promoted horizontal processes of learning between national courts.

A paradigmatic example concerning the development of the division of labour is the case law concerning the Unfair Contract Terms Directive. In the first decades after the adoption of the Directive, the CJEU emphasised the role of national courts and expressly restricted its own role to that of an interpreter of the general criteria of unfairness. The CJEU noted that 'it should not rule on the application of these general criteria to a particular term, which must be considered in the light of the particular circumstances of the case in question', with due consideration given to national background law.[100] Without formally changing this position, the CJEU later developed the role of the Directive towards a more free-standing European consumer protection instrument, as reflected for example in the 'reasonable supplier standard'[101] introduced in the *Mohamed Aziz* case.[102] This move can have broad implications with regard to European and national consumer law conceptuality. The narrative is still waiting to be finalised.

In this area, the division of labour between national courts and the CJEU has changed as a consequence of an increased activity and creativity of the CJEU. In the terminology of Takis Tridimas,[103] the CJEU has moved from a policy of 'deference cases' in which the decision is deferred to the national court, towards 'guidance cases' in which more guidelines are provided by the CJEU (whilst the cases are usually not 'outcome cases' in which the national court is provided with a ready-made solution). Depending on the case the division of labour between the CJEU and the national courts may be different and vary over time, as their cooperation is 'based on an incomplete and somewhat unstable political bargain'.[104] In practice, there is a broad

[97] See the partially empirical analysis by Krommendijk (2021: 163).
[98] See eg Pollack (2017: 587–92).
[99] Pollack (2017: 590).
[100] Case C-237/02 *Freiburger Kommunalbauten GmbH Baugesellschaft & Co. KG v Ludger Hofstetter and Ulrike Hofstetter*, ECLI:EU:C:2004:209, citation at [22], as well as several subsequent cases.
[101] Micklitz and Reich (2014: 790), also called a 'possible agreement test', Howells, Twigg-Flesner and Wilhelmsson (2018: 148).
[102] Case C-415/11 *Mohamed Aziz v Caixa d'Estalvis de Catalunya, Tarragona i Manresa (Catalunyacaixa)*, ECLI:EU:C:2013:164, [77].
[103] Tridimas (2015: 408–409).
[104] ibid (404).

variety of motives for a national court to refer a case to the CJEU or to neglect the opportunity.[105] The course of Europeanised narratives can take many shapes.

I have here pictured the CJEU as one entity that produces legal materials. From the point of view of legal reasoning this is a natural approach. Needless to say, however, behind the decisions of the Court are not only its judges. Many other actors, such as the lawyers of the parties, the national courts formulating the questions to the CJEU, the Commission as an intervening repeat player, the intervening Member States, and the Advocate General contribute to the outcome. Detailed 'EU Law Stories' have been told on the CJEU landmark cases, showing how a multitude of actors have an impact on the way in which the case is decided and justified.[106] For example, the French junior judge Etienne Rigal and the Spanish judge José María Fernández Seijo played crucial and very conscious roles as referring judges in the development of the procedural safeguards for the enforcement of the Unfair Contract Terms Directive.[107] Even though the main responsibility lies with the CJEU itself, this illustrates how many legal actors carry some personal moral responsibility for the direction of legal narratives.

The narratives in which European actors are involved may be related in various ways to the national context. Some narratives proceed predominantly within the realm of EU law. The European legislation, CJEU case law, and scholarly comments on EU law easily create the impression of an autonomous narrative concerning some developments in EU law alone. The main actors are the European actors and the end result is a rule of EU law. Contrary to this, in other narratives the context is clearly a domestic one, the main actors are national ones, and the EU actor appears rather as an additional participant. However, even though one may make such a distinction between European and national narratives to simplify the discussion, one cannot maintain any deep dichotomy of this kind. On the one hand, there are no 'pure' EU law narratives. The CJEU may rely on knowledge (experimental learning) regarding national laws, and even when this is not the case, there is always a national component in every narrative on EU law, as EU law has to be executed by national legal actors. On the other hand, 'purely national' narratives are not isolated from EU law either: even in such environments that at the outset appear to be EU-safe, some impact of EU law may suddenly appear like a Jack-in-the-Box – such as in the far-reaching procedural decisions concerning the Unfair Contract Terms Directive – and change the course of the narrative. As mentioned above, 'spillovers' from EU law may even affect domestic law in areas outside the competences of the European actors. In other words, many narratives are mixed narratives, even when they have a predominantly European or domestic perspective.

The Europeanisation of private law not only adds important new actors to the narratives on legal change, but also affects and changes the roles of the national actors. EU law limits the field of what is considered 'legally possible' for the national legislator, even though the latter has various techniques for extending the margin

[105] Krommendijk (2021: 168) lists a 'myriad of motives', including both politico-strategic reasons and non-political considerations, like formalism/pragmatism, personal, psychological and institutional reasons.

[106] See the interesting volume Nicola and Davies (2017).

[107] Nicola and Tichadou (2017: 384–85, 389).

for domestic policy choices. The dialogue between the CJEU and national courts has an impact on what national courts feel it is possible to do. In addition to having such a vertical impact, European actors may also affect the internal balance between national actors. The judicial dialogue within the EU has, for example, been conceived of 'as a tool that empowers national courts against the national legislature',[108] and the CJEU has expressly taken up the task of protecting the independence of national courts.[109] National governments and legislators on the other hand may use the CJEU as a means to promote their interests and develop strategies for influencing the direction of European case law.[110] These kinds of aspirations and influences add to the complexity of the scene in the Europeanised narratives. The complexity is a reflection of the fact that in such narratives the national court has to 'serve three masters': the domestic legislator; the European legislator; and the CJEU.[111]

In addition to the public actors on the European level, the EU legislator and the CJEU, various private actors, like those mentioned in chapter 4 section V, can participate in the Europeanised narratives. European standardisation, for example, has an increasing impact on the narratives of private law.[112] The European Committee for Standardization (CEN), the European Committee for Electrotechnical Standardization (CENELEC) and the European Telecommunications Standards Institute are important actors that directly fill EU law with concrete content.[113] Private regulation may in various ways be included in European legal narratives and examples are abundant.[114] The participation of such private actors adds another layer of complexity to the cast of European narratives that can be both necessary and detrimental. Technological standardisation is needed, but critical discourse condemns the growing role of private regulatory actors for replacing democratic deliberation with bargaining between stakeholder interests with often unequal representation.[115] In addition, as Kaarlo Tuori has noted, this kind of soft-law type normativity typical of transnational law even 'makes it impossible to draw a sharp and unequivocal boundary between law and non-law'.[116] In this context, I will not discuss these elements of the complexity further. For good reasons they have attracted research projects of their own.

I have not yet touched upon another group of important actors in the Europeanised narratives, namely scholars. The reason is not an attempt to downplay their importance in this context. On the contrary, the role of academics is crucial with regard to the Europeanisation of legal narratives. I have therefore saved the issue of the role of scholars for a more thorough analysis under separate headings later in this chapter.

[108] Cafaggi and Law (2017: 14).
[109] Case C-64/16 *Associação Sindical dos Juízes Portugueses v Tribunal de Contas*, ECLI:EU:C:2018:117.
[110] See eg Bulterman and Wissels (2013).
[111] Möllers (2020: 478).
[112] See eg van Leeuwen (2017), Cantero Gamito and Micklitz (2020) and V Mak (2020) ch 8.
[113] See eg Cantero Gamito (2020).
[114] See eg Cafaggi (2011). Vallejo (2021) has even proposed a new concept, 'private administrative law', to grasp the development of EU law in this respect.
[115] Tuori (2021: 281). See Büthe and Mattli (2011) for a comprehensive analysis of winners and losers in global private regulation.
[116] Tuori (2021: 222).

The participation of many actors tends to make the story-telling dynamic. In such a dynamic narrative, the most important issue is not necessarily the formal division of power between various levels of regulation, an issue that has often been to the fore when discussing the multi-level governance structure of the EU. It is equally important to look at the dynamics of the system, how the interactions between the participants in the narratives are governed. In the context of uncertainty and experimentalism it is often a question of managing diversity[117] rather than finding unified solutions. The constitutional agonies that relate to the perceived need to understand the legal hierarchies and conflicting claims on supremacy upon which the EU is built and have led to various interesting theories on 'constitutional pluralism'[118] have not given rise to equally intense debates within the field of private law. In the context of an experimental vision of private law it feels quite natural not to focus on hierarchy, but instead to emphasise the continuous interaction between European and national actors that interlinks the European and domestic narratives on legal change. In fact, some perspectives on constitutional pluralism seem to point in the same direction, towards a 'process-oriented approach' that is based on 'a philosophy of communication, dialogue and compromise which allows constructive coexistence',[119] and thereby becomes a vehicle of mutual learning.[120]

It is easy to lament the multitude and various involvement of actors in the Europeanised narratives for leading to difficult complexity, but one should not forget the positive consequences of involving such a many-sided and versatile cast. Different actors fulfil different roles and they can all be useful to support good legal narratives. The European main actors, the European legislator and the CJEU, cater for the need for harmonised rules for the internal market. In addition, in the experimental field of private law in Europe they also function as channels of legal learning across the borders. At the same time, they may function as powerful instances of creating new practical solutions unbound by national conceptual structures, contributing to the modernisation of national laws. The domestic actors, on the other hand, are required both to connect legal decision-making sufficiently to culturally and locally defined real life and to infuse a degree of legitimacy in the narratives that the European institutions are unable to provide.

In other words, various legal actors make use of the European laboratory in different ways. The European legislator and the European courts produce sources that directly become a part of the domestic narratives. As they often base their decisions on knowledge about the experiences of the Member States, they may also be the most active drivers of cross-border learning within the EU. Even though their activity today is practically the most important form of Europeanisation of private law, I will not discuss it further. As mentioned in the introduction, I will look at the ultimate step towards Europeanisation: domestic decision-makers using learning directly across

[117] For an interesting example concerning new technological challenges, see Purnhagen (2019); on managing diversity (2019: 1388).
[118] See eg the collection by Davies and Avbelj (2018).
[119] Davies (2018: 323–24).
[120] Avbelj and Davies (2018: 7).

Member State borders as part of their reasoning. Such horizontal movement of legal ideas represents a deeper commitment to Europeanisation.

III. FREE MOVEMENT OF LEGAL IDEAS: LEARNING HORIZONTALLY ACROSS THE BORDERS

The horizontal use of comparative knowledge across borders is sufficiently common to have been characterised with the help of a variety of metaphors. If someone prefers a biological metaphor rather than the pedagogical 'cross-border learning', a good candidate is 'cross-fertilisation'.[121] In economic terms one finds similar trends described as an 'international marketplace for judgments'.[122]

Horizontal learning of this kind questions the traditional dichotomic way of posing validity questions. A concept pair like 'national' and 'transnational' should not be understood as an either-or dichotomy, but rather as a scale on which domestic and foreign elements are blended in various proportions depending on the context. The same goes for concepts like 'legal source'. Instead of asking whether a certain item is to be considered a legal source or not, one should discuss what kind of argumentative force that item has in a particular context, and how much force it has. I will discuss this issue further in chapter eight.

Learning from the law of other countries has traditionally been a standard procedure among national legislators. They have mostly been the primary actors in the 'transplantations' or 'transpositions' of foreign legal ideas into their national law. As cross-border learning through legislation is common, it does not require further documentation in this context.[123] It is only worth noting that the variety of ways in which national legislators have used the experience of others is broad. Some have even introduced large bodies of law from other countries as a basis of their private law, the best example being the many receptions of *Code Civil* and *Bürgerliches Gesetzbuch* around the world. Others have taken over smaller pieces, like the spreading of the Products Liability Directive far outside the EU. Sometimes the reception is limited to solutions to singular problems only. The learning obtained may be used more or less identically, simply translated, or only in a societally and legally adjusted form. Some may use the experience of one or a few admired model countries, whilst others base their work on broad comparisons and combinations of models from different sources. There is more than one way only of using comparative experience in legislative practice.

This kind of comparative exercise is often not limited to other Member States only, but reaches further. One may assume, however, that experience from other EU countries is particularly interesting, both because of the relative similarity of the societies and due to a possible European ethos. In particular, when national legislators deal with implementation of EU legislation, including the adjustment of the surrounding legal landscape, the natural direction to look is at other Member States.

[121] This term is mentioned eg by Lohse (2011: 283).
[122] Andenas and Fairgrieve (2004: xxvii, xxviii).
[123] See eg Lupo and Scaffardi (2014) on comparative law in legislative drafting.

The use of experience from other Member States by national legislators is obviously the most important way that legal ideas move horizontally within the EU. The cross-border use of European domestic experience, however, is not a prerogative of legislators alone. The small narratives on change include all levels of legal practices: learning can take place in legislation, in legal doctrine, in court practice, as well as in administrative practice. An experimental European ethos, if taken seriously, implies an increasingly positive attitude towards the crossing of European internal borders by all legal actors. The use of learning across the borders in concrete legal decision-making and scholarship reflects more deeply the idea of European experimentalism. It is such free movement of legal ideas that really challenges traditional approaches to 'national law' and 'legal sources'.

Among legal decision-makers, I will concentrate on the activities of courts. It is worth saying, however, that the ability to learn across the borders is not limited to courts alone. Various kinds of cooperative structures between other national decision-makers in Europe have been established in order to facilitate cross-border learning. The networking between European administrative enforcement networks in the area of consumer law is an important example.[124]

Much of what I will say about the experimental learning expected from courts also applies to legal scholars. In view of their particularly important role in these processes I will address their challenges and opportunities separately.

I will discuss horizontal learning by courts and scholars because the legal legitimacy of cross-border learning comes most clearly to the fore in this context. Decision-makers relying on materials from foreign law – even when it is the law of another Member State – cannot avoid a justificatory burden[125] if one does not accept a purely arbitrary use of such experience that happens to be within reach. One could claim that the acceptance of the increased value of cross-border learning requires a Europeanisation of legal methodology and a European doctrine of precedents.[126] A lighter and more vague claim, more in line with the acknowledgement of fragmentation and diversity, would be that most of the various legal methodologies in the EU Member States seem to need a stronger and more express European component. In the rest of the book I will analyse features of this European methodological component. 'Free movement of legal ideas' is discussed as a methodological credo concerning legal reasoning[127] in an EU that takes its experimental learning potential seriously.

In the context of decision-making, legal 'learning' implies some level of legal justification. Of course, a court can use the experience of foreign legislators and decision-makers only in order to find substantive arguments for a solution. It may

[124] Deeply analysed by Cafaggi (2017). See also Regulation (EU) 2017/2394 of the European Parliament and of the Council of 12 December 2017 on cooperation between national authorities responsible for the enforcement of consumer protection laws and repealing Regulation (EC) No 2006/2004. Also in other areas Member State authorities are ordered to exchange experiences and best practices, see eg Basedow (2021: 309–10).

[125] Walker (2019: 367).

[126] Berger (2001: 886–92). See, however, ch 9 section II below.

[127] Not to be confused with the procedural principle of recognition of judgments that has been called 'free movement of judicial decisions', so eg Lenaerts (2020: 32), or with easy cross-border access to justice, www.e-codex.eu.

treat a foreign case simply as a source of information concerning a societal fact comparable to any other information concerning possible solutions to a societal problem. In that case, the cross-border learning appears to be merely a practical way of finding good substantive arguments. Even though the substance of the information is of crucial importance, however, the use of a foreign source often adds at least a drop of authoritative value to the substantive reasoning. The recognition of such an authoritative value – which may appear in stronger, decisive fashion, but also, and probably more often in weaker forms just adding some weight to the reasoning – is a central point in a Europeanised legal methodology. I will discuss this issue more in detail in chapter nine.

The use of foreign sources is part of the legal heritage of many countries. Evidence of this is the considerable amount of doctrinal discourse on the issue.[128] Often, however, such cases have been based on national traditions to use material from particular countries – like the frequent use of German case law by countries in the Germanic tradition and the use by Nordic scholars and judges of material from other Nordic countries than one's own – or on traditions within particular branches of law – like the use of English maritime law cases almost all over the globe. In other words, the tradition of using foreign sources is established in many countries, but the challenge at hand is whether and to what extent such a tradition should be expanded towards a broader use of legal experience from across the whole EU.

There are indications concerning some development of legal practice in this direction. Many have felt that domestic legal actors in various jurisdictions have become more open-minded towards European learning processes. The frequency of using European comparative law in domestic decision-making is said to be growing.[129] Some even claim that domestic courts have increased the use of comparative materials 'to an unprecedented extent'.[130] The cases are in most countries[131] not abundant, however, and other scholars instead underline the relative scarcity of such cases.[132] In the present chapter, I will not discuss the quasi-empirical question about the frequency of such cases further. It is sufficient to note that many European jurisdictions at least acknowledge a possibility of using comparative arguments in domestic legal reasoning.

With regard to both normative expectations and practical ease one should distinguish between different types of contexts in which domestic courts could use foreign legal experience. The knowledge interest in a case that relates to the

[128] See eg Drobnig and van Erp (1999); Canivet, Andenas and Fairgrieve (2004); Markesinis and Fedtke (2006); Bobek (2013); Andenas and Fairgrieve (2015); and Smits (2019). See also E Mak (2013), with a constitutional and empirical approach. The collection Markesinis (1994), despite its title, focuses on concrete comparative studies rather than on a general discussion of the influence of foreign sources on English law.

[129] Michaels and Jansen (2006: 863); Cafaggi (2017: 232).

[130] Andenas and Fairgrieve (2015a: 9).

[131] However, on Swiss law, *cf* Kadner Graziano (2015: 40), according to which the Swiss Federal Court has made reference to foreign law in 10% (in tort law 20%) of cases.

[132] eg Bobek (2013: 14, 192), claiming that there is no universal trend in this direction, and that the number of such decisions is very low. Riesenhuber (2018: 721–22), in his broad critique of the idea of comparative law as a method of interpretation, finds few indications of such use even in the practice of the CJEU.

interpretation and application of EU legislation and national legislation based on EU law differs from what kind of guidance one seeks when such a connection to joint legislation is lacking. Admittedly, the line between these two groups is by no means sharp.

In cases relating to EU law, the use of materials from other Member States is easier to justify. It resembles a situation in which a national lower court contemplates the use of a decision from another lower court in the same jurisdiction. Probably according to most European legal methodologies the court is not obliged to take into account that decision, but has the opportunity to make argumentative use of it. A similar approach seems natural with regard to the use of materials concerning EU legislation from another Member State. As to the national Supreme Courts, their obligation according to EU law to ask for a preliminary ruling might often solve the issue,[133] but the CJEU has in addition explicitly ruled that the court has to ask for a preliminary ruling if there are conflicting decisions of lower national courts concerning a concept used in EU secondary legislation.[134] The CJEU in this way has nudged the national courts to avoid conflicting interpretations. One may also argue in favour of the relevance of foreign sources in more practical everyday language: 'for the court that has to interpret national law in conformity with a directive, it might be useful to consider foreign case law'.[135] There are, in other words, normative and practical pressures on the courts towards the use of comparative sources when applying EU law. I will analyse these normative pressures further in chapter nine.

Even though comparative studies have not focused much attention on the implementation and application of EU directives,[136] one can presume a growing movement of legal experience concerning the application and interpretation of EU law across national borders, often supported by the reporting of case law in legal writings. For example, courts across the Union are inspired by landmark cases on the Products Liability Directive, in particular from the larger jurisdictions. It is difficult, however, to produce a documentation of the extent of such use of foreign experience directly by the courts,[137] as the use is not always transparent. At least in some legal traditions it is considered less proper to cite foreign materials in the reasoning of the court and also in other jurisdictions courts may be reluctant to make references to foreign materials, perhaps because of the enhanced risk of displaying mistakes concerning the alien jurisdiction. In cases where one can discern an obvious influence from experience from abroad, the decision of the court often lacks an express reference to that experience. As a parallel example of this, one might mention case law concerning the UN Convention on Contracts for the International Sale of Goods (CISG), ratified by almost all EU countries. Even though the idea of a shared law based on shared scholarship and shared precedents is so strong that it has been described as 'the global

[133] Tjong Tjin Tai and Teuben (2008: 841) mention this as the reason why domestic courts do not consult each other's decisions when interpreting EU law.

[134] Case C-160/14 *João Filipe Ferreira da Silva e Brito and Others v Estado português*, ECLI:EU:C:2015:565.

[135] Smits (2004: 235). Howells and Watson (2015: 624 *et seq*) show how UK courts have been willing to use comparative materials in decisions related to EU consumer law.

[136] Smits (2004: 235) at that time found such studies to be largely absent.

[137] According to Markesinis and Fedtke (2006: 137) courts do not appear to have used much comparative materials in such cases.

jurisconsultorium of the CISG',[138] cases with an express reference to case law from other countries are scarce.[139] In a transparent movement of legal ideas, however, one should attempt to overcome such a reluctance to show the true sources of a decision. Argumentative transparency is an important way of safeguarding the rule of law.[140]

The possibilities of using foreign materials are relatively self-evident in many national paradigms of legal decision-making related to EU law. The opportunities of an experimental, learning law are not limited, however, to the use of cross-border knowledge concerning the interpretation and application of existing EU norms. The experimental perspective is brought a step further in cases where the learning is not directly connected with some common piece of European legislation. Such free-standing movement of pieces of legal experience is the ultimate expression of the idea of a free movement of legal ideas within the EU. The existence of such cases is a kind of litmus test concerning the relevance and viability of the idea.

In comparative law discourse, one much-cited paradigmatic example is the English case *White v Jones*.[141] The case was about the liability of a solicitor towards the presumptive beneficiaries of a will for failing to follow the instructions of the later deceased person when drafting his will. As the solicitor had not changed the will in the way he was instructed, the plaintiffs could not receive the sums indicated and they consequently sued the solicitor. Lord Goff noted, referring to a broad description of cases from a variety of countries, that 'the problems which arise in cases such as the present have troubled the courts in many jurisdictions, both common law and civil law', indicating 'that they are of their very nature difficult to accommodate within the ordinary principles of the law of obligations'. He then sought a solution based on a long discussion of 'German experience' that could be used 'thanks to material published in our language by distinguished comparatists'. House of Lords in this case in other words expressly chose to make use of experience across borders in discussing a hard domestic case.

This is a paradigmatic example for many reasons. It shows how courts can fruitfully use experience even across the border between common law and civil law. The case also illustrates how a court can integrate foreign experience in legal reasoning both transparently and deeply, narrowing the gap between the context of discovery and the context of justification in a way that is exemplary for an ideal European private law based on the free movement of legal ideas. Further one should note the role that the court expressly gives to comparative research as translator and transmitter of the foreign experience.

Finally, the case also shows how the use of foreign materials may require a redefining of the legal description of the problem in order to overcome the legal cultural barriers related to the variations in conceptual structures between different legal systems. The Court did not find the different ways of classifying the issue at hand in the dichotomy of contractual and tortious liability in Germany and England as

[138] Baasch Andersen (2011: 35).

[139] Baasch Andersen (2011: 40–43). However, cases are also reported in which a court cites up to 40 foreign decisions, Ferreri (2012: 50).

[140] I analyse this issue further in ch 8.

[141] [1995] 1 All ER 691.

relevant, as the focus was put on the concrete real-life issue at hand. Cross-border movement of legal ideas supports a development of a legal language that is closer to real life than the traditional dogmatic structures of private law.[142]

This is not the only English case in which the court has made use of comparative law methodology. Already around the turn of the century, one could speak about a series of judgments.[143] Nor is this merely an English peculiarity. As mentioned above, one can find traditional case law in many countries that refers to the law of some geographically or culturally close neighbour. The experimental value of the EU, however, is fully used only when one can take into account experience from other countries than traditional 'legal allies'.

Learning across borders does not take place easily, even if the inclination of the courts to use experience from colleagues in other Member States would seem to be growing, as I assume is the case. The use of foreign material as a legal source is challenging for several reasons. There may be problems of legitimacy and of linguistic and cultural understanding, and one should not underestimate the practical challenges related to finding and accessing foreign material.

As to legitimacy, there is a recurring argument that the use of foreign sources in legal decision-making would be in conflict with democratic self-governance, as expressed through democratically adopted national legislation.[144] Predominantly, the legitimacy discussion has related to the interpretation of constitutional law, where the tension between national democracy and foreign legal sources is clearly visible.[145] In private law, where the influx of various elements of transnational private ordering into the legal realm is traditionally strong, it is more difficult to take a principled position against the use of foreign sources as such. Through private law history, various kinds of materials have gained a kind of 'informal authority' with great importance for the development of legal practice.[146] Instead of discussing the legitimacy of the use of foreign sources in a dichotomic yes-or-no fashion, one should therefore rather relate the question to the relative weight of foreign sources. More precisely, if the focus is on democracy, it is a question of the weight of national legislation in front of the foreign material. Here one should recall[147] that the question whether foreign sources may be used is relevant primarily in hard cases. In routine cases that can be directly solved on the basis of the clear wording of a national statute, there is little room for discussing the use of other sources, be they domestic or foreign ones. Democracy should not be overrun by lawyers, either domestic or foreign. One should recall, however, that there is no clear line between hard cases and easy cases. Convincing foreign materials may be used to bring a previously established domestic interpretation into question and turn a former easy case into a hard one. Many legal orders even acknowledge some opportunities for decision-making *contra legem*.[148] The more flexible the national

[142] I will return to this issue in ch 8 section V.
[143] See eg Berger (2001: 886) and Markesinis and Fedtke (2006: 67–68).
[144] This argument is noted eg by Kadner Graziano (2015: 27).
[145] See eg Hwang (2019) with references.
[146] See eg Jansen (2016).
[147] See ch 1 section IV.
[148] On EU law as a reason for domestic decision-making *contra legem*, see Möllers (2020).

legal orders become, as a consequence of contemporary uncertainty, the more room there will be for a horizontal movement of legal ideas across borders. Later, I will return to the undoubtedly relevant legal queries that relate to the important need to respect the rule of law in a democracy.

The weight of the question of legitimacy obviously correlates with the importance of the societal issue to be decided. This does not stop courts from making path-breaking decisions making use of comparative materials. A good example is offered by the British private law case, *Arthur J.S. Hall & Co. v Simmons*,[149] in which the House of Lords put an end to a traditional immunity of advocates from negligence claims, even though it 'was said that the sky would fall in'.[150] This decision could be made on the basis of an analysis of legal practice in other countries.

The challenges related to the linguistic and cultural understanding of foreign materials are obvious, and are a standard concern uttered by comparative lawyers. The recurring discussion concerning the possibility and meaning of 'legal transplants' is an expression of this concern. As stated above, however, learning across borders does not mean copying, but rather a process based on a sufficient understanding of the context of the foreign legal experience and an adaptation of this knowledge to the domestic legal and societal environment.[151] In principle, this means a much deeper societally and culturally embedded process of thought than just a pure translation and direct use of the source. *White v Jones* indicates how legal cultural analysis is often required before one can use foreign sources convincingly. As this is a challenging demand, and hard to fulfil in day-to-day court practice, it focuses the limelight on the role of legal scholars. The reasoning of Lord Goff in *White v Jones* shows, however, that the challenges can be met also in decision-making by the courts.

In other words, without forgetting the broad number of cases in which courts in Europe have been using comparative sources, I assume that the prime engines for a movement of legal sources across European borders must be legal scholars. Foreign cases have entered into many decisions through the 'filter' of comparative research.[152] Scholars can dig deeper and produce the necessary cultural and societal contextualisations needed for successful learning processes. Comparative scholars can also perform the linguistic task of setting the source at the disposal of the national court in a language it masters – a task that in due course may be handled by translation programmes. In *White v Jones*, Lord Goff expressly acknowledged that his reasoning was based on material in English produced by scholars of comparative law.

Finally, one encounters obvious practical problems when using foreign materials. As discussed later in this chapter, digitalisation may mitigate at least part of these problems, but so far it is still difficult to get sufficient access to and opportunity to search relevant material in foreign databases, and no EU-wide search is presently available. Only concerning particular issues, such as international case law on

[149] [2002] 1 AC 615.
[150] Steyn (2006: 637).
[151] Schiek (2011: 445), regarding the interpretation of Community law: 'isolating the specific cultural backgrounds … and adapting them to the national court's legal system as necessary.'
[152] Smits (2019: 511).

CISG,[153] is a truly international or European search possible. Again, assistance must come from legal scholars who have better opportunities than the courts to dive into the vast river of comparative material. The availability of analytical backup within a court, however, may improve its opportunities to engage in a deeper comparative discourse.[154]

Scholars, in other words, play a key role in promoting the movement of legal ideas across European borders. I will in the following look more closely at their role. This should not be read, however, as an attempt to downgrade the role of courts. Much has been also done by courts, and there are indications that the use of comparative sources within the EU is increasing. One might even assume that courts in Europe are actively promoting this tendency through organised forms of collaboration. The active cooperation between the European courts in the European Judicial Network in civil and commercial matters[155] and in the Superior Courts Network established by the ECHR,[156] as well as the training of judges, is driving the development.[157] More generally, both formal and informal transnational networking of judges has clearly been increasing.[158] The Europeanisation effect of this networking probably lies in the development of the mentalities of judges towards a greater openness, rather than offering fora for concrete discussions on joint legal issues.[159]

IV. THE ROLE OF SCHOLARS

A legal science that transcends national borders is an essential prerequisite for a European private law. As shown above, for practical reasons courts often use foreign material that is provided by legal comparative research. This corresponds with legal sociological studies on the globalisation of law, showing that this process is 'mainly an exercise of legal science and international organisations and has not as yet reached far into judicial practice.'[160]

The crucial role of legal research in facilitating the movement of legal ideas corresponds to what was said in chapter four about the key role of scholarly work in small narratives on legal change. In the same way as scholarly conceptualisation is considered important for stabilising new steps and making them lasting in domestic narratives, sufficient academic input is also significant with regard to the success of Europeanised narratives. As scholars are shaping and developing the deeper level of legal thinking – legal culture – they are particularly important as developers of a Europeanised legal culture that supports joint learning processes within the EU.

[153] See www.cisg.law.pace.edu.
[154] Bobek (2013: 46–47).
[155] See e-justice.europa.eu/content_european_judicial_network_in_civil_and_commercial_matters-21-en.do.
[156] See www.echr.coe.int/Pages/home.aspx?p=court/dialoguecourts/network&c.
[157] Smits (2012: 20).
[158] See eg E Mak (2013: 5, 83–98) and Claes and de Visser (2012).
[159] See the convincing critique by Bobek (2013: 48–50).
[160] Gessner (1998: 434).

Legal scholars are not bound by such conventions concerning acceptable justification patterns that may make courts reluctant to refer to foreign materials openly. The obstacles to narrowing the gap between the context of discovery and the context of justification are not present in the same way in legal doctrine. Legal scholars are traditionally free to embrace the opportunities of European cross-border learning transparently. For example, in Germany legal scholars have for decades recognised the value of foreign sources more broadly than the reluctant courts.[161]

Even the European Parliament has stressed the importance of academic comparative work in this context.[162] This was at a time when many academics were engaged in projects of harmonisation of private law. It has been suggested that academic support for EU law-making has been reduced since the heydays of Europeanisation.[163] This, however, does not necessarily imply a reduction of academic influence on cross-border learning. As will be discussed later, the input from cross-border academic contributions does not need to strive for Europeanisation in order to be relevant in this context. For cross-border learning, critical analysis of unreflective processes of Europeanisation is equally important.

Academics do not only play an important role as producers of Europeanised legal research; with regard to the development of a receptive Europeanised legal culture, the education and training of future legal professionals may have an even greater impact. By promoting more Europeanised curricula, and by performing such teaching, scholars can participate in building a Europeanised legal culture. The issue of the impact of legal education on the processes of legal integration has attracted much scholarly attention.[164] As I am focusing on legal reasoning, I will not discuss legal education further.

Not only do legal needs for development support the use of foreign materials in scholarly writings; the general scientific community also creates pressures that support the growth of cross-border legal research. In view of scientific logic – and more crudely, in view of research funding – cross-border legal research is a very 'natural' endeavour. As science is intrinsically international, legal scholarship should be as well. Academic legal scholars from different countries should be able to talk to each other as scientists do: 'If legal science is to be worthy of the name "science", it is essential that legal discourse is not limited to the confines of the domestic state.'[165] The European laboratory offers the academic a natural and fruitful way of crossing national borders.

In other words, a legal researcher cannot escape the 'double citizenship' in both the legal community and the scientific community that Kaarlo Tuori has analysed so well.[166] A realist doctrine of legal sources acknowledges that the scholar follows

[161] Ranieri (2006).
[162] See the Parliament resolution on the Commission Communication 15 November 2001. In the report (Report A5-0384/2001) the importance of comparative analysis is stressed and the Commission is requested to secure legal advice from academic bodies, inter alia from the Lando-Commission and the Study Group on a European Civil Code.
[163] Muir, Dawson and de Witte (2013: 2).
[164] Already early eg Friedman and Teubner (1986).
[165] Hondius (2011: 553), claiming that 'The future obviously is in a global legal science'.
[166] Tuori (2002: 285).

partially a different path than a judge, because the scholar also has to take into account the rules of the scientific community. This is why the possible reluctance of courts to draw openly on foreign experience does not hinder scholars from doing so. Even black-letter scholars do not have to obey precisely the same doctrine on legal sources as case law. For a legal scholar, the sources used are not only sources of law, but also research material that has to be chosen, assessed and used in accordance with the research question at hand.[167]

In the domestic setting addressed in chapter four, I emphasised the systematising and conceptualising role of scholars, as that is the part of their task that cannot be performed by anybody else. With regard to cross-border learning, legal research can play a decisive role not only as a systematiser, but also both as a screener and transmitter of foreign sources and as a critical and contextual analyst of such material. Legal research can find useful foreign experience, choose what to use, conceptualise and contextualise that material, and discuss the material in relation to the domestic context. Such analyses can then lead to starting, supporting and stabilising Europeanised narratives on legal change. This is not to say that the conceptual tasks of legal research would be less important in the Europeanised context. Successful learning requires conceptual understanding and creativity in all phases of the study. Not only experience concerning solutions to practical problems, but also conceptual and systematising ideas may move across the borders.

Unlike courts and similar legal actors, whose ultimate task is to make legally legitimate decisions concerning concrete issues, legal research has a plurality of aims, from mimicking legal decision-making to criticism of law and legal decisions. There is accordingly a broad range of variations in the ways in which domestic legal research can use and has used foreign materials. Even within the particular field of comparative law methodological approaches vary[168] to the extent that 'The sea of comparative law' (maritime metaphors seem to be popular in this area) has been said to be 'full of … vessels, icebergs and small fragmented groups, differing routes and destinations.'[169] Legal research can position itself more as a participant in legal narratives or more as an outside spectator, but in the latter case the forced 'double citizenship' of legal scholars means that the scholar cannot take a completely outside position.[170] A comparative lawyer can try to adopt an outsider's view by just analysing the comparative materials, without taking a stand on whether this should have an impact on any national or European law. Even in this position, however, the researcher cannot escape the fact that the research can be used in domestic and European narratives on legal change, as was done, for example, in *White v Jones*. This is not a criticism, as such use only indicates that the work is of good quality. Another scholar may be more inclined to produce legal dogmatics (black-letter law), taking a direct stand on how existing domestic law should be interpreted, but using cross-border material as argument. In

[167] Doublet and Bernt (1993: 25) emphasise the difference between juridical method and legal-scholarly method.

[168] See eg the collection by Van Hoecke (2004). For a critique of various approaches, see Frankenberg (2016).

[169] Husa (2005: 93).

[170] Comparativists are perhaps not alone in the crowded room of black-letter law, *cf* Husa (2022) ch 1.

such a case, the scholar acknowledges the normative value of the foreign material more openly, but again the further use of the reasoning is dependent on its quality. The precise way in which comparative material is processed in legal research may in other words vary, and the argumentative impact may be different. From the point of view of how research can promote the movement of legal ideas across the borders, however, the differences are differences of weight rather than fundamental ones.

Europeanisation has also led to the development of new ways of presenting comparative materials that are in principle based on the 'outsider's view' but are clearly meant to encourage the movement of source material across European borders. The broad work on developing *Ius Commune Casebooks for the Common Law of Europe*[171] directly aims at supporting a Europeanised private law discourse. The Common Core of European Private Law project has in turn brought together hundreds of scholars to analyse and discuss concrete real-life issues, as they are presently regulated in national laws, to offer a basis for a critical discussion on future restatements or codifications at the European level.[172] Projects like these contribute to a development in which a movement of sources across the borders becomes increasingly natural, even though the projects refrain from recommendations as to the development of national laws. They also contribute to the development of a joint legal-cultural conceptuality that is a necessary precondition for a fruitful understanding and learning across the borders.

The fact that both comparative studies with an outsider's perspective and black-letter studies can contribute to the movement of legal sources across borders does not mean that both play a similar role in such movements. Comparative law is a traditional and established field of legal research, but its impact on the day-to-day decision-making of courts has remained relatively limited. Even though there is a growing number of cases in which comparative studies are cited, an increasing use of cross-border material in domestic legal dogmatic work would obviously have a stronger impact on the movement of legal ideas across borders, at least in the short term. Those producing national black-letter law are probably the key actors with regard to the inclusion of cross-border legal sources in small narratives.

The Europeanisation effect of including foreign materials in domestic dogmatics does not only relate to the concrete issues under scrutiny. In the long run, such works can have a more general impact on legal methodology. The more common the use of cross-border material in dogmatic studies becomes, the stronger it directs general thinking about legal sources in a Europeanised direction. The doctrine of legal sources is after all a combination of actual practice and normative expectations.[173] Growth in the use of cross-border sources forces the domestic doctrine of legal sources to acknowledge the role of cross-border material, even though it may do so reluctantly.[174]

[171] See www.bloomsburyprofessional.com/uk/series/ius-commune-casebooks-for-the-common-law-of-europe/?pg=2. For tort law, see van Gerven, Lever and Larouche (2000) and for contract law, Beale, Fauvarque-Cosson, Rutgers and Vogenauer (2019).

[172] See www.cambridge.org/core/series/common-core-of-european-private-law/9A1F0195629A3C0607233F14029C3A25.

[173] For a critique of traditional doctrines of legal sources, see ch 8 section II.

[174] For example in the Nordic countries the common cross-border use of Nordic material is clearly downplayed (often mentioned either very briefly or not at all) in Nordic legal theory.

With regard to cross-border horizontal learning within the EU, I did above distinguish between issues relating to EU legislation and issues in which the direct relationship to EU law is lacking. In the first case, sources from other Member States are self-evidently relevant, as it is clear that, for example, decisions from national courts in other Member States enlarge the available knowledge base. In dogmatic studies, such material is indeed often used, even though the principles concerning how and from what Member States the material is chosen are not always revealed. One might even claim that there is a stronger normative requirement for scholars than for courts to make use of foreign materials in these kinds of cases. This follows from the 'double citizenship' of legal scholars in both the legal and the academic world. The principles of good science seem to require the use of legal research from other Member States when discussing domestic law based on a detailed directive, such as the Products Liability Directive. As research should be built on previous research, the ignorance of research on a more or less identical text in another country would seem problematic from a scientific point of view, at least if that research is published in a fairly accessible language. In cases where a joint European legislative basis is lacking, there is not a similar pressure from research ethics towards the use of cross-border materials.

In fact, the harmonised area has witnessed for decades the advent of a European doctrine, expressly detached from any national basis. In treatises on, for example, European consumer law, often written together by scholars from different jurisdictions, the focus is on a joint understanding of EU instruments.[175] Jürgen Basedow's in-depth analysis of EU private law as a growing legal order is a recent important contribution to this discourse.[176] This genre usually contains an element of learning across the borders, as national experience often is used as a contributor of questions and materials to the European discourse. National cases and discussions may be referred to both as illustrations of particular problems and as guidance for how to tackle these problems.

A convincing critical use of foreign sources has to be transparent. One cannot ignore the societal commitments that every process of screening and choosing foreign material is based on. Also in a functional approach the definition of problems and functions includes value judgements.[177] The ideal of transparency requires that a scholar should openly and honestly account for the reasons for the choices made when using foreign sources. The common way of approaching this challenge by just referring to 'practical' or 'research-economic' reasons – like the language ability of the researcher or the availability of sources, leading to the predominant use of common law as well as German and French law – sounds increasingly unconvincing if no other reasons are mentioned.

The increasing use of foreign materials in many ways challenges the established methods of legal dogmatic research. The traditional approach of national doctrine has been based on an ideal of completeness. A good analysis of a legal problem has

[175] See eg Weatherill (2013); Reich, Micklitz, Rott and Tonner (2014); Howells, Twigg-Flesner and Wilhelmsson (2018) as well as Micklitz and Weatherill (1993).

[176] Basedow (2021).

[177] eg Rühl (2018: 485), analysing the criticism of the functional approach.

traditionally required an account of 'all' relevant legal sources available within the national legal order, and if any sorting out has been made, it has been based more on the silent practical experience of the scholar than on an explicit methodology. Europeanisation challenges this starting point. It has been said that 'research methodology has been turned upside down' by globalisation and digitalisation,[178] and Europeanisation is increasingly having the same effect. From an ideal of a complete coverage of sources in a delimited field, legal studies are moving towards a situation in which abundant material is available in a field with fluid borderlines. The ideals for how this abundance should be exploited, however, are not yet well developed.[179]

The development requires more thought-through and precise ways of framing the research questions than has been the tradition in legal dogmatic research. The research question determines the method and material, and many alternatives are available even for black-letter law research in the multi-dimensional and increasingly borderless contemporary legal world. As these alternatives are even more enhanced by the opportunities provided by digitalisation, I will follow up this point in the discussion of the digital future below. Here I only want to remind the reader about the need for critical contextualisation of cross-border material. Legal scholars do not only have the task of screening, conceptualising and transmitting foreign sources, but should also be able to discuss them in their societal context and relate them to domestic societal needs. Obviously, legal scholars who are equipped with methods and practices of societal research are in the best position to carry out this task. It is easy to agree with Jan Smits when he claims that an 'interdisciplinary approach is indispensable for the discipline of European private law'.[180] The growing need for various kinds of interdisciplinary approaches in dealing with the foreign material makes the clear framing of research questions even more important.

V. SCHOLARS AS CREATORS OF EUROPEAN 'PRINCIPLES'

Legal research, as a builder of normative structures, can further the movement of legal ideas in a more systematised way than the courts with their focus on decision-making in individual cases. The academic integration of cross-border experience in legal reasoning can therefore also be performed indirectly, in a two-step fashion. Scholars have used the comparative material to construct 'European principles' and then these principles are integrated into both domestic and European legal reasoning. Both comparative lawyers and private lawyers have contributed to such academic Europeanisation. The academic groups that have created 'European principles' have played important roles in the Europeanisation of private law narratives.

Obviously, the term 'principles' in this context has been understood in a variety of ways. The understanding of 'European principles' that would best correspond

[178] Germain (2007: 139).
[179] I will discuss the required ideals further in particular in chs 8 and 9.
[180] Smits (2004: 243). With regard to the globalisation of law, Walker (2017: 111) in a similar vein demands 'greater cross-disciplinary awareness'.

with what is generally meant by legal principles would be doctrinal reconstructions of relatively general norms that would be common to most European jurisdictions. Indeed, some scholars speak about 'European principles' in this way. Examples include the principles that 'penalty clauses are enforceable in principle but subject to judicial control of reasonableness' and 'an offer is revocable except when the offeror explicitly or impliedly made it irrevocable'.[181] Some have even sketched the birth of a 'European legal doctrine' that would focus on the development of such principles, including both European human rights principles, European private law principles and common general principles of law, as well as a new conceptual framework.[182] Scholarly work of this kind lowers the threshold for cross-border learning and can offer useful building blocks for the common legal-cultural language that is a prerequisite for a smooth movement of legal ideas within the EU.

However, today 'European principles' in the context of private law usually refers to something much more concrete and detailed. The 'principles' are code-like structures built by academic groups, combining comparative knowledge from various Member States with openly legal-political reasoning concerning the 'best' available solution. The impressive work done in creating such concrete European principles has superseded a less ambitious search for more general principles that could truly be called common for Europe. This is not to say that there is no relationship between law-like principles and general principles. On the contrary, to be credible, the drafters of law-like principles have to respect possible joint European general principles as well.

In the EU the concrete constructing of principles started with the work of the Lando Commission, creating the Principles of European Contract Law (PECL)[183] that set the tone for further work in this direction. The PECL were devised to provide a foundation for EU legislation; to offer a package of norms that could be chosen by the parties to a contract; to formulate what could be called a modern *lex mercatoria*; and to provide a 'Model for Judicial and Legislative Development of Contract Law' as well as a basis for harmonisation.[184] The collection was initially fairly successful; it was used as a model for legislation in some of the former socialist countries when they were reforming their private laws,[185] and they had an impact even on German and French modernisation of their civil codes.[186] References to the PECL were made both in court decisions[187] and in arbitral awards.[188] The PECL became acknowledged as a source of law among domestic scholars as well.[189] If the PECL had remained the

[181] Hesselink (2013: 240).
[182] Van Hoecke and Ost (1998: 211–15). Basedow (2021) Book II discusses legal community principles, market principles and solidarity principles in EU private law.
[183] Lando and Beale (2000) and Lando, Clive, Prüm and Zimmermann (2003). I had the pleasure of working in this group after Finland became a member of the EU in 1995.
[184] Lando and Beale (2000: xxiii–xxiv).
[185] See eg Varul (2008) and Varul (2011: 288) on Estonia.
[186] See eg Jansen (2010: 149–50); Ackermann (2018a); and Fauvarque-Cosson (2018).
[187] See eg Vendrell Cervantes (2008) on PECL in Spanish courts and Busch (2008) on PECL in Dutch courts. The Lithuanian Supreme Court seems to have been very active in referring to all the collections of principles, see eg Kadner Graziano (2015:43).
[188] See eg Heidemann (2011: 182–86).
[189] Jansen (2011: 35) with references.

only effort in the area of contract law, it could have become a quite widely used reference text in EU private law discourse. Later projects, like the Draft Common Frame of Reference (DCFR), diminished the source value of the PECL by offering competing collections. However, it should be noted that the DCFR was strongly influenced by the decisions made in the PECL.[190]

After the creation of the PECL, a huge project that covered broader areas of private law was started. The Study Group on a European Civil Code and (to some extent) the Research Group on EC Private Law (Acquis Group)[191] produced the DCFR,[192] which had a coverage that included, in addition to general contract law, specific contracts, non-contractual obligations and some movable property law. This made the multi-layered structure more civil code-like and more difficult to use in a pragmatic problem-oriented fashion.[193] In the debate, criticism was indeed voiced against the choice of an abstract structure, and a contract code was suggested as a more pragmatic approach.[194] In general, the DCFR has been described both as more doctrinal and as substantively a step backwards in comparison with the PECL.[195] Perhaps for this reason the legislative consequences of the DCFR have not been as great as was probably expected. As even the project concerning a Common European Sales Law (CESL),[196] related to the DCFR, failed, it is easy to see that the DCFR did not really have the impact that the participants in the heyday of Europeanisation hoped for.

Other European principles, such as the Principles of European Tort Law (PETL), drafted by the European Group of Tort Law,[197] later stirred the broth still further.[198] In addition, regional collections are possible.[199] For a court or a legislator desiring to base its work on 'European principles' there are several collections to make use of. For a globally minded decision-maker, the UNIDROIT Principles of International Commercial Contracts (UPICC) that in many ways resemble the PECL, increases the choices.[200] The UPICC has already been published in four versions, each expanding on the previous version.[201]

Even though this multiplicity of collections complicates the choice for the decision-maker, it has the positive effect of pushing the user to avoid superficial recognition of some academic 'principle' without looking more closely at the elements of cross-border learning behind the principle. The competition between collections of

[190] Well analysed by Clive (2012).

[191] See Acquis Group (2007). I had the pleasure of participating in the work of this group.

[192] The outline edition was published in 2009: DCFR (2009).

[193] Beale (2011: 125) describes the more complicated structure of the DCFR.

[194] eg Grundmann (2008) and Schulze and Wilhelmsson (2008).

[195] Jansen (2011: 56).

[196] COM(2011) 635 final. See eg Dannemann and Vogenauer (2013). An offshoot of this work is the new Consumer Sales Directive, Directive (EU) 2019/771.

[197] See www.egtl.org.

[198] PETL has also been referred to in domestic legislation and case law, even in the famous *Urgenda* case (in its footnote 35), see eg Martín-Casals (2023).

[199] The Restatement of Nordic Contract Law, created by Lando et al (2016), has gained little attention.

[200] The use of UPICC as a source of law (in particular by arbitrators) is discussed eg by Heidemann (2007).

[201] The first version was published in 1994 (see eg Bonell (1994)) and the latest version is from 2016: www.unidroit.org/instruments/commercial-contracts/unidroit-principles-2016.

principles saves the dynamic of Europeanised private law. For good reasons, some have applauded the competition between legal ideas that the multitude of principle groups would result in[202] and have suggested a deliberate opening of the field for competition between different groups.[203] From the point of view of an experimentalist European private law, one should view the pluralism as an asset rather than a problem.

This does not mean, however, that the DCFR has minor relevance. In Europe one finds a growing number of court decisions in which the court expressly refers to the DCFR as an argument.[204] It is also increasingly common that legal scholars use the DCFR as part of their reasoning. Because of the academic origin of the DCFR and the general expectation that legal scholars should be forerunners in using comparative materials, it is natural to expect the scholarly use of the DCFR to offer the first sign of its relevance in a domestic context. Sometimes, however, the loop is started at the other end: scholars say they refer to the DCFR because the courts do so.[205]

Small narratives are developing and legal ideas are spreading through the collections of principles. The principle-creating groups have become considerable actors in Europeanised narratives. Scholars contribute to strengthening the impact of what the groups have achieved by discussing and analysing the collections on a kind of meta-doctrinal level.[206]

With regard to the learning function of the principles, one should note their peculiar status, combining comparative knowledge and legal-political decisionism. The creators of the principles constantly navigate between the existing law and a good law. Some are more inclined towards creating 'good law' in the societal sense, the best example probably being the European Social Contract Group (EuSoCo) and its Principles of Life Time Contracts,[207] whilst others seem more focused on a restatement-like endeavour, but all groups are clearly standing on both legs. In the diverse European private law landscape one cannot produce a 'restatement' without making choices.

The principle groups have made numerous choices among alternatives offered by the laws of the Member States. With regard to the learning a free movement of legal ideas could provide, the principles reduce the available experience. This reduction, however, is not necessarily bad as such. Legal research can efficiently contribute to the movement of legal ideas only by screening and choosing from the large bulk of available material. When evaluating the role of the principle groups, a key issue is therefore transparency.[208] How openly do the groups present the choices that they have made,

[202] eg Wagner (2003).
[203] eg Grundmann (2010).
[204] See eg Håstad (2015) and Samuelsson (2016) on Swedish courts, the latter claiming (2016: 209) that the Swedish and the Spanish supreme courts are the most active in this respect. See also Mossberg (2020: 214), with references, on the discussion in Sweden whether the DCFR should be termed a 'legal source'. In Finnish law, see eg the cases KKO (Supreme Court) 2015:26 and 2018:37. The latter case is particularly interesting as both the majority and the minority of the court referred to the DCFR, but partially to different provisions.
[205] See Samuelsson (2016: 212).
[206] See eg Jansen and Zimmermann (2018).
[207] Nogler and Reifner (2014).
[208] The importance of transparency with regard to rule of law is discussed further in ch 8.

and how well do they make clear the diversity prevailing in the national material? A reflective user has to be able to ascertain the depth of the comparative research that the principles are based on.[209] The accuracy and usefulness of the notes on Member State law that are published together with the principles[210] are of key importance in this respect. If the notes are clear and the reasoning concerning the choices is transparent, the use of the principles as learning vehicles is less objectionable.

If the principles are used as such, without reflection on the choices made, there is a risk for a 'blind' movement of sources, for an adoption of simplified solutions based on similarities on the surface level, without digging deeper into the legal-cultural layers and cultivating real plurality.[211] The principles can be used as a kind of easy 'shortcut to Europe'.[212] As the cost of information on comparative law is reduced by the DCFR,[213] there is an obvious risk that the principles will be used in such a superficial way.

A perspective that sees the suggested norms as an 'objective' product of experiences of national traditions distilled by 'pure science' is particularly worrying with regard to the need for a forward-looking approach. A less reflective direct use of the principles easily clashes with the need for dynamism in contemporary law. The *Professorenmodell* of the nineteenth century has indeed been criticised for being an outdated way of creating law in the twenty-first century.[214] As the basic ingredients for the new cocktail are taken from existing national laws, one could reasonably expect that the perspective would tend to look towards the past rather than the future. Learning through principles can have a backward-looking and static edge,[215] risking 'exacerbating petrification and obsolescence'.[216] This picture, however, is not unambiguous. For example, the Spanish Supreme Court seems to have used the collections of principles to modernise the application of the Spanish Civil Code.[217]

The potentially backward-looking character of the principles might be expected to strengthen conservative legal-political ideals. Such an assessment, however, is not self-evident either. Even some scholars committed to promoting social justice in private law have characterised the DCFR as fairly balanced, although there is still room for improvement.[218] Be that as it may, it is obvious that the principles contain important value choices that should be openly discussed in a decision-making that strives to be transparent.[219]

A similar demand for improved transparency and deeper reasoning can be made with regard to interdisciplinarity. The drafting groups have rightly been criticised for not making use of other social sciences when making choices.[220]

[209] Berger (2001: 883).
[210] The publications of PECL and DCFR contain such notes, whilst they are lacking in the global UPICC.
[211] Andersson (2016: 42).
[212] Samuelsson (2016: 212).
[213] Möslein (2010: 187).
[214] Micklitz and Cafaggi (2010: xxv–xxxii).
[215] Such criticism for being backward-looking is presented eg by Niglia (2006: 406).
[216] Möslein (2010: 187), concerning the DCFR.
[217] Trías (2018: 87–89); Requejo Isidro and Otero Crespo (2015: 558).
[218] Hesselink (2008: 85).
[219] Sefton-Green (2009) argues for openness concerning the moral-political dimension of the DCFR.
[220] See eg Grundmann (2010: 39–40) and Gomez (2010).

Even though one may claim that forward-looking learning requires cautiousness in the use of academic principles, this does not mean that one has to take a negative stance on the role of principles in the process of Europeanisation. As noted above, the assessments and choices made by experienced academics may assist legal decision-makers. In addition, the collections of principles are important as contributors to the creation of something that one could call a common European legal language. As Mark Van Hoecke and Mark Warrington have rightly underlined, the development of 'some conceptual meta-language' is a 'necessary condition for a real development of comparative law' and the development of such a language is the task of legal doctrine.[221] The idea of an experimental and cross-border learning law presupposes a minimum basis of understanding between legal players from different national environments, a common 'legal language'. It is not a question of pushing a common language in the linguistic sense – the strong position of the English language in the preparation and application of the principles has understandably been criticised[222] – but in a legal-cultural sense. By creating new legal concepts and agreeing on the understanding of existing ones, the drafters of the principles can contribute to cross-border understanding. The principles together with the notes on national laws can function as a kind of dictionary on Europeanised legal concepts.[223] Projects that formulate principles can in other words contribute to a conceptual basis for a fruitful European legal discourse.

An illustrative example concerning a conceptual decision by the principle creators that can facilitate the exchange of contract law experience across the borders is the introduction of so-called 'control liability' as a basis of liability in contract law. This rule was originally created as a compromise between common law and continental law in the UN Convention on Contracts for the International Sale of Goods (CISG),[224] but was included as the basis of contractual liability for all kinds of contracts in the PECL[225] and the DCFR.[226] The adoption of such a common starting point may also lead to the adoption of control liability in national contexts,[227] but even when this is not the case, it offers a common frame of reference when studying and discussing the experience of others. The concept facilitates exchange of experience on several levels of abstraction. As the definition of control liability is relatively flexible, it is open to a variety of more concrete assessments of the fair placement of risks in which it is possible to take into account national experiences. The definition of control liability offers both an object of comparison in relation to other possible forms of liability

[221] Van Hoecke and Warrington (1998: 525–26, 530).

[222] eg Sefton-Green (2008).

[223] Other projects have directly focused on creating uniform European terminology, see eg Ajani and Ebers (2005).

[224] Art 79(1): 'A party is not liable for a failure to perform any of his obligations if he proves that the failure was due to an impediment beyond his control and that he could not reasonably be expected to have taken the impediment into account at the time of the conclusion of the contract or to have avoided or overcome it or its consequences.'

[225] Art 8:108(1).

[226] Art III.–3:104.

[227] As has been done in the Nordic Sales Acts in the 1980s.

and a common language concerning how one should allocate concrete risks between the parties.

In conclusion, as long as the projects that develop principles produce 'soft law' and 'soft legal knowledge', they probably tend to facilitate the experimental and fragmented movement of ideas within the EU rather than hamper it, as a formally adopted code would do. The idea of a free movement of legal ideas does not imply any dissociation from European principle-building projects as such, as long as they do not result in a code-like legislation that would petrify the legal situation. If the collections remain as they are, simply competing academic collections (that may also be revised academically), they can be used as a legal-cultural support for deeper attempts to acquire learning across the borders.

VI. THE DIGITAL FUTURE

There is a growing number of cases that illustrate a horizontal movement of legal sources across borders, but in relative numbers such cases are still scarce. The idea of a learning European private law that can make extensive use of the experience of 27 legal orders still seems to belong to the sphere of the possible rather than of the real, even though the opportunities are increasingly made use of. However, the world is changing rapidly, and law is bound to change with it. The greatly enhanced opportunities that digitalisation brings with regard to accessing and processing foreign materials will no doubt encourage the development in a direction in which the free movement of legal ideas becomes closer to everyday legal reality.

The national doctrines of legal sources usually blend a descriptive and a normative account of the justification patterns of legal decision-making. They are both a description of how courts and other decision-makers tend to use sources of law and a corpus of source principles for good decision-making. The doctrines are therefore always to some extent dependent on how sources are actually used in domestic practice. When practice changes, the doctrine of legal sources will eventually change too. Practice again is not only changing because of theoretical advancement, but also due to practical convenience. It is well known that both decision-makers and scholars tend to prefer material that is within easy reach.[228] That is why digitalisation is bound to change both judicial and scholarly practice, and the practical changes must ultimately have an effect on the understanding of law and legal sources itself. The easier the access to foreign material becomes, the more our understanding of the deep divide between domestic law and foreign materials will be eroded.

The impact of digitalisation on law and private law has been discussed for decades. This discussion has to a large extent focused on substantive issues that are outside the scope of the present book. With regard to issues of legal method and decision-making, much interest has been devoted to the opportunities of automatised legal decision-making that artificial intelligence and machine learning are opening up.[229]

[228] See eg the Swedish survey by Sandgren (1999–2000: 592).

[229] See eg de Elizalde (2022) on opportunities for automated enforcement of EU consumer law.

Shorter steps in this direction can be taken through digital devices that offer automatised support for decision-making, by for example identifying potentially unfair clauses in standard form conditions.[230] Extensive databases and advanced management software products have been developed to support legal practice. The contemporary rapid advancement of artificial intelligence will undoubtedly increase the opportunities probably in ways that are hard to imagine.

In the present context, however, I will not delve into the complex issues of automatised decision-making. In practice, much of the development relates to routine cases in limited and specialised areas of law.[231] When I speak here about a learning law and a free movement of legal ideas, however, the searchlight is on hard issues. As mentioned above, the use of experience across borders involves societal analysis and legal-cultural understanding that one cannot easily infuse into automatised decision-making. In addition, even if the role of automatic legal decision-makers increases, one should bear in mind what I said above about the differences between the legal method used by a court and the opportunities that are available for legal research. The opportunities of automatic decision-making do not limit the scope of human scientific creativity.

I am here only looking at what impact digitalisation can have with regard to the use of legal sources across the borders. How can it improve the opportunities of horizontal legal learning in Europe?

In a way, my perspective is the opposite to that employed in the discourse on automatised legal decision-making. In this discourse the main question is in what ways digitalisation can replace or support traditional legal decision-making. One asks to what extent a machine can copy (and improve) the way in which a human decision-maker performs legal reasoning and uses legal sources. From this perspective, legal reasoning as such remains basically unchanged. My approach moves in the other direction: I will look at legal reasoning from the perspective of the available digital tools and ask how these tools might possibly change the ways in which legal reasoning is conducted. The focus is on whether and to what extent digitalisation affects the movement of legal ideas.

In legal literature, some scholars have discussed the impact of digitalisation on legal method, though the extent of this discussion seems much more limited than discussions related to substantive digitalisation issues and automatised decision-making. For example, in Europe, Giovanni Sartor predicted in 2011 that legal theory and legal informatics would be increasingly integrated in both directions, implying 'new models of legal reasoning'.[232] Christine Kirchberger has presented a vision concerning a step from a traditional doctrine of legal sources to a doctrine of legal information.[233] In the Nordics, Peter Blume in the 1990s posed the question: how does digitalisation change the sources of law?[234]

[230] See eg the interesting attempt to create such software by Micklitz, Palka and Panagis (2017).

[231] See also the US discussion on the lack of ability of a machine to produce hard analogical reasoning, Katz (2013: 956).

[232] Sartor (2011: 15).

[233] Kirchberger (2010).

[234] Blume (1999).

Digitalisation puts within easy reach many such sources that were previously difficult to access, such as case law from lower courts or decisions of various administrative bodies. This will have an impact on the use of legal sources and eventually change the prevailing doctrines of legal sources, depending on what was hitherto available in the national context. In the same way, digitalisation can affect the use of foreign source material and thereby have an impact on legal learning across borders. In her extensive paper on legal information management in the global and digital age, Claire Germain noted that 'The world is shrinking, and it is now difficult to distinguish between domestic and foreign and international law in a global setting.'[235] Peter Blume predicted in 1999 that the fact that international and foreign sources were becoming more easily available would lead to a decision-making pattern where solutions would be based on a combination of domestic and foreign sources.[236] This tendency that he could recognise with respect to international law would probably include foreign domestic law as well, even if this was not yet evident.[237] Even though one cannot yet note any dramatic change in this direction, increasing digital availability most certainly lowers the threshold for the 'lazy' lawyer to use cross-border material. Digitalisation supports the vision of a private law that is able to make good use of experimental learning across borders.

One reason why European private law is not there yet lies in the insufficiency of the available tools. With contemporary tools the practical threshold for using foreign sources is still relatively high. The development is rapid, however, and what is difficult today may be in use, at least by the avant-garde, tomorrow.

The first steps were taken decades ago. In the Member States the most important legal material is usually available in digital form. As the best databases in some countries are commercially operated, availability might be blocked by a paywall – even though access to legal sources should be free in a society based on the rule of law.[238] As open legal databases are made available not only by public authorities, but also by other agents like educational institutions, legal information institutes, professional associations and law firms, one could anyway claim that the most elementary level of digital service, the digital availability of legal material, is already by and large in order. There are also global collections of national databases, like the one offered by the World Legal Information Institute.[239] In some areas, for example concerning the CISG,[240] there are databases that connect national material from several countries.

More than this is needed, however, before digital tools can really contribute more deeply to the development of legal method. Improved availability is not the same as improved usefulness. The ease with which one can conduct a search in the various databases varies a great deal. Some databases only publish legal documents in their traditional form, in different formats, whilst other databases contain a plethora of metadata and hyperlinks. A lawyer who wants to use foreign material from different

[235] Germain (2007: 138).
[236] Blume (1999: 328).
[237] ibid (333).
[238] As underlined by the international Free Access to Law Movement, see eg en.wikipedia.org/wiki/Free_Access_to_Law_Movement.
[239] www.worldlii.org.
[240] www.cisg.law.pace.edu.

countries extensively encounters a lack of such joint standards and protocols that would make a broad search on European national solutions easy to perform. With regard to national decisions related to EU law the situation is somewhat better, as the EU law database Eur-Lex nowadays presents such material[241] and ACA Europe[242] runs a portal that provides access to national decisions on EU law.[243] In general, however, we have not yet reached the vision of a legal semantic web that would make national legal information from Member States available in automatically readable form for each and every one. The development is rapid, however, and what is not possible today may be commonplace tomorrow. Digital access and search functions that would boost the free movement of legal ideas are not a reality yet, but they are just around the corner. What today is happening in only a relatively few cases may then become a regular part of the lawyer's toolkit.

Artificial intelligence and machine learning are developing rapidly, continuously creating new opportunities. Legal information can to an increasing extent be processed automatically. Active work is being done, for example, on the issue how relevant legal arguments can be sought from corpuses of case law.[244] One can imagine what new approaches and questions such use of big data may open for European legal research. In the same way as 'digital humanities' has produced fascinating achievements within the humanistic disciplines, legal scholarship is bound to find new research challenges along this path. Many new perspectives are opening up for researchers who are willing and able to make use of the opportunities that increasingly present themselves behind the term big data.

Improved tools for access and process, however, cannot remove the need for creative legal scholarship. Such improvements do not solve all challenges with regard to the development of a European legal sphere that recognises the value of a free movement of legal ideas. The use of foreign sources in a way that means real learning requires an understanding of the sources in their context. This requirement relates both to linguistic and to cultural understanding.

As to linguistic access, the development of translation programmes based on machine learning are advancing so rapidly that the purely technical translation of a language will soon not be a problem. The development advances at a different speed related to different languages, with the smallest languages probably being the last to become accessible.

Linguistic access will not solve the challenge of cultural and legal-cultural understanding. Search tools and machine translation will not eliminate the problems related to this challenge. The discussion concerning the possibility of cross-border understanding continues to be topical in a developed digital environment. Sufficient cross-border understanding requires not only linguistic understanding, but also some kind of a culturally related 'common legal language'. In addition, as underlined several times above, a superficial automatic application of foreign legal sources removed

[241] Available at eur-lex.europa.eu.

[242] Association of Councils of State and Supreme Administrative Courts, which of course primarily focuses on public law.

[243] The database Jurifast, available at www.aca-europe.eu.

[244] Kerikmäe and Särav (2017: 212).

from their cultural and societal context does not lead to real legal learning. The learning process should involve a discussion of the sources both in their own societal context and in relation to the societal needs of the learning jurisdiction. These assessments also involve value judgements. In such an analysis, the opportunities offered by digitalisation might lead to the petrification of conservative solutions, as digitalisation increases the availability and statistically convincing nature of long-established practices.[245] Digital tools may on the other hand help to bring new forward-looking solutions from the cross-border material on the national legal agenda. Even in the digitalised world, such choices must be made.

Digitalisation, in other words, offers new opportunities for legal scholars interested in learning across borders, but it also carries new challenges. It brings to the table questions of method that are not necessarily new, but will receive considerably more weight in the digital environment. Above I noted how the increasing use of foreign materials questions the established methods of legal research that are based on an 'ideal of completeness', as the available foreign material is abundant and located within a field of fluid borderlines. When digital access advances, this challenge becomes much more serious. It forces legal research, even in the form of black-letter law, to look more closely at its methodological underpinnings.

As I noted above, the many alternatives that are available as source materials in a borderless legal environment underline the need for precise framing of research questions in legal research, including black-letter law. When digital opportunities increase, the need to think through the questions and transparently present them becomes even more pertinent. When one crosses national borders, does one do it in order to find good questions or good answers; does one seek guidance from authoritative sources that for some reason are considered to express an expert view; or does one seek in a critical approach the borderlines for what could be called the 'legally possible'? The choice of materials is at least partially dependent on the question posed.

The recognition of the need to make choices requires legal research to use more transparent relevance criteria. One has to be able to justify why the used material is interesting with regard to the research question. From where does one want to retrieve learning across borders and why – in particular when language abilities no longer play a decisive role? How does one select the cases or the legal literature one wants to consult – when availability is no longer a problem? Without diving deeper into this issue at this stage, I merely want to underline the value of explicitness and transparency concerning the choices with regard to both the relevance and the selection of material. As I explain in chapter eight, I regard transparency of legal reasoning to be a key mechanism for safeguarding the rule of law in today's fragmented legal culture.

The search in the wealth of available legal data is often conducted with the help of algorithms that the legal researcher does not completely master. In order to be able to evaluate findings critically, however, the scholar should ideally be able to look behind the veils of algorithms. Having said that, one has to admit that the ideal is increasingly difficult or even impossible to reach as the algorithmic

[245] See Blume (1999: 330). Algorithms that reproduce discriminatory structures in their training data is a good example of this, see eg Koulu and Pakaslahti (2018: 34–35).

solutions become ever more complex. Transparency with regard to search methods is a natural, but perhaps an impossible, requirement. What this means in a technological landscape that rapidly changes is hard to say. An illustrative example is the study of Henrik Palmer Olsen and Magnus Esmark on the question of to what extent algorithms can find legally important decisions of the European Court of Human Rights and thereby support traditional legal-dogmatic research. They note that the question how premise-based networks can work as a basis for legal-dogmatic research is still largely unexplored.[246]

Many questions with regard to the effects of digitalisation on legal reasoning are still open, and new questions will arise as technology advances. It is safe to assume that digitalisation will affect legal methods and legal research as the easy use of new source materials is gradually improved. As Kaarlo Tuori notes, digitalisation has 'a potentially revolutionary impact' on legal practices, but we can still only guess in what ways.[247] This also applies to the use of foreign legal sources and cross-border learning. In general terms it seems well-founded to expect digitalisation to facilitate and support the movement of legal ideas across borders. It can contribute to making the examples of cross-border learning more mainstream.

VII. CONTEXTUALLY ASSESSED AND EXPERIMENTAL LEARNING INSTEAD OF CREEPING HARMONISATION

As I stated earlier, learning across borders does not mean copying across borders. The societal context of the ideas to be moved and their suitability in the context to which they will be 'transplanted' have to be analysed and assessed. This means, among other things, a questioning of dogmatic and conceptual structures that hamper cross-border learning processes. In the previous chapter I noted the tendency and aspiration to steer legal language towards a language closer to real life. The need and pressure for such a development of contextual language is even stronger in connection with attempts to learn across borders. Real learning based on societal and cultural assessments often requires the framing of the issue in problem-oriented real-life language. As is very well illustrated by the *White v Jones* case, the willingness of a court (or a scholar) to transcend doctrinal categories can be essential with regard to the opportunity to fall back on sources from abroad. A pragmatic focus on the functioning of the legal system tends to lead the decision-maker to ponder how the factual problem at hand should be solved instead of diving into theoretical and systematical controversies.[248]

This does not mean, however, that all cross-border learning should take place in an extremely fragmented mode. A small Europeanised narrative may also contain borrowing and further development of conceptual fragments. The free movement of legal ideas includes the opportunity to move both legal concepts and principles.

[246] Palmer Olsen and Esmark (2018: 79). For a critique of their analysis, see Bogetoft (2020).
[247] Tuori (2021: 280).
[248] Berger (2001: 890). I will discuss the conceptual orientation towards 'real life' further in ch 8 section V.

These concepts and principles, however, do not necessarily remain on the same level of legal abstraction than those threatened by learning from abroad. Conceptual ideas may be problem-oriented and close to the concepts of real life.

The focus on problems rather than concepts does not imply a presumption that all problems are functionally similar across the borders. On the contrary, certain problems and functions may be so specifically linked to some jurisdiction that there is no room for movement of the solutions to other jurisdictions.

Some scholars understand, however, the growing number of examples of learning across the borders in the EU as steps towards a kind of 'creeping harmonisation'.[249] As the project for creating a European Civil Code has been buried, some have set their hopes on courts and scholars, suggesting that a similar result could be reached in a piecemeal fashion, through gradual adaptation of the national rules to an imagined European standard.

The basic ethos of such an idea is the thought that harmonisation is always 'good'. Small narratives that bring the laws of the Member States closer to each other would as such be 'good narratives'. The ethos would be the same as what on a more general level of globalisation is discussed under the heading of 'universalism'.[250] Both in German and English case law, judges have in various wordings recognised European harmonisation as a goal in itself.[251] The former President of the German *Bundesgerichtshof*, Walter Odersky, very clearly expressed his view in the 1990s that in their decision-making national courts should take into account the opportunity to serve European harmonisation and that the frequency of such reasoning should increase as European integration progresses.[252] Also scholars have advocated a movement in the direction of a new European *ius commune*.[253]

It is not self-evident, even in an ideologically pro-European approach, however, that harmonisation should be considered an ultimate goal in itself. As the strength of the European edifice and perhaps even the identity of the EU are built on the maxim 'united in diversity', this should also be taken seriously in the legal field.[254] In academic debate, the legal culture within the EU has indeed been described as a legal culture 'between Unity and Diversity'.[255] Rather than a one-way street, the intertwinement of the national and the European is pictured as a 'dialectics without synthesis'.[256] European harmony is not reached by unification but by accepting differences and by organising them.[257] The concept of 'reflexive harmonisation' is used to describe the need both for the contextual reception of rules across the borders and for

[249] The expression 'creeping harmonisation' is used by Lando (2000a: 359), who borrows 'creeping' from Berger (1999).

[250] See more closely below, ch 9 section V.

[251] See eg Berger (2001: 885–86).

[252] Odersky (1994: 2).

[253] eg Markesinis (1994: 2).

[254] The normative authority of this catchword is discussed in ch 9 section IV.

[255] Semmelmann (2014).

[256] Tontti (2001: 49).

[257] Delmas-Marty (1994: 184).

the reinforcement of necessary diversity.[258] Burkhard Schäfer and Zenon Bankowski eloquently picture the fundamental openness of private law in the EU:

> It will not be fixed in the unique equality of commodity exchange but will, in a never ending cycle, take the outside in and try to make it coherent. Thus the integration will always be in flux and the journey will never end.[259]

Mark Van Hoecke and François Ost have expressed the same sense of endlessness in theological-linguistic terms:

> In order to avoid a 'legal Babel', already superseded by the facts, or an utopic 'legal Esperanto', we need a constant dialogue between legal cultures, without a necessary final synthesis and unification of all these cultures.[260]

From the perspective of this work, it is easy to join the camp that does not regard harmonisation as a general and ultimate goal in itself. It would be contrary to the picture of contemporary legal development as small narratives proceeding without any strong master plan. Some, even many, narratives increase the level of harmonisation, but that does not rule out narratives proceeding in another direction. Understanding the EU as a laboratory in which national laws provide experience for an experimental development is not compatible with the ideal of a totally harmonised body of private law, at least if this would be of a comprehensive kind that resembles a civil code. Experimentation requires diversity and an opportunity to increase diversity when this seems justified. One may even claim that 'without diversity the stock of knowledge and experience on which the learning process depends is necessarily limited in scope' and therefore 'diversity of national systems is an objective in its own right.'[261] As Christian Joerges puts it, the task of European private law is to 'instigate innovation and change', not uniformity.[262]

The arguments that I presented in chapter two against a comprehensive European codification are in other words also applicable to the ultimate goal of creeping harmonisation. The force of these arguments, however, is obviously weaker in relation to creeping harmonisation than to fully fledged codification. Even though one could consider harmonisation to be an obstacle to experimentation, some argue that from an economic point of view one should not deem this argument to be decisive, as experience can be brought in from elsewhere and it is not necessarily more costly to change a harmonised rule.[263] In particular, creeping harmonisation can hardly be expected to result in a broad and comprehensive code-like structure that would be very difficult to amend. A partial harmonisation that is built on step-by-step learning would be more open to new narratives on change.

Even though harmonisation should not be seen as a goal in itself, there are in many cases good reasons speaking for a harmonised solution. The well-known general harmonisation arguments have their natural place in the assessment of the learning

[258] Andreadakis (2011). See also Schiek (2011: 446) ('reflexive convergence').
[259] Schäfer and Bankowski (2003: 504).
[260] Van Hoecke and Ost (1998: 215).
[261] Andreadakis (2011: 62–63).
[262] Joerges (2004: 195).
[263] Gomez and Ganuza (2011: 125–27).

one can bring in from other Member States. The facilitation of cross-border trade, the provision of equal conditions of competition as well as equality as to the level of protection, are relevant arguments when discussing harmonising solutions. However, they are not equally relevant in all kinds of cases. Instead of making harmonisation a goal in itself, one should rather use and assess the arguments in the specific context, in addition to the societal assessment that anyway has to be made when a legal idea is moved. Such reasoning would better fulfil the requirement of transparency that can be considered one of the safeguards for the rule of law in the contemporary state of uncertainty. Instead of justifying a decision or a standpoint with reference to an abstract goal of harmonisation, the decision-maker or the scholar can increase the transparency of reasoning by expressly arguing why a harmonised solution would seem important with regard to the issue at hand.

Even when a harmonised solution in the light of some argument would be recommendable, however, this does not necessarily help the legal actor to find the solution. Looking across the borders does not always offer any guidance as to what decision would lead to a higher degree of harmonisation. Only in cases where a majority of the Member States have adopted one solution would the adherence of a minority state to that solution obviously mean a step towards European harmonisation. As the variety of solutions on offer is usually much broader, the use of a harmonisation argument often brings little help to the decision-maker. In such cases, some might treat the various scholarly collections of European principles, like the PECL and the DCFR, as proxies for the 'European solution'. As the principles are by no means 'restatements' of what the national laws of the Member States contain, a superficial use of the decisions offered by the principles, without considering their background in various national laws, would not fulfil the ideal of transparency, as noted above.

In other words, harmonisation is just one goal among others that should be recognised in a small narrative on legal change. The value of experimentalism means that one should occasionally accept and cherish changes that might decrease the level of harmonisation. Some Member States may be more innovative concerning some legal issues than others and may function as forerunners for a new way of solving them. Such innovations, when they depart from what is the traditionally accepted view in most Member States, decrease the level of harmonisation. They might still be a valuable outcome of the experimental approach to private law.

An episode in Nordic legislative decision-making illustrates well such a thinking in which experimentalism rather than harmonisation is preferred. Large parts of private law have been very similar in the Nordic countries and the goal of Nordic harmonisation or even unification was widely accepted. The Helsinki agreement on cooperation between the Nordic countries from 1962 contained an express obligation for the Nordic countries to make their private laws as similar as possible.[264] However, when the political drive towards improving consumer protection was becoming important, this generally accepted ideal of harmonisation gave way to national experimentation. At the Nordic lawyers' meeting in 1972, the Swedish Minister of Justice, Carl Lidbom,

[264] Samarbetsöverenskommelse mellan Danmark, Finland, Island, Norge och Sverige (in Finland published in FördrS 28/1962), Art 4.

expressly argued that the traditional policy of identical legislation was less appealing in contemporary society, as politically controversial issues were usually not suitable for law drafting cooperation aiming at far-reaching harmonisation.[265] According to his opinion one country (read Sweden) could act as a pioneer and others learn from its experience; Swedish marketing legislation that was studied – and to some extent followed – by the other Nordic countries was a good example.[266] The other Nordic countries did use the Swedish experience, even though Lidbom's approach was not greeted with joy among Nordic lawyers. Swedish experimentalism moved things forward faster than a harmonising project would have done.

From the point of view of European harmonisation, the movement of legal ideas is a delicate exercise. If done well, it contains a transparent assessment of the societal issues involved, including the harmonisation arguments. A legal actor should not hide behind foreign authority, even when it appears as relatively harmonised, in order to disguise the fact that these operations are inevitably value laden.

The opportunity to look across the borders broadens the range of choices available for the decision-maker. References to foreign legal experience can be used to break up petrified structures of national law that hamper development. Foreign material may help turning a routine case into a hard one. Impulses from abroad might function as 'legal irritants' that can start processes of change in national law.[267] In this sense, the opportunity to use cross-border sources tends to enlarge the area of the legally possible.

The European twist, in other words, does not alter the moral responsibility of the legal actor to strive to contribute to well-argued 'good' small narratives.[268] What one should add when discussing the desirable qualities of a Europeanised legal decision-maker and scholar is an emphasis on open-mindedness.[269] In order to be able to enjoy the fruits of an experimental European law the legal actor should be open to impulses from other parts of the EU than the domestic jurisdiction. Openness and transparency are keywords when describing the *modus operandi* of a good contemporary European legal actor.

VIII. IN OTHER WORDS

The metaphor of law as a dynamic collection of small narratives on legal change gains new elements when one adds the European perspective. The opportunity to learn from legal experience across the borders illustrates concretely a way of fulfilling the learning function of contemporary law. The EU can in fact be described as a legal laboratory, making the experimental development of law in Europe possible. Europeans can make productive use of the diversity of their experience.

[265] Lidbom (1975: 53–59).
[266] ibid (68–69).
[267] Teubner (1998).
[268] As discussed in ch 4 section VII.
[269] Kahneman, Sibony and Sunstein (2021: 370): The best judges are 'actively open-minded'. E Mak (2013: 4, 102–09) has demonstrated that the individual judge's personal approach is 'a highly determinative factor' with regard to the use of foreign sources.

Europeanisation enlarges the cast of the narratives considerably. It adds to the picture European actors, such as the European legislator and the CJEU. These actors have their particular roles to play, and they might under favourable conditions support the modernisation of domestic laws.

In addition to the vertical learning processes steered by these actors, however, learning may also occur horizontally directly across the borders. Courts and scholars may use materials from other Member States in domestic legal reasoning. In this and the following chapters, the focus is on this kind of horizontal learning, as it represents the boldest step towards an efficient use of the experiences of the European laboratory. It more deeply challenges established conceptions of national law and legal sources. The catchphrase that I use in this context is the free movement of legal ideas.

In contemporary case law, one can find good examples of such free movement, but decision-making of this kind can hardly be called mainstream. Digitalisation, however, is improving the tools for access and use of sources across borders. The free movement sketched here happens occasionally today, but may be commonplace tomorrow. When digital development makes the available materials abundant legal reasoning must become more transparent when justifying the choice and selection of materials.

Even though courts and other decision-makers are in a key position with regard to the acknowledgement of foreign legal material as relevant sources, legal scholars play a crucial role in Europeanising legal discourse. They have the resources to become the main actors in creating a European legal culture that acknowledges the value of cross-border experience. Legal scholars have the ability to find, choose, conceptualise and contextualise useful foreign materials and discuss them in relation to the domestic context. The collections of European principles prepared by scholarly working groups is but one way of contributing to the cross-border discourse, and they should not be used in a superficial way.

Learning across borders does not mean a blind transplantation of ideas from abroad. True learning implies that foreign experience is understood in its legal, cultural and societal context and is assessed in relation to the conditions of the recipient Member State. The reliance on foreign sources does not relieve the decision-maker and scholar from making value judgements related to the use of the material. The personal moral responsibility of legal actors concerning how they contribute to the Europeanised narratives remains.

In making these decisions one should not understand harmonisation as a goal in itself. From the perspective of an experimental legal laboratory, diversity is also important. One has to assess concretely, in relation to each issue at hand, how to balance the need for harmonisation with the value of diversity in a Union 'united in diversity'.

6

The European Way – A Grand Narrative After All?

IN THE PREVIOUS chapters I described the dynamics of contemporary private law with the help of a metaphor of small narratives on legal change that are emerging, proceeding and coming to an end without any grand master plan. In such an understanding of law, Europeanisation is pictured as scattered pieces of European learning affecting the course of the narratives. New learning is acquired both vertically, within the European hierarchies, and horizontally, across the borders, but the learning does not necessarily push the decision-maker in any predetermined direction.

Is this, however, a good picture? The suggestion in the heading of the chapter – a European Way? – posits an alternative. It implies the possibility of grand European narratives on legal development. Could one imagine the emergence of some European grand narratives that have an impact on private law development in Europe?

The notion of a grand narrative refers to a structure of thought, an ideology or a theory that more generally would set the direction of the small narratives on legal change. The acknowledgement of such grand narratives would contradict the claim that there is no ready-made map steering the development. The small private law narratives would not be narratives on their own, but parts of a larger one.

In the search for such grand narratives, not every abstract idea that legal actors have referred to qualifies as a candidate. Legal decision-makers relay on many kinds of 'theories' that are natural parts of the small narratives. Only if the ideas are both sufficiently broad to offer a general picture of the direction of change and sufficiently concrete to determine the range of possible choices for a legal decision-maker or scholar one could call them grand narratives in the present sense. In addition, to refute the claim that a grand master plan is lacking they must be recognised as having enough argumentative strength to really influence development in a more or less coherent direction.

In this chapter, I will discuss some candidates for the position of European grand narratives. One may reasonably doubt, however, whether Europe is the right level for the search. Having recognised the central role of national legal cultures in the small narratives one cannot avoid asking about a possible role of domestic grand narratives. Legal actors in various Member States might rely on domestic grand narratives as master plans for developing their private law.

Noting this possibility, I will not here dive deeper into the variety of domestic legal narratives. Looking at the issue from a European perspective one can assume their force to be less than grand. An only domestically recognised grand narrative at least to some extent would collide with the impact of EU law. The existence of a domestic grand narrative would therefore hardly endanger the fragmentation thesis. In this context, it is also worth noting that the 'European' narratives that I analyse in this chapter (the European social model and fundamental rights) are also good candidates for domestic use. My reasoning concerning these narratives applies in both European and domestic settings.

I have here presented small narratives of learning across the borders as a fragmented approach to Europeanisation of private law. This implies that law becomes and should become 'more European' instead of remaining or becoming 'more national'. Is the analysis, in other words, based on a grand narrative in disguise, a grand narrative on Europeanisation? Below I will first discuss whether and in what respect a kind of grand narrative on Europeanisation forms a basis of this work, and what this starting point means with regard to my views on the development of European private law.

'Europeanisation' as such does not necessarily tell much about the content of the narrative. It only means replacing something 'national' with something 'European'. 'The European way', however, could be understood to have a societal content as well. Often one encounters a claim about the existence of a 'European social model' that has been able to combine market economy and welfarism in a unique European way. This claim is often used apologetically, implying a superiority of the European model. Be it as it may, the narrative on the European social model is told so often from both a leftist and a rightist perspective that it should be looked at as one of the candidates for the position of a European grand narrative with relevance also for private law.

In legal-societal discourse, one often encounters references to 'European values'. The interpretation of these may vary, but from a legal point of view, at least some elements are obvious. All states that wish to become members of the EU have to adhere to democratic principles, protect fundamental rights and comply with the rule of law. One could speak about the European 'Holy Trinity', consisting of democracy, human rights and rule of law.[1] These values are essential in any normative analysis of law in the EU, and they are and should be taken seriously as guiding values. They clearly belong to what Kaarlo Tuori has described as the deep structure of law that unites all Member States of the EU.[2]

Both democracy and the rule of law, however, are predominantly procedural values. They relate primarily to the procedures of decision-making, rather than to its content. Good things as well as bad things (as long as they are not extremely bad) can be made in a democratic procedure and be implemented through the rule of law. With regard to private law in particular, they do not define any substantive vision concerning the direction in which the law should be developed. They are not offering a decision-maker any substantive grand narrative behind which the decision-maker could hide in concrete private law decision-making. In fact, there is even a certain

[1] eg Weiler (2020: 96).
[2] Tuori (2018: 55).

tension between respect for democracy and the idea of a substantive grand narrative on the development of law. Some have on good grounds claimed that democratic decision-making is not compatible with the idea of one single value or principle guiding the decisions.[3] Democracy requires at least some pluralism.

The rule of law is of more direct relevance to this work. Related to values like legal certainty and predictability, as well as to lack of arbitrariness, it challenges the fragmentation and flexibility thesis. I have therefore devoted the next three chapters of the book to these challenges. In the chapters I discuss both how seriously legal fragmentation hurts the rule of law and what one can and should do to defend the rule of law (by increasing transparency) in the contemporary world of uncertainty.

The third leg of the 'Holy Trinity' – human rights or fundamental rights – relates to both procedure and content. The fundamental rights narrative is indeed a serious candidate to the position as a European grand narrative also in relation to private law. As the role of fundamental rights has been a prominent theme in private law discourse both on European level and on domestic level in many Member States, I have devoted the end of this chapter to a closer look at that narrative.

I. EUROPEANISATION AS A GRAND NARRATIVE OF PRIVATE LAW?

For several decades one could see Europeanisation as a grand narrative that steered much societal development in Europe. The narrative on ever deeper integration within the EU was combined with the narrative on enlargement, and the only question posed was often how to combine and focus the continuous processes of vertical and horizontal integration.

This is no longer the case. The EU is in a situation in which simultaneous processes of integration and disintegration occur. Influential nationalist movements, denying to varying degrees the value of Europeanisation, have taken root in most Member States. The ultimate expression of this is Brexit, but similar views have been voiced in other countries. Because of the problems connected with Brexit and due to the relatively high and growing popular support for the EU, many of the nationalist movements have toned down their aspirations of de-Europeanisation, but the fundamental ethos remains. The reactions of the Member State governments to the refugee challenge and the COVID-19 pandemic may even indicate a more general loss of pan-European solidarity. The war in Ukraine on the other hand seems to have strengthened the European cooperative spirit, but it is hard to predict its long-term effects. One can expect the Europeanisation narrative to be challenged by nationalist narratives in the future.

Europeanisation, however, does not lack supporters in social theory.[4] The giants of societal diagnoses, Ulrich Beck, Anthony Giddens and Jürgen Habermas, have suggested more Europe and deeper integration as the best solution for the perceived

[3] Hesselink (2021: 9).

[4] One of course also finds critique of the complacency of political and legal theory; see eg the critique by Joerges and Kreuder-Sonnen (2017) of the lack of response to the quasi-authoritarian emergency politics of the EU related to the financial crisis.

European crisis.[5] At least as a normative standpoint, as a possible alternative, the narrative of Europeanisation is still well and alive.

This work is built on such a positive approach to Europeanisation. In the introductory chapter, I expressly positioned this book as an analysis of the opportunities of a European-minded lawyer in the contemporary state of uncertainty. I understand this positioning, however, as a conscious normative choice. The commitment to the grand narrative on Europeanisation is of a normative nature, and one could equally well have toned down the European perspective. Making the roads by walking them,[6] one can choose to walk in the European direction. The scholar making this choice is certainly supported by many others walking in the same direction, even though the grand narrative on Europeanisation is hardly generally accepted within the European legal community.

Even if the narrative on Europeanisation were to be largely acknowledged, however, it would not necessarily offer the master plan that one would expect from a grand narrative. As I have argued previously, Europeanisation does not necessarily mean harmonisation. The vision of a Union 'united in diversity' cherishes difference as well as likeness. This goes for law in the same way as for other societal and cultural structures. This is why my commitment to Europeanisation has not prevented me from claiming that the idea of a European Civil Code is not in tune with societal reality and from refraining to see 'creeping harmonisation' as goal in itself. The key is only to embrace a European ethos in the legal activity.

In this view, diversity is not an evil as such. Some may even claim that the multi-level governance structure of the EU, with its pluralist and fragmented approach to law, is one of the advantages of the EU in the legal sphere. The breach of the positivist coupling between law and the national state opens up for more fragmentation and flexibility, as required by contemporary society. From a federalist point of view, such features would be regarded as temporary deficiencies in the EU that will be remedied in due course, but 'To the post-modernist, the polymorphic structure of the EU is simply the reflection of the post-modern condition, and quite likely permanent.'[7] According to this view, the idea of a unified harmonisation of the law of Europe may even be at odds with the basic function and idea of the EU itself. This pluralist ethos also relates to private law: 'there is no true way for the development of European private law in its multi-level environment. All is to play for.'[8]

If Europeanisation of private law does not mean harmonisation of law, or at least not only harmonisation, what do I refer to when speaking about a European ethos? In chapter five, I described it as an ethos that takes European experimentalism seriously, as a source of learning across the borders. Europeanisation in such a context means openness to new ideas, even when they originate in some other Member State. It is a state of mind that implies a willingness to listen to experiences of others and to make use of this learning. Such a grand narrative on Europeanisation is easy to subscribe to also if one is not a supporter of a wholesale European codification or harmonisation.

[5] Beck (2012); Giddens (2013); and Habermas (2012).
[6] Bauman (1995: 17).
[7] Caporaso (1996: 49).
[8] Weatherill (2011: 319).

A growing openness towards ideas and experiences across the borders requires European legal actors to develop at least some sense of a community. I am convinced that such a Europeanised community is emerging, both as a result of a more Europeanised legal education and as a consequence of continuous vertical interaction within the multi-level structures of Europe. As Michele Graziadei has shown, both extensive Europeanised scholarly work and case law from the European courts have led to a European legal consciousness in the fields of contract and consumer law that did not exist 30–40 years ago.[9] A grand narrative on Europeanisation as a growing willingness to listen, learn and interact across the borders is therefore not only a normative commitment of the author of this book, but also in many ways a realistic description of what is happening in European private law.

An obvious counter-argument to this rather optimistic view on Europeanisation relates to the variety of legal cultures in Europe. Even though the basic elements of the legal deep structure, like the rule of law and protection of fundamental rights, should prevail in all Member States, this does not change the fact that national legal cultures (and commercial cultures) differ in many ways. The basic cleavage between common law and civil law, which Pierre Legrand found so deep that for him a cross-border understanding was impossible,[10] is the paradigmatic example, but one can draw many other borderlines as well. Hans-W Micklitz eloquently contrasts the English model of private law, 'a liberal and pragmatic design fit for commercial use'; the French model, 'an intellectual political design of a (just) society'; and the German model, 'a paternalistic market design'.[11] Another variety, the particular nature of Nordic law, was also mentioned in the introductory chapter of this book. The previously socialist Member States may also retain elements of their legal culture that relate to their particular history. The possible differences between eastern and western EU might be more important than one can see[12] in the mainstream comparative discourse that emphasises German, French and English law. The examples of cultural borderlines could be multiplied. Would the vision of a European legal community not require at least an increasing harmonisation of legal culture?

In my understanding of Europeanisation, however, there is no necessary normative pressure towards a strongly harmonised legal culture. A Europeanised legal professional can well be able to combine this role with a national legal identity, as long as adequate cross-cultural understanding within Europe is possible. As was noted in chapter 5 section I, when discussing 'legal transplants', partial understandings are sufficient for creating a community. I believe in the possibility of sufficient partial understanding of this kind. The Trento Common Core of European Private Law project has clearly demonstrated that even though 'the differences that separate the common- and civil-law mentalities and cultures are irreducible and incommensurable, they nevertheless are not beyond the understanding of participants of both legal systems.'[13] If this is the case with regard to this traditionally deep legal-cultural divide, it is certainly also true for other legal-cultural borderlines within the EU.

[9] Graziadei (2016: 106).
[10] Legrand (1996).
[11] Micklitz (2018: 47–118).
[12] Kukovec (2015) presents a forceful argumentation for the importance of the centre-periphery divide.
[13] Curran (2003: 66).

Even though not normatively required, however, Europeanisation in the form advocated here may in the long run lead to some convergence of legal cultures. Understanding others and learning from them inevitably affects the understanding of one's own legal culture.

In this loose sense, this work is based on the normative choice of a grand narrative on Europeanisation. This choice, however, does not alter the picture of a private law that develops through small narratives without following some grand scheme. The narrative on Europeanisation in the form adopted here is a procedural narrative related to the ways in which European sources can be introduced in the small narratives. Openness and willingness to learn across European borders are key elements of the narrative on Europeanisation. Such an acknowledgement of the value of a free movement of legal ideas does not reveal much about the substantive content of the learning. Small Europeanised narratives may carry the private laws of the Member States in various directions in an equally fragmented manner as purely domestic narratives.

II. THE EUROPEAN SOCIAL MODEL AND PRIVATE LAW

The recognition of a European social model is another candidate for the position as a grand narrative. Could one draft such a model that could be used to push the development of private law in Europe in a more coherent direction?

At least until the financial crisis one version was obvious. It is not far-fetched to claim that the belief in a free globalised market represented a widely accepted grand narrative. Through the retreat of a diversity of values related to local societies and economies, the world experienced a belief in a relatively pure market-liberalist ethos on a global scale. This relatively unquestioned dominance of a global market ideology, however, came to its end in the financial crisis. Other phenomena, like the rising populism related to growing economic and social cleavages, added to the burden, and the collapse of international distribution chains due to the pandemic and the war in Ukraine brought in new question marks in the debate. Today an unqualified global free market narrative would probably only convince those who are already saved.

Some might describe this as an opportunity to renew the belief in some kind of European social model as a competitor to the capitalism of the US.[14] Traditionally in the Member States, and increasingly in the EU itself, the market approach has been balanced by aspects of welfarism, by interventions to support disadvantaged groups and to offer public services. The welfare state is basically a European invention. Even though the discussions on the 'crisis of the welfare state' have been going on at least since the 1980s, the welfare state is still a core concept in the political ideology of many European countries – perhaps with some doubt regarding some of the new Member States – and it also has a strong popular support.

This idea of a 'European social model' is reflected in the normative basis of the EU as well.[15] The Treaty itself sets the task for the Union to promote 'a highly competitive

[14] Rifkin (2004) emphasised the European dream in such a context.
[15] Damjanovic and de Witte (2008).

social market economy, aiming at full employment and social progress, and a high level of protection and improvement of the quality of the environment.'[16] One could claim that market economy combined with welfarism is a part of the European identity, a part of the narrative of Europe.

On the other hand, in the context of the EU, one could also claim that the market narrative is strongly emphasised by the internal market agenda that is a hallmark of the Union. One cannot deny the particular 'constitutional' position of internal market arguments in the European Union, as the Union is built on the recognition of the four freedoms, with implications on private law as well.[17] Some have indeed argued that the idea of a functioning market can be understood as an unwritten fundamental right in line with other fundamental rights.[18] One could accordingly see the narrative of the internal market as the grand narrative of European law. Market integration would be the basic principle on which the norm-production of the EU rests.[19]

However, this does not necessarily imply that one has to understand the market narrative as the only or the dominating narrative in the context of EU law.[20] Market integration is not the same as a free market. Some have argued that the European economic constitution as a whole is rather pluralist and does not favour any particular socio-economic paradigm,[21] allowing for very different approaches to regulation. In fact, when looking at what the internal market agenda has meant with regard to regulation, it was already in the 1990s characterised as a 'Janus-face'.[22] As it balances between dismantling national mandatory rules that can constitute barriers of trade and harmonising such mandatory rules in the interest of weaker parties such as consumers, it produces both market-liberalising rules and mandatory rules of the welfarist type. In the present Treaties, the position of the welfarist elements has been strengthened, meaning that the Janus-face is expected to look at the social more often or more deeply than before. Even in the much-debated *Laval*[23] and *Viking Line*[24] cases in which the CJEU seemed to favour a liberal free movement agenda to the detriment of social rights of employees, the result was based on a social rhetoric and balancing of the clashing values.[25] The internal market agenda, in other words, is not a grand substantive tool that could remove the need for contextually geared welfarist private law narratives. It rather adds a new and complicating element to the small narratives. Much of what is said at the end of this chapter on the role of fundamental rights in the small narratives also applies *mutatis mutandis* to the four freedoms.

[16] Treaty on European Union, Art 3(3).

[17] See eg Remien (2003).

[18] Pöyhönen (2000: 82).

[19] eg Franck (2006: 433). For a critique of the presumed dominance of an 'internal market rationality', see Bartl (2015).

[20] See also Mulder (2018), arguing for 'a dialogue of mutual responsiveness' regarding social legitimacy in the internal market (discussing free movement law, competition law and state aid law).

[21] Kaupa (2016).

[22] Reich (1993: 45) on European consumer law.

[23] C-341/05, ECLI:EU:C:2007:809.

[24] C-438/05, ECLI:EU:C:2007:772.

[25] See eg Reich (2008). Kukovec (2015: 424 *et seq*) argues that the cases rather reflect the conflict between centre and periphery, obscuring the concerns of the periphery.

However, even if one could recognise a European social model built on market economy and welfarism, it would not help much in the search for a European grand narrative on the development of private law. It is difficult to draw conclusions from such a social model on the desirable substance of private law, because of the inherent tension between market and welfare in the model. The tension makes it possible in principle to derive many kinds of private law regimes – ranging from relatively liberalist to relatively welfarist – from the same general model. The social model does not offer sufficient guidance, as it combines a belief in market forces creating the economic basis of the welfare with interventions in the market to support redistribution and social security, without specifying, in what ways and by what legal instruments the interventions should be made. The social model therefore does not require, even though it supports, a private law influenced by welfarist goals, protecting weak parties. One could also imagine, at least in theory, a welfare state that tries to reach its goals by a market-oriented contract law combined with a redistributive social security and tax legislation.

The loose coupling between the European social model and private law is illustrated by the private law options available in the processes of privatisation and marketisation, through which the relationship between state, market and civil society has been reorganised in many Member States. Public functions have been relocated to private bodies and market-oriented steering mechanisms have been introduced in the public sector, resulting in a more disintegrated and partially privatised welfarism, sometimes called a welfare mix or a welfare pluralism. Interestingly, the consequences for private law of this alleged dismantling of the welfare state vary.[26] One would assume that market-liberal societal reforms would walk hand-in-hand with a more market-liberal private law, and many examples affirm this assumption. A clear-cut example is the reduction of the protection of tenants in contracts for lease of dwellings related to the liberalisation of the housing market in Finland as well as in some other Member States. Market-liberal reforms, however, may also push private law in the other direction. A privatisation of public tasks, moving them to become offered on a contractual basis, often requires stronger mandatory private law rules as a counterweight.[27] More broadly, if the direct public steering of private activities is decreasing, there is an increasing demand for private law to fill the perceived gaps. Private law rules and litigation can be used as an alternative to public law regulation. By noting this pressure towards more welfarist functions of private law, I do not want to claim that the use of private law for this task would be more efficient than the public law approach. I just want to illustrate that the coupling between the social model and private law is not straightforward. A profoundly market-liberal societal approach does not necessarily imply only market-liberal solutions in private law.

The juxtaposition of market and welfarism has been typical for many descriptions of private law. As mentioned already before, the development of contract law has been pictured with the help of dichotomies like freedom and solidarity,[28] individualism and altruism[29] and market-individualism and consumer-welfarism,[30] to mention

[26] See eg the collection of essays Wilhelmsson and Hurri (1999).

[27] In the Nordics, see eg the early analysis by Stridbeck (1992) of the electricity contract.

[28] Unger (1983: 616 *et seq*).

[29] Kennedy (1976: 1713 *et seq*).

[30] Adams and Brownsword (1987: 52 *et seq*).

only a few.[31] This dualism continues also in contemporary European discourse on the development of private law. Even though the expressly formulated leading principles of the Draft Common Frame of Reference – freedom, security, justice and efficiency[32] – seem to emphasise the market-liberal narrative – and this may be one reason why the DCFR has been criticised for being conservative and out of tune with modern European contract law[33] – one also finds the mandatory provisions of the *acquis* included in the rulebook. Despite its leading principles, the DCFR has not been able to avoid the challenge of balancing market and welfarism. Even the DCFR discusses the principle of solidarity and social responsibility as well as the principle of protection and promotion of welfare as possible overriding principles 'of a high political nature'.[34]

This duality of the pressures on private law has long roots[35] and the discourse on the issue points in many directions. If looked at from a perspective that also includes national models, the European social model is vague. The implicit 'European economic constitution' is incomplete.[36] Also within the EU, one encounters several varieties of capitalism[37] that balance market and welfare in various ways. In building the model, one cannot overlook the social, economic and cultural differences between Member States. In the context of each Member State, the tradition against which the direction of a change should be assessed is not the same. There are clear differences between the private laws of the Member States with regard to the balance between the two poles.[38] Therefore, the general model does not offer a blueprint for the development of private law. It keeps the doors open for many kinds of small narratives and the tension between conflicting goals may even broaden the area of the legally possible. Within the dichotomy of the social model, steps both in a welfarist direction and towards market-rational ideals are possible.

This is how the situation looks like from the point of view of a detached observer. Normatively, however, one may opt for promoting a grand narrative on change that proceeds towards one of the poles of the dichotomy. One may strive to promote market-liberal ideals in private law or attempt to further a welfarist vision. Could one sketch such grand narratives with a capacity to steer concrete legal development that a legal actor could deliberately choose to use?

Looking first at the market-liberal narrative, one could claim that private law, or at least contract law, could be coherently built on market-liberal ideals, as these are the rules that constitute the market.[39] Indeed, in the discourse concerning a European civil code some seemed to have such an agenda: a European codification was seen as

[31] For more examples, see above ch 2 section V.

[32] DCFR (2009: 60).

[33] Hesselink (2011).

[34] DCFR (2009: 14–16). Why these are more 'political' than the others is not explained.

[35] A classic text on the social role of private law: von Gierke (1889; in English 2018).

[36] Collins (2009a: 82).

[37] On varieties of capitalism see Hall and Soskice (2001), and for Europe eg Nieminen (2005: 157 *et seq*) and Zumbansen and Saam (2007).

[38] See eg Lurger (2002: 217).

[39] In this context I pass over the fact that in the legal sphere the market narrative suffers from an unavoidable circularity: as the market is constituted by its legal ground rules – there is no market without such rules – the ground rules cannot, at least in their entirety, be deduced from the idea of the market they constitute.

a way of restoring the right balance between the rules for standard cases honouring private autonomy and the exceptional cases of the *acquis*.[40] This normative position is possible, and it can be supported with concrete examples, for example related to the deregulation of the housing market.

The choice of a market-liberal narrative, however, does not relieve the decision-maker from the pain of taking a stand on concrete issues. Default rules may also have various ethical roots. Also within the commercial sphere, one finds various 'sub-cultures' with different understandings of morally acceptable behaviour. There is a general tension, for example, between rules that further co-operation and rules that reward self-interest. In Europe, English law is considered to be in the more competitive camp,[41] whilst German law attaches relatively greater weight to cooperative behaviour. These cultural differences are reflected for example in different attitudes towards pre-contractual information duties and good faith.[42] The often cited remark by Lord Ackner in *Walford v Miles*[43] that 'the duty to carry on negotiations in good faith is inherently repugnant to the adversarial position of the parties when involved in negotiations' is easy to contrast with more cooperative approaches to contracting on the continent. This and many other examples show that even the market-liberal narrative is not an identical European one, but at least partially path-dependent on national traditions. A market-liberal vision of private law in other words cannot offer a ready-made master plan for European legal development, as the commercial cultures and the understandings of market-rationality vary. Even if one would lean more in the direction of market-liberalism than I personally find necessary, one cannot escape the need for pragmatic contextual assessments.

It would anyway be difficult to formulate a credible one-sided market-liberal grand narrative, taking into account the nature of the *acquis* and the development of fields like consumer law already during the last century. Contemporary legal experience in Europe does not support an approach, in which one sees market-liberalism as the only key to coherence. The European legislative interventions in contract law have been focused on mandatory regulation.[44] In addition, not only the legislator has demonstrated some degree of social ethos. During recent years the strong and persistent interventions by the CJEU in order to protect consumers against unfair terms – and against harsh consequences of the financial crisis – have almost become a paradigmatic example of social responsiveness.[45]

The value of a purely market-liberal vision as a normative grand narrative is in other words limited. What about the other alternative, a welfarist grand narrative of private law? Would it be possible to create a grand narrative that in a coherent fashion could guide the small narratives in a welfarist direction? As the development of contemporary private law in Europe includes many examples of advances in this direction, I will look more closely at this alternative in the following.

[40] So Tilmann (1993: 278).

[41] Perhaps because its main focus is on contracts between businesses of some size; so Beale (2018: 22–23).

[42] See eg Brownsword, Hird and Howells (1999).

[43] [1992] AC 128, 138.

[44] See eg the many analyses of justifications of limits to party autonomy in Grundmann, Kerber and Weatherill (2001).

[45] See eg Beka (2018); about the financial crisis (2018: 359).

III. VARIETIES OF WELFARISM AND PRIVATE LAW NARRATIVES

To say it from the start: it is hard to imagine a coherent model for a completely welfarist private law. The tension between welfarist regulation and market-liberal rules requires a balancing act that easily becomes fragmented and contextual, as was noted above. However, if one could construct a coherent theory of welfarism behind the various interventions, one could at least limit the sphere of alternatives available in the balancing.

A coherent narrative on welfarist private law would require a coherent idea of the welfare state as a starting point. The idea of the welfare state, however, is a blend of several elements such as guaranteeing the members of the society a minimum standard of income, protecting them against some of the uncertainties in life and offering them some social services.[46] These elements appear in different combinations and proportions in different Member States. Some, like the Nordic ones, have traditionally been public service states, whilst others lay stronger emphasis on income transfers.[47] There is no general blueprint of a European welfare state, but only a situation of family resemblance between the welfarist Member States.

The European idea of the welfare state, in other words, is too vague to provide decision-makers with the tools that they need for an analytical discussion of welfarism in private law. In addition, the welfarist ideals relate to features not closely connected with the private law discourse. The ideals leave room for a large spectre of varieties of welfarism in private law. In other words, one cannot create a grand narrative of welfarism in private law based on the general ideals of the welfare state.

Instead, one could look at the concrete development of private law in the search for a possible grand narrative of welfarist private law. Also this endeavour, however, is challenging. Already terminologically, one can sense the challenges. As has been noted before, the headings under which the authors describe a possible welfarist paradigm, vary. Some speak generally about 'social justice'.[48] Within contract law, other variants are for example 'contractual solidarity'[49] or a 'principle of regard and fairness'.[50] What term one wants to use is primarily a question of convenience. Linguistically, 'social justice' is probably broader than 'welfarism', as it may contain also other forms of justice than those intuitively connected with welfarist thinking. I have here preferred to use the term 'welfarism', both to express the connection to the ideals of the welfare state,[51] and to delimit the elements to include in the search for a European welfarist narrative.

The creation of a welfarist narrative based on existing legal materials requires a definition of the elements that should be included in the welfarist paradigm. The views on this issue are probably diverging. Looking at contract law, one should at least include two kinds of rules: first, rules that aim to protect the weaker party in a contractual relationship (including a party who aspires to enter a relationship); and,

[46] Eräsaari (1984: 113).
[47] A detailed discussion concerning the different welfare state models can be found eg in Kosonen (1994: 60 *et seq*).
[48] eg the Study Group on Social Justice in European Private Law (2004).
[49] Lurger (1998).
[50] Lurger (2011).
[51] Also Micklitz (2011: 3–4) expressly relates social justice in private law to the rise of the welfare state.

secondly, rules that aim at the advancement of some public goal, such as protection of the environment (if the public goal can be termed welfarist). In other parts of private law, the welfarist elements may be described differently. In tort law, for example, instances of strict liability and obligatory insurance may be good examples of welfarist rules, at least to the extent that they aim to protect vulnerable persons (or ordinary persons) or to further public goals.[52]

Such a vague description of welfarism in private law, however, is not sufficient to guide the classification of private law rules as 'welfarist'. What in one perspective appears as a welfarist measure may from another welfarist point of view be regarded as problematic depending on how one defines the weaker party. Many information requirements are of this kind. Mandatory rules that oblige a bank to give certain information to consumers when concluding credit contracts could be classified as welfarist, as they aim to improve the position of the consumer in relation to the creditor. From the point of view of distributive justice, however, such rules may be less welfarist, as they rather improve the position of strong consumers. Fifty years ago studies showed that the improvement, if any, of the interest awareness due to truth-in-lending regulation seemed to be concentrated in higher-income groups[53] and that credit shopping induced by the regulation occurred to a greater extent among these groups.[54] In so far as information regulation in practice benefits the rich more than the poor, it appears as counterproductive in a distributive understanding of welfarism.

This small example illustrates the difficulties in building a coherent vision of a welfarist private law. The welfarist bag can be filled with various elements that are not necessarily based on similar ideals concerning the needs of weaker parties and the understanding of public good. I will illustrate this with a short description of an analysis of varieties of welfarism in EU contract law that was published in 2004.[55]

In the paper, I analysed the varieties of welfarism with the help of five dichotomies,[56] reflecting features that have been important in the development of welfarism in EU contract law. Based on these categories, I constructed a welfarist assessment scheme, distinguishing six types of contract law welfarism:

1. Market-rational welfarism	Regulation aimed at improving party autonomy and the function of the market mechanism (eg disclosure and transparency rules)
2. Market-rectifying welfarism	Regulation aimed at rectifying outcomes of the market mechanism in order to promote acceptable contractual behaviour (eg substantive fairness rules and substantive mandatory rules)
3. Internally redistributive welfarism	Regulation aimed at redistributing benefits in favour of the weaker party in a contractual relationship (eg rules affecting the price and the main subject matter of the contract)

(continued)

[52] Keren-Paz (2018) argues for an egalitarian tort law that should be instrumentalist, pluralist, contextual and progressive.

[53] Whitford (1973: 414).

[54] ibid (418, 420).

[55] Wilhelmsson (2004). The scheme has been developed further by Reich (2014: 34–36).

[56] Market-rational regulation/market-rectifying regulation, commutative justice/distributive justice, internal perspective/external perspective, ability-orientation/need-orientation, and protection of parties/protection of other values.

(Continued)

4. Externally redistributive welfarism	Regulation aimed at redistributing benefits in favour of the disadvantaged in comparison with the better off, within a group of contract parties in similar situations (eg equality rules)
5. Need-rational welfarism	Regulation aimed at giving benefits to parties with special needs in comparison with other parties in similar situations (eg rules on *social force majeure*)
6. Public values welfarism	Regulation aimed at giving contract law protection to interests and values not directly related to the parties (eg protection of environmental values and human rights)

The list starts from the type of welfarism that is most closely linked to traditional market-liberal contract thinking and it proceeds towards more clear expressions of welfarism. As I showed in the paper, all the boxes are in use in EU contract law or domestic contract laws or both, in various combinations.

When discussing the level of welfarism, the strictness of a legal measure is also relevant. For example, when discussing externally redistributive welfarism the goals can be set at various levels. Even though EU regulation on discrimination in various forms is fairly dense, making it possible decades ago to formulate a European principle of non-discrimination,[57] this does not necessarily imply a fight against discrimination on economic grounds.[58] However, some have read the introduction of the concept 'vulnerable consumer' in the Unfair Commercial Practices Directive[59] as a kind of recognition of the relevance of economic discrimination in EU private law.[60] In addition, the privatisation of public services has further pushed EU to regulate access to such services in a non-discriminatory fashion, implying a combat against economic discrimination.[61]

Obviously, the range of possible public values welfarism is also broad and cannot easily be defined. One can find, for example, occasional discussions on whether environmental reasons could be used to constitute non-conformity according to the original Consumer Sales Directive;[62] in the new Consumer Sales Directive 'durability' is mentioned in this context, as 'longer durability of goods is important for achieving more sustainable consumption patterns'.[63] The commitment of the EU to climate goals is changing the picture and sustainability concerns are now entering contract law discourse more broadly on European level.[64] Micro-political climate change litigation will probably bring these concerns more visibly on both the EU and the national agendas.

[57] eg Schiek (2000). In his recent study of the politics of justice in European private law, Micklitz (2018: 161–279) has considered the provisions against discrimination in EU law to be a hallmark of the EU regulation.

[58] *cf* Caplovitz (1963): 'the poor pay more'.

[59] Art 5 (3).

[60] In her interesting analysis of consumer vulnerability in mortgage contracts Domurath (2017) discusses, for example, the position of 'low-net-worth consumers' (2017: 116).

[61] Micklitz (2018: 277).

[62] See eg Rott (2003) and Wilhelmsson (2004a: 233–235) with further references.

[63] Directive (EU) 2019/771, Preamble at 32.

[64] See eg Eftestøl-Wilhelmsson (2016); Demeyere and Sagaert (2020); and Schirmer (2021).

The analysis of the varieties of welfarism in EU contract law highlights the difficulties of constructing, even normatively, a coherent grand narrative on welfarism that would be sufficiently concrete to limit the range of available choices when developing the law. When one adds the domestic Member State layer to the picture, it becomes even more blurred.[65] Welfarist contract law is based on a variety of different interpretations of welfarism that cannot easily be combined into a coherent edifice. Adding other areas of private law obviously increases the range of possible combinations. The welfarist approach is 'unlikely ever to attain the consistency of its market-individualist rival.'[66] The choice of a welfarist narrative does not relieve legal actors from the need to take a stand on topical questions on a contextual basis.

As mentioned above, however, Hans-W Micklitz has recently published an impressive attempt to construct a comprehensive picture of 'the politics of justice' in European private law, with the concept of 'access justice' in the centre. He draws a picture of the EU moving from a common market towards 'an Internal Market with a social outlook'[67] – what in the terminology of this book could be called a welfarist internal market. Micklitz constructs a 'Post-Classical Private Law', a 'Tripartite Private Law Order',[68] built on three pillars: first, on the universal service obligations that reflect access justice; secondly, on the law on the consumer and labour market that reflects both access justice and social justice; and, thirdly, on the societal private law that 'is the laboratory that is about to contribute to European society building'[69] and reflects societal justice. The structure resembles a proposal for a grand narrative on welfarist private law in the EU. Even though it offers much inspiration for a welfarist agenda, however, it is hardly sufficiently concrete to determine the range of possible choices for actors involved in developing private law in Europe. There is also a tension between the two expressions of welfarism, between what Micklitz calls social justice and access justice,[70] that challenges the use of the model as a grand narrative. The tripartite private law order rather looks like a well-systematised private law toolbox that offers many kinds of useful instruments for private law change rather than a narrative that would determine the use of the various tools. The order is also expressly related to EU private law only, whilst the national narratives may follow other lines. This is also acknowledged by the author. Despite his model-building, he describes European private law as 'highly fragmented' and EU law as not being 'bound and tied to thinking and operating in legal boxes' and having an 'innovative character'.[71] Micklitz in other words does not offer his systematisation as a steering grand narrative that would eliminate the variety of available small narratives. His path-breaking analysis of access justice rather broadens the area of the legally possible in a new welfarist direction.

Another interesting attempt to define normatively welfarism in European contract law is presented by the European Social Contract Group (EuSoCo). It proposes that

[65] On the absence of a European model of social justice in private law, see Comparato (2014: 161–68).
[66] Adams and Brownsword (1987: 165).
[67] Micklitz (2018: 276).
[68] ibid, Part III.
[69] ibid (359).
[70] Tuori (2014: 399) shows how the European access justice threatens 'national solidaristic social justice'.
[71] Micklitz (2018: 392–93).

one should choose the rules governing social long-term contracts, like consumer credit contracts, labour contracts and tenancy contracts, as the starting point for the development of European contract law.[72] As the principles elaborated by the Group are very general, and cover only a limited area of private law, they cannot really aspire to reach a position of a grand narrative in the sense that this concept is used here. The proposal, however, opens up yet another new path of possible development that broadens the alternatives available for the legal decision-maker and the scholar.

Martijn Hesselink has recently published a proposal concerning a progressive European code of private law. In this revival of the European Civil Code debate, however, the code would look very different than traditional codes. The proposed mandatory and constitutional European code would consist of fundamental principles instead of detailed rules, and it would be radically democratic instead of technocratic. It would be based on 'justice' rather than economic growth.[73] This proposal indeed looks like the missing grand narrative of European private law. However, even though the proposal is appealing, it is not yet convincing as a grand narrative.[74] The system of fundamental principles is presented only in very general terms: the code should be based on substantive equality and autonomy, and it should be based on both distributive and relational justice.[75] The potential tension between democratically adopted principles and social principles is also not solved, even though Hesselink sees the problem and discusses the issue.[76] The relatively few fundamental principles that Hesselink envisages[77] may function as triggers for various good small narratives on changes in private law rather than as a comprehensive model for the development. In this sense he might not be far away from his inspirer, Katharina Pistor, who proposes incremental changes, 'roll-back strategies', of various kinds – in my terminology 'small narratives'[78] – to counteract what she calls the code of capital.[79]

The fact that welfarism in private law cannot be reduced to one coherent formula may be disturbing from the point of view of those who defend a systematic development of private law. However, the goals of welfarism may in fact be better off in a more fragmented approach. As the needs of the weak and the vulnerable are evolving and public values are changing, the pursuit of welfarism requires an experimental law. The solutions are too decisionistic to be carved in stone once for all. The input from national level is also important, in order to keep the experimental progression going.

Even though it is hard to imagine a coherent narrative of welfarism that could offer a solid ground for developing EU private law, welfarism, in all its varieties, occupies an important normative place in the European project. Welfarist arguments should have a considerable weight in the processes of Europeanisation. It is legitimate to

[72] Nogler and Reifner (2014).
[73] Hesselink (2022), as summarised on (2022: 343).
[74] See also the critique by Beckers (2022), who shows how legal institutions are both dynamic and conflictual and do not serve only one interest.
[75] Hesselink (2022: 323, 327).
[76] ibid (328), relying on Habermasian democratic deliberation. See also Hesselink (2021: 107–08) on this tension in the recent French reform of contract law.
[77] Hesselink (2022: 326): a 'few dozen'.
[78] The strategies include the familiar elements claims for compensation, punitive damages and class actions, Pistor (2019: 227), and they might be implemented gradually, 'one step at a time' (2019: 233).
[79] ibid (224–29).

choose the welfarist perspective as an agenda-setter for the flexible learning processes through which European private law is developed – but the choice does not relieve decision-makers from the responsibility to assess contextually what kind of welfarist solutions it seems appropriate to promote.

> The lawyers' cry echoes from afar: what are the (right) answers? Which values shall we adopt and which distributive consequences are preferable? This is the democratic and European challenge we have to face.[80]

IV. FUNDAMENTAL RIGHTS AS THE LAWYER'S GRAND NARRATIVE?

The decline of the authority of ethical systems and ethical expertise does not eliminate the discourse on ethical systems that would suit the world of today. The candidates are many. From a legal point of view, the most important of these endeavours is the attempt to systematise societal ethics in the language of human rights. The doctrine on human rights aspires to occupy a central place in an ethical world order. Realistically, there is a weak basis for any real global consensus, as the acceptance of human rights in many countries seems more rhetorical than real. It even seems that the weight of human rights thinking during the last decade has been shrinking, as there has been a backlash towards authoritarianism in many countries. However, within the European Union there is a relatively broad agreement concerning these issues, first based on the European Convention on Human Rights. The fundamental rights were expressly included in the EU *acquis* by the European Court of Justice.[81] Then, in the year 2000, in connection with the Treaty of Nice, the Charter of Fundamental Rights of the European Union was adopted. The Charter applies to the EU institutions and bodies and to Member States when they implement EU law.[82]

The COVID-19 pandemic has brought the fundamental rights discourse even more strongly on the agenda. National measures to fight the pandemic could endanger fundamental rights of the citizens. Many debates on the measures have focused on how to balance the emergency requirements and the need to secure fundamental rights.

In a traditional private law discourse, respecting the public/private divide, the emphasis on fundamental rights in the legal-ethical debate could have passed without considerable attention. In contemporary law, however, there has been a remarkable change in the discourse patterns. Private law doctrine and practice increasingly use fundamental rights arguments, be it in the form of a direct or an indirect horizontal effect.[83] The scholarly discussion of this issue had become intense already in the beginning of the present century.[84]

The pioneering theses by Olha Cherednychenko and Chantal Mak brought the issue more firmly on the European agenda,[85] and the debate has continued

[80] Sefton-Green (2006: 286).
[81] See already *ERT*, Case C-260/89, ECLI:EU:C:1991:254, [41]–[45].
[82] Art 51. On how this connects the Charter to EU contract law, see eg Collins (2017a: 11–16).
[83] On the various forms of horizontal effect (in European private law), see eg Besson (2009: 24–30).
[84] See eg Canaris (1999); Friedmann and Barak-Erez (2001); C Mak (2004); Simon (2004); and Wright (2001). In Finland there has been much debate as well: eg Pöyhönen (2000) and Länsineva (2002).
[85] Cherednychenko (2007) and C Mak (2008). See also eg Hesselink (2003).

ever since.[86] Fundamental rights reasoning has become mainstream also among scholars of private law, to the extent that some speak about 'constitutionalisation of private law'.[87] The use of the Charter of Fundamental Rights has been said to 'represent a profound change in the rule of recognition' in the Member States of the EU.[88] In case law, the CJEU has recurrently made use of the Charter in private law cases, for example of the rule on effective judicial protection.[89] 'The Fundamental Rights Action Plan' organised under the auspices of the European Commission even produced a practical tool for judges on how to use fundamental rights in private law cases, with many concrete examples.[90] Fundamental rights have indeed figured in such a prominent role in the discussion on European private law that one has to take a closer look at the matter when pondering about grand narratives of Europeanisation.

At this point, I must make a terminological remark. I have referred both to fundamental rights and to human rights. These terms are to a large extent, but not fully, overlapping. In some discourses 'fundamental rights' are used when referring to national constitutional rights, including the EU Charter of Fundamental Rights, whilst 'human rights' rather denote rights included in the European Convention on Human Rights or acknowledged by global human rights documents. The main bulk of the 'human rights' certainly are also 'fundamental rights'. In the context of discussing European private law, it is difficult to use a distinction between fundamental rights and human rights, as the private law discourse in some Member States mainly refers to the local constitution, whilst the debate in other countries to a greater extent relates to the European Convention on Human Rights.[91] With regard to the possibility of a grand narrative regarding private law, it is not necessary to make the distinction. I will, therefore, in the following only speak about fundamental rights, including human rights in this concept.

In the last century, some were sceptical against giving fundamental rights a strong role in legal reasoning, as the rights could fulfil a conservative function in the field of private law. For example, constitutional protection of ownership could be used in this way. To an increasing extent, however, fundamental rights are applied for welfarist purposes. A variety of fundamental rights principles have been used in such contexts. National courts have used fundamental rights to prohibit discrimination, to protect weaker parties, privacy, political rights and the environment and to valorise non-economic interests.[92] Rights to housing[93] and to consumer credit[94] have been

[86] See eg Colombi Ciacchi, Brüggemeier and Comandé (2010); Micklitz (2014a); and Collins (2017). More globally: Siliquini-Cinelli and Hutchison (2019). A different kind of issue is the impact of the compensation rule in Art 41 of the European Convention of Human Rights on tort law; see eg Somers (2018) and Andersson (2016).

[87] eg Kumm (2006); Cherednychenko (2007); and Micklitz (2014a).

[88] Collins (2018: 335).

[89] Safjan and Düsterhaus (2014).

[90] Busch and Schulte-Nölke (2011).

[91] C Mak (2008: 25).

[92] Colombi Ciacchi (2014: 126) has found these six major policy trends by analysing cases from nine Member States.

[93] See eg Rutgers (2017) – though she finds less impact than expected (2017: 136).

[94] Analysed by Cherednychenko (2017) – though she does not expect ground-breaking improvements (2017: 164).

discussed in relation to the Charter of Fundamental Rights. Some have expressly seen the Charter as a reflection of the welfarist nature of European capitalism, offering a political mandate to reform private law in this direction.[95] In particular, when the constitutions recognise social rights as a part of the package of fundamental rights, a welfarist use of the rights is possible.[96] The welfarist opportunities may explain the enthusiasm of some scholars concerning the growing role of fundamental rights in private law. Even though there are good examples in this direction, one should be aware, however, that nothing prevents turning the use of fundamental rights in another direction; for example, using freedom rights against welfarist contract law regulation.[97]

A couple of concrete examples on the use of fundamental rights in a private law context have been much cited in European private law doctrine. The landmark case in the European discourse is the German surety case, regularly cited in European and comparative discussions.[98] The decision of the German Constitutional Court concerned the validity of a contract to act as a guarantor. An uneducated and poor woman had made the commitment for the business debt of her father. After the Supreme Court of Germany upheld a claim of the bank against the daughter, she appealed successfully to the Constitutional Court. It held that the courts had a constitutional obligation to intervene, on the basis of the general clauses of the *BGB*, in contracts that were exceptionally onerous because of a structural imbalance of bargaining power. The Court reached the result by referring to the fundamental rights protection not only of private autonomy, but also of the social state (the so-called *Sozialstaatsklausel*[99]).[100]

The connection between the welfarist agenda inherent in the *Sozialstaatsklausel* and contract law is easy to see. If social rights are protected as fundamental rights, they can function as a counterweight to the freedom rights of private autonomy and property. Perhaps more surprisingly, other fundamental rights may occasionally also be relied on in contract cases. For example, in an Italian case, the court relied on the freedom of association as it deemed it to be contrary to good faith for an insurance company to uphold a life insurance contract when the owner of the insurance company (Mr Berlusconi) supported his political party with the help of the acquisition network of the company. The insured should not have to contribute economically to a political party that he disliked.[101] In a German case, freedom of speech, understood as including the freedom to receive information, was used to allow a Turkish tenant to install a satellite dish to receive Turkish TV programmes, despite the landlord's contract-based refusal to grant permission.[102] One could give many additional

[95] Mattei and Nicola (2007: 48).

[96] Collins (2008: 108) notes that the UK courts have no such social rights to refer to.

[97] See the excellent critique by Bartl and Leone (2017) – under the heading 'Difficult Times Ahead for Social Legislation?' – of the CJEU Case C-426/11 *Alemo-Herron and others v Parkwood Leisure Ltd*, ECLI:EU:C:2013:521 in which the Court used the freedom to conduct a business to disallow a UK employee protection rule that went further than a minimum directive.

[98] Cherednychenko (2007: 3) starts her thesis by describing this case.

[99] The German *Grundgesetz* Arts 20 and 28.

[100] BVerfGE 89, 214; NJW 1994, 36.

[101] Trib Milano, 30 March 1994, Foro it., 1994, I, 1572, cit per Hesselink (2003: 4).

[102] BVerfGE 90, 27.

examples of creative use of fundamental rights by the courts in order to legitimate a result that differed from what 'pure' private law reasoning might have led to.

With regard to the contemporary need for a law that is flexible, fragmented, contextual and experimental, it is not surprising that the weight of fundamental rights reasoning in private law is increasing.[103] As the above-mentioned examples indicate, fundamental rights reasoning is a dynamic tool that can be used in a flexible way to overcome a static private law edifice when its consequences seem ethically unacceptable. Even those who tend to favour a formal understanding and interpretation of traditional private law may be convinced by a fundamental rights argument. The turn towards fundamental rights in private law, in other words, is both understandable and commendable against the background of the needs of late modern society.

Fundamental rights arguments have become useful tools of micro-political legal actions as well. Many climate change cases offer a good illustration of this. Fundamental rights, like the right to a healthy environment and the rights of future generations, have been referred to as one basis of the claims.[104] The responsibility of businesses for maintaining and defending human rights across their sphere of influence is also a topical issue.

The increasing emphasis on fundamental rights reasoning in private law has the advantage that it opens private law to more transparent moral reasoning. It makes it possible 'to foster self-reflection' within the field.[105] The potential of fundamental rights as tools to achieve morally acceptable solutions when established private law would produce unjust results forces the legal actor openly to analyse the ethical perspectives involved in the issue at hand. Chantal Mak has elegantly shown, on the basis of a thorough analysis of German, Dutch, Italian and English case law, how fundamental rights arguments function as instruments to raise the awareness[106] of the courts and make them reflect on the political stakes present in contract law, related to the balance between autonomy and solidarity.[107] This line of reasoning opens up the discourse to recognise the real moral and political issues involved. In the words of the author herself:

> The case studies in this Chapter have shown how fundamental rights seem to address the underlying policy issues in any case in which they are applied. As mediators between politics and law, they define the values shared in society that have to be integrated into the solution to contract cases. In this sense, their meaning is more unambiguous than that of any principles of contract law, for the latter seem to suggest an objectivity which they cannot live up to, whereas the former do not pretend to give any 'right answer'. And as such, the application of fundamental rights may play an important role in keeping contract law, especially its general clauses, in line with societal views on autonomy as well as 'social justice'.[108]

[103] In his 'euroconstitutionalism' Gerstenberg (2018) defends the contemporary use of fundamental rights as a device for 'democratic experimentalism' (eg 2018: 161).

[104] See eg de Vilchez Moragues (2022: 228 *et seq*).

[105] Eller (2020: 1402).

[106] The 'awareness thesis', C Mak (2008: 181).

[107] ibid, Part II.

[108] ibid (289).

Aurelia Colombi Ciacchi has reached a very similar conclusion in her study of the fundamental rights based decision-making of national courts concerning private law relationships in nine EU Member States. The fundamental rights reasoning opens the decision-making of the courts, and thereby

> it enables legal actors to deal with the balancing of conflicting interests and policies in private relationships more explicitly, under a broader and supranational perspective. The substantive core of judicial reasoning becomes more transparent, more suitable to cross-border comparison and mutual learning processes.[109]

Fundamental rights reasoning in private law cases usually relates to the context of the particular case. The cases mentioned above illustrate this very clearly. The German surety case does not deal with the prerequisites of surety agreements in general; it focuses on the fundamental rights implications of the particularly weak situation of the daughter. The satellite dish case relates to the position of the Turkish immigrant; it does not rule on the right of a landlord to forbid the use of satellite dishes in general. In fact, in many cases in which the courts have given fundamental rights a horizontal effect, they have done so by using private law general clauses on good morals and good faith.[110] The fundamental rights agenda, in other words, provides tools for filling late modern society's increasing need for contextual moral assessment.

The advantages of fundamental rights reasoning can only be realised if the arguments are used in a transparent fashion. If the fundamental rights perspective develops into a very specialised form of legal-technical discourse, in which only constitutional lawyers and human rights lawyers are regarded to have sufficient expertise, these advantages are to a large extent lost. The moral transparency would become blurred in yet another playground of a specialised legal expertise. In extreme form, this could imply a shift of power in favour of 'élite lawyers and élite courts',[111] a transformation of the state into 'a constitutional juristocracy'.[112] There is undoubtedly a risk for a too far-reaching specialisation. The case law of the European Court of Human Rights is so immense that it requires particular expertise to understand the messages from Strasbourg. As mentioned before, the need for creating particular algorithms to find legally important decisions of the Court has been discussed.[113] The Court has also been criticised for putting too much emphasis on issues that for a non-expert spectator appears as *petitesses*.[114] In addition, the risk that fundamental rights discourse slips into expert-driven legal-technicality is not related to the ECHR alone. A similar risk exists also in national settings. A criticism of fundamental rights reasoning that is based on doubts why lawyers should have a privileged position in assessing such value issues is not uncommon in domestic discourses, in particular if fundamental rights are used to alter the consequences of democratically adopted legislation.

The risk of letting the fundamental rights discourse in private law slip into a clash between two types of legal-technicalities – formal private law and formal fundamental

[109] Colombi Ciacchi (2014: 133–34).
[110] Hesselink (2003: 8–9) and Hesselink (2002: 182).
[111] Kennedy (2020: 112).
[112] Kumm (2006: 343).
[113] Palmer Olsen and Esmark (2018).
[114] See Andersson (2016: 61).

rights law – is avoidable. Fundamental rights should be used primarily as a kind of markers that some arguments are considered important, without eliminating a transparent assessment of the situation that can be understood also by others than the fundamental rights expertise. Only in this way, one can retain the transparency that is important for rule of law in contemporary society.[115]

The acknowledgement that the occasional use of fundamental rights in private law – if done in a transparent, non-technical fashion – can be assessed in a positive light, does not yet say much about the role of fundamental rights reasoning as a possible grand narrative that would give the development of private law in Europe a sense of structure and direction. Can the emphasis on fundamental rights provide private law with the longed-for map that could steer the small narratives on legal change in a coherent manner?

Some have indeed seen fundamental rights as the sought-for key to bring coherence into contemporary private law. The discussion on constitutionalisation of private law contains such nuances, though often described in a vague manner. Fundamental rights are presented as a kind of guidelines for the development of private law: 'the construction of the science of law, of legal reasoning, of the elaboration of the fundamental principles on which a legal system is based, finds in the constitution an immediate, certain and necessary reference'.[116] In the context of the EU it seems conceivable to search for a joint grand narrative on fundamental rights, as they are a part of the common European deep structure of legal thinking,[117] and therefore have been described as a 'key to legitimation' of European harmonisation.[118] Indeed, the fundamental rights narrative is referred to as something that might offer some alleviation of the problem of fragmentation that is connected both with the societal uncertainty and with the multi-cultural nature of the Union.[119]

The recommendations are cautious, however, and probably do not really defend a grand narrative of the sort that would subordinate private law to fundamental rights. Such subordination is also not endorsed by Olha Cherednychenko, who in her thesis analysed whether the protection of the weaker party in European private law should be achieved by subordinating private law to European fundamental rights.[120] Her standpoint is clear: it would be 'frightening' to attempt to construct a detailed solution for a particular issue on the basis of broadly phrased EU fundamental rights and Member States should not be hindered from experimenting with different levels of contract law protection of the weaker party.[121]

It is easy to share Cherednychenko's scepticism against a reasoning in which the fundamental rights narrative would directly determine the development of private law. It is difficult to conceive such a grand fundamental rights narrative, for two reasons.

[115] See ch 8.
[116] Alpa (2004: 737).
[117] Fundamental rights as part of the deep structure is one of the recurring themes in Tuori (2002).
[118] Delmas-Marty (2002: 187).
[119] See Hesselink (2002: 177–78). In Hesselink (2016) he seems to advocate a more restrained use of fundamental rights.
[120] Cherednychenko (2007: 161, 225).
[121] ibid (558).

The first reason relates to the content of and interrelations between various fundamental rights. Fundamental rights reasoning could offer a master plan for private law only if the fundamental rights themselves would form a coherent system. The European fundamental rights landscape, however, is complex, as to both norms and actors, and is often described as fragmented itself.[122] In addition, even if one would choose the perspective of the European Charter only and disregard the differences between it and national fundamental rights as well as international human rights, the European fundamental rights cannot be squeezed into a coherent system to guide the development. There are several generations of fundamental rights, traditional freedom rights, economic and social rights and collective rights, with roots in different ethical environments. This variety is reflected in the European Charter, containing chapters on dignity, freedoms, equality, solidarity, citizen's rights and justice, with unavoidable internal tensions. Even those who believe in the systematic nature of fundamental rights have to admit the tensions, for example, between freedom rights and economic and social rights and between formal and real equality. In a private law context, the tensions often appear as a conflict between the fundamental rights of both parties.

The solution advocated by fundamental rights enthusiasts is a contextual balancing of the various fundamental rights principles against each other. Instead of offering a direction-setting grand narrative, fundamental rights reasoning brings us back to square one: a fragmented and flexible law that develops through small narratives on legal change. Fundamental rights based decision-making can be studied as a legal governance that 'implies accommodating and balancing different policy objectives and interests of different actors'.[123] In other words, moral contextualism cannot be avoided with the help of fundamental rights, but is rather strengthened by fundamental rights thinking.

The second reason looks at the relationship between many private law issues and fundamental rights. In most cases, this relationship is so distant that a fundamental rights based understanding of the private law issues appears as artificial. The fundamental rights based litigation concerning private relationships has in practice focused on details related to a number of issues, such as the prohibition of discrimination and the protection of weak parties, privacy and the environment, but private law covers a multitude of other issues. How, for example, can one connect the perhaps most important contract law issue, the definition of the proper basic liability rule – strict liability, control liability or negligence – to the realm of fundamental rights? The rule that a party should be responsible for his or her own sphere of control[124] could perhaps in very general terms be connected to the value of freedom and freedom-related responsibility, but a similar connection could also be made for other liability rules. And can fundamental rights reasoning offer any real guidance when discussing other topical issues; for example, the definition of non-conformity or the obligation to give notice concerning breach of contract in a contract of sale? Similar examples could be added almost endlessly. Although important choices are reflected in these

[122] Brems and Ouald-Chaib (2018); Violini and Baraggia (2018).
[123] Colombi Ciacchi (2014: 125).
[124] The liability rule in CISG, Art 79.

questions – many apparently 'technical rules' in private law may reflect deeper ideological commitments[125] – they are politico-moral choices that have to be made within the realm that the fundamental rights leave open to the decision-makers, rather than to be determined by these rights. The task of fundamental rights is to define the frames, within which democratic and judicial decision-making can seek good decisions, not to eliminate the opportunities of such decision-making.

Fundamental rights reasoning, in other words, does not offer a grand narrative that would lead the development of private law in Europe in a particular pre-set direction. It tends to open up private law to more transparent moral assessment and contextual judgement, and it is in this sense in line with the needs of contemporary society, but it cannot offer a systematic key for creating a general and coherent system of private law. Fundamental rights reasoning only becomes an additional element in small narratives on legal change.

The systemic effect of fundamental rights reasoning may even be the opposite to that of a steering grand narrative, extending the range of alternatives rather than limiting the options. By introducing new arguments for a decision-maker or a scholar, it makes it possible to reach decisions that would be difficult to defend without the fundamental rights argument. Expressed in a more metaphorical language, it introduces 'an instrument of self-criticism' in private law.[126] In addition, it brings in new actors, such as the European Court of Human Rights and the national constitutional courts, on the private law scene. It also changes the role of other actors in the private law setting. Civil courts may become constitutional actors, acquiring the task of a dynamic European polity building in the hybrid decision-making between national and European law.[127] By adding new arguments and new actors to the small narratives, fundamental rights reasoning broadens the sphere of the legally possible.

The climate change cases are a good example of how fundamental rights reasoning can extend the options of private law actors. Laura Burgers has shown, how the legitimacy of such case law – making the courts willing to make what seems to be rather 'political' decisions – is related to the process of constitutionalisation of the environment.[128] The variety of standpoints concerning the legal character of these cases, according to Burgers, can be explained by the fact that the legal understanding of this process is still in transition.[129] The cross-border narrative of constitutionalisation of the environment, in other words, is not yet finalised.

Even though fundamental rights reasoning cannot supply European private law with a grand narrative, legal-culturally it may have an impact on the narrative of Europeanisation. It may more loosely serve the building of connections between domestic and European law. As has been noted before,[130] the exchange of legal experience within the EU requires a joint 'legal language' of some kind. The fundamental rights perspective, belonging to the shared European deep-structure, can contribute

[125] Collins (2008: 105).
[126] Wielsch (2014: 378).
[127] As suggested in the Utopia of C Mak (2020).
[128] Burgers (2020a: 69 *et seq*).
[129] ibid (71).
[130] See in particular ch 5.

with some elements to this language. The Charter of Fundamental Rights can function as an instrument to translate private law principles into arguments that can interact with EU law.[131] In the words of Aurelia Colombi Ciacchi, the fundamental rights perspective can make private law reasoning more adaptive to mutual learning processes.[132]

V. IN OTHER WORDS

In the preceding chapters, I dealt with a variety of issues from a European perspective. In this sense, there certainly is a 'European way'. In this chapter, however, I asked whether it is possible to pinpoint a European grand narrative that would form a master plan for the development of European private law. Could one construe a grand European narrative that would falsify the claim that contemporary private law develops in a fragmented manner?

The adherence to the first candidate – the narrative on Europeanisation of law – is a normative choice on which this book is based. As the ideal of Europeanisation recognises a Europe 'united in diversity', the narrative is primarily procedural. It relates to how cross-border and European elements can be introduced in legal decision-making and scholarship. It requires legal actors to be open to learning across the European borders, but it does not contain a substantive grand narrative that could steer the development of private law.

Narratives on the European social model, combining market and welfarism, do not provide private law with a coherent master plan either. The tension between the two elements of the model allows the choice of a broad variety of private law solutions within the confines of the model. In addition, even if one would normatively decide to choose, for example, the welfarist perspective as an agenda-setter, one would not find the sought-for master plan. Due to its internal complexity, the ideal of welfarism can only function as a basis for flexible learning processes. It does not relieve the legal actors from the responsibility to make contextual assessments of available welfarist solutions. A continuing development of the welfarist perspective requires an experimental approach.

The same goes for the important role of fundamental rights reasoning. It does not offer a grand narrative, as it cannot guide the private law narratives into a system of pre-set solutions. What it can do, however, is opening up private law to transparent moral assessment and contextual judgement. The narrative can broaden the available choices by enabling new arguments to question traditional private law structures.

Finally, in Europe the rule of law is an important grand narrative. The following chapters are devoted to an analysis of how one can understand and defend the rule of law in the fragmented legal landscape of small narratives.

[131] Sieburgh (2013: 1188).
[132] Colombi Ciacchi (2014: 134).

7

The Legal Queries: Coherence, Predictability and Equality

THE TOUR ACROSS possible grand narratives in the preceding chapter ended in mentioning the rule of law. Few would deny the central position of this value in the self-understanding of the EU. According to the Treaty, the Union 'is founded on the values of respect for human dignity, freedom, democracy, equality, the rule of law and respect for human rights'.[1] The acknowledgement of the role of the rule of law, however, poses questions with regard to the leading theme of the previous chapters, the claim that the contemporary world of uncertainty needs a fragmented and flexible law. How is it possible to accept more fragmentation and flexibility, in the light of the value of the rule of law?

I will here discuss this question with particular focus on fragmentation, as most of the criticism against the impact of the Europeanisation on private law relates to its fragmenting effects. Many regard the opposite to fragmentation, coherence, to be an important pillar in support of the rule of law. In many continental visions, in particular, coherence plays a central role in the rule of law discourse. Coherence supports the justification and legitimacy of law.[2]

In fact, a 'mythology of coherence' dominates much intellectual discourse.[3] Social science searches for connections, trying to paint coherent pictures of the issues at hand. Legal scholars emphasise the systematising task of legal dogmatics with reference to both scientific and legal ideals. Constructing a 'false' coherence, however, in areas in which fragmentation dominates, should not be a true scientific goal – but it might be a legal goal, as legal dogmatic research contributes to building the legal system. When discussing the weight of this legal goal, one must ask how serious the problems are that decreasing coherence might cause for the rule of law. By analysing coherence, one may reach a deeper understanding of what fragmentation of law really means.

[1] Art 2 of the Treaty on European Union.
[2] Smits (2012: 12); Ackermann (2018: 745 *et seq*).
[3] In his well-known critique of the history of ideas, Skinner (1969: 16 *et seq*) speaks about such a 'mythology'.

Predictability and equal treatment of equal cases are the most important benefits that scholars attach to coherence.[4] I will here look more closely at these two goals. Before that, it is necessary to analyse the concept of coherence of law itself. Despite the recurring references to the concept, scholars often use it rather vaguely.

The concept of coherence, as used here, refers to the structure of the legal order. The focus is on the relationships between the normative pieces (both principles and rules) that the legal order acknowledges. The coherence questions in this chapter concern the systematical aspects of the substantive legal order.

Legal coherence has also been analysed in other meanings. Within the EU, with European and national courts sharing the responsibility for applying EU law, the coherence of the judicial system (the court system) and its impact on the rule of law is an important issue.[5] As my focus is on private law, I will not discuss this procedural aspect of coherence further.[6]

In legal theory some 'coherence theories' relate to the coherence of legal reasoning in particular cases. The structure of the reasoning and the internal harmony of the arguments are the key questions.[7] This form of coherence is not necessarily dependent on the coherence of the legal order.[8] One should recognise, however, that the two perspectives are at least partially interlinked. The coherence of reasoning may support the coherence of the system.[9] The connection between reasoning and system is visible in the present work as well. Even though I discuss the coherence of the system, the response to the challenges that I present in this and the next chapters relate to legal reasoning. The keyword, however, is transparency, not coherence.

Some discuss coherence of law in the light of aesthetics. A well-structured law is a beautiful law. Coherence 'is something that comes naturally, something deeply rooted in our cognitive makeup.'[10] Who can deny this? But is it really important? The task of law is to support building a just society, not to offer additions to the treasures of poetry. The law is for the people rather than for the connoisseurs of style. I will not use further space to discuss coherence as an expression of legal aesthetics.

I. COHERENCE AS A VAGUE IDEAL

The concept of 'coherence' is frequently used in legal discourse. For some the recognition that law should form a coherent system is almost a self-evident

[4] See eg Tuori (2011: 165).
[5] See eg Lenaerts (2007).
[6] On the various roles of the legal actors in the European setting, see ch 5 section II.
[7] See as examples Alexy and Peczenik (1990); Soriano (2003); Paunio (2013: 84 *et seq*); and Amaya (2015).
[8] Soriano (2003: 305).
[9] Paunio (2013: 83).
[10] Schäfer and Bankowski (2003: 501).

prerequisite for legal thinking. The issue of coherence was at the forefront in the debates concerning the need for creating and developing a European contract law and a European civil code. European legal scholars criticised both the perceived incoherence of national law caused by the punctual *acquis* and the incoherence of the *acquis* itself. The European Commission early underlined to need for a more coherent contract law.[11] But what do the proponents of coherence mean by coherence?

The preoccupation with coherence is primarily a continental European concern. In the US, it is not part of the everyday private law discourse, perhaps because 'US law is so thoroughly lacking in coherence that no one would think it useful either to criticize it or to reform it with coherence in mind.'[12] There is not, however, a complete lack of interest in coherence among US scholars. The *Stanford Encyclopedia of Philosophy* states that 'coherence theories … have more recently found their way into the philosophy of law.'[13] One can, for example, find scholars, who recognise 'legal coherentism' as a traditional approach, but claim that coherence in the modern administrative state does no longer function as the standard of excellence for an instrumental law and that legal research therefore should shift its focus from legal coherence to legal effectiveness.[14] In the UK, it is even after Brexit possible to discuss 'coherentism' as a competitor to 'regulatory-instrumentalism'.[15] Also in common law, in other words, occasionally one encounters coherence reasoning.

In the debate on the need for coherence, relatively little is said about the concept of coherence itself. The meaning of coherence is often taken as granted. The discussants only mention a few examples to illustrate unacceptable cases of incoherence. For example, when criticising EU law one may refer to variations in the consumer concept in different legal acts or to varying withdrawal periods and technicalities in the original directives on the right of withdrawal.[16] There is often no further analysis of what (in)coherence really means in the examples used. So when discussing the role and value of coherence one has first to look more closely at the concept of coherence itself.

I have previously published an analysis of the possibility to reach more European coherence through a generalisation of the *acquis*.[17] Looking at the examples used by scholars when discussing the (in)coherence of private law I could distinguish six understandings of coherence:

[11] COM(2003) 68 final: 'A More Coherent European Contract Law. An Action Plan'.
[12] Kennedy (2006: 10).
[13] Dickson (2005).
[14] So Rubin (2017: 328).
[15] Brownsword (2018).
[16] *cf* eg the Doorstep Selling Directive (85/577/EEC); the Distance Selling Directive (97/7/EC); the Distance Marketing of Financial Services Directive (2002/65/EC); and the two Timeshare Directives (94/47/EC and 2008/122/EC), as well as the Consumer Rights Directive (2011/83/EU), repealing the two first ones.
[17] Wilhelmsson (2008).

Form of coherence strived for	Perceived problem of incoherence	Examples of incoherence
Coherence of presentation	'Wrong' place of norm	Choice of place of certain paragraphs in the German *BGB*[18]
Logical consistency	Contradictory norms	One rule prescribing what another rule forbids
Coherence of scope or systematics	Varying scopes of instruments, fluid borders between branches	Variations of the consumer concept
Coherence of concepts	Varying content of basic legal concepts	Various understandings of concepts like 'negligence'
Coherence of particular norms	Similar situations regulated in different ways	EU withdrawal rules
Coherence of principles	Conflicting basic principles or values	'Liberalist' and 'welfarist' rules

This analysis of the European private law discourse shows how the concept of coherence has been used in a variety of meanings. One should bear in mind the variations in the understanding of the concept when assessing its significance.

With regard to the rule of law, not all forms of coherence are equally interesting. Coherence of presentation is not at the core of the concept, as it relates to legal aesthetics rather than content. With regard to logical consistency, lawyers have adequate instruments to deal with the problems (like *lex specialis derogat legi generali* and other collision norms). Below, I will focus on the other forms of coherence, with particular emphasis on the coherence of principles.

The discussion on coherence often takes place within the framework of a particular branch of law. The increasingly specialised legal doctrine is less interested in the coherence of the legal order as a whole. Probably few earnestly believe in the possibility of such general coherence – whatever that would mean. As Duncan Kennedy says, 'everyone knows it's impossible'.[19] In the same spirit, Kaarlo Tuori emphasises that 'the unity of the entire legal order, its *total coherence*' is no longer at issue, coherence as a goal concerns 'merely *local coherence*'.[20]

The analysis of coherence, in other words, must be related to the division of private law into branches of law. The emergence of ever narrower branches of law is in fact one of the expressions of the process of fragmentation.

When scholars constitute a branch of law, they usually refer to principles and rules that reflect a deeper coherence of its content than only a punctual coherence of scope, concepts or particular norms. A number of principles and rules are acknowledged as a branch of law if it seems possible to arrange them into a systematical whole. The substantive norms must be related to each other in a way that makes the branch of law seem as coherent as possible. For lack of a better term, I have called this 'coherence of principles'.

[18] See eg Zimmermann (2005: 458–60).
[19] Kennedy (2006: 11).
[20] Tuori (2011: 162).

The definitions of what this form of coherence in a deeper sense actually could mean are vague. At first sight, one might believe it to be clear to every legal professional how to understand such coherence. The frequent use of the concept indicates that there exists a kind of intuitive understanding of how a coherent systematisation of a branch of law looks like. It is, however, hard to find a clear definition. When discussing deeper coherence of law, scholars have often resorted to metaphors like 'the law speaking with just one voice'[21] and to other figurative expressions.[22] Law is described as a jigsaw puzzle and coherence the guideline that make us put the pieces in their right places.[23] Legal norms are said to be coherent if there is 'a set of principles that are either consistent with one another or apportioned to parts of the system according to a coherent set of meta-principles',[24] or if 'they give the expression to the same general principle or to a set of matching principles'.[25] Coherence is understood to mean 'that principles, rules and cases are all seen as part of an overall system, allowing analogous interpretation'.[26] In German doctrine substantive coherence is said to imply the idea of a teleological order in which the more concrete norms are tied to and coherent with more fundamental general principles.[27] Franz Bydlinski has presented a prominent concretisation of this, by identifying 131 legal principles in private law.[28] The Germanic understanding of coherence has been applied in the analysis of the *acquis* as well.[29] But what does 'one voice', 'system' and 'order' really mean?

Coherent constructions of ethical systems usually rest on the idea of a leading principle, be it of substantive character, like in utilitarianism, or procedural, like in Rawlsian ethics. It is difficult, however, to designate one single leading principle, or even only a few leading principles, that would constitute the system within a branch of law.[30] The attempts to do so are often not very convincing in the light of law as it stands and are easy to 'falsify' with examples in which other principles have been put in a dominant position, even if one recognises that coherence is an aspiration that does not rule out occasional errors.[31] Branches of law may be built on a multitude of principles that are not necessarily well interconnected, and those who attempt to construct systems of legal principles are forced to include many principles in their structure.

For example, as has been mentioned many times before, contemporary contract law reflects values that pull in different directions. Scholars have described the development in terms of opposites such as freedom and solidarity, individualism

[21] Stemming from Cicero, see eg Besson (2004: 257).
[22] See Paunio (2013: 83).
[23] Bergslid Salvesen (2021: 415).
[24] Kennedy (2006: 11).
[25] Tuori (2011: 165).
[26] Smits (2012: 10).
[27] The German classic being Canaris (1983). More recently Jansen (2005: 768): A system '*erfordert die Herstellung innerer Kohärenz im Sinne eines durch Begründungsrelationen verbundenen Ganzen von Aussagen*'.
[28] Bydlinski (1996).
[29] Riesenhuber (2003: 5 *et seq*).
[30] What Hesselink (2021: 5–6) criticises as contract law 'essentialism', or its 'monistic sting' (2021: 268).
[31] Weinrib (2012: 13).

and altruism, or market-individualism and consumer-welfarism. As was shown in the previous chapter, even the varieties of welfarism present in European contract law cannot be concentrated in one principle. Admittedly, the relevance of seemingly different values does not rule out the possibility of a substantive coherence of a branch of law, if one could solve the value conflicts by developing coherent meta-principles. This, however, is not easy to do in a convincing manner.

One might attempt to save the ideal of coherence of principles by using the Dworkinian distinction between principles and policies.[32] Even though policies may be contradictory, a coherent set of principles could nevertheless be developed and employed.[33] The distinction between principles and policies, however, is not easy to grasp, for example, when discussing the above-mentioned contract law dichotomies. If one could make such a distinction, the principles would have to be so general that one could pursue only a loose local coherence.[34]

The more complex the clashes between the conflicting principles become, the harder it is to develop meta-principles to save the coherence of the system. Fragmentation pressures the opportunities to create coherent systems of principles to ever more limited branches of law. Only by acknowledging increasingly narrow (sometimes even quite artificial) definitions of branches of law, can one maintain the vague ideal of coherence of principles. A branch of law formed around one single well-prepared piece of legislation might seem coherent, but this is something different than the coherence of a larger branch of law in traditional systematics. The ideal of coherence, in other words, moves from large traditional branches of law towards more local spots of coherence: 'Coherence is created locally, not globally, and the larger system can therefore remain in permanent flux, even if its smaller subunits are internally coherent'.[35]

For example, in contract law the division of the branch into a growing number of sub-branches tends to preserve an illusion of at least some local coherence. Obviously different value constellations – meta-principles – dominate, for example, maritime law, insurance law, landlord and tenant law, and consumer contract law, and newcomers like the law of contracts of electronic commerce are becoming increasingly independent from the principles of general contract law. Some have suggested particular principles to be developed for 'social long-term contracts'.[36] Even in general contract theory one finds acknowledgement and even celebration of the fragmentation into contract types. The choice theory of contracts developed by Hanoch Dagan and Michael Heller is built on the idea of autonomy of choice between a multiplicity of contract types, reflecting various combination of values, with much less room left for a 'general' contract law.[37]

The complexity of private law systematics is increased by the fact that the logic of formation of sub-branches seems to vary. Whilst some sub-branches reflect the

[32] Dworkin (1978), ch 4.
[33] Some note also the possibility of coherence of policies; Smits and Letto-Vanamo (2012: 2–3); Smits (2012: 12).
[34] This seems to be the opinion of Tuori (2011: 168).
[35] Schäfer and Bankowski (2003: 490).
[36] Nogler and Reifner (2014).
[37] Dagan and Heller (2017).

traditional division of contract law in contract types described in an abstract legal fashion, other sub-branches may come into existence because of the need to regulate a particular factual situation. Such new branches are developing for example in relation to the sectorisation of markets.[38] Special branches related to services of general interest, combining public law and private law measures, are good examples of branches that have emerged in this way. The keys for constructing coherence are different, depending on whether the issue is looked at from the traditional legal or the factual perspective.

The concept of coherence is vague and pictures an ideal rather than a concrete and detailed edifice. 'The law speaking with one voice' only sets the tone, and that tone does not imply a general harmony. One should understand coherence as a concept of degree and not as an on/off way of describing the legal situation.[39] Rather than discussing whether law should be coherent or not, one could ask, for example, how much coherence the law would need to achieve legitimacy. In such an approach, one can recognise that the degree of coherence in different branches of law is varying, and that the desired degree of coherence could be higher in smaller units. Whilst the rules concerning some particular type of contract might appear as highly coherent, the degree of coherence within general contract law, combining many smaller units, would remain on a lower level. Obviously, accepting such a fluid concept of coherence makes it more difficult to deplore, in a convincing manner, the loss of coherence of law.

The analysis of the coherence discourse discloses many question marks concerning the usefulness of the concept of coherence as a buttress of the rule of law. The vagueness of the concept makes a general discourse on coherence and the rule of law less interesting. One should also recognise that the ideal of coherence and the metaphor of small narratives on legal change are not completely contradictory. Their relationship can be fruitfully described by a metaphor that recognises coherence, picturing the structure of law as islands of coherence in a fragmented legal sea. Overall coherence is shrinking because of fragmentation (the degree of generality of the parts of the system can be considered as one measure of coherence[40]), but that does not rule out higher degrees of coherence on some of the smaller sub-areas. Even in the context of shrinking branches, however, coherence escapes a precise definition, although it may be easier to address in a narrower context.

Coherence building is a task of legal doctrine. The systematic structure of private law is created by legal scholars as an instrument for achieving order in the law.[41] As emphasised in chapter four, scholars play an important role as creators of legal concepts and stabilisers of changes by developing the conceptual structure. Every new concept means a proposal for a new element of coherence. One should not read, in other words, my comments on the vagueness of legal coherence talk as a general critique against legal concepts and principles that may improve coherence. Concepts and principles should just be seen as important parts of a dynamic structure of small

[38] Also called 'verticalisation', Cantero Gamito (2020: 7).
[39] Alexy and Peczenik (1990: 145): 'Coherence is a matter of degree.'
[40] See eg Alexy and Peczenik (1990: 140–41).
[41] Ackermann (2018: 747).

narratives rather than as elements of a given static system. Scholars contribute to building and defending, and sometimes also enlarging, the islands of coherence in the fragmented environment, but doctrine should not be coherence-expansionist at all cost. In contemporary society, the concept building should be kept on a level that is compatible with what is needed by a problem-oriented learning law.

The demand for coherence has a legal-political dimension. There is a tension between the value of coherence of law and democracy. The stronger the demand for coherence appears in legal discourse, the more the power of the legislature is circumscribed by the power of legal scholarship. The responsiveness of small narratives on legal change to the needs of contemporary society requires leaving sufficient power to the legislator, and the value of democracy should not be undermined by strict doctrine. The discourse on the development of consumer law, familiar in many jurisdictions, is a good illustration of how coherence reasoning has been used to criticise the emergence of new legislation, as breaking the harmony of the private law system.[42]

More generally, coherence arguments should not be used against sensible contextual solutions. In a consumer law perspective, the coherence of substantive law is a less important value than the aim to reach practically working solutions.[43] To mention one example, when the original Consumer Sales Directive was prepared, the Commission suggested the introduction of a right of the consumer to direct action concerning lack of conformity against the producer of the goods.[44] This could have become a useful tool for both improving consumer protection and strengthening the trust in the internal market. The proposal was turned down, however, because it was seen to be in conflict with the traditional system of contract law (privity of contract). Coherence reasoning ran over pragmatic legal policy.

This is not to say, however, that legal concept-building is always conservative. Scholars may engage in creating forward-looking, even emancipatory concepts that contribute to push the narratives on legal change in progressive directions. Micro-political activity may sometimes aim at the development of new legal-systematic perspectives on the issue at hand.

I have here discussed the vagueness of the concept of coherence in order to show the difficulty in making a convincing general claim that the rule of law requires coherence. The vagueness of the concept, on the other hand, does not exclude that fragmentation could have negative effects on rule of law. In the analysis of whether this is the case, one has to look directly at the rule of law effects that one can relate to coherence. The most used arguments in this context refer to the values of predictability and equality. I will now turn to these values and their relationship to coherence. Does increasing fragmentation really endanger predictability and equality?

[42] See eg on the German debate on *Sonderprivatrecht* Damm (1978) and Gilles (1980).

[43] Consumer law research has always included relatively strong elements of socio-legal and empirical research. For a new account of parts of this paradigm, see Micklitz, Sibony and Esposito (2018a).

[44] COM(93) 509 final, 86–88.

II. PREDICTABILITY – AN OVER-VALUED EFFECT OF COHERENCE?

Loss of predictability is a natural corollary to the general features of societal development described in chapters two and three. As society becomes more complex and quickly changing, it becomes more unpredictable. This also has an impact on law. The idea of a learning law is based on the need for a law that can adjust to a fast-changing society. One may assume that law tends to become more unpredictable in contemporary society.

The question here is to what extent legal coherence reasoning is needed to counteract this tendency. How much weight does the argument carry that coherence is required in order to preserve sufficient predictability of law? Does the acknowledgement of the importance of predictability require a strong adherence to the value of coherence?

One cannot deny the prima facie value of predictability, as a central element of legal certainty. The understanding of legal certainty varies between jurisdictions and between various fields of law,[45] but it always contains an element of formal legal certainty, the predictability of legal consequences. Even though formal legal certainty has to be balanced with material legal certainty, predictability is one of the key elements of the rule of law. This is true also in critical narratives that want to use law as an instrument for protection of weak and vulnerable groups: a precise rule can give the weak a better protection than flexible judges, even when they are empathetic.

In the analysis of predictability, one should also note that the concept has been used in two different meanings in legal discourse. The value of predictability is not only related to the foreseeability of the outcome of a legal case; it has also been referred to in a broader societal meaning, as a prerequisite of a market economy.[46] For contracting parties, it is important that they are able during contract negotiations to foresee the consequences of the contract in various possible situations. Paradoxically, formally precise rules do not necessarily provide more foreseeable grounds for decision-making than flexible ones at this stage. Common law traditionally considers itself to offer a high degree of legal predictability based on a relatively strict adherence to a literal interpretation of the contract.[47] In this legal environment, for the parties to be able to foresee the consequences of the contract, the contract has to address as many scenarios as possible in detail and from various angles – which has led to a complex and expensive Anglo-American contract practice. If the parties do not engage in writing detailed and comprehensive contract terms, the risk grows that the contract might lead to unreasonable results. A more flexible legal approach, in which the courts have wider possibilities to take into account the purpose of the contract and the actual circumstances, might prevent contract parties from suffering surprising unfair consequences. Flexible rules might promote certainty, as they

[45] On various meanings of legal certainty in a comparative perspective, see Fenwick, Siems and Wrbka (2017).

[46] Tuori (2011: 165).

[47] Zweigert and Kötz (1998: 406).

make it possible to enforce what the parties reasonably expect.[48] In other words, if one seeks to justify predictability with reference to the need of the market, the issue is not as simple as one might imagine. Occasionally a flexible principle can support market-predictability, even though it might make the outcome of a court or arbitral procedure less predictable. Having noted this ambiguity in the discourse on predictability, I will leave the broader market-related perspective, and use the concept of predictability to refer only to the possibility to foresee the outcome of a legal case. From the point of view of the rule of law, this is the focal issue.

The weight of predictability varies in different contexts and jurisdictions. I will not discuss the weight of this value further, as my aim here is to analyse the relationship between coherence and predictability. The concept of coherence is vague. Does the emphasis on such an ideal really contribute to legal predictability? The issue is of importance mainly in so-called hard cases, as no deeper legal argumentation is required to reach the result in routine cases. Hence, one could rephrase the question as follows: does fragmentation increase the number of hard cases and hard issues at the expense of the bulk of routine issues, and to what extent?

It is not self-evident that fragmentation contributes to a considerable decline of predictability. A fragmented legislation concerning a particular issue might be very detailed and predictable, and case law and academic writing may result in a very stable legal situation in a particular limited area of law. The fact that Finnish law for a long time applied different rules to accidents caused by cars and by trams – an example I will refer to in the next section – instead of having one comprehensive system did not reduce predictability. Even the promotion of the idea of a flexible and learning law that develops in small narratives on legal change does not imply ever-growing deficits of predictability. A good small narrative on legal change can end in a fragmented legal situation becoming stabilised and predictable in future cases. It is fair to assume, however, that an increase in number and a decrease in size of the islands of coherence in the fragmented sea of private law probably to some extent tend to expand the overall frequency of hard issues.

Even in such cases, however, coherence reasoning is not necessarily the key to predictability. In hard cases, reference to coherence is only a part of the reasoning that can be used to solve the case. The argumentative tool for producing coherence is analogy – but as lawyers know, an argument in favour of analogy can often be met by a claim based on reasoning *e contrario*. The choice must be made with reference to other arguments than the need for coherence as such. Analogy may function as a justificatory dressing for a decision that primarily is made on other grounds.

It seems, in other words, that the practical importance of coherence-based predictability is overvalued. Small and fragmented narratives on legal change do not threaten the predictability aspect of rule of law as much as many seem to imagine. This is not to say that coherence reasoning could not contribute to predictability in hard cases. It is just a question of proportions. Even though coherence probably has some value in this regard, it seems that the fragmentation of private law discussed in

[48] Collins (1999: 271). For a similar reasoning on consumer law, see Willett (2018: 183).

this book can do much less damage to predictability than assumed by the most vehement defenders of the value of coherence.

Legal research seeks coherent structures in a complex world. Legal scholars play a crucial role in creating coherence. I will conclude this section with a few notes on this role of legal scholars and its effects on predictability.

Legal scholars, who formulate concepts and principles, usually strive to improve both coherence and predictability. Legal conceptualisation can indeed stabilise the normative situation and increase predictability for the future. Scholars as builders of the conceptual legal infrastructure are said to strive to increase consensus in the legal community.[49] At the outset, it seems clear that scholarly coherence-driven systematisations are both aimed to support and tends to achieve increased predictability.

The real picture, however, is more complex. As there is a continuous tension between systematic coherence and the fragmenting effects of a learning law, the predictability effects of systematisations vary, depending on how they reflect this tension. The academic creators of concepts and principles can process the tension in ways that may sharpen it. On the one hand, scholars can make conceptual suggestions, perhaps inspired by micro-politics, to make visible weak signals of change in the legal material. They may seek the legally possible rather than the already widely accepted. Such new (alternative) systematisations can function as forerunners in narratives on change. The proposed concept or principle weakens the predictability of legal outcomes rather than strengthens it, at least until the proposal is stabilised or discarded.[50] On the other hand, if a scholar disregards new legal fragments and attempts to capture a branch of law by using a seemingly coherent but outdated structure of concepts and principles, the structure affects the dynamic between main rules and exceptions without being able to remove the exceptions. The latter only remain less visible in the total picture. This might increase the probability of surprising decisions, and in this sense decrease predictability. Various Jack-in-the-Box phenomena in which legal argumentation comes to differ drastically from what parties could reasonably assume might become more frequent. In other words, whatever choice scholars make when there is a tension between traditional conceptuality and new fragments, there is always a possibility that scholarly systematisations decrease predictability rather than increase it.

Legal scholars, in other words, may choose various approaches when developing the coherence structures of private law, both forward- and backward-looking and both actively developing the law and preventing such a development.[51] Therefore, the position of scholarly doctrines in relation to predictability is ambiguous. Coherence built by scholars may support predictability, but not as much as one might assume.

Some have suggested that scholars should take into account the situational sensitivity required by late modern society by developing more flexible principles and

[49] Helin (1998: 1034).

[50] Kennedy (2006: 14–15), speaks about reformulation or reconfiguration as reducing the sense of impact in a particular field.

[51] See also ch 4 section VI.

systematisations. The task of legal-systematic development would no longer be to build 'a substantive classificatory system of norms but a looser, principle-based coherence.'[52] This seems like a balanced and realistic adaptation of coherence building to late modern legal fragmentation. Flexible principles are certainly better suited to accommodate the increasingly fragmented legal material than a more strictly built system. As Mark Van Hoecke and François Ost have emphasised, the complexity of contemporary society requires 'more flexible and more complex forms of systematisation … to order things without unifying them, to work out the requirements for compatibility, rather than to impose strict uniformity … to find probabilities rather than to assert certainties.'[53] The use of such systematic tools is characterised by balancing rather than interpretation and application. From the point of view of predictability in the traditional sense, however, this move does not change the picture that I have drawn here. Flexible concepts and principles may seemingly improve predictability of outcome, but the mere fact that the tools are flexible and are used in balancing warns one not to overrate their predictability effects.

The appreciation of the role of flexible principles requires another understanding of predictability. Instead of drawing the attention to the predictability of the outcome, one could emphasise the predictability of reasoning. Although the outcome may not be easy to predict when using flexible principles, the parties should be able to foresee what kind of arguments legal actors consider relevant in the situation. To function this way, the flexible principles must reflect the fragmented legal material at hand and the real arguments should not be hidden behind fictitious reasoning. Indeed, and more generally, in today's fragmented legal reality, transparency of reasoning is a key element of the rule of law.[54]

III. EQUALITY – BUT COMPARED TO WHAT?

The value of coherence is also linked to the principle of equality. The law should treat similar cases in a similar fashion and different cases differently, with due regard to the nature of the differences. Law should not favour anybody, but should treat all legal subjects alike.

The principle of equality is a cornerstone of the rule of law. I do not wish to denounce the importance of the principle – even though the hero of Scandinavian realism Alf Ross called a general principle of equality a legally empty principle.[55] The question here, however, is whether and to what extent the principle of equality requires law to be coherent. Such claims are often put forward. Some have even discussed whether there is a constitutional claim for legislation being coherent, based, inter alia, on the general principle of equality.[56]

[52] Tuori (2011: 166).

[53] Van Hoecke and Ost (1998: 209).

[54] See ch 8.

[55] Ross (1966: 371). If the principle specifically demanded, for example, similar treatment irrespective of gender or race, the principle had a meaning (ibid).

[56] On German law, see O'Hara (2018: 140 *et seq*).

Looked at from a particular standpoint, incoherence may indeed be perceived as resulting in injustice. For example, if the application of some rules would lead to a better treatment of average consumers than vulnerable ones, one would not accept this as a just situation.[57] However, the link between the principle of equality and coherence is not as straightforward as one might think at first sight. The challenge lies in how one should compare the situations discussed. Equality requires comparison, but according to what criteria? Should one seek the keys to comparison within the conceptual structures of traditional private law, as might be assumed by those emphasising legal coherence, or should one choose another perspective?

In other words, one may question to what extent fragmentation really endangers equality. For example, it was not considered to be a problem of equality that in Finland compensation for injuries caused by cars and trams had to be claimed through systems that were very different even in their substance, as trams followed the rules for railways. When in 1999 the responsibility for damages caused by tram traffic was brought closer to the responsibility based on the motor insurance system, equality was mentioned only in passing in the Government Bill.[58] The object of comparison only changed from railway traffic to road traffic.

The most obvious expression of the principle of equality is in the fundamental right not to be exposed to discrimination. The Charter of Fundamental Rights of the European Union declares as prohibited 'Any discrimination based on any ground such as sex, race, colour, ethnic or social origin, genetic features, language, religion or belief, political or any other opinion, membership of a national minority, property, birth, disability, age or sexual orientation'.[59] This prohibition also has an impact on private law.[60] Anti-discrimination rules, therefore, are included also in the DCFR. The book on contracts and other juridical acts contains a chapter on non-discrimination, covering discrimination on grounds of sex or ethnic or racial origin.[61] According to the definition in the DCFR, discrimination occurs if 'one person is treated less favourably than another person is, has been or would be treated in a comparable situation'.[62]

The principle of non-discrimination requires equal treatment of different groups of people. As pointed out in the DCFR, establishing discrimination requires comparison: somebody should not be treated less favourably than another 'in a comparable situation'. It is not self-evident, however, what key one should use to find comparable situations. The comparison often focuses on people and groups of people in relatively concrete situations rather than on the legal systematisations that connects different situations. From a prohibition of discrimination related to a concrete situation, one cannot easily draw conclusions on how coherent a specific branch of law should be with regard to different situations. If law is equally incoherent for persons from different groups, there is no violation of the principle of non-discrimination. Only if the

[57] Sibony (2018: 182).
[58] *Hallituksen esitys* (Government Bill) 234/1997, s 3.
[59] Art 21(1).
[60] Reich (2014: 60) speaks about 'spill-over' effects on private law.
[61] DCFR II.–2:101.
[62] DCFR II.–2:102(1)(a).

perceived incoherence has indirect discriminating effects, is it forbidden in the same way as direct discrimination. For example, the above-mentioned example concerning liability for cars and trams would be problematic only if one could show that accidents caused by trams systematically hit different groups than those caused by cars. The establishment of indirect discrimination, in other words, requires empirical reasoning and focusing on the societal context rather than using a legal conceptuality. A variety of keys to comparison are on offer and traditional legal systematisations are not necessarily the first choice.

The principle of equality, as a basic principle of legal thinking, has a broader reach than the principle of non-discrimination alone. Even when such particular personal qualities that are expressly mentioned in non-discrimination principles are not involved, the principle of equality and the rule of law require that law should treat legal subjects equally in similar circumstances. The question is whether coherence of law can offer the needed key for pinpointing breaches of such a broader principle of equality.

The application of the principle of equality requires similarity of circumstances. The assessment of similarity, however, can be made in several ways. What is equal in a relevant way is not an 'objective' matter. The distinction technique, known from common law, illustrates how easily a similarity claim can be warded off when the legal actor does not accept the result. Essentially, the way matters are systematised determines the equality assessment. Similarity is always an abstraction made from a chosen point of view.[63]

In private law, one may seek the key to comparison in various quarters. One may choose the perspective of the traditional systematisation of private law or of some particular branch of law. In this perspective, legal coherence would offer the tools for comparison. On the other hand, however, one may also seek the similarities in actual social situations or societal needs, across traditional legal boundaries. It might even appear as more natural to base the assessment of equality on conceptions of similarity of real situations rather than on an abstract system of legal concepts. One can focus on similarity in practical experience and empirical analysis rather than in conceptual structures.[64] The best choice is not self-evident. Below I will mention some examples that illustrate the difficulties in choosing the key to comparison in the multitude of perspectives at hand.

Assessing equality from the perspective of general private law conceptuality often does not provide a sufficient solution. In private law, circumstances that conceptually and systematically are similar are not necessarily treated similarly. For example, the rules on terminating contracts are very different with regard to different contract types. The fact that the provisions on terminating commercial agency contracts, insurance contracts and tenancy contracts are different does not concern supporters of equality (and rightly so), although, from an abstract legal point of view, the situations are equal. The societal substance of the situations is different. There are

[63] Often cited in this context is Gustav Radbruch: '*Gleichheit ist immer nur Abstraktion von gegebener Ungleichheit unter einem bestimmten Gesichtspunkt*'.
[64] Sibony (2018: 182).

no clear criteria, however, for how different the societal situations should be, in order to trigger different solutions. Is it a problem of equality that the law protects a commercial agent[65] differently than other subordinate traders?

As has been noted above, contemporary law tends to be divided into an increasing number of branches of law with their own understanding of local coherence. A branch-related perspective may offer one starting point for reasoning on equality. It does not challenge, however, the process of fragmentation of contemporary law, but rather makes use of it. The focus on branches of law may even overcome the opposite between a legal conceptuality and a societal real-life perspective. The development of new branches of law reflects the fact that late modern law increasingly takes care of the regulatory needs of the society through contextually bound legislation and practice. The construction of branches and their principles that in this way emanates from the factual substance of the situations supports societal understandings of equality.

Not even on the level of branches of law, however, is there a straightforward relationship between coherence and equality. One may ask why the general doctrines of each branch of law should be the starting point for the equality assessment, rather than, for example, a problem-focused approach that would link different branches of law with each other.[66] From such a contextual perspective, the internal coherence of branches of law would be left to a secondary position in the assessment.

The picture of the relationship between coherence and equality becomes even more blurred when one adds the European dimension to the reasoning. It might require a comparison across the borders. A particular European discourse on equality relates to the equality between persons from different Member States. With regard to businesses, this kind of equality thinking is in the basic DNA of the EU, in the form of protection of equal conditions of competition. With regard to other persons, it also has argumentative relevance. If, for example, a similar consumer problem appears in different Member States, it would seem contrary to the equality principle if consumers in some countries were protected, whilst consumers in others were not. The development of European consumer law, even though it started from internal market concerns, is to some extent carried by such equality reasoning. European legislation on the harmonisation of consumer law, in other words, might increase the equality between European consumers. On the other hand, however, the punctual consumer law directives are often criticised for being one of the main causes of fragmentation of domestic private law. Measures that increase fragmentation domestically may support equality on the European level.

Even though it seems difficult to establish that fragmentation would have a general negative impact on equality, there are types of fragmentation that may seem more doubtful in this respect. The examples of fragmentation that I have referred to in this book are of a kind that one could call 'situational fragmentation'. Various fragmented rules on strict liability in tort law have evolved for particular types of situations and the different rules on termination of contracts are situational too. The European

[65] Covered by the Commercial Agents Directive (Directive 86/653/EEC).

[66] In Finnish doctrine eg Kangas (1982), discussing the legal position of widows across legal disciplines.

consumer law directives regulate particular problematic situations. Fragmentation, however, may also be personal. Such personal fragmentation is more open to critique from the point of view of equality.

The issue of personalisation is not new in private law. The use of arguments related to the ability or even the needs of the parties[67] has long been discussed.[68] Digitalisation and big data, however, have brought a new perspective to the table. The proponents of a personalised law speak about the opportunities of a law that is adapted to the personal properties of the individual, catering for the personal needs and demands of the parties. For example, the application of the negligence standard could be more closely related to the abilities of the possible tortfeasor;[69] the contractual default rules could be more closely tied to the preference structures of the parties;[70] and consumer law information duties could be tailored to the needs of the individual consumer.[71] Personalisation could build, for example, on both the financial status and the personality type of the party.[72]

Such personalisation is obviously at least debatable from the point of view of the principle of equality.[73] This is clear in particular when different rules would be applicable because of sensitive and regulated features as ethnic origin,[74] but equality concerns cannot be avoided also in other cases. As personalised rules mean that people are treated differently in the same situation, one should at least demand rational reasons for accepting such a difference.[75] It might be difficult, however, to produce sufficient reasons to counter the weight of the principle of equality. Some scholars have suggested putting emphasis on the consequences of the application of the rules: if the same rules benefit only some actors, but are not needed by others, it would violate equality to apply them also to the latter. According to this view, if the rules were personalised, it would, therefore, rather increase equality than decrease it.[76] In general words, equality is said to require that different people should be treated differently.[77]

At least if the use of different rules are dependent on some personal feature alone, it seems difficult to defend personalisation. In cases in which the personal element is only a part of a broader assessment, including situational factors, the person-related reasoning can be more convincing. Even traditional legal thinking accepts references to personal abilities (eg professionalism) in a negligence assessment or to personal needs in a decision concerning contractual fairness. In such a context, one might even

[67] On need-rationality in private law, see Wilhelmsson (1992).
[68] For a critique of the use of the actual need of the parties, see eg Ripstein (2006: 1429 *et seq*).
[69] Ben-Shahar and Porat (2016); Ben-Shahar and Porat (2021: 61 *et seq*).
[70] Critical: Bender (2020).
[71] eg Busch (2019). For a critique of personalisation of consumer information, see eg Poludniak-Gierz (2018).
[72] Porat and Strahilevitz (2014).
[73] Ben-Shahar and Porat (2021) ch 8 discusses the issue mainly in light of the US Constitution (The Fourteenth Amendment Equal Protection Clause).
[74] Bender (2020: 400–04). This obviously also applies to other features covered by non-discrimination rules.
[75] So Bender (2020: 404–05).
[76] Hacker (2017: 660).
[77] Ben-Shahar and Porat (2021: 14).

discuss the possibility of creating need-oriented private law concepts.[78] This is not the place, however, to pursue this discussion. It suffices to note that whilst situational fragmentation does not seem to form a significant threat to equality, personalised fragmentation might bring in difficult equality issues on the table.

As the principle of equality requires similar treatment in similar situations, but the possible keys to similarity are manifold, the need to respect the principle turns the spotlight on legal reasoning, again. A decision-maker or a scholar discussing a hard issue has to produce arguments, on the one hand, on which grounds two apparently similar situations are treated differently, or, on the other hand, why guidance to a solution is sought from a situation that at first sight seems different. They should clearly reveal their key for the equality assessment. The application of the principle of equality requires transparency of reasoning concerning the comparison that it involves.

IV. IN OTHER WORDS

The small narratives on legal change imply a fragmentation of law that challenges the traditional value of legal coherence. Continental legal discourse, in particular, has emphasised the importance of this value.

A closer look at the coherence discourse, however, reveals a relatively vague understanding of what legal coherence means. The fundamental tests are expressed in words like having the law speaking with one voice or seeing the law as a teleological order tied together by a number of fundamental principles. The vague ideal of coherence does not appear as a convincing reason to worry about the process of fragmentation of law. This is not to say that coherence is not important. However, it often appears as a playmate of, rather than an opposite to fragmentation. In the increasingly fragmented legal world, the value of coherence is related to ever more narrow branches of law.

In this interaction, the concept-building function of legal academia, striving at creating and expanding the islands of coherence, is still an important activity. The doubts with regard to the value of coherence as such do not question the systematising role of legal scholarship.

The demonstration of the vagueness of the concept of coherence is not sufficient to show that fragmentation does not pose challenges to the rule of law. One has to look closer at the reasons why coherence has been regarded as important. From the point of view of the rule of law, many have related the significance of coherence to the values of predictability and equality.

A fragmented law in many cases has as predictable outcomes as a more coherent legal order (whatever that means). Fragmented detailed rules may sometimes lead to more predictable results than broad principles that appear as coherent. Even though one may assume that the shrinking of the islands of coherence in the sea of

[78] As I have suggested in Wilhelmsson (1992: 151–52).

fragmented law expands the overall number of hard issues, the negative impact of fragmentation on predictability seems highly overrated.

The same goes for the relationship between coherence and equality. Even though it is clear that incoherence in some situations can lead to a sense of inequality, there is not a clear-cut relationship between the values of equality and coherence. An assessment of inequality requires a comparison, but between what? Should one seek the coherence key in the structure and conceptuality of private law or in the similarity of concrete social situations? In a European perspective, measures that lead to more fragmentation of national law may improve the equality between persons from different Member States. Situation-related fragmentation, in other words, does not pose an unequivocal threat to equality.

The small narratives on legal change may contain elements of unpredictability and inequality. Change means doing things differently than before. When developing the narratives, from the point of view of the rule of law it is important to control arbitrariness. How can one cater for that need in the setting of a flexible and fragmented learning private law? This is the issue to be discussed in the next chapter.

8

Transparent Reasoning Supporting the Rule of Law

DESPITE THE FLUIDITY of late modern law, the small narratives on legal change are also tied by legal chains in late modernity. These narratives navigate the area between the already legally accepted and the legally possible. If they would not be so bound, they would not be legal narratives. The rule of law requires the law to rule. What does this mean in today's fragmented and flexible legal environment?

One important element of the rule of law is related to the constraints of legal decision-making. The rule of law requires a decision-making that is not felt to be arbitrary[1] and does not allow the abuse of legal power. The rule of law means controlling and fighting arbitrariness.

Here I focus on this aspect of the rule of law, as the movement of legal ideas across European borders obviously produces question marks with regard to this feature. I have not found it necessary here to explore other elements – institutional,[2] procedural and substantive – that have been mentioned in the extensive discussions on the rule of law.[3] It suffices to refer to the Rule of Law Checklist created by the Venice Commission, a useful guide to the various elements that may be included in the concept of the rule of law.[4] Needless to say, the guide also mentions the prevention of abuse and misuse of powers as one of the elements, meaning, *inter alia*, that legal decisions should be based on adequate reasoning:

> Are public authorities required to provide adequate reasons for their decisions, in particular when they affect the rights of individuals? Is the failure to state reasons a valid ground for challenging such decisions in courts?[5]

The need to control arbitrariness directs the focus to the reasoning applied in legal decision-making. As it is hard to emphasise a static predictability of outcomes in an uncertain environment in which new needs and challenges constantly arise, one

[1] So eg the last paper of Joseph Raz (2019).
[2] My metaphor of small narratives, in which various legal actors participate, brings to the fore the multiplicity of checks and balances, an important institutional element of the rule of law.
[3] See eg the volume by Engelbrekt, Moberg and Nergelius (2021), taking stock of the institutional perspective on the rule of law in the EU, with a particular focus on the eastward enlargement.
[4] Venice Commission (2016).
[5] ibid (29).

could instead look at the predictability of arguments and ways of reasoning. And even though it is difficult to realistically discuss equality of outcomes in a diverse and constantly changing society, one may successfully analyse the equality of reasoning. Predictability and equality in ways of reasoning support the rule of law.

In other words, one can aspire to control arbitrariness not only from top to bottom, from the perspective of the system and its coherence, but also from bottom up, from the acceptability of the reasoning used in hard cases. The importance of the latter grows as the impact of the former shrinks.

The rule of law in this sense, focusing on legal reasoning, can be upheld only if the reasoning is accounted for openly and truthfully. Therefore, the key concept here is the transparency of legal reasoning. In this chapter, I will look more closely at the transparency of legal reasoning as a mechanism for supporting the rule of law in a flexible and fragmented legal context.

I. TRANSPARENT REASONING AS A SOLUTION

Looking for the key to the rule of law in legal reasoning changes the perspective on how legal certainty can be promoted. Commenting on the usefulness of the analysis of legal rhetoric, Hans Petter Graver claims that in hard cases the focus on arguments supports predictability rather than weakens it, as an open account of credible legal arguments makes it easier to foresee in what direction legal decision-makers may be convinced to move in the future.[6] Or, as Elina Paunio puts it, instead of a formal and system-oriented legal certainty, one could speak about a 'discursive legal certainty' that understands legal decision-making and legal reasoning as a communicative process in which, for example, a court communicates a message to its addressees.[7] According to Jan Smits, in a diverse European law one should 'move away from a focus on rules, principles and concepts … towards an identification of *arguments* for and against certain solutions.'[8] In different wordings, the scholars suggest reasoning and arguments rather than a coherent order to be safeguards of the rule of law.

As mentioned in the previous chapter, some scholars have moved coherence discourse from the coherence of the system towards the micro-perspective on the coherence of legal reasoning. This approach, however, is not pictured as static, as a system-oriented coherence discourse would easily be. Coherence in legal adjudication is seen as a 'continuous process of generating coherence' rather than building a final coherent edifice of reasons,[9] just like a small narrative on legal change that continuously seeks an end in a new legal equilibrium, from which a new small narrative may start again when the time is ripe. The focus, in other words, is on the dynamics of open reasoning. In addition, in this view the equilibrium sought must contain both authoritative legal elements and substantive elements that relate to the fairness of the

[6] Graver (2007: 558).
[7] Paunio (2013: 136), focusing on the European Court of Justice.
[8] Smits (2011: 334).
[9] Soriano (2003: 307).

outcome.[10] Legal reasoning must at least be acceptable both in a legal and in a societal sense. Obviously, in such a complex structure of reasoning there is no closed list of relevant arguments. Therefore, it is essential for an assessment of the acceptability of the reasoning that the decision-maker reports the arguments used as truthfully and completely as possible.

Transparency is a popular metaphor in contemporary societal debate.[11] It has become a 'magic concept' that is hard to object to.[12] In a transparent society, one should avoid secret deals made behind closed doors. A transparent activity can be assessed and criticised, and arbitrariness can be detected and fought in a transparent environment. Transparency in societal decision-making, therefore, is understood as an important feature of a functioning democracy. A rationality that is both discursive and communicative is 'at the bottom of representative democracy.'[13]

In the legal setting, it is a prerequisite for a democratic society that legal decision-making is public. Self-evidently, as a matter of definition, in a society based on the rule of law, secret legal decisions should not be made behind closed doors. But the requirement of openness could go further than that. Transparency taken seriously not only requires decision-making to be accessible, but also relates to how openly legal decisions and scholarly standpoints are justified. It has to do with the honesty of legal reasoning. A transparent legal reasoning accounts for all the arguments that have influenced the decision. Such transparency makes it possible to exert democratic assessment and criticism concerning the ways in which law fulfils it tasks. A transparency requirement of this sort can function as a tool for fighting arbitrariness and for enhancing the legal and democratic legitimacy of legal decision-making. Open reasoning makes it possible to discuss and assess legal decisions both within the legal community and in society.

Lawyers and legal theorists rightly emphasise that the heuristic process when reaching a decision is different than the justification offered for the decision. The context of discovery differs from the context of justification. In a transparent legal decision-making, however, one should strive to make this difference as small as possible.

Needless to say, transparency of reasoning is not an on/off criterion. In complicated issues it is seldom possible for anybody to present all the reasons that have led to a certain standpoint. The *Vorverständnis* of legal actors affects legal reasoning more than one would like to admit. Rather than using a dichotomy between transparent and non-transparent reasoning, one should speak about a scale on which various degrees of transparency are encountered. There can be more or less transparency in legal reasoning. From the point of view of the rule of law, one should support increasing transparency, as much as is practically possible.

Legal reasoning builds on much tacit knowledge on what is to be considered an acceptable argument and how it should be weighed in the relevant legal order. This

[10] ibid (306).

[11] See eg the multidisciplinary collection of essays in August and Osrecki (2019), as well as Koivisto (2022), who (critically) analyses the concept as a governance ideal.

[12] Koivisto (2022: 22).

[13] La Torre (2002: 81).

facilitates the communication between legal actors. An open and truthful reasoning, however, should also strive to picture essential pieces of the tacit knowledge. Even though one cannot escape the impact of the legal culture in which one is raised, the attempt to put knowledge into words makes the decision-maker more aware of tacit biases and facilitates a thorough critique of the decision. By clearly formulating the more fundamental arguments behind a standpoint, one may also be better equipped to escape what Martijn Hesselink, analysing European contract law and political philosophies, has called 'normative intuitionism'.[14]

In cases in which the reasoning includes a possible movement of legal sources across the borders, the usefulness of an express explication of the various national patterns of reasoning is obvious. From the point of view of Europeanisation, the building of some joint legal tacit knowledge on a European level requires open reasoning in the domestic settings. In the words of Walter van Gerven:

> In order to allow each of these traditions to make a valuable input in shaping a *ius commune Europaeum*, judges … must be made aware of the need to use language which is comprehensible to lawyers not belonging to their own legal systems. That would mean for the common law judges to be more concise, for the judges who have adopted the German style to be less academic, and for those who have adopted the French style to be less cryptic.[15]

Some even claim that the comparative perspective as such enhances the quality and openness of national decision-making. As the comparative perspective brings the national court to 'focus on the facts, interests and socio-economic framework of the foreign case', it may lead to 'a better understanding of the facts and legal issues which are at stake in the dispute before a judge.'[16] I will discuss a transparent cross-border use of sources more closely in the next chapter.

Not only should one expressly recognise tacit knowledge and cultural patterns, but there is also a need to overcome patterns that hamper an open account of the arguments. There are restrictive habits in many countries with regard to the reasons that courts expressly refer to. As noted in chapter five section III, in some countries there is a high threshold for the courts to refer to foreign sources, even when they clearly have used such material. 'The notion of foreign precedent is – simply put – uncomfortable.'[17] In the context of movement of legal sources across the borders, these kinds of restrictions do not fulfil the requirement of transparency. From the point of view of European private law, it would be beneficial if such traditions were toned down. For understanding a decision that actually was inspired by a foreign source, it would be desirable to communicate the relevance of this source.

Transparency does not mean the same thing in different contexts. In her analysis of discursive legal certainty and the judicial reasoning of the European Court of Justice, Elina Paunio distinguishes different communicative spheres to which the reasoning is addressed: the parties, the interveners and the involved national courts; the broader context of similar cases; the discussion in legal doctrine; the attention in

[14] Hesselink (2021: 3).
[15] van Gerven (2004: 15).
[16] Berger (2001: 890).
[17] Baasch Andersen (2011: 42), giving an illuminating example.

media; and society at large.[18] This analysis shows how the need to open up tacit legal knowledge has to vary depending on the context. Clearly, for example, the media and the public at large require different and more numerous explanations than the legal actors. What balance one should strike between the legal and the societal audience in this respect is difficult to tell. On the one hand, the persuasiveness of reasoning among legal specialists may sometimes be the best safeguard for the legitimacy of a decision.[19] On the other hand, however, the more societally interesting a legal case appears to be, the more clearly democratic legitimacy and criticism require an extensive account also of the tacit legal knowledge.

Not only are the variations between different receivers of legal reasoning relevant, but the demands made on different legal actors may also vary. Even though the transparency requirements in principle concern all the actors, it is obvious that they are not identical for each and every actor. Both courts and scholars should be transparent in their reasoning, but the content of the requirement is not the same. As scholars also have to fulfil the fundamental scholarly commitments to openness of the scientific community,[20] their reasoning should be transparent on a deeper level. Legal scholars have the best resources to meet the challenging expectation of a thorough account of their reasoning, including the tacit knowledge involved.

II. TOWARDS A TRANSPARENT DOCTRINE OF LEGAL SOURCES

The control of legal reasoning in a way that minimises arbitrariness has traditionally been one of the main preoccupations of legal theory. Theory has developed doctrines of legal sources to provide a tool for predictable decision-making. A doctrine of legal sources is meant to equip the legal actors with a machinery that can make the adopted outcomes seem more 'objective'. In other words, one could see the doctrine of legal sources as a way to create the required transparency of legal reasoning. However, there are drawbacks in many such doctrines that may hamper an open account of the arguments used. A doctrine of legal sources is not necessarily the same as a transparent doctrine of legal sources.

The name of the doctrine of legal sources in German and in the Nordic languages is metaphorical. The German *Rechtsquellenlehre*, the Swedish *rättskälleläran* and the Finnish *oikeuslähdeoppi* all paint a picture of a well from which the materials used in legal reasoning can be scooped. One may criticise such a metaphor for tending to compress the variety of arguments that can be used into something that can be fetched from a few 'wells'.[21] It pictures a relatively schematic doctrine of legal sources, a doctrine that typically presents itself in the form of a 'catalogue of the sources'.[22] Such a doctrine may display features that are not helpful when trying to

[18] Paunio (2013: 137–39).
[19] Smits (2010: 21).
[20] Tuori (2021: 106).
[21] Makkonen (1998: 77).
[22] Aarnio (1987: 78).

draw a transparent picture of legal reasoning. At worst, it tends to obscure rather than illuminate the reality of legal reasoning.

The risk of a cleavage between the picture conveyed by a doctrine of legal sources and actual legal reasoning is well known. Developers of doctrines of legal sources often expressly admit it. They may attempt to circumvent the challenge, for example by distinguishing between the doctrine of legal sources, listing the sources, and a theory of argumentation that defines '*how* the sources should be used in the argumentation in order to guarantee the maximal acceptability of the reasoning'.[23] The problematic features that I will analyse in the following therefore reflect a simplified and generalised picture that does not offer a complete image of the actual doctrines of legal sources.

So, what are the challenges? Firstly, a doctrine of legal sources may use a schematic language that reflects a thinking in alternatives rather than degrees. The idea of a particular category of arguments that can be termed legal sources easily pushes the discussion in the direction of binary on/off questions. In such a discourse, one would ask whether a certain item should be considered a legal source or not. For example, when discussing the role of the European collections of principles, some approach the issue by asking whether the PECL or the DCFR can be considered a 'legal source' in the national setting.[24] However, in practice, legal argumentation is seldom so schematically structured. It rather moves in hermeneutic circles in which both the content of the sources and their 'status' as well as other possible arguments interact with each other. A realistic analysis therefore requires much more nuanced questions than crude dichotomous ones. A schematic binary approach may also hamper the possibilities to detect minor changes and trends in modes of legal reasoning.

For example, the Swedish Supreme Court judge, Torgny Håstad, pictures the reasoning of the Court in cases where it has made reference to the DCFR in a somewhat puzzling way. He claims that the references are 'always of an informative or supportive nature' and not 'a source of binding domestic law', but at the same time he notes that 'disputing parties must be aware that the Supreme Court is familiar with DCFR and may be inspired by its solutions.'[25] The dichotomic language of legal sources clearly does not offer sufficient tools for Håstad to describe how the DCFR is used, as he needs other concepts as well, such as 'inspiration'. I will be looking more closely at the use of DCFR as a legal source in the next section of this chapter.

Secondly, the way in which the list of legal sources is presented often conveys the picture of a complete and closed list. It explicitly or implicitly hints at a kind of *numerus clausus* of legal sources, inspiring recurrent discussions on whether some new item should be added to the list. In practice, however, such closure does not reflect the great variety of arguments used in legal reasoning.

Admittedly, many doctrines of legal sources alleviate this sense of closedness by including an open-ended category, covering most of the arguments one can imagine to be relevant. For example, in Nordic legal theory what is called *reella hänsyn* – factual

[23] Aarnio (2011: 149).
[24] See eg Samuelsson (2016: 216) (critical to the discussion) with further references.
[25] Håstad (2015: 184). Could one express it more vaguely?

or practical arguments – is usually mentioned as a source of law, in the instrumental Nordic legal culture even an important one. Such a category of practical arguments covers a wide range of different types of arguments, both economic, social and historical. This leaves out only a small category of 'forbidden sources', such as 'arguments that are against the law or good practice and those that are openly political.'[26]

However, even within doctrines of legal sources that include an open-ended category the problem of a closed list may remain in another form. The difficulty follows from the distinction between authoritative and substantive reasons.[27] Even though this is not a clear-cut distinction, it adds another perspective to the question of how closed the list of legal sources appears to be. The category of practical arguments that seems to open the list of legal sources usually contains various kinds of substantive reasons, whilst the possible authoritative reasons are strictly listed. As this listing of the authoritative sources, containing legislation, case law, perhaps *travaux prèparatoires* and *Stand der Lehre*, appears to be closed, new candidates for the position of authoritative argument easily trigger discussions on whether the established list should be opened.

The example of the use of the DCFR as an argument in national legal reasoning illustrates this well. The DCFR is an example of a potential source that can have both substantive and authoritative impact. On the one hand, the DCFR can function as a source of good substantive reasons; on the other hand, there is often at least an authoritative element present in reasoning based on the DCFR. The recognition of such an authoritative status immediately raises the question whether the DCFR could be included in the closed list of authoritative sources. Therefore, it is not surprising that the question whether the DCFR can be considered to be a legal source has also been raised in Swedish discourse, despite the open-ended Nordic doctrine of legal sources. A similar question can be raised with regard to the use of comparative materials in legal decision-making.

As noted above, the list of legal sources may also be closed from the other end, by describing a number of 'forbidden sources'. In practice, however, the content of this delimitation is not very clear. For example, one can on good grounds condemn the use of 'openly political' arguments (usually meaning arguments related to party politics), but can one really draw a generally acceptable line between 'openly political' and other substantive arguments that would amount to any more than criticising the way in which the argument is formulated? Or to give another example: the Goddess of Justice is often pictured as blind-folded in order to emphasise that every person, rich or poor, young or old, should be treated alike, and that the person's qualities and condition should be ignored when making a legal decision. Person-related arguments therefore would seem to fall under the category of forbidden sources. However, as I have shown elsewhere, in Finnish and Nordic private law one may in certain situations take into account the poor financial and social position of a party as a legally relevant fact, for example when discussing the adjustment of contracts or of damages in tort or the doctrine of *social force majeure*. In this way, the blind-folded Goddess

[26] Aarnio (2011: 151).

[27] For a definition, see below in this chapter. I will also apply this distinction in ch 9.

of Justice is forced to look at the parties and accept a portion of need-rationality in private law.[28] Also from the point of view of forbidden sources, practice appears to be more flexible than a rigid doctrine of legal sources would foresee.

Thirdly, the doctrine of legal sources is often presented as a hierarchical edifice. A much-used example is the tripartite classification introduced by Aleksander Peczenik, distinguishing sources that 'ought to be' used, 'should' be used and are 'permitted' to be used.[29] One could in other words group legal sources in strongly binding sources (legislation), weakly binding sources (precedents and *travaux préparatoires*), and permitted sources (recommendations, legal literature and foreign law). It should be noted, however, that for Peczenik the hierarchy of legal sources was only a prima facie order that could be bypassed in concrete legal reasoning.

A presentation of the sources of law as a hierarchy accurately reflects our understanding that different arguments have different relative weights in legal reasoning. In reality, however, legal reasoning is much more varied, relative to the content of the sources and the context in which they are used. In one case, case law may play a leading role, while in another case substantive arguments may lead the court to play down the role of previous cases. Sometimes solutions *contra legem* are adopted, even though legislation is in the highest category of sources. For example, during the pandemic there were situations where the rule of law seemed to be eroded, and this also related to the enforcement of legislation concerning private law issues.[30] The age of the legal sources, their fitness with regard to the actual case and even their subjective weight – for example in references to legal scholarship, the opinion of a well-known scholar may be given more weight than that of others – can all have an impact on their role in the reasoning. Often the reasoning is built on a multitude of arguments in a way that makes it difficult to say whether an argument has been used in a decisive role or only as an additional support for the outcome.

A schematic, closed and hierarchic doctrine of legal sources does not picture legal reasoning in hard cases very well. As already stated, however, a doctrine of legal sources does not have to appear to be such a schematic, closed and hierarchic edifice. When I occasionally use the term 'legal sources' in this book it is in a less formalistic sense, referring only to the possibility of using a certain item as an argument in legal reasoning. This is because a formalistic doctrine of legal sources does not correspond to our tacit knowledge, or even to our openly described knowledge about the complexity of legal reasoning.

The mismatch between a formalistic doctrine of legal sources and the reality of legal reasoning means that a picture conveyed through the lens of such a doctrine is not very transparent. At worst, a formal application of a doctrine of legal sources – for example a pure reference to the wording of a legal text without any analysis of the particular context, or a reference to a case without a closer look at its reasoning – impairs the transparency of the real reasons. To achieve transparency, one has to look behind any formal doctrine of legal sources and ask further questions.

[28] See Wilhelmsson (1992).
[29] Peczenik (1975: 7 *et seq*), (1989: ch 6), (1995: 213 *et seq*).
[30] See eg Fassiaux (2021) on EU passenger rights.

This does not mean that the formal doctrines of legal sources would be 'false' or useless. They convey a picture of how legal reasoning usually treats certain categories of arguments. They express some basic features of the legal culture in question, for example (in continental law) the primacy of legislation, the roles of case law in various jurisdictions or the strong position of *travaux préparatoires* in certain countries. In fact, the doctrines may picture large parts of legal decision-making and legal reasoning quite accurately. So-called easy cases or routine cases can usually be described in terms of a relatively formal doctrine of legal sources. They are 'easy' precisely because the result seems to follow directly from the applicable sources.

In hard cases,[31] however, the application of a formal doctrine of sources does not appear convincing. If it were, the case would not be hard. As a deep discussion on legal reasoning must focus on hard cases, a doctrine of legal sources that catches only the easy ones is not sufficient. In addition, one should bear in mind that there is always the possibility that an easy case in a particular situation becomes a hard case. A small narrative on legal change may start in the form of a novel legal reaction to something that in the stable phase has been treated as an easy case. A legal actor may even rethink the relationship between sources, for example between legislation and case law: in relation to climate cases some have framed the issue as a tension between the task of politics and the task of courts.[32] Be that as it may, in climate cases, from various parts of the world, there seems to be 'a shared understanding of the need to reach to a multiplicity of legal sources to properly determine the obligations of the state'.[33] A formal doctrine of legal sources does not reflect the transparency required to prevent arbitrariness in such landmark cases.

In other words, transparent reasoning requires answering a more complex web of questions than those that can be framed within a formal doctrine of legal sources. In the following section, I will look more closely at the various types of questions that appear to be relevant in this context. I will start by picturing a concrete and, in the context of this book, topical example.

III. THE DRAFT COMMON FRAME OF REFERENCE AS AN EXAMPLE

To illustrate what kind of questions one should address in a transparent mode of reasoning I will return to the example of the DCFR as a potential legal source. The DCFR, the PECL and other collections of principles have brought a new type of possible legal source on the agenda. As noted in chapter 5 section V, the PECL has been referred to in national court decisions and arbitral awards as well as in legal dogmatic literature. The same goes for the DCFR succeeding the PECL. If one wants to embark on this road, the value of transparency requires express answers to several questions. In the following, I will look at the use of the most ambitious collection of principles, the DCFR, as an argument in domestic legal reasoning and discuss what

[31] See ch 1 section IV on the distinction and on the focus of the book on hard cases.
[32] Weller and Tran (2021: 603).
[33] de Vilchez Moragues (2022: 16).

kind of questions need to be answered in order to make the reasoning as transparent as possible.

As mentioned above in this chapter, the references to the DCFR by the Swedish Supreme Court has triggered a discussion on whether the DCFR can be considered a source of law in Sweden. I have argued that such a question is too schematic and needs to be replaced by more analytic questions. One should dig deeper into the issue of why a court or a scholar wants to make reference to the collection of principles. A short overview of Swedish and Finnish cases in which the Court has referred to the DCFR offers sufficient fuel for the analysis of what questions one should address.

Looking at the Swedish Supreme Court, which has already referred to the DCFR in about 20 cases, one finds an obvious explanation of this activity. Two judges, Torgny Håstad and Johnny Herre, have been participating actively, often as drafting judge, in cases where the DCFR has been expressly mentioned in the reasoning of the Court. These judges also participated in the drafting of the DCFR. The establishment of the habit to consult the DCFR can in other words be explained in causal terms by the coincidental fact that two of the DCFR drafters happened to be members of the Supreme Court at the time when the question of the source value of the DCFR was topical.[34] Håstad himself admits this openly:

> One reason for the amount of references may be that I was a justice of the Supreme Court up to 2011 and that Johnny Herre is a justice there from 2009. Both of us were members of the group working out the DCFR and thus familiar with its contents.[35]

Such a causal explanation, however, is not the type of argument one hopes for when demanding open and transparent reasoning. Arguments related to the person of the judge are of the kind that could be called 'forbidden sources', even though they might have a high explanatory value.[36] Causes are not necessarily acceptable reasons.

In his attempt to explain the justificatory use of the DCFR in the Swedish Supreme Court, Håstad claims that the references to DCFR are 'of an informative or supportive nature.' He then mentions four ways of using the collection as part of the Court's reasoning. First, the DCFR might just be used as a comparative law source, as a kind of 'summary of foreign law'. Secondly, it has been used 'to demonstrate that Swedish law or the Supreme Court ruling is in line with foreign law', which might be of importance in a particular line of business. Thirdly, it can be used as a source of 'inspiration' when there is no clear solution offered by domestic law. Finally, sometimes the reference to the DCFR simply forms 'part of a broad introduction'.[37]

One finds similar kinds of use in the two Finnish cases in which the Supreme Court has referred to the DCFR. In one of the cases, the Court first referred to its own previous case law and then noted that the DCFR had adopted a similar standpoint; the reason for the reference might be that the case dealt with financial leasing, a relatively international line of business.[38] In this case, the status of the DCFR argument is

[34] Samuelsson (2016: 210).
[35] Håstad (2015: 179).
[36] One of the classic texts is Frank (1963; first published 1930).
[37] Håstad (2015: 184).
[38] Finnish Supreme Court, KKO 2015:26.

unclear. The Court could have reached the same solution based on previous case law, without referring to the DCFR at all. In the other case, however, concerning termination of a long-term contract, the Court expressly used the DCFR to fill in a lacuna in Finnish law.[39] The Court reached parts of its solution by using a relevant provision of the DCFR as justification.

The Swedish and Finnish cases illustrate some of the questions that call for an answer when using the DCFR as a legal source in domestic law. This description is not meant to be exhaustive. Other kinds of questions may also arise.[40]

First, one has to take a stand on the basic question, why the DCFR is considered to be a relevant argument. The use of the DCFR usually has to be based on substantive meta-level reasons. One possible approach is a reference to the expertise of the drafters of the DCFR. The collection of principles is an attempt to combine the knowledge of positive law with an assessment of what is considered to be a good rule. The elite of European legal scholars, among them also experts with thorough practical knowledge, participated in the drafting of the rules. Another possible line of argument relates to the presumed advantages of European harmonisation. If one, for various possible reasons, finds European harmonisation desirable, the DCFR may be used as a device for promoting such a development. In this context, one may also discuss whether it is more natural to use the DCFR when dealing with internationalised issues rather than with domestic ones.

One might also analyse more deeply how one uses the DCFR from the point of view of the division between authoritative and substantive legal sources. As noted above, the DCFR is a source that cannot be put in only one of the boxes of the dichotomy. Is one using the material gathered in the collection only as a cornucopia of good substantive arguments, through which one can learn what works elsewhere in Europe, or is the reference to the DCFR considered to give additional authoritative weight to the argument? One might recognise that 'there is something authoritative about the laws of others'[41] and that DCFR as a kind of compilation of national laws carries this authority as well. Usually the substantive and the authoritative elements are combined in legal reasoning using the DCFR, but either flavour may sometimes be predominant. In a transparent mode of reasoning, one should openly discuss the balance between these elements.

Secondly, one has to address the role and weight of the DCFR as an argument concerning the issue at hand. It is possible that one gives the DCFR a fairly strong position and uses it to develop domestic law, even going so far as to criticise and push for changes in established domestic law. In a somewhat weaker role, it is only referred to in order to fill gaps in domestic law. It is given still less normative force when it is used only as an additional argument to support the result reached on the basis of other arguments. One may, for example, in this way give substantive arguments a kind of legal spice, as the DCFR functions as a safeguard that the substantive

[39] Finnish Supreme Court, KKO 2018:37.

[40] Like the choice of language: should one only use the English version? For a critique, see Sefton-Green (2008).

[41] Walker (2019: 368).

arguments are sound.[42] Finally, the DCFR may also be used as one of the building blocks when the general principles of the domestic private law are developed.[43] A transparent reasoning would indicate on which of these levels the DCFR is used, and why this approach has been chosen.

As the DCFR lacks formal status, it is usually not convincing to use a reference to the DCFR as the sole argument to decide an issue. There is usually a need for some substantive reasoning concerning the suitability of the rule to be applied in the context of the domestic legal and societal environment. Transparency related to the weight of the DCFR in other words normally requires a sufficient account of the substantive consequences of the application of the rule in question. One has to analyse what the introduction of the solution of the DCFR means in substantive terms with regard to the domestic society.

Thirdly, as many of the reasons for using the DCFR apply to other similar collections as well and also to comparative knowledge in general, one should provide an explicit justification of the choice of the DCFR as the source to use. A scholar who refers to the DCFR should make it clear why this collection has been given particular attention, instead of, for example, the PECL or the UNIDROIT Principles. The justification may be sought in substantive reasoning related to each concrete issue at hand, but it might also be of a more systematic nature. In legal dogmatic scholarship, a systematic approach is particularly important, as the results are not convincing if the source used seems to vary arbitrarily.

Such more systematic reasons, related to the use of the source as such, may for example be the comprehensive nature of the DCFR, its semi-official status, as supported by the Commission, and an assessment that this collection is the best device to use if European harmonisation is sought for. It is easy to see that such arguments can be met by good counter-arguments – as described in chapter five section V, many have considered the DCFR to be more doctrinal and less pragmatic than the PECL – but that simply underlines the importance of the transparency of the reasoning. It may lead to other solutions, for example a parallel use of the collections of principles: if all the relevant collections point in the same direction, it certainly strengthens the argument.

In this context one should also discuss the issue why the DCFR, or the other collections of principles, are used instead of comparative materials from other Member States. Why not opt for a free movement of legal ideas directly across the borders instead of choosing the indirect way of using the DCFR as source of Europeanised learning? Reasons of research economy or decision-making economy may make this solution appealing, but these reasons should be openly accounted for. As shown in chapter 5 section VI, digitalisation may within the foreseeable future decrease the weight of such reasons. As was also discussed in chapter 5 section V, the transparency of the comparative notes attached to the DCFR are essential. If these are accurate and sufficiently extensive, it makes the use of the DCFR less objectionable from a comparative point of view. In fact, there are cases in which the notes of the DCFR

[42] Janssen and Schultze (2011: 249) speak about a *Kontrollfunktion* of comparative law.
[43] Norros (2007: 39).

have been used to demonstrate the comparative law experience, for example that rules concerning the issue vary between the Member States.[44]

When discussing this issue, one should recall the different roles, opportunities and traditions of courts and scholars. It seems more legitimate for a court to use the DCFR as a kind of shortcut to Europe that makes it possible to use already collected and processed comparative knowledge.[45] For legal scholars, the same kind of reasoning is less convincing. A scholar who uses the DCFR encounters a basic question of importance in the scientific community: to what extent can research rely on the results of previous research without questioning it? The DCFR of course is not a research result in the traditional sense, and nobody has suggested that it would represent some kind of average European private law. This does not mean, however, that one should not from time to time question the comparative information on which the DCFR rests, in particular as the drafters of the DCFR themselves have stated that 'The DCFR is an academic text' that 'sets out the results of a large European research project and invites evaluation from that perspective.'[46] Scholars who make use of the DCFR should at least openly address the question why they are relying on the collection instead of on the experience that can be brought directly across the borders from other Member States.[47]

I have looked more closely at the use of the DCFR here, not only because it relates to the Europeanisation theme of the book, but also because it offers a good example of the large variety of questions that in a transparent reasoning can be made concerning one argument alone. The questions that can be posed in general, not only concerning the DCFR, are of course multifold. In the following, I will sketch some traits of the broader picture.

IV. A TRANSPARENT INTERPLAY BETWEEN AUTHORITATIVE AND SUBSTANTIVE ARGUMENTS

As the example of the DCFR has shown, a transparent legal reasoning may address a multitude of questions. They relate both to the range of possible arguments and to the relative weight of each argument.

The nature of the arguments vary. Above, I have referred to the distinction between substantive and authoritative reasons. Substantive reasons may contain, for example, references to economic or social consequences of a decision or to moral principles. Their value as arguments is directly dependent on how convincing they are as to their substantive content. Authoritative reasons, on the other hand, do not derive their value primarily from their substance, but from the institutional position of the source, like acts of legislation, court cases, in many countries the *travaux préparatoires* and in some even statements in legal literature (*Stand der Lehre*). What is expressed in an

[44] eg the Swedish case NJA 2010 p 629.

[45] Samuelsson (2016: 212) uses the shortcut metaphor in this context.

[46] DCFR (2009: 7).

[47] *cf* also Schmidt-Kessel (2006: 328), who argues that the character of the PECL as a comparative work should affect its interpretation.

authoritative source has value as an argument primarily because it is stated in such a source.

Legal reasoning is usually based on a combination of authoritative and substantive arguments. This dichotomy is therefore a useful starting point when analysing some of the requirements of an open argumentation, even though some arguments, as has already been noted, appear to have both authoritative and substantive features. Transparent legal reasoning, in hard cases, typically combines both kinds of reasons and both should be openly accounted for.

The roles of the two groups of arguments differ, at least in principle. Authoritative arguments make the reasoning legal. Legislation, case law and other authoritative arguments render the reasoning a legal flavour. One might say that these arguments draw 'a boundary between what is legal and what is not.'[48] Therefore, a legal decision or analysis usually has to include some reference to an authoritative source, at least to position the issue on the legal map. In order to make a small narrative on change legal, there has to be some authoritative element involved in the narrative.

If the express wording of the most important authoritative source or sources undoubtedly cover the issue at hand, the case would typically be classified as an easy case. In such a situation, reference only to the authoritative argument, for example to the wording of the applicable legislation, might seem sufficient. However, as mentioned before, even an easy issue may in a particular situation or when societal and ethical conditions have changed be questioned and turned into a hard one. There is in other words always a more or less hidden potential of questioning authoritative arguments, even in an easy case, by bringing new substantive arguments into the equation. If the substantive arguments are strong, a legal actor who reasons in pure authoritative terms without reference to critical substantive reasons may appear to be hiding behind a too formal approach. A truly transparent legal reasoning would also open up the substantive queries in such a situation.

Concerning many issues, authoritative sources only draw the boundaries around possible solutions. They determine what could be deemed 'legally possible'. Even if one cannot define the exact answer to a legal question so that everyone would agree, there are certainly always alternatives that so clearly fall outside the authoritative boundaries that no (sane) legally educated person from the jurisdiction would find them legally possible. The boundaries are not, however, precise and stable. The point of the metaphor of small narratives on legal change is indeed that each step of the narrative involves a displacement of the boundaries of the legally possible, opening up for new steps that were formerly not acceptable. Both the moves within the boundaries and the pressure towards moving the boundaries typically require some substantive elements in the reasoning. In addition to the legally possible, one also has to search for the societally desirable. A transparent reasoning requires an open account of the substantive reasons for these moves.

Such moves can also be made by introducing new authoritative arguments to the scene. A good example is the possible use of comparative materials as well as the DCFR and other collections of principles as sources of authoritative arguments.

[48] Aarnio (2011: 147), referring, however, to the doctrine of legal sources as a whole.

The knowledge that a certain solution is adopted in some other countries that are deemed important may suffice to overcome the 'national ought'[49] and move the domestic boundaries of what is considered legally possible, and thereby open up the field for a narrative on legal change. In a cross-border micro-political legal strategy, this function may be used to promote issues that the activists are supporting. Transparency requires, however, that substantive goals and effects are openly acknowledged. In the words of David Kennedy, comparative law projects should come 'with an ideological and interest "impact statement"'.[50]

A reference to fundamental rights is another example of how an authoritative argument can be used to open up traditional reasoning and make it possible to introduce new substantive arguments into private law.[51] The acknowledgement of fundamental rights reasoning in private law can have a positive influence on the transparency of argumentation, as it allows a more open resort to a value-related discourse than the traditional private law paradigm.

Even though the use of authoritative arguments is what makes a reasoning legal, substantive arguments are important in a transparent presentation of the reasoning, in particular in hard cases.[52] The focus on situations in which law learns from reality through small narratives on legal change underlines the need for substantive reasoning. A learning law that aspires to respond flexibly to new societal demands should attempt to reach a deep understanding of the societal implications of the issues at hand. Substantive arguments cannot be avoided in the small narratives that are carrying the processes of legal learning. As has been said, a truly European private law would to some extent require an interdisciplinary approach, including economics, history and empirical evidence, which would support a 'demystification of national private law.'[53]

The substantive arguments may be of various kinds, from common sense assessments to fully fledged empirical analysis of the causality chains involved. They may also concern ethical and philosophical issues,[54] taking into account societal changes that affect moral perceptions. A transparent reasoning requires the decision-maker expressly to address the latent values behind the reasoning. Obviously, the requirement of transparency must be different with regard to courts and academics. Where the use of common sense reasoning by the courts may be acceptable, as long as it is sufficiently transparent to make it possible to question the assumptions, scholars face a stronger demand to discuss the assumptions in the light of scientific evidence, if that evidence is available.

[49] This expression is used by Coendet (2014: 3), when criticising comparative-law-sceptic legal positivism.

[50] Kennedy (2003: 206). In the same vein, Frankenberg (2016: 231), who advocates a reflexive and critical turn of comparative law: 'How, for what purpose and for whose benefit does one compare laws … ?'

[51] See ch 6 section IV.

[52] Alexy (1989: 286) claims more generally that 'practical arguments' are always necessary in the last analysis, as 'Statements of legal dogmatics cannot continue to be justified by even more statements of legal dogmatics'.

[53] Smits (2004: 243).

[54] See also Hesselink (2021) – and earlier (2011a) – analysing the relationship between theories of political philosophy and European contract law.

V. REASONING IN A REAL-LIFE LANGUAGE

Above, I underlined the importance of a truthful reporting of the substantive arguments involved as an element of transparency. Decisions in which the societal consequences have had an impact on the outcome should not be hidden behind 'pure' legal reasoning. The account of substantive arguments, be it commonsense reasoning or a research-based analysis, cannot, however, easily be made in a very formal and abstract legal conceptuality. The emphasis on substantive arguments pushes legal discourse in the direction of using more ordinary language. I have noted above the accentuation of ordinary language or 'real-life language' as both a tendency and a normative demand in several contexts.[55]

The development of the language of legal discourse to include concepts closer to real life can support both pragmatic reasoning, democratic control and critique of law.

The further away the language of the legal world is from the language of the real world, the more likely one creates translation errors when moving from one to the other. A legal actor using abstract legal reasoning often has some real-life examples in mind – in a court case the case at hand – and the reasons connected with the examples are not necessarily good ones when confronted with other situations covered by the same abstract concepts. In pragmatic reasoning that focuses more clearly on the real-life situation, this risk is diminished. It makes sense to use categories that are easier to recognise, both for lawyers and for lay persons.[56]

At least in principle the use of real-life language increases the opportunities of democratic control of arbitrariness, as it facilitates the assessment of the substantive parts of the reasoning by others than professional legal experts. A transparent law that wishes to address important societal problems in a language that can be understood by the media and the public should not lock itself up in highly abstract and self-referential language. Legal professionals have to open the doors to their conceptual ivory towers. As legal realists have shown, doctrinalism can function as an improper shield against critique from non-lawyers.[57]

In critical discourse, legal language is pictured as a language of lawyer domination. Adam Gearey notes that even radical legal thinking may reproduce forms of domination through legal language. Therefore, a radical lawyer, according to his view, should not hide behind technical languages.[58] Such a lawyer should rather focus on problem-solving in a way that resembles how 'ordinary folks' approach challenges.[59] More generally, the use of law as an instrument of micro-politics pushes the language in a real-life direction. It favours the use of words of real life that can be understood by both the media and other non-legal societal players. The causes of micro-politics, like climate change, are usually real-life issues, which cannot be neatly ordered into traditional legal categories.

[55] See, in particular, chs 2 and 3.
[56] So also Hesselink (2002: 242).
[57] Dagan (2015: 1893).
[58] Gearey (2018: 116).
[59] ibid (124 *et seq*).

This is not to say, however, that one should abandon the use of formal legal concepts. The process is not an either-or one. Legal reasoning requires some basis in tradition.[60] Legal experts can often best defend the rule of law by presenting the most fundamental critique of flawed and arbitrary decision-making. The task of academic scholars is also to contribute to the development of law by creating and refining legal concepts. Because of the increasing need for transparency in legal reasoning, however, such development easily implies the introduction of new real-life elements into legal conceptuality.

The wishes for a legal language closer to real life are not unique for contemporary law.[61] Various strands of pragmatism, like American and Scandinavian realism, and subsequent analytical schools have strived at directing attention towards the solution of concrete problems and diminishing the role of general legal concepts (regarded as 'metaphysical'). They have underlined the value of substantive arguments. One could therefore picture the contemporary voyage towards more real life in legal language as a continuation of what realist and analytical movements have achieved. For two reasons, however, I find it important to underline the contemporary pressures towards increasing real-life reasoning. First, the American and Scandinavian turn to pragmatism did not necessarily appear in Europe as a whole.[62] Secondly, the rapidly growing uncertainty of contemporary society, including an ever more rapid pace of change, presumably increases the pressures on a fragmentation of law into real-life pieces.

The length of the steps to be taken in this direction may vary according to different domestic legal traditions. As far as it is the case that, in the words of Basil Markesinis, 'common law judges still seem to talk to everyone who is prepared to listen … , German judges only talk to intellectual equals, and French judges … keep their thoughts to themselves',[63] the pressures towards increasing real-life language in legal discourse must take different shapes in these countries. However, this hardly eliminates these pressures for any legal order. All (European) legal orders use abstract legal concepts that appear as more or less unintelligible for the general public.

Looking analytically at the pressure towards reasoning in real-life language, one might distinguish two aspects of the development. On the one hand, the speech about real-life language indicates a move towards a more concrete legal language. Broad legal concepts are replaced by narrower ones, which still, however, appear as legal abstractions. Many of the achievements of realist-analytical approaches are of this kind.[64] On the other hand, it implies a development of legal language towards a language closer to ordinary language. The concepts are formed not through more detailed legal-analytical analysis, but based on descriptions of the real world in the language of this world. These two aspects are not always easy to distinguish. They are almost necessarily interwoven, as on the one hand legal-analytical improvement requires an understanding of the empirical reality, and on the other hand concepts

[60] See also Dagan (2015: 1916) on why realists also tend to accept a certain doctrinalism.
[61] Early on, von Gierke (1889) defended problem-oriented law as being more popular or vernacular (*volkstümlich*).
[62] I have discussed the turn towards legal pragmatism more fully in ch 4 section I.
[63] Markesinis (1994: 30).
[64] Like the realist analysis of ownership, see eg Helin (1988: 211 *et seq*) on Scandinavian realism.

based on ordinary language require some connection to traditional legal conceptuality to be recognised as legally relevant. The increasing real-life orientation, in other words, takes place in a constant interaction between legal and ordinary language.

As the relation between real-life and abstract legal concepts represents a mixture in which the real-life elements successively gain greater weight, it is not necessary or even possible to define precisely what 'real-life' means in this context. A few concrete examples on moves (and insufficient moves) in this direction may suffice.

In tort law, this kind of development has been quite obvious. In his analysis of European tort law, Christian von Bar has expressly noted that 'modern tort law's specific instances are … defined not by legal categories but in terms of real-life circumstances which form the bases of the causes of action.'[65] This can be illustrated by the example mentioned several times before, namely the development of rules concerning strict liability for dangerous activities. Many Member States in some form have recognised such a principle, also mentioned in the Principles of European Tort Law.[66] The discourse on the issue, however, is often focused on concrete situations rather than on legal-conceptual analysis. One may ask directly, how one should assess damage caused by explosives,[67] by leaking pipelines[68] or by car races,[69] to mention some examples from the Nordic countries. The general principle of liability for dangerous activity is scattered into small pieces of case law and legislation concerning specific activities defined very much in a real-life fashion.

In contract law, it is illustrative to compare the two first parts of the PECL with the third part, dealing with what could be called principles of the general law of obligations. According to Ole Lando, the authors of the PECL had a focus on real life in the sense that they 'tried to avoid legal concepts and used factual language, which is easier to translate'.[70] In the spirit of the CISG, they strove to avoid abstract concepts and to use plain language referring to things and events.[71] The Principles should be understood both by lawyers and by business people.[72] Other scholars have also praised the less formal approach by the PECL.[73] However, these praises can honestly be related only to Parts I–II, the purely contract law parts of the book. Part III[74] appears as much more abstract than the rest of the collection, and the relationship to real life is more distant. The reason lies in the considerably shorter timeframe of the drafting of the third part that did not allow the group sufficient opportunities to proceed behind the prevailing conceptual structures. The quality of the PECL would have been higher without the third part. The fact that the follower of the PECL, the DCFR, did not have the expected success as an instrument of European legislation

[65] von Bar (1996: 13).
[66] PETL 5:101(1).
[67] See eg the Finnish Supreme Court KKO 1957 II 10 and 1963 II 63 and the Swedish Supreme Court NJA 1966 p 248.
[68] See eg the Swedish Supreme Court NJA 1991 p 720, 1997 p 468 and 2001 p 368 and the Danish Supreme Court U 1983.866 H and U 1983.895 H.
[69] See the Finnish Supreme Court KKO 1972 II 97.
[70] Lando (2001: 5).
[71] Lando (2006: 483).
[72] Joint Response (2001: 65).
[73] eg Jansen (2011: 56). See also above, ch 5 section V.
[74] Lando, Clive, Prüm and Zimmermann (2003).

might also have been due to its abstract nature, not being in line with the demands of real-life orientation.

The 'real life' described in the above examples is situational. As noted earlier, personal fragmentation may occur as well. This may lead to the emergence of corresponding real-life concepts. I have earlier discussed the possibility of private law concepts like a 'debtor with limited means', a 'debtor in need of housing', a 'low income debtor', an 'unemployed debtor', an 'ill debtor', a 'debtor burdened with considerable maintenance liabilities' and a 'small-enterprise debtor of limited financial strength'.[75] The legal discourse would obviously be quite different if it would use such real-life terms instead of, or in addition to, the abstract 'debtor' and 'creditor' or 'seller' and 'buyer'.[76] One may assume, however, that the principle of equality sets some (vague) borderlines against too far-reaching personalisation[77] and use of person-related real-life concepts. One has to balance the advantages of recognising the 'real' people involved with the ideal of a blindfolded Goddess of Justice who cannot see the parties when delivering justice.

'Real-life language' or 'ordinary language' is not a fixed and clearly defined way of communication. Language varies with context. For example, in relation to consumer rights, emphasis should be on real life as experienced by the ordinary consumer. The legal language and way of communication should be understood directly by consumers, without the help of professional lawyers. When discussing purely commercial matters, on the other hand, 'real life' could also mean the realities of commercial life, which tend to be expressed in a language of commercial actors. An intrusion of business language into legal language is obviously taking place. To some extent, one has to accept this tendency as a fact, but one should also recognise the risk that the development of one expert language, legal language, through the influence of another expert language, the language of business, may decrease transparency in relation to those who do not master these languages. In so far as fragmentation of the law leads to small, expert-driven regulatory silos, the risk of adopting a language that is barely comprehensible to other than experts is obvious.[78]

The risk that the openings towards real life can lead to the introduction of another closed expert language has caused concerns in particular with regard to various kinds of technical standards that are acquiring increasing importance in the palette of legal instruments. Standards concerning technological issues and the rules of financial markets are often so specialised that not even a legal professional is able to decipher them. Some might think that a progressive law would require a 'de-technification' of their language.[79] Be that as it may, this example again shows the ambiguity related to most tendencies of legal development. What is presented as a 'democratic' tendency towards a transparent use of language may include 'undemocratic' aspects as well.

The pressures towards real-life language are obvious in the context of EU legislation and court practice. The pragmatic nature of much EU law leads European

[75] Wilhelmsson (1992: 151–52).

[76] See also Domurath (2017: 125), who speaks about a 'real-life mortgagor'.

[77] See ch 7 section III on personalisation and equality.

[78] Criticised by Hesselink (2021: 131).

[79] Micklitz (2022: 407) poses the question, but would prefer to strengthen the judicial review of the standards.

actors consciously to avoid the use of national legal concepts that would be heavily burdened by legal tradition. Real life – the use of 'de-legalised terms'[80] – is a natural starting point for EU law.

This also goes for the Europeanisation of private law more generally. With regard to the particular focus of this book, Europeanisation through the free movement of legal ideas, the pressure towards a language closer to real life is obvious. Borrowing arguments is easier the closer to real life the legal concepts are. As a French judge who was interviewed about the use of foreign sources noted, the general tendency in French judging to focus more on 'categories of factual situations' has an impact on the use of comparative law.[81] A transparent discussion of the reasons for borrowing a solution from another jurisdiction requires an explicit attempt to understand the effects of the solution on national law and society and this is often easier to achieve in a language closer to real life. The discourse in real-life terms is in other words commonplace for comparative lawyers, using the functional method of comparison: the issue to be studied 'must be posed in purely functional terms; the problem must be stated without any reference to the concepts of one's own legal system.'[82] In the academic work related to the Europeanisation of private law, this problem-oriented approach has been developed by the Trento Project that has been searching for the 'common core' of European private law comparing how factual questions are solved in various European jurisdictions.[83]

In the landmark case, *White v Jones*,[84] cited many times before, Lord Goff discussed the concrete issue in a comparative light, disregarding the fact that the conceptual treatment of the issue, being based on contract or tort, was different in English and German law:

> In these circumstances, the effect of the special characteristics of any particular system of law is likely to be, as indeed appears from the authorities I have cited, not so much that no remedy is recognised, but rather that the system in question will choose its own special means for granting a remedy notwithstanding the doctrinal difficulties involved.

In this case, the move from an abstract legal conceptual structure towards a focus on the concrete issue, the liability of a solicitor towards the presumptive beneficiary of a will, was carried out transparently. Gradually, such European learning processes are bound to affect the abstract legal conceptuality involved and push the legal concepts and the legal discourse closer to the language of real life.

VI. IN OTHER WORDS

The increasing fragmentation and flexibility of private law raises worries about the role of the rule of law. One important element of the rule of law is the prevention

[80] Sefton-Green (2012: 40) uses this expression in connection with Europeanisation.
[81] Interviewed by E Mak (2013: 159).
[82] Zweigert and Kötz (1998: 34).
[83] See common-core.org.
[84] [1995] 1 All ER 691.

of arbitrary decision-making. From this perspective, increased transparency of legal reasoning appears to be at least part of the solution. I argue that transparent reasoning is one way of supporting the checks and balances of contemporary society. This turns the focus towards discursive rather than system-oriented legal security. By transparently accounting for all the arguments involved in a legal decision or a legal analysis the legal actor opens up the reasoning for both professional and democratic criticism and control of arbitrariness.

In order to be transparent, the reasoning should explicitly note all the arguments that the decision-maker or scholar has used. Different demands in this respect can obviously be made with regard to courts and scholars respectively, as the latter are also bound by the strict openness requirements of the scientific community.

At the outset, legal decision-making is steered by doctrines of legal sources. Many traditional doctrines, however, are too formal to grasp all the features of truly transparent reasoning. The great variety of modes of legal reasoning in hard cases cannot be understood by a schematic, closed and hierarchic doctrine. Transparent reasoning has to be broader than many of the doctrines of legal sources envisage.

In hard cases, a legal reasoning that aspires to be transparent usually has to include both authoritative and substantive arguments. Reasoning that hides behind authority alone, without disclosing the societal impact of the solution, lacks transparency. A legal analysis that truly aids learning is aware of the societal implications of the issues at hand and openly accounts for the substantive arguments involved.

The focus on substance has implications concerning legal language. There is a pressure on legal language to become closer to real life. Learning across borders also requires a functional approach related to factual situations and described in such terms. The development of the language of legal discourse in this direction can support both pragmatic reasoning, democratic control and a critique of law.

The ideal of transparent reasoning is here illustrated through an analysis of the possible use of the DCFR as an argument in domestic legal reasoning. A transparent use of the DCFR would require a discussion that covers several questions, such as the reasons for referring to such a collection, the role and weight given to the collection and the reasons for the choice of the DCFR in particular. In the next chapter, I will proceed further in analysing questions of this kind, as I will discuss what transparent reasoning means in relation to the free movement of legal ideas directly across the borders.

9

Transparent Movement of Legal Ideas

IN CHAPTER FIVE, I showed how the EU can function as a legal laboratory, facilitating the experimentalism required from law in times of epistemological and ethical uncertainty. The ultimate expression of a truly experimental ethos is a horizontal legal learning across national borders, what I have called a free movement of legal ideas within the EU. In particular, I have chosen to look at the cross-border use of legal materials in the practice of domestic courts and in the reasoning of national legal writing, as this is the ultimate expression of a joint legal area of experimental learning. I discuss the voluntary use by courts and scholars of materials from other EU jurisdictions in applying their domestic laws.[1] Such cross-border learning processes are not pure theory, created in the minds of committed adherents to the idea of a European legal space; they also occur in contemporary legal practice.[2]

In this chapter, I will discuss the question of how one should use such materials, coping with the aspirations to develop a transparent Europeanised legal reasoning.[3] As there is a justificatory burden on those who wish to rely on foreign sources,[4] one has to ask how the requirements posed by this burden could be fulfilled. How can a decision to refer to cross-border materials be sufficiently justified in legal reasoning that aspires to be transparent?

A transparent justification requires courts and scholars to provide open and honest answers to a multitude of questions related to the reasons for using such material and to the ways in which such material is used. To illustrate the issues, I will look at some patterns of reasoning that can be traced in case law, including the accounts of judges regarding their decision-making,[5] as well as in legal dogmatics in various European countries. I am using such cases, however, only as illustrative examples, without any ambition to create a comprehensive picture of the situation in various Member States. My aim is to show what kind of justification one could and should include in a transparent use of foreign sources in an ideal legal Europe.

The full utilisation of the European 'laboratory' requires a growing openness towards the use of materials across the borders. This does not imply, however, that

[1] In other words, it does not cover the 'mandatory' use of foreign law, for example as demanded by domestic private international law, see also Bobek (2013: 19–20).
[2] As exemplified above, in ch 5 section III.
[3] The chapter is partially based on my paper Wilhelmsson (2014), though much expanded and developed.
[4] Walker (2019: 367).
[5] See also the study on the use of foreign sources based on interviews with judges by E Mak (2013).

all legal decision-making should make use of these materials or that the use of such materials would automatically lead to a 'good' result. As mentioned before, the relevance of cross-border materials seems legitimate primarily in so-called hard cases. The cases in which courts have been looking at foreign law in Europe have indeed concerned new issues, often controversial ones, for which national law does not provide a solution.[6] In an easy case, the possibility of using foreign sources does not necessarily arise at all. Having said that, however, I also wish to recall that the line between hard and easy cases is not clear, and that convincing foreign materials may be used to bring a previously established domestic rule into question.[7] Foreign law may play the role of a 'critical resource'.[8]

In this sense, some have called comparative law a subversive discipline[9] and a discipline that can contribute to enlarging the horizon of decision-makers,[10] by increasing the 'stock of solutions' regarding legal problems.[11] The learning brought from abroad may contribute to enlarging the scope of what one considers legally possible. A solution that, based on domestic sources alone, seems to be out of reach for a court or a scholar discussing the issue, may become acceptable when convincing foreign sources are added to the reasoning. This is one reason why learning across borders can be a useful means for emerging legal micro-politics.[12] As Thijmen Koopmans has suggested, the need for cross-border learning by the courts is strong, for example with regard to new social problems, challenges related to biotechnology, new forms of communication, urban decay, pollution and migration as well as situations characterised by loss of authoritative power in moral matters. The difficulties of political institutions to solve such issues, and the limited support given by traditional legal sources, make it natural to look for inspiration abroad.[13] Whether such comparative learning or even subversive enlargement of the sphere of the legally possible is 'good' or not, ultimately depends on a substantive assessment of the issue at hand. As I will note later, transparent reasoning involving foreign legal experience should usually include some substantive arguments as well.

To focus the analysis I will concentrate on what one could call a 'spontaneous'[14] use of foreign materials by domestic courts and scholars. As noted before, foreign materials are also flowing across the borders through the mediation of European courts like the CJEU and the ECHR. If they have based their decisions on comparative national materials, national sources gain indirect influence through the decisions. When domestic courts use such European materials the foreign national experience is already processed once, and the requirements regarding transparency of the reasoning

[6] Smits (2019: 508). Bobek (2013: 196) notes that comparative reasoning has been used by courts in 'important cases, significant for their novelty, contentiousness, or political sensitivity.' Also, a French judge, interviewed by E Mak (2013: 191), noted that comparative analysis was reserved for important cases.

[7] For examples on cases in which foreign law has been used to change established practice, see eg Kadner Graziano (2015: 49–50).

[8] Waldron (2005: 141).

[9] Muir Watt (2004: 33).

[10] Canivet (2004: 188).

[11] Already Ernst Zitelmann, cited per Coendet (2014: 1).

[12] See ch 3.

[13] Koopmans (1996: 549).

[14] *cf* Riedl (2002: 45), who speaks about 'spontaneous' harmonisation.

are obviously different from those regarding direct borrowing across the borders. I will here only discuss the direct use of foreign national sources by domestic courts and scholars, leaving aside the indirect import through the case law of the CJEU and the ECHR. Equally indirect cross-border learning through a collection of principles, like the DCFR, is not in focus in this chapter either.[15]

I. TOWARDS A TRANSPARENT JUSTIFICATION

If used properly, the 'laboratory of the EU' can support the improvement of domestic legal orders. At the same time, however, such use of foreign sources involves a certain degree of arbitrariness which might be difficult to reconcile with fundamental legal principles related to the rule of law. By explaining in detail why the comparative material is used and justified in a certain situation, one may at least partially mitigate this problem. Transparent reasoning makes it possible openly to face and discuss the question why the use and the selection of foreign sources can appear to be legitimate in relation to the issue at hand.

One obstacle to transparent legal reasoning was mentioned earlier: the more frequent use of comparative materials in the context of discovery than in the context of justification.[16] As legal reasoning, in particular in courts, is to some extent based on informal norms or tacit knowledge concerning the acceptable range of arguments, these norms may prevent an express reference to foreign materials even in cases in which the court has used such material. The traditional standard example is French law, where the reasoning of the courts is generally very short, and leaves most of the arguments, including foreign materials, unmentioned, even though other sources such as the opinion of the Advocate-General indicate that foreign law had been the object of scrutiny.[17] In many countries, it may also for reasons of sovereignty be considered inappropriate for a national court to make explicit reference to foreign legal actors. The prevailing schematic doctrines of legal sources may as such counteract the express use of foreign materials.[18] Sometimes a practical fear of making mistakes concerning foreign law[19] prevents the express reference to foreign materials even in cases where such materials have been used in the deliberations. Self-evidently, such traditions of non-disclosure of used foreign materials do not fulfil the demands of transparent reasoning. One may only hope that national tacit knowledge-based traditions of this kind would successively surrender to more open forms of European learning in which the cross-border dialogue between legal actors would be visible. Only by doing this transparently can courts make use of the cross-border learning without sliding into a decision-making that appears too arbitrary.

[15] On DCFR as a source, see above ch 8 section III.

[16] This difference is also observed by E Mak (2013: 4).

[17] Bobek (2013) ch 6, Smits (2019: 509–10). Markesinis and Fedtke (2006: 62–66) describe France and Italy as legal orders that are 'Doing it but not admitting' (using foreign law). There is perhaps now some development towards openness in French law, see Andenas and Fairgrieve (2015a: 11).

[18] On the less transparent nature of (some) such doctrines, see ch 8 section II.

[19] Bobek (2013: 233) speaks about the 'transparency trap': the more argument a decision-maker uses, the easier it is to criticise the decision.

In other words, it is a minimum requirement of transparency that the decision-maker informs the public about the cross-border learning it has used, if the decision-maker has indeed been inspired by foreign experience. It is interesting to note that even a French President of *Cour de Cassation* has emphasised the need for such transparency:

> Because the methods of courts ought in all circumstances to be transparent, it is obvious that the comparative analysis which the judge intends to include among the elements under examination ought to be … explicit.[20]

Transparent reasoning means more, however, than a simple reference to the foreign sources that the decision-maker has made use of. A decision-maker who resorts to foreign materials in order to find something to build the decision on, only because the material appears to be useful in the case, moves close to a purely arbitrary use of sources. Even though it is often easy to agree with the claim that comparative sources are useful, many questions remain: Why are they considered useful? How are sources deemed to be useful chosen? Transparent reasoning also requires an open account of such deliberations.

In practice, such demands are often not fulfilled. Sometimes scholars and courts seem to use the materials just 'because it's there'.[21] The reason for using foreign law might simply be intellectual laziness, as it is more comfortable to resort to a ready-made foreign solution than to make the difficult analysis of the issue oneself. Judges may refer to foreign decisions because it helps rescue them 'from a feeling of intellectual nakedness'.[22] The reference to foreign law may be given for 'ornamental purposes' to demonstrate the learning of the judge or scholar.[23] National traditions may be based on 'pragmatic indolence, using foreign law in an unsystematic way on the basis of availability and linguistic accessibility.'[24] Clearly, these are not satisfactory reasons. Even though the true heuristic explanation for the use of foreign materials might well be 'because it's there', there certainly ought to be some further reason for the use, making it legally legitimate. A transparent legal reasoning requires a deeper analysis and an open account of the reasons.[25]

In chapter 8 section III, I discussed, as an example, the kinds of questions that one ought to answer, when using the DCFR as a legal argument. One may apply a similar typology of questions when discussing what issues a transparent use of cross-border materials should address. First and foremost, as the use of comparative materials is not a self-evident part of most national traditions, one should offer express reasons explaining why these materials are considered relevant in the case at hand. Is there, for example, particular authority for using certain comparative arguments; is the use perhaps based on a belief in the value of European harmonisation; or is it relying on the trust in the substantive or legal expertise of the producer of the material? Secondly, it is important to account for the normative strength

[20] Canivet (2006: 1398). *cf* Canivet (2015: 477), where he only notes the French structural obstacle to refer to foreign law.

[21] Claimed by a well-known critic of comparative reasoning, Scalia (2004: 308).

[22] Waldron (2005: 138).

[23] Smits (2019: 514).

[24] Heirbaut and Storme (2006: 645), on Belgian law.

[25] Waldron (2005: 130) even requires the judge to offer a 'theory' related to the citation of foreign law.

of the cross-border experience. Is it used only to fill gaps in domestic law; to give substantive arguments a kind of legal flavour; or more boldly to open up new paths for domestic law? Finally, one should also be able to demonstrate on what basis the choice of materials is made, that it is not only a result of arbitrary 'cherry-picking'.[26] Are there other reasons than linguistic ability and easy access – neither seems to be a legally very convincing reason, even though they often offer the best explanations of the choices[27] – to justify why materials from certain jurisdictions and not others have been included?

There may be other relevant questions in addition to these. Particularly important is the analysis of the relationship between the authoritative use of foreign materials and the substantive arguments involved in decision-making. As I will show below, in hard cases the decision-maker usually has to rely on a blend of authoritative and substantive reasons.

As I have noted many times before, one cannot impose precisely the same transparency requirements on courts and on legal scholars. Traditions that in many jurisdictions may make it difficult for a court to make an express reference to foreign materials do not form the same kind of obstacle for scholars. The practical difficulties of offering deep justifications in the hectic day-to-day life of a court – the use of foreign law has indeed been called a 'luxurious' type of legal analysis 'that cannot be expected from every judge'[28] – do not affect the legal scholar in the same way. There is a double pressure on the scholar to dig deeper, as the scholar does not only have to fulfil the transparency demands of the rule of law, but also those of the scientific community. Whilst a court might reach some minimum level of transparency by shortly stating what foreign materials it has used, and why, legal scholars should be able to address the issues in a broad and more analytic fashion. As analysed in chapter 5 section IV, digitalisation also drives legal writing further away from the traditional 'ideal of completeness' and thereby demands a more open account of the choice of sources and methods of retrieving them.

In this chapter, I will look more closely at the types of questions that should be transparently addressed, in particular by scholars, but in an ideal world also by courts, when their reasoning is based on cross-border experience. Before proceeding to these questions, however, I have to clarify my understanding of what pressures cross-border legal learning puts on the domestic traditions concerning legal reasoning.

II. A UNIFIED EUROPEAN DOCTRINE OF FOREIGN LEGAL SOURCES?

The national traditions concerning the use of legal sources vary considerably between the Member States. Whilst for the (remaining) common law Member States case law is the determining factor in legal reasoning and judges are the leading stars in the legal universe, in continental Member States other types of arguments are important, in addition to case law. In German legal reasoning, the views of the scholarly

[26] See Kadner Graziano (2015: 29–30), who claims that court practice does not show such a tendency.
[27] See the empirical analysis by Gelter and Siems (2012: 93, 95).
[28] Smits (2019: 508).

community, *Stand der Lehre*, are recognised as a central source and the leading legal stars are renowned scholars. In a famous work on judges, legislators and professors, RC van Caenegem compares judge-made English law, legislation-shaped French law and scholarly developed German law.[29] In addition, in the Nordic countries, the *travaux prèparatoires* to legislation are probably valued higher than in many other countries. Digging deeper, even the way in which sources are used as arguments may vary between jurisdictions: the different ways in which common law courts and continental courts rely on previous case law offer a good example.[30] These are just a few well-known examples concerning variations between the national argumentative traditions. Many others could be added. Even though national doctrines of legal sources do not necessarily convey a very accurate and transparent picture of actual legal reasoning in hard cases,[31] such variations between the doctrines certainly reflect real differences in reasoning.

This leads to the question: what impact can national variations in the use of sources have on the ideal of a transparent movement of legal sources across the borders? In the previous section, I noted one consequence of the transparency requirement on traditional domestic patterns of legal reasoning. Transparency requires courts and scholars to refer expressly to foreign legal materials when such materials have been used, even when references to foreign materials have not traditionally been considered appropriate in the domestic legal culture. That recommendation, however, does not yet say anything about what foreign materials a legal actor should refer to. German courts might prefer to cite textbooks from other countries,[32] whilst common law courts might cite foreign case law instead. Is this a problem with regard to the transparent movement of legal sources?

The most radical answer is the claim that a transparent learning across borders is possible only within a reasonably unified tradition of legal reasoning. A movement of legal ideas could be truly transparent only if the transparency were not hampered by diverging national methodological traditions. The vision of a European area of legal learning would require a unified European legal methodology, a Europeanised doctrine of legal sources.

Some have indeed put forward proposals regarding the need for such Europeanisation of legal methodology. In an often-cited paper, Hans Peter Berger has proposed a Europeanisation of legal methodology which would include a European doctrine of precedents and be 'strongly influenced by the increasing significance of comparative law'.[33] He has even claimed that a joint European methodology is necessary (*notwendig*) with regard to the successful harmonisation of European private law.[34] Others, in particular German scholars, have advocated a European legal method as well.[35]

[29] van Caenegem (1987).
[30] Komárek (2013).
[31] For more detail, see ch 8 section II.
[32] Unberath (2004: 308).
[33] Berger (2001: 886–87).
[34] Berger (2001a: 6–8). See also Vogenauer (2005: 235): '*Vereinheitlichung des Rechts erfordert Vereinheitlichung der juristischen Methode*.'
[35] eg Flessner (2002) and Vogenauer (2005). See also Jansen (2005).

If the aim is a harmonised European law, a development of a joint European view on applicable sources is certainly tempting. There is some merit in the claim that harmonisation of law requires harmonisation of legal method. With regard to transparency, a harmonisation of legal methods in Europe would have advantages. Cross-border transparency could increase, as it would be easier to understand foreign case law and other legal materials if the basic method of producing them would be familiar.

A harmonised method, however, would also have several drawbacks with regard to transparency. As national doctrines of legal sources do not picture actual legal reasoning very well, often being too schematic, closed and hierarchic,[36] a Europeanised doctrine of legal sources could easily be hit by a similar fate. The Europeanised doctrine would then rather obstruct transparency than promote it. In addition, the national methodological traditions are fairly strong and difficult to change in a radical manner. A wholesale adoption of a Europeanised methodology – if that could be accomplished – would run the risk of concealing the differences rather than removing them. Beneath the Europeanised surface at least some impact of national traditions might continue, but in a way that would be more difficult to observe.

The idea of a European legal laboratory and learning law does not aspire to harmonisation as a goal in itself.[37] Learning across the borders is a process in which legal ideas from other countries are processed and inserted in the legal and societal context of the receiving country. The process does not require Member States to harmonise their methodologies, as long as they appear as reasonably transparent. For an expansion of the free movement of legal sources across the borders, only some development of the way in which legal sources are used is necessary. Legal reasoning should be more open towards cross-border influences to make full use of the experimental value of the European legal area. Such an increasing open-mindedness towards cross-border learning should be transparently reflected in a more express use of foreign sources.

The cross-border learning processes may also push national methodologies to become more alike in some other respects, but this is not because methodological convergence would be a necessary prerequisite for the free movement of legal ideas. The instances of convergence would rather be just examples of a learning across borders on the methodological level. The convergence might even be a consequence of such mundane issues as the availability of materials in the right linguistic form. For example, the increasing use of foreign materials from outside of common law in English courts is brought about by the availability of comparative legal literature, which is used as the primary source.[38] Scholarly work has in this way received greater attention than what has earlier been the case within common law.

I have already mentioned another possible pressure on national methodologies. The experimental and learning law pushes legal conceptuality towards a language that is closer to real life.[39] The free movement of legal ideas across the borders

[36] See ch 8 section II.
[37] See ch 5 section VII.
[38] Smits (2019: 511). See also eg Lord Goff in the paradigmatic *White v Jones* [1995] 1 All ER 691.
[39] See ch 8 section V.

strengthens the demand for more real life instead of abstract doctrine. Europeanisation tends to support a legal methodology that is more focused on the specificity of cases rather than on sophisticated national dogmatic frameworks.[40] As Jan Smits notes, it is easier to compare the issue to be decided to similar situations in foreign case law than to solutions in abstract statutes.[41] This may mean, in other words, a stronger focus on case law in such national settings in which abstract doctrine and legislation have been more important.

To avoid any misunderstandings, it is important to reiterate that the choice of focus on cases or on conceptual structures is not an either-or decision. Both perspectives have their legitimate place in mature legal reasoning. I have deliberately not spoken about the free movement of legal solutions, but of legal ideas, as learning may occur not only with regard to good solutions in real-life cases, but also concerning useful legal structures and concepts.[42] When using foreign conceptual materials in legal reasoning, requirements concerning sufficiently transparent justification must include a deeper analysis of how the foreign concept would interact with the prevailing doctrinal structures in the domestic setting. Obviously, both the prevailing national legal structures and the role of conceptuality in legal reasoning vary to the extent that a joint European method of moving concepts does not appear to be feasible.

In other words, there are many reasons for not believing in a more or less fully fledged Europeanised methodology, even though some Europeanisation of legal reasoning is required in order to facilitate legal understanding across the borders. There is a pluralism of approaches to legal sources, and the picture is not completely stable, as the methodological tools are also part of the learning processes. The uncertainty as to method underlines the requirement of open reasoning.

The lack of a joint methodology implies that there are no clear European answers to the question when one should use cross-border materials in legal decision-making. A European approach merely requires open-mindedness as to cross-border learning and the requirement of transparent reasoning demands open discussion of the use and choice of comparative arguments. In the following section, I will list some questions that should be addressed in a transparent discourse on this issue.

III. AUTHORITATIVE AND SUBSTANTIVE JUSTIFICATION OF FOREIGN SOURCES

In some discourses on the use of foreign materials in legal reasoning, the questions are set in a binary and formal way: is the foreign material considered a real 'legal source' or is it just 'of an informative or supportive nature'?[43] Is the authority accorded to

[40] Berger (2001: 890), advocating a 'functional comparative process'.

[41] Smits (2019: 521).

[42] An illustrative example is the French case law adoption of the German and Italian distinction between obligations to achieve a result and obligations to use reasonable care, see Albarian (2015: 488).

[43] Håstad (2015: 184), on the use of the DCFR see above ch 8 section III.

foreign law 'conclusive' or 'persuasive'.[44] Can it be classified as 'binding', 'persuasive' or purely 'inspirational'?[45] Such strict conceptual classifications, typical of schematic doctrines of legal sources,[46] are not, however, sufficient with regard to a transparent account of the use of foreign materials. Legal reasoning is much more nuanced. Foreign sources may be used in a multitude of ways in legal reasoning.[47] Their status and weight as arguments can vary and the ways of legitimating their use vary accordingly. Their weight depends on the other arguments available in the case as well: it is easier to turn to cross-border learning if the decision-maker feels that there is a real gap in domestic law.[48] Judges that use comparative law have indicated in interviews that they are looking for good arguments rather than considering the formal status of the sources.[49] Reasoning that uses foreign materials could in other words rather be characterised by terms like 'liquidity'[50] and 'degrees of persuasiveness'.[51]

A dichotomy that is related to the above ones is the distinction between substantive and authoritative arguments. I defined this dichotomy and discussed it in general terms above in chapter eight. Repeating it briefly, a substantive argument receives its force from the content of the argument, whilst an authoritative argument receives its source value from being stated in a particular source, like in legislation, in a case, in the *travaux préparatoires* or in a statement in legal literature, if the decision-maker acknowledges such value for the particular source.

The dichotomy, however, is not understood in an on-off manner. A legal argument may at the same time be both authoritative and substantive. The use of a particular source is often considered legitimate for both authoritative and substantive reasons. A court case is not only relevant because it contains a statement by a legal authority; it might be considered even more relevant if the reasoning in the case is considered to be substantively justified. In fact, the use of foreign materials regularly displays, explicitly or implicitly, both substantive and authoritative features.

When calling an argument substantive or authoritative, I refer to the way a judge or scholar uses the argument in legal reasoning. It is a question of the role that the actual decision-maker can give the argument when taking a stand on a particular issue. This may vary, and this is why the distinction is important when discussing transparent reasoning. Openness requires the express justification of the cross-border use of sources, and this justification may be (predominantly) either substantive or authoritative.

In practice, one may assume there are at least a minimum of substantive assessment attached to more or less all use of foreign legal sources: it is hardly conceivable that a decision-maker would use a foreign source if, according to the views of the

[44] eg Waldron (2005: 129). See also Bobek (2013: 212 *et seq*), according to which the use of comparative material should be (i) persuasive, (ii) subsidiary, (iii) additional and (iv) just defendable and by necessity selective. Kadner Graziano (2015: 38) also emphasises that foreign law can only have persuasive authority.

[45] Markesinis and Fedtke (2006: 5) as well as Baasch Andersen (2011: 46–48) (on CISG).

[46] See ch 8 section II.

[47] Andenas and Fairgrieve (2015a: 12) present a typology of seven ways of using comparative law.

[48] See eg Canivet (2006: 1391).

[49] E Mak (2013: 4, 215).

[50] See eg Cotterrell and Del Mar (2016: 5) and Krisch (2016) (on transnational legal authority).

[51] Cotterrell and Del Mar (2016: 12).

decision-maker, it would result in a substantively 'bad' decision. As discussed in chapter 5 section I, a successful 'transplantation' of a legal idea from one national context to another must involve an analysis of how the foreign piece legally and societally fits into the new national context, that is a substantive reasoning concerning the working of the borrowed source. As there regularly has to be some substantive assessment accompanying the comparative material, it is easy to understand normative claims that the authority of a foreign source should be only 'persuasive'. Another thing is how much additional support of this kind one wishes to demand; a European-minded legal actor might not require as much as someone more nationally inclined.

As discussed below, there is usually also at least a drop of authority involved in cases of this kind. This mixture of substantive and authoritative reasons, however, does not remove the analytical usefulness of the distinction. The relationship between the elements in a particular case is an important feature with regard to how it should be transparently presented.[52] When a legal actor uses a foreign source, the actor should openly state to what extent its use is based on some authoritative value in addition to its substantive value. The justification of recognising some authoritative value of a foreign source is a central issue when assessing the legitimacy of the use of foreign legal sources in legal decision-making.

Sometimes foreign legal materials are used predominantly as sources of substantive arguments. In such cases the methodological issue does not primarily relate to the question why foreign sources are used in decision-making, but the question is rather a practical one: how and where can one best find and learn good arguments? For example, cross-border references to black letter legal research can sometimes be understood in this way. Legal scholars cite foreign authors, not because of their authority, but because of the arguments these authors offer. The citation is not there to increase the value of the argument; rather, it is required by the ethical rules of science. It is a tribute to the expectations of the community of researchers rather than to the weight of legal argumentation. Such a primarily 'scientific' rather than 'legal' movement of sources is particularly obvious in relation to the movement of legal concepts and constructions. Europeanised scholarly discourse may induce movement of conceptual ideas based purely on the scientifically convincing nature of the systematisations. This does not mean, however, that legal scholars do not use authoritative reasoning as well when referring to other scholars. Even though some of the references to foreign scholars in legal dogmatics are made primarily for scientific reasons and not because of the legal authority of the source, often such references are used with authoritative weight as well, in particular when the scholar mentioned has a strong international reputation.

The accounts of the use of comparative sources in the practice of courts and scholars are often couched in a language implying that the use is motivated by the substantive knowledge those sources contain or express. For example, foreign sources are said to be used to 'cast an empirical light on the consequences of different

[52] The typology of Andenas and Fairgrieve (2015a: 12) contains both clearly authoritative ('to overturn authority in domestic law') and typically substantive ('to review factual assumptions about the consequences of legal rules') cases.

solutions to a common legal problem',[53] 'to ascertain whether a rule has successfully fulfilled its function',[54] to see whether a concept or institution 'had been successfully tested in other legal systems',[55] or to 'help disprove locally expressed fears about the consequences of a particular legal solution'.[56] The comparative material may be used only as a kind of 'fitness check', to show that the solution can be seen as fair and effective,[57] as it has worked elsewhere. In most cases, however, the foreign source does not present such a scientifically credible and extensive presentation of its arguments of substance that one could convincingly claim that only the substance was important. One cannot epistemologically compare a foreign case to a real scientific analysis of the societal issue at hand. Therefore, obviously in most cases when a foreign source, for example a foreign case, is cited the reference means more than just a hint on where the decision-maker has found the substantive reasons used. The reference acquires some additional (not necessarily decisive) value by being a 'legal' source. For a legal professional it feels more convincing to cite a case than just the substantive arguments of the case. A domestic professional tends to respect the reasoning of a foreign colleague. In other words, in most cases some added authoritative value seems to be attached to the foreign legal source. Citing a foreign case gives the decision a more convincing justification.

As case law and scholarly study should not be looked at as a branch of social science, it is natural to attach an element of authority to foreign cases and legal literature. This is important, as it means that a cross-border source can be admitted on the basis of a typically legal common sense fitness check alone, without requiring a thorough scientific study on the suitability of the solution. This presupposes, however, a sufficient justification for rendering the foreign material such authority. Some possible grounds will be analysed in the following sections of this chapter.

A foreign source may in practice have various degrees of authoritative value. Terms like 'binding', 'persuasive' and 'inspirational' reflect such variations, even though the terms might be misleading if used too schematically. The foreign source may have only weak authority, somehow contributing to giving the substantive arguments a legal flavour.[58] As has been said, a judge might 'in the end, be inspired more by the mechanisms of interpretative decoding he will find in a legal culture that is not his own than by ready-made solutions'.[59] The source may also be needed simply to convince the reader that a certain solution can be considered legally possible. In other cases, the foreign source may acquire stronger authority, being a positive or even a decisive argument for the adopted solution. The role of a foreign source is not only dependent on the source itself, but also on the relevance and weight of other available (domestic) reasons. In the analysis below of possible justifications for acknowledging authoritative value to a foreign source, I will include both weaker and

[53] *Printz v United States* 521 US 898, 921 (1997).
[54] Canivet (2004: 187). Markesinis and Fedtke (2006: 135) speak about evidence that a solution has 'worked'.
[55] Unberath (2004: 312).
[56] Markesinis and Fedtke (2006: 127).
[57] Canivet (2006: 1394).
[58] A kind of *Kontrollfunktion*, Janssen and Schulze (2011: 249).
[59] Canivet (2004: 189).

stronger forms of authoritative value, without pursuing this distinction further, as the variations in practice rather can be placed on a scale than within a dichotomy.[60] A completely transparent reasoning, however, should address both the grounds for authority and the weight given to the argument.

In the following, I will discuss some grounds on which foreign sources may be given authoritative value, a value emanating to some extent from the position of the source itself and not exclusively from its substantive arguments. My perspective is the requirement of transparent reasoning. I am not aspiring to recommend some particular way of reasoning, but rather to demonstrate the kinds of reasoning that are available for a legal actor who wants to offer a transparent justification of a reference to a foreign source.

IV. THE EUROPEAN AUTHORITY ARGUMENT

The use of foreign sources in legal reasoning is not a new phenomenon. On various grounds, courts and scholars have used materials from other countries in developing their own legal order. By exploring such cases, one gets a hint on a possible way of justifying an authoritative use of European sources across the borders.

Sometimes the foreign materials form part of an established process of exchange and learning between particular national laws. Common law cases, in particular from the English courts, are referred to around the common law world. French materials concerning *Code Civil* are used in countries that have been inspired by this codification. Therefore, Italian lawyers do not consider French law to be really foreign.[61] A similar export of sources concerning the German *Bürgerliches Gesetzbuch* takes place to countries that have adopted the *BGB*. The legal actors often do not experience these cases as a use of genuinely 'foreign' sources. The sources are understood as 'quasi-domestic' materials, available as a kind of 'insider' legal knowledge. They appear as a 'giveaway', a benefit given to countries that have bought the basic product (common law, *Code civil*, *BGB*). In cases where a foreign model is expressly used, one might argue that this implies a mandate for the decision-maker to refer to sources from the parent jurisdiction.[62]

Another example of a similar quasi-domestic movement of sources is found in Nordic law. In private law, there is a Nordic tradition of using sources from other Nordic countries. This is true for legal scholarship, but the courts also occasionally refer to cases from other Nordic countries. This joint legal tradition makes the Nordic material appear as almost domestic in legal reasoning.[63]

It would be tempting to justify the use of sources from other EU Member States by applying a similar notion of a kind of 'quasi-domestic' legal materials. All Member State law is part of the legal structure of the Union. European legal actors

[60] As Bobek (2013: 68) notes, it is in reality often impossible to discern the argumentative value of the comparative argument in a decision.

[61] Alpa (2004a: 196).

[62] Bobek (2013: 29).

[63] See more closely eg Wilhelmsson (2021).

should therefore understand the laws of all the Member States to be part of a larger legal home. Sources from other Member States could be a natural part of legal reasoning in the same way as US courts can look across state borders. In comparative law discourse, the use of comparative law in the European setting is indeed considered to be different from the use of comparative law in general.[64]

The acknowledgement of some kind of quasi-domestic role of sources from other Member States would mean a recognition that an authoritative source from one EU Member State would retain at least some (maybe minimal) authority in another Member State only because it is European. One could call this the European authority argument. Could such an argument be convincingly justified in a transparent legal discourse?

Looking more closely at the 'quasi-domestic' uses of foreign materials within smaller groups of Member States one may, on the meta-level, find several ways to construct a legally acceptable justification for such a use. Leaving aside for the time being various forms of substantive meta-justifications and looking at purely authoritative meta-level legal reasoning, one can envisage at least two possible ways of justifying a cross-border legal authority for sources from other Member States. First, one might base the European authority argument on a meta-level authoritative source of some kind. Secondly, one could refer to an evolving legal custom in the EU. Below, I discuss these grounds for the European authority argument. Needless to say, a decision-maker should in a transparent legal reasoning disclose the reliance on such a ground.

A claim concerning the authority of foreign legal materials would be strong if one could refer to some acknowledged meta-level authority to support the claim. One could then speak about authority based on express meta-level legal authority. To illustrate what I mean by such meta-level authority I will first mention other examples of this kind of argument, before discussing the question whether one could convincingly rely on express meta-level support for the European authority argument.

A meta-level authority can be derived from an enactment or some other authoritative source that normatively asserts the authoritative value of foreign sources. For example, a constitution might state that foreign law may be taken into account when interpreting it.[65] In private law, one might refer to the Nordic so-called Helsinki Treaty (the 1962 Treaty of Co-operation between Denmark, Finland, Iceland, Norway and Sweden).[66] According to Article 4 of the Treaty, 'The High Contracting Parties shall continue their co-operation in the field of law with the aim of attaining the greatest possible uniformity in the field of private law.' One could imagine decision-makers experiencing such a clear harmonisation order as an important legal basis for using Nordic sources. However, this is pure theory. In practice, courts and scholars never explicitly refer to the Treaty as a justification for the cross-border use of Nordic sources. The Nordic area of legal reasoning was developed – long before 1962 – as a legal custom rather than something based on direct meta-level authority.

[64] Freedland (2004: xviii).

[65] For example, the South African Constitution of 1996, Art 39(c). See eg Rautenbach and du Plessis (2013).

[66] The Treaty was signed on 23 March 1962 and entered into force on 1 July 1962.

A similar type of authoritative support for regional harmonisation, but more limited in scope, can be found in the recent bilateral agreement on cooperation and integration between France and Germany.[67] In this the two countries agree to strive at a stronger bilateral harmonisation in the area of economic law: '*Beide Staaten vertiefen die Integration ihrer Volkswirtschaften hin zu einem deutsch-französischen Wirtschaftsraum mit gemeinsamen Regeln.*'[68] It is too early to tell whether this agreement will be understood as offering authoritative support for using sources across the French–German border. The Nordic experience shows that agreements like this do not necessarily have a strong effect on the way in which legal sources are used in everyday legal reasoning.

An example at global level is Article 7(1) of the United Nations Convention on Contracts for the International Sale of Goods (CISG), according to which in the interpretation of the Convention, 'regard is to be had to its international character and to the need to promote uniformity in its application'. This Article should lower the threshold to rely on sources from other CISG countries. Despite this command, however, there seems to be relatively few instances of express references to foreign case law in the application of the CISG.[69] More generally, one may also find a similar internationalised attitude to the interpretation of other international conventions, for example in the area of transport law,[70] so one may doubt whether the express command of CISG Article 7(1) in practice adds much to the status of foreign sources. One may generally assume that for international conventions there is at least an implicit authority for attempts to harmonise interpretation through the use of foreign materials. International conventions are a special case, however, that does not tell how one should justify the movement of sources with respect to other issues.

The obvious question here is whether EU law offers any meta-level authoritative support for the movement of legal sources within the Union. The Treaties are not helpful in this respect. The Treaty on the Functioning of the European Union does not consider legal harmonisation to be a task in itself, as long as it is not required by the building of the internal market. Article 81 on judicial cooperation in civil matters, for example, only states that such cooperation 'may include the adoption of measures for the approximation of the laws and regulations of the Member States'. In fact, the idea of a Union that is 'united in diversity'[71] is reflected in the Treaty on European Union, Article 3(3), according to which the Union 'shall respect its rich cultural and linguistic diversity'. One can hardly extract any clear general command towards legal harmonisation from the Treaties.

[67] *Vertrag zwischen der Bundesrepublik Deutschland und der Französischen Republik über die deutsch-französische Zusammenarbeit und Integration (Vertrag vom Aachen vom 22. Januar 2019).*

[68] Art 20(1) of the Agreement.

[69] See above ch 5 section III.

[70] Unberath (2004: 308), Markesinis and Fedtke (2006: 136) and Janssen and Schulze (2011: 249). Illustrative is Lord Diplock in *Fothergill v Monarch Airliners Ltd*. House of Lords [1981] AC 251, 281–82: 'The language of an international convention has not been chosen by an English parliamentary draftsman … It should be interpreted … unconstrained by technical rules of English law, or by English legal precedent, but on broad principles on general acceptation.' See also Sisula-Tulokas (2019–20), criticising the less open reasoning of the CJEU.

[71] This phrase is nowadays presented as the motto of the EU; see europa.eu/about-eu/basic-information/symbols/motto/.

However, the interpretation of statutes based on directives harmonising the law might be a special case. It resembles the interpretation of international conventions,[72] mentioned above. However, it is not self-evident what this means with regard to the possible authoritative support for learning across the borders in Europe. Directives are usually, in line with the wording of Articles 114–115 of the Treaty on the Functioning of the European Union, expressly aiming only at 'approximation', not unification, of the law. This might at least in some cases make the claim that the presence of a directive as such would authoritatively oblige the decision-makers to make use of foreign European experience in the area less convincing, in particular in situations in which the CJEU has recognised the need for a margin of national decision-making.[73] The whole institutional setting, however, in which EU law is implemented, with the CJEU giving preliminary rulings on the interpretation of Union law[74] and the highest courts being obliged to ask for such rulings,[75] indicates an expectation that EU law should be given a similar interpretation in all Member States. In addition, the CJEU has indirectly promoted a kind of obligation of national Supreme Courts to learn across the borders. According to the CJEU, in a case in which there are conflicting decisions of lower national courts concerning a concept used in EU secondary legislation,

> the third paragraph of Article 267 TFEU must be construed as meaning that a court or tribunal against whose decisions there is no judicial remedy under national law is obliged to make a reference to the Court for a preliminary ruling concerning the interpretation of that concept.[76]

This decision has been said to promote a horizontal dialogue between national courts.[77] The case supports a right of domestic courts to use cross-border materials when applying national law based on EU secondary law. The decision-maker can use the case as an expression of meta-level authority for justifying references to cross-border materials in the application of EU law.

In particular cases, one may find other scattered efforts to render additional meta-level support to cross-border learning concerning application of EU law. A striking example is the attempts by the Commission to unify the domestic application of the Commercial Agents Directive. In its report on the application of the Directive it at least indirectly recommends the use of German law as the basis of interpretation:

> The Commission considers that this Report, which gives detailed information, particularly concerning the method of calculation of the indemnity as it is carried out in Germany, provides further clarification of Article 17 of the Directive and secondly, by so-doing should facilitate a more uniform interpretation of Article 17 of the Directive.[78]

[72] Hartkamp (2004: 230) claims the situation to be 'practically identical'.

[73] The paradigmatic example being the unfair contract terms Case C-237/02 *Freiburger Kommunalbauten GmbH Baugesellschaft & Co. KG v Ludger Hofstetter and Ulrike Hofstetter*, ECLI:EU:C:2004:209.

[74] Treaty on European Union, Art 19(3)(b).

[75] Treaty on the Functioning of the European Union, Art 267(4).

[76] Case C-160/14 *João Filipe Ferreira da Silva e Brito and Others v Estado português*, ECLI:EU:C:2015:565.

[77] Cafaggi and Law (2017: 7).

[78] COM(96) 364 final 10.

As the Commission does not have adjudicative power, the authoritative value of this statement is limited. It might be mentioned, however, in a transparent justification of cross-border use of German sources concerning commercial agents.

Summing up, there is limited meta-level authoritative and convincing justification of a general use of sources from other Member States. Only in the application of EU legislation might one refer to arguments of an authoritative legal character that support at least an opportunity for national courts to use cross-border learning. If one wants to defend a European authority argument with a more general scope, the foundations must be sought elsewhere.

Another possible basis of meta-level authority is custom. In most legal systems, the doctrine of legal sources develops through case law and legal theory and can normatively be defined as a part of customary law. If the doctrines of legal sources develop towards the establishment of a custom with a more international outlook, the meta-authority for using cross-border sources could be based on such a renewed customary law. One might claim that, for example, foreign judgments through regular use could become acknowledged as sources in domestic cases.[79]

One can certainly 'discover signs evidencing the progressive development of a specifically European way of looking at things'.[80] The idea of a European methodology, discussed earlier in this chapter, offers a systematic perspective in this direction. Even though I do not believe, at least at this stage, in a fully fledged Europeanisation of the doctrines of legal sources, on the domestic level some kind of customary acceptance of cross-border European sources could develop. To be a convincing part of customary law, however, the new doctrine would have to contain some rules on how and under what conditions the use of sources from other Member States would be considered legitimate or even required. As long as a more elaborate understanding has not emerged, a claim that the use of foreign sources could be given an authoritative legitimation by customary law is not convincing. Nor have I seen anybody use such language of legitimation. An emerging custom might, however, be referred to as a supportive element in a broader justification of a cross-border use of sources from other Member States.

This is the case in particular with regard to the application of EU legislation and national legislation based on EU law. In such cases, one may claim that in many countries a custom that at least allows the use of sources from other Member States has emerged. In particular, if the field is harmonised in a fairly detailed way, as, for example, product liability, it seems customary at least occasionally to use cases and materials from other European jurisdictions. The Dutch experience that a foreign background to the legislation to be applied lowers the threshold for considering foreign sources[81] can be attested in many other jurisdictions as well.[82] As has been stated above, deep normative justifications of the use of foreign law in cases in which

[79] See E Mak (2013: 33).

[80] Canivet (2004: 190).

[81] Hartkamp (2004: 231).

[82] *cf* the American 'borrowed statute' doctrine, Smits (2019: 507). In his general report, Drobnig (1999) distinguishes between comparison in cases of rules with an international element and of purely domestic rules. See also comments on CISG above in this section.

EU law is applied are not necessarily required. The situation resembles the one in which a national lower court refers to case law from another lower court: such references are not required, but are certainly legitimate.

In legal academic writing this emerging custom may be supported by the custom of the scientific community. One could even claim that an analysis of a detailed piece of EU legislation without references to research on the same issue from other Member States would be at least dubious with regard to research ethics. A researcher should account for previous research in the field, and research from foreign Member States has to be regarded as relevant previous research. Language abilities (still) put some limits on what a researcher can do in this respect.

Theorising about the legitimacy of using foreign sources is one thing, the practical opportunities to make such use is another.[83] Practical issues in due course affect what one considers to be custom. Therefore, such matters as availability, access and language are of paramount importance. Sources available in broadly known languages such as English, French and German – and among the Nordic countries sources written in a Scandinavian language – are more likely to be used outside their own jurisdiction and to be included in the customary apparatus of sources in the receiving jurisdiction. The rapid development of electronic means will undoubtedly in the future greatly increase our practical opportunities to make use of foreign legal sources. When I have argued that custom does not offer much additional weight to the European authority argument, my perspective has been on the current situation. However, custom is not static, but undergoes continuous change. As I have stated before,[84] the digital future may create many new opportunities for legal actors to use foreign materials and this might very well have a considerable impact on prevailing customs. When materials from the whole Union are digitally easily accessible and searchable as well as automatically translated, it would be strange if this expansion of the corpus of legal materials would not have any impact on the way the sources are used in legal practice. But, as I have said before, we are not there yet.

Even when one understands an increasing use of materials from other Member States in legal reasoning as something that is worth striving for in an experimental and learning European legal community, the requirement concerning transparent legal reasoning usually cannot be satisfied by a pure authority argument. One cannot be contended with a general claim that within the Union a source from another Member State would have some legal authority only because of its origin. More is needed to make the reasoning convincing. One should require additional argumentation for the cross-border use of sources, at least when the issue is not related to the application of EU law.

I will in what follows look at some possible patterns of such additional justification. As the issue of a legitimate use of foreign sources is not an on-off issue, several types of arguments may influence how convincing one finds a particular foreign source to be with regard to a particular issue.

[83] For example, the growth of trans-border law firms may also increase the use of cross-border materials, Glenn (2004: 226).

[84] ch 5 section VI.

V. A COMMUNITY OF VALUES AS AN ARGUMENT

In the debate on the globalisation of law some – often constitutional or international lawyers[85] – have advocated theories concerning the use of foreign sources based on the idea that law could be seen as a field of universal normative knowledge. According to Jeremy Waldron, legal solutions to certain problems 'might get established in the way that scientific theories are established'.[86] He envisages something that he calls a 'modern *ius gentium*' based on a possible international consensus on any particular subject.[87] As Neil Walker notes, recognising the authoritative value of the laws of others might imply 'some notion of a realm of *universal* normativity'.[88] Klaus Günther indeed speaks about a 'universal code of legality' with a certain factual validity containing basic legal concepts and rules.[89] From a practical-methodological point of view, one could speak about 'a global community of courts'[90] and 'a transnational legal science' as the developers of a transnational legal doctrine.[91] 'Universal concepts of law' may be regarded as legitimate arguments in domestic legal reasoning.[92] In this approach, the use of foreign sources becomes a value in itself, as an expression of some sort of universal legality. In its modern version, universal legality is not based on any conception of natural law, but on the development of transnational legal practice and transnational discourse.

As to the structure of legal reasoning one may indeed find some largely cherished general features. Legal professionals everywhere are educated to focus their questions in a particular legal way. They are trained to distill from a large pool of facts what is to be considered 'legally relevant', and from a collection of source-materials what is to be considered 'legally possible'. The idea of a modern and universal *ius gentium*, however, goes further than that. It also implies a recognition of some common substantive legal values.

A good illustration of this type of thinking from case law is the often-cited passage from *Fairchild v Glenhaven Funeral Services Ltd*: 'In a shrinking world … there must be some virtue in uniformity of outcome'.[93] In this case, Lord Bingham justified the extensive reference to foreign sources in a rather transparent fashion:

> Development of the law in this country cannot of course depend on a head-count of decisions and codes adopted in other countries around the world …. If, however, a decision is given in this country which offends one's basic sense of justice, and if consideration of international sources suggests that a different and more acceptable decision would be given in most other jurisdictions, whatever their legal tradition, this must prompt anxious review of the decision in question.[94]

[85] Waldron (2005: 129), however, expressly includes private law in his analysis. For a critique of Waldron, see eg Tripkovic (2014).

[86] Waldron (2005: 144).

[87] ibid (146).

[88] Walker (2019: 368). See also Walker (2015: 85).

[89] Günther (2008: 16).

[90] Slaughter (2003).

[91] Michaels and Jansen (2006: 878–79).

[92] Coendet (2014: 2).

[93] [2003] 1 AC 32, para 32 (referring to authority from common law, Germany, Norway, France, the Netherlands and Greece).

[94] ibid.

Hardly anybody argues that one could construct a truly universal legal code. It is a question of 'a universalism of the parts', rather than a holistic top-down universalism;[95] 'the universal code of legality' is not a homogeneous system as it contains both indeterminate and contested universals.[96] In addition, the basic values expressed by the legal orders of various countries might be so far away from what a Western spectator would expect that general claims on universalism with a global reach might seem uncomfortable. Some, therefore, may limit legal 'universalism' to cover only the laws of states that share Western values.[97] There are also doubts whether there are such public values prevailing at the global level that could really enrich private law, as there is no state to provide such values.[98]

As the focus in this book is on European private law and the use of the 'European laboratory', there is no need to discuss the difficult issue whether one should distinguish between more and less acceptable jurisdictions, and more generally whether one should believe in the existence of some universal legal content based on legal practice and discourse.[99] The discussion on joint values, however, underlines the relevance of the following question: as far as the EU is built on the idea of joint legal values, can this be used as an argument for referring to sources from other Member States along the lines of a kind of regional universalism?

A suggestion that points in this direction is Samantha Besson's plea for a European law that speaks with one voice. She applies the Dworkinian moral demand of integrity, according to which legal decision-making should be made as coherent as possible in relation to previous laws and decisions, to the European political community, making the decisions part of 'a complex and pluralist but single European order'.[100] This would mean that 'all authorities should take into account past laws and decisions of other European authorities, be they national or strictly European, and try to make their own laws and decisions fit with them as far as possible'.[101] This principle should cover not only EU-related law, but the legal order in its entirety.[102] In practical terms, the extreme quantity and diversity of European legal material would seem like an obstacle, but the author is convinced that this problem will shrink as the social and cultural diversity between Member States decreases.[103] In this sense, the approach seems to be built on the idea of the EU as a community of values.

The EU is indeed often portrayed as a Union based on joint values. In Article 2 of the Treaty on the European Union, the joint value-basis is expressed:

> The Union is founded on the values of respect for human dignity, freedom, democracy, equality, the rule of law and respect for human rights, including the rights of persons belonging to minorities. These values are common to the Member States in a society in which pluralism, non-discrimination, tolerance, justice, solidarity and equality between women and men prevail.

[95] Walker (2019: 369–71).
[96] Günther (2008: 18–19).
[97] Waldron (2005: 145).
[98] eg Michaels and Jansen (2006: 873).
[99] The issue of a possible global *lex mercatoria*, see eg Berger (2010), falls outside the scope of this book.
[100] Besson (2004: 259).
[101] ibid (263).
[102] ibid (264).
[103] ibid (265–66).

Earlier, I analysed the European social model and the growing weight of fundamental rights reasoning as possible grand narratives of European law.[104] I did not consider these narratives to be sufficient, however, to function as ready-made maps for the development of European private law. Still, one should not rule out the possibility that more limited European narratives could receive their normative fuel from a joint European value-basis, or more humbly from a joint epistemic normative community. The question is whether and to what extent such a reference to joint normative understandings offers a convincing and transparent justification of the use of cross-border sources within the EU.

A claim that a certain foreign source is relevant because it reflects a European joint value or a common understanding could be described as a use of heavy argumentative artillery. It is hard to see that a reference to one single source from another jurisdiction within the EU could be convincingly defended by just calling it an expression of a joint value-basis of the Union. The 'modern *ius gentium*' is based on an idea of 'a dense and mutually reinforced consensus'.[105] A single or a few pieces of legal material do not represent such a consensus. The argument concerning a joint European understanding requires more than that in order to be convincing.

The reasoning based on a consensus-type argument, in other words, requires some breadth, even though it does not necessarily require evidence of a real consensus between all Member States. The reasoning in this pattern of argumentation focuses on tendencies rather than on individual cases. If one can show that within other Member States a tendency prevails to develop the law in a certain way, this might be a relevant argument for developing the domestic law in the same direction. Such reasoning related to tendencies within the EU seems to be gaining ground. For example, the discussion concerning the modernisation of the German law of obligations has been said to support the breakthrough of a new way of argumentation, according to which the compatibility with international collections of rules and with European development tendencies is seen as an indication of the quality and usefulness of the solutions.[106] In case law, one may also occasionally find references to comparative materials as expressions of tendencies in European legal practice. The reference may also be formulated as an indication of the dominant view in Europe or more loosely of something that many have adopted.[107]

Sometimes such tendencies or dominant views are described as 'European principles'. Even the CJEU has occasionally constructed what it calls 'general principles of civil law'. It has thus been able to justify interpretations and gap-filling of directives, for example, in the area of consumer law.[108] Inspiration for such constructions could be taken from the provision in the Treaty on the Functioning of the European Union Article 340(2) on non-contractual liability of the Union. The Article prescribes

[104] ch 6.

[105] Waldron (2005: 145).

[106] Schulze (2004: 85).

[107] For a Swedish example, see the case NJA 2005 p 608 (referring to 'many foreign legal systems', but with references mainly to European sources).

[108] See eg Case C-412/06 *Annelore Hamilton v Volksbank Filder* [2008] ECR I-2383 and Case C-489/07 *Pia Messner v Firma Stefan Krüger* [2009] ECR I-7315. Critique by Weatherill (2010).

that the Union shall make good damage 'in accordance with the general principles common to the laws of the Member States'. Domestic courts and scholars may be inspired by these recognitions of the idea of some joint European principles of private law. One may discuss, however, how much evidence one needs to make a claim concerning the existence of a joint European general principle convincing. When it seems natural to make such a claim, the joint European principle might be of so general a nature that it does not contribute much to the solution of the issue at hand.[109] Searching for more concrete European principles, domestic courts have used, for example, academic collections, such as the DCFR, as indicators of European tendencies.[110] It is well known, however, that it is hard to claim that the adopted solutions in the collections reflect a joint European principle with regard to many issues. All in all, in truly transparent reasoning, references to 'general principles of civil law' in Europe should be given a firmer anchorage in comparative materials than is often the case. Convincing open reasoning under a heading of 'joint European general principles' usually requires more than just a reference to a few European jurisdictions or to a collection of academic principles.

Even when one might convince the reader of the emergence of a European tendency, this is not necessarily a sufficient argument for adopting the same solution. As was argued above,[111] in an understanding of the EU as a laboratory for experimental legal learning, the harmonisation of law is not a value in itself. Diversity is the growing bed for new ideas that may spread across the borders if they prove to be valuable. In such a perspective, the development of law needs a never-ending process of reflexive harmonisation that includes both a contextual harmonisation and a reinforcement of diversity.[112] In completely transparent reasoning, the European tendency argument therefore often requires some additional support. The tendency may, for example, be endorsed because it is considered to indicate that the solution is well-functioning, or it may be supported by substantive reasoning concerning the value of harmonisation of the rules in the area.

A reference to a tendency or a dominant view may play a variety of roles in the argumentation. In some situations it can function as a push for a new solution that is developing domestic law – if other Member States are moving in this direction, we should also do so. It can also be used, however, as a device to hamper development. The argument then reads: even though the present solution is not good, one should not domestically amend it, as it reflects a generally recognised principle in Europe. To be transparent one needs additional substantive reasoning indicating the role of the European tendency argument with regard to the dynamic development of the law.

A reasoning that refers to some kind of universal normativity based on joint values seems most convincing when it deals with strongly value-laden issues relating to

[109] *cf* Reich (2014) on the 'general principles of EU civil law', finding seven such principles: the principles of 'framed autonomy', 'protection of the weaker party', 'non-discrimination', 'effectiveness', 'balancing', 'proportionality' and 'good faith'. The principles of EU law is another issue than joint European domestic principles, but the list illustrates how principles on a high level of abstraction may look like.

[110] See ch 8 section III.

[111] ch 5.

[112] Andreadakis (2011).

morality and societal justice. When values are changing, an evolving series of legal measures in Europe that follows this change may also be a rather convincing argument for accepting it on the domestic level. A good example is the development of the rules on same-sex marriages. Concerning this issue, national legislators have been able to use inspiration from other Member States when modernising their laws. In most cases, this has primarily involved legislative learning, but it has affected the reasoning of courts and scholars too. More generally, private law issues that trigger questions, for example, related to human rights, minority protection, pluralism, non-discrimination, tolerance, justice, solidarity and equality between women and men, as mentioned in Article 2 of the Treaty on the European Union, might appear to be more closely related to the joint value-basis of the Union. Concerning such issues, a reference to European tendencies may be enlightening and convincing as such. One should note, however, that even in this case there are various ways to rely on a 'tendency': in a forward-looking perspective materials that indicate a 'tendency' might not yet represent the law of the majority of the Member States.

A reference to joint European legal values might have different weight in different areas of law. In some fields, the legal actors have formed closer communities with stronger interaction than in other fields, and this may support the emergence of patterns of reasoning relating to more concrete joint values and principles. In the area of consumer law one could speak about the existence of a kind of epistemic community since the 1970s.[113] Some have even spoken about the emergence of a European legal consciousness in this area.[114] The considerable amount of EU consumer law legislation has further facilitated the growth of a genuinely cross-border consumer law discourse in Europe. It is still, however, premature to speak about a joint value-basis of European consumer law. As the discussions concerning the consumer image in European law indicate,[115] there are fairly deep cleavages both between various domestic approaches and between domestic and European approaches. The consumer law community does also not include all legal actors in the area, but predominantly legal scholars and other actors with an interest in consumer protection. This does not mean, however, that the existence of a consumer law community has no relevance at all with regard to the development of joint European consumer law principles. The scholarly discourse certainly provides instruments for identification of such common ground, and may also push the development in a harmonising direction. Since the consumer law community predominantly consists of scholars, one may expect it to be supportive in particular of the cross-border use of scholarly products, like concepts, systematisations and methods.[116] The epistemic community also helps good substantive arguments, often based on thorough research, to move across the borders. In these cases, however, the use of cross-border materials may be justified with reference to the requirements of good scientific practice rather than invoking some presumed joint European value-base.

[113] See the collection of papers by Micklitz (2021).
[114] eg Graziadei (2016: 106), on consumer and contract law.
[115] See eg Micklitz (1996) and Leczykiewicz and Weatherill (2016).
[116] On research methods in consumer law (in particular behavioural research), see Micklitz, Sibony and Esposito (2018a).

VI. AUTHORITY BASED ON PERCEIVED QUALITY

The ideal of a free movement of legal ideas implies a possibility of learning across the borders of all jurisdictions of the EU. This is often impractical, with the exception of possible collections or reporting of sources concerning some particular legislation, like the CISG[117] or the Products Liability Directive.[118] The digital future may change the scene, but today cross-border learning in practice normally occurs in relation to some, usually only a few, selected jurisdictions. The selection varies from Member State to Member State. Those contemporary judges who tend to refer to foreign cases seem to make their choice primarily based on legal tradition, language and the prestige of the foreign court.[119]

For example, when making reference to foreign jurisdictions, German courts usually prefer to cite cases from other members of what is called the German legal family, such as Austria and Switzerland.[120] The same community also works in the other direction. Austrian and Swiss courts rely predominantly on cases from German courts.[121] In common law jurisdictions, the majority of references to foreign materials relate to other common law jurisdictions.[122] The Nordic legal cooperation and its impact on cross-border learning between the Nordic countries has already been touched upon above.

Cross-border legal communities are often based on perceived similarities of legal culture. Learning from a foreign source is easier if a court or a scholar recognises concepts and principles as being familiar. This also relates to legal methodology. The more similar the decision-maker perceives the reasoning to be, the easier it is to exchange sources. Linguistic abilities or preferences may also determine the selection. The Germanic, the common law and the Nordic groupings are tied together not only by legal culture, but also by language. A striking example of the importance of language is offered by Belgian legal culture in which French-speaking lawyers seem to have leaned towards French law, whilst Flemish-speaking lawyers have looked for inspiration from Dutch law.[123] These kinds of cultural-linguistic groupings, based on legal tradition, will probably survive a broader Europeanisation. They are also not necessarily in conflict with broader learning patterns, but may even promote the development of a comprehensive European view. If the actors of a legal culture are used to look at foreign materials from within a certain grouping, the hurdle for looking even beyond that group will probably feel lower than it is for an actor used only to domestic materials.

[117] www.cisg.law.pace.edu/.

[118] See eg the reporting that has been offered by Hogan Lovells in the European Product Liability Review, later the International Product Liability Review.

[119] E Mak (2013: 4, 206 *et seq*). On the interpretation of a Convention, see also Lord Diplock in *Fothergill v Monarch Airliners Ltd*. [1981] AC 251, 284: 'As respects decisions of foreign courts, the persuasive value of a particular court's decision must depend upon its reputation and its status, the extent to which its decisions are binding upon courts of co-ordinate and inferior jurisdiction in its own country and the coverage of the national law reporting system.'.

[120] Janssen and Schulze (2011: 249); Gelter and Siems (2012: 93–94); Smits (2019: 509).

[121] Gelter and Siems (2012: 93); Smits (2019: 520).

[122] Bobek (2013: 90, 93); Smits (2019: 519–20).

[123] Heirbaut and Storme (2006: 659–60).

In a truly Europeanised area of experimental legal learning, however, one should be able to overcome borderlines created by such informal groupings of jurisdictions. The paradigmatic case *White v Jones*[124] is an example of such a move, reaching out from common law to German and other continental law. From the point of view of European-wide free movement, it is particularly interesting to discuss a transparent justification of such cross-border learning that looks beyond the regional and cultural silos. When selecting materials within a truly Europeanised legal community, one needs other arguments than culture and language. As discussed above, a fully Europeanised tradition or custom concerning the use of foreign materials has not yet emerged.

Even though a Europeanised approach in principle requires openness towards learning from all parts of the Union, one cannot (today) easily take all available learning on board. One still needs arguments for making a selection of jurisdictions to study. When one discusses what kinds of arguments that are possible, it is useful to look at the underlying reasoning in contemporary case law and scholarship within the more limited communities of legal interaction.

The metaphor of a learning law offers a useful inroad into the issue. The aim must be finding a good 'teacher'. In general, one recognises as a good teacher a person in whose level of knowledge and intellectual ability one can trust. In legal reasoning, one accordingly recognises such foreign actors that one believes to be capable of teaching something that improves one's legal order. One may for this reason attach authority to particular legal orders, to particular courts and legal decision-makers or to certain persons or groups of persons.

Certain foreign legal orders may enjoy a particularly good reputation in the minds of decision-makers. For example, Italians find French and German law prestigious,[125] whilst others might turn to common law. The prestige may be caused by societal power, cultural dominance and similar external factors, but from the point of view of a learning law, a key element ought to be the perception of the quality of the legal order and the legal actors that a decision-maker intends to cite.

As there is no generally accepted way to measure the quality of law, there are various understandings of what the good quality of law is all about. Those who prefer citing German law may do so because of its systematic nature and conceptual consistency, those looking at common law may emphasise its pragmatic approach to problem-solving. Some large jurisdictions are also cited considerably more often than the law of smaller countries.[126] This practice may also be based on a quality aspect: the larger quantity of case law and black letter research creates the expectation that many issues have been the object of deeper thinking in such jurisdictions. Some may even speak about leading legal systems in the EU, usually referring to German, French and English law (before Brexit).[127] Be that as it may, the reasons for attaching particular value to a certain legal order should be openly analysed and discussed.

[124] [1995] All ER 691.

[125] Alpa (2004a: 209).

[126] Gelter and Siems (2012: 95). Bobek (2013: 41–42) notes that smaller jurisdictions might look to larger ones as a practical necessity.

[127] These countries are also said to function as legal 'origin countries', see eg Gelter and Siems (2012: 97).

The prevailing business culture behind a national jurisdiction may make this jurisdiction particularly attractive for some actors. The tendency to lean on experience from English courts may relate to the perception that the British commercial culture is more competitive than the more cooperative Nordic and, to a lesser degree, German commercial cultures. When these kinds of reasons lie behind the choice of materials, the choice is not necessarily based on quality, but on the substantive consequences of the choice, as there are variations between these countries with regard to the expectations of moral behaviour in the marketplace.[128] As I have stressed repeatedly, transparent reasoning requires the disclosure of such substantive reasons as well.

Perceptions of expertise may relate to particular issues or fields. The paradigmatic example is the widespread use of English sources in maritime law.[129] In the context of the EU, such reference to particular expertise may relate to directives that are based on the experiences of some Member States. The inspirational status of German law with regard to the interpretation of the Commercial Agents Directive has been mentioned before as a good example.

The 'good teacher' argument usually relates to a legal order in general. However, a particular court or institution may develop such a reputation that its decisions are considered especially valuable – it may acquire 'leadership amongst one's peers' in a horizontal dialogue.[130] For example, a court or a judge that has produced many highly appreciated judgments may reach a particularly authoritative status. More generally, in business law cases the level of experience of the court with regard to trade issues may be a criterion for assessing its value as creator of new learning.[131]

Even the perceived quality of individual cases may be relevant. In the emerging 'international market place for judgments' the quality and form of a judgment may determine its persuasiveness.[132] When this is the case, however, the predominant reason for using the source seems to be of a substantive rather than an authoritative nature.

In jurisdictions in which legal dogmatics formally or practically functions as a source of law, some scholars might be cited more often because of their reputation and the quality of their writings. Such reputation may extend across the borders. For example in Nordic law, some scholars have been cited regularly throughout the region.[133] However, so far the weight of scholarly reputation often seems to correlate with the importance of the jurisdiction about which the scholar is writing. When speaking about scholarship on domestic law – and not about scholarship on EU law – it is not easy to name many scholars that are regularly cited across the EU.

[128] For the various attitudes towards pre-contractual information duties in these countries, see eg Brownsword, Hird and Howells (1999).

[129] On German practice using English maritime law, see Drobnig (1999a: 136) and Unberath (2004: 308).

[130] E Mak (2013: 80) uses this metaphor.

[131] See Baasch Andersen (2011: 48).

[132] Andenas and Fairgrieve (2004: xxxv).

[133] Scholars like Jan Hellner (Sweden), Carl Jacob Arnholm (Norway) and Henry Ussing (Denmark) – not to mention many living ones – have received many citations across the Nordic countries.

Summing up, it is clear that one of the ways of producing legitimation for the use of foreign sources is related to the quality of the material. This gives rise to a multitude of follow-up questions: how does one define quality? Is the perception of quality derived from experience or from particular approaches to legal issues? Should one focus on the quality of particular legal orders or of particular courts or institutions? Obviously, there is no agreement on these questions. One has to accept the existence of different views as part of the experimental setting. It is important, however, that such questions are raised. Only by openly discussing such issues can decision-makers avoid choosing their sources in a completely arbitrary way.

In future discussions, one might ask whether there could be some division of legal labour within the EU. As English courts are considered to be experts in maritime law, others might be recognised as having expertise in other fields. Could the Nordic countries aspire to a position as experts in, for example, consumer law, whilst other jurisdictions could contribute in depth to the development of other fields? As market actors constantly produce new types of business models and contracts, emerging areas that require experimental legal responses may offer opportunities for both smaller and larger jurisdictions to create solutions to be followed by others.

The assessment whether a foreign solution is a forerunner or a backlash cannot be done based on authoritative sources alone. The choice of 'high quality' usually includes a substantive evaluation of the situation. Transparency requires openness concerning the substantive arguments. In the following section I will look closer at some such arguments.

VII. SUBSTANTIVE JUSTIFICATION OF A HARMONISING USE OF FOREIGN SOURCES

When using foreign materials a court or a scholar may refer to substantive arguments that directly concern the concrete legal issue to be decided or analysed. I have above addressed the need for transparent substantive reasoning when foreign sources are used.

In addition, substantive arguments may be used on a meta-level to justify the resort to foreign sources. When a particular foreign source is used as an argument with some authoritative value, the meta-legitimation for the authority may be based on substantive reasons. As there is no self-evident authority of foreign sources, one may argue substantively for establishing such authority. In the following, I will look more closely at what a transparent substantive meta-legitimation of authority of a foreign source may contain.

Within the EU, substantive reasoning of this kind is familiar from the debates on the desirability of harmonisation of European private law and of a European Civil Code. As I have argued in chapter two, the vision concerning a fully fledged European Civil Code is not in tune with contemporary society. 'Creeping harmonisation' should also not be seen as a goal in itself in a European legal setting that values experimentalism.[134] The substantive arguments behind these visions, however, are

[134] See ch 5 section VII.

still relevant when one attempts to justify cross-border learning processes concerning more limited issues. Familiar substantive arguments for harmonisation are, for example, the need to facilitate cross-border transactions and to create equal conditions of competition, the value of building a European identity and of equal treatment of European citizens. Other substantive arguments for justifying cross-border authority of sources in Europe could of course be added to the list. I will not discuss the arguments as such, as many have done so elsewhere. I only want to note that the substantive arguments for giving foreign sources authority have different weight depending on the circumstances. One of the arguments might be relevant in one type of situation and another in another type of case. This is important with regard to what one should include in a transparent legal reasoning.

The practical needs of commercial actors are often cited as a primary reason for harmonisation. According to this argument, common rules facilitate cross-border transactions. This argument seems forceful when discussing the legislative harmonisation of particular fields of law, like the law on some particular type of contract. The argument is not always convincing when discussing issues of detail alone. With regard to certain private law issues, however, joint approaches can be important for the parties to cross-border transactions. Hugh Beale has called these issues 'traps'.[135] Rules on giving notice, on limitation periods and on securities in movables can easily cause hidden traps for businesses. Even more basic domestic starting points, such as the effect of *cause* in French law and consideration in English law, may lead to surprises.[136] The avoidance of hidden traps is a good substantive argument for looking across the borders.

In other cases, the harmonisation argument relates to the need to create equal conditions of competition. This argument has been used, for example, as justification for the harmonisation of mandatory rules for protecting consumers. As equal conditions of competition hardly require harmonisation in details that have minor economic impact, the argument is relevant in particular when the economic consequences of the rules are considerable. For example, in cases that might require an economically significant change of behaviour in relation to a large number of customers, the equal conditions of competition argument supports looking across the border. As another kind of example, one could mention that the French *Cour de cassation* has taken into account the situation in other Member States when deciding on the validity of exemption clauses in contracts for delivery by couriers in order not to burden the French operators more than their European competitors.[137]

A different kind of harmonisation argument celebrates the building of a European identity. According to this argument, a joint private law would strengthen the common identity of Europeans. This argument, if relevant at all, rather relates to codification projects and has less relevance for the micro-level movement of legal sources. Admittedly, for example in cases with strong emotional appeal and broad media coverage, similar approaches across the borders may contribute to a shared

[135] Beale (2002).
[136] Kadner Graziano (2005: 525–28) describes these as examples of an '*Überraschungseffekt*'.
[137] Canivet (2006: 1394).

feeling of being European. For example, if domestic legal actors react in the same way to widely observed commercial practices that offend the basic values of many citizens,[138] it might create a sense of European togetherness. This comes close to what I have described above as reasoning based on the idea of Europe as a union of values.

One may also refer to the value of equality as an argument for harmonising decision-making. If the citizens of the Union feel that they are treated differently in different Member States, it may hurt their sense of justice. The principle of equal treatment has indeed been offered as a methodological basis for the Europeanisation of private law.[139] This argument, however, is not generally convincing, as the Europeans cherish the idea of being united in diversity, of being ruled by their domestic legal orders. In some cases, in particular concerning the protection of individual rights, the equality argument may have more force. Some have mentioned privacy law in this context.[140] The harmonisation of European consumer law is also to some extent supported by the idea of equality between consumers from different Member States. Differing rules protecting weaker parties may not be applauded by parties from a Member State with less stringent standards, in particular in broadly discussed cases. For example, it would seem natural to solve much-discussed medical care liability cases (eg breast implant and hip replacement cases) in the same way across the Union. One could also argue for a harmonised approach to tobacco liability, even though different views about risk taking and smoking habits might lead to differing conclusions.[141] As Neil Walker has argued (on a global level), 'there is something authoritative about the laws of others just in view of the weight of the argument that like cases should be treated alike across legal orders'.[142]

I have tried to show how the weight of the substantive arguments for cross-border learning varies depending on the issue. Even though there is hardly any agreement concerning the situational weight of the arguments, this does not eliminate the need for an analysis. Only by openly using arguments of this kind can legal decision-making and legal scholarship become transparent in a way that makes it possible to discuss the solutions on rational grounds. An analysis of the relevance of substantive arguments supporting harmonisation in a case has to be much more nuanced than reasoning built on a general acceptance of cross-border sources. In such a discourse one is able to openly balance the harmonisation value of a foreign source against other arguments related to a case.

The insistence on transparent reasoning relates also to the choice of the sources to use. The harmonisation arguments that I have commented on here are obviously often quite weak if there is no dominant view in the laws within the EU. Some might find it possible to refer to the needs of cross-border trade and the elimination of hidden traps in order to support a convergence dominated by the large jurisdictions, because these are better known and linguistically accessible for businesses.

[138] Matters of taste and decency were left outside the scope of the Unfair Commercial Practices Directive. See Howells, Micklitz and Wilhelmsson (2006: 59–62).
[139] Berger (2001: 888).
[140] Canivet (2004: 190).
[141] See Howells (2011).
[142] Walker (2019: 368).

Value-laden experience, on the other hand, might be sought in countries that have established themselves as value-leaders and frontrunners in some area of law. In such a case, the reasoning leaves the harmonisation narrative and falls back on what I described earlier as argumentation related to quality and trust. In comprehensive transparent reasoning, arguments mentioned under different headings can be mixed into a variety of cocktails.

VIII. IN OTHER WORDS

The focus of this chapter is on how courts and scholars may use cross-border European (domestic) sources as transparently as possible. I am normatively discussing what kind of reasoning one may convincingly use to justify references to foreign sources.

There are various ways to justify the use of a foreign source as an argument with some degree of authority. First, the authoritative status of the foreign source may be based on some meta-level authority, like legislation or custom. In the European context, there might be emerging a kind of custom-based authority allowing the use of foreign sources in the interpretation of domestic law implementing EU law. Secondly, particularly in some value-laden cases, the view on the EU as a union of values may be a possible argument for making use of knowledge concerning prevailing legal tendencies in the EU. Thirdly, the authority of the foreign source can be based on a particular trust in the legal quality of the source. The trust may relate to the perceived expertise gathered in some particular jurisdiction or it may be based on the belief in the competence of a particular foreign court or scholar. Fourthly, the authority of the foreign source may be based on meta-level substantive arguments related to the value of European harmonisation. Depending on the circumstances, one might use different arguments: the needs of cross-border trade, the importance of equal conditions of competition, the striving for a European identity or the requirement of equal justice for all Europeans.

A transparent use of foreign sources can usually not rely on legal authority alone. Substantive reasoning that relates to the issue at hand is also needed. A court or a scholar would hardly use cross-border learning to reach a solution that they find substantively 'bad'. On the other hand, when one perceives proceeding in a direction to be 'good', foreign sources may at best expand the area of the legally possible and offer tools for breaking with old petrified structures. From the point of view of transparent reasoning, it is important that substantive arguments related to the goodness of the decision are openly accounted for.

The presented typology does not offer a readily applicable formula that would increase predictability as to the outcome of cases. With regard to the rule of law, however, also the quality of reasoning matters. A line of reasoning that makes use of an analysis of the type presented here is more transparent and controllable than a use of foreign sources that lacks express justification. A more general adoption of such advanced transparent reasoning may today seem as wishful thinking, but it is a way to support the rule of law in a legal world in which the ideal of a relatively stable and coherent legal order is no longer convincing.

10

Closing the Book(s)

THE JOURNEY THAT resulted in this book started from the debate on a European civil code decades ago. The debate forced the participants to position themselves in relation to a multitude of general questions on the role and function of (private) law and legal reasoning. Even though the idea of a European civil code has faded away, the general issues related to the future of private law in Europe remain. An analysis of the Europeanisation of private law requires answers to many questions concerning issues like the societal functions of private law; the role of the rule of law in an uncertain and dynamic world; the options of a critical legal science and practice in contemporary society; and Europeanisation and nationalism in private law, to mention only a few. By combining the discussion of such issues I have sketched one perspective on how private law is being and could be developed in a European setting by a free movement of legal ideas.

The starting point for the creation of this picture was a diagnosis of contemporary society. During the latter half of the twentieth century, the increasing degree of epistemic and ethical uncertainty caught the attention of societal discourse. Globalisation and digitalisation have considerably deepened the sense of uncertainty, and the COVID-19 pandemic has demonstrated the profound character of the development. In such a state of uncertainty, rigid and stable legal structures, like a European civil code, cannot respond well to the regulatory needs of society. The alternative solution is an experimental and learning law that can continuously draw on experiences from and adapt to various challenges posed by today's uncertain societal environment. A law that can learn and develop in such an experimental fashion must become more flexible and fragmented. Flexibility and fragmentation are keywords when describing legal development in contemporary society.

To illustrate how flexibility interacts with necessary but fragmented islands and periods of stability, I have introduced a metaphor called 'small narratives on legal change'. The metaphor focuses on processes of change rather than on the 'snapshot content' of law at a given moment. It is a story of how a particular, larger or smaller part of the law is moved from a relatively stable position to a new position, through the activity of various legal actors. The metaphor includes all legal actors, both legislators, courts and legal scholars that may have an influence on the direction of the narratives. It shows the constant interaction within law between active periods of development and periods of stability when the narrative has ended in a new position. The 'smallness' of the narratives hints at a lack of a great masterplan, allowing changes in various directions based on contextual and experimental learning (societally, the narrative can be very 'big', related for example to the combat against climate change). As a small narrative on change may start unexpectedly, the presumption of legal stability may occasionally turn out to be an illusion.

The metaphor of small narratives on legal change is useful in both domestic and Europeanised contexts. Adding the European perspective introduces a new layer of complexity into the narrative. The various national actors are accompanied by European legal actors, such as the European legislator, European courts and European legal scholarship. All these can bring European learning into domestic legal narratives. This is legal everyday life. Theoretically more far-reaching, however, is the emerging acknowledgement of a possibility to learn directly across the borders within the EU, even without the mediation of European-level legal actors. Such a practice means an efficient use of the learning acquired across the whole of the 'European legal laboratory'. Therefore, I have focused in particular on the opportunity of such horizontal learning processes between domestic actors, even though they still are not very frequent in practice.

Even though there is no grand master plan that could clearly steer the development, some European grand narratives may contribute to the development of small narratives. The philosophy of European welfarism as well as the strong European belief in fundamental rights can open up narratives that search for new alternatives. They cannot, however, provide an increasingly fragmented private law with a coherent legal structure that would seriously challenge the growth of flexibility and fragmentation.

An important European value is the rule of law. Many have questioned how one can maintain the position of this value in a flexible and fragmented legal environment. Even though the loss of coherence of law does not necessarily imply an equally strong deterioration of the essential goals of predictability and equality, it is clear that the relationship between the value of the rule of law and the experimental free movement of legal ideas is not an easy issue. The solution that I offer here is the increased transparency of legal reasoning. Even in an experimental and constantly learning European setting, one can counteract arbitrary decision-making by making radically stronger demands on the openness of the reasoning of courts and scholars. By expressly opening up the reasoning, a legal actor offers a basis for assessment and critique as important devices of the rule of law.

The increased openness means an honest account of both the substantive and the authoritative arguments that legal actors use to solve a legal issue. In connection with a horizontal movement of legal ideas, transparency requires an open discussion of why and to what extent inspiration is drawn from foreign materials. As horizontal use of sources usually has to be supported by substantive arguments, such substantive reasoning should not be hidden behind the formal authority of the material. The societal significance of the solution – the perception concerning its 'goodness' – should be spelled out.

This is the narrative of the present book, compressed into a few pages. As one can see, the conclusions drawn from the societal starting point, after travelling through the legal landscape, are both descriptive and normative. There are pressures towards a more flexible and fragmented law, whether one likes it or not. To this quasi-empirical starting point, I have added a normative perspective. One should try not only to withstand the changes, but also to make positive use of them. I offer a normative vision concerning the opportunities of a fruitful Europeanisation of private law in a contemporary society of uncertainty, realised with sufficient respect for the demands of the rule of law.

The vision should not be understood as a suggestion concerning a deep change of paradigm of legal reasoning. It is built on experiences from contemporary European practice and doctrinal analysis. My approach is not based on an 'either-or', but on a 'both-and' logic. One should not look at the development in a binary fashion,[1] but rather as movement along a scale in which fragmentation and flexibility receive increasing weight. Such an approach better reflects the complexity of law.

I. FAMILIAR THEMES WITH A NEW TWIST

One should not strive to reinvent the wheel. Many of my themes have been discussed before, sometimes in the same terms, sometimes in a different terminology. Scholars have acknowledged, and usually deplored, the increasing fragmentation and flexibility of private law. In comparative law discourse, the possibility of 'transplantation' of pieces of law across borders has been a fashionable theme for a long time. These are just two examples on how my analysis relates to previous debates. As the reader is no doubt aware, one could add many other examples.

My contribution lies in the storyline that combines the different strands of theoretical discourse. I have attempted to write a coherent theoretical story on incoherence (fragmentation and flexibility) as a prerequisite for a societally advantageous Europeanisation of private law. My litmus test concerning the force of the analysis is how well the parts of the story fit together.

This does not mean, however, that there are no personal twists relating to the individual parts. On the contrary, the input from various theoretical debates has been adapted to the basic perspective of the work. In what follows, I will give a couple of examples on how I have (mis)treated some familiar issues.

My less negative or even positive twist (without forgetting the negative features) on the increased fragmentation and flexibility of private law is related to the perceived need for law to become more experimental and learning in contemporary society. The focus on learning and change implies a dynamic perspective on law. A static snapshot of the 'law as it is' or 'the law in force', as often presented in black-letter research, reveals only a partial understanding of the legal situation. Without denying the value of such snapshots, my aim is to present a picture that focuses on legal change, embodied in the metaphor small narratives on legal change. The focus on change does not imply, however, that there is no stability in the legal order. The theory builds on an understanding that the law concerning a particular issue oscillates between periods of stability and of change. The metaphor is intended to focus the interest on the mechanisms of change.

In addition, the metaphor underlines the role of all legal actors in developing such narratives. I have chosen to focus my main attention on the work of courts

[1] This is one of the starting points of Tuori (2021) in his analysis of the properties of law.

and scholars. This does not mean that I want to deny the central role of the (hopefully) democratic legislator in developing the law. The role of legislation, however, is relatively self-evident in a dynamic perspective of law, even though there are also limitations to legislative power. I have therefore wanted to direct attention towards the 'micro-management' of law by courts, scholars and other similar legal actors. It is on this level that the perspective on change brings forward new opportunities and responsibilities, and broadens our understanding of what is included in the 'legal order'. The main theme of the book – the free movement of legal sources – is therefore analysed with particular focus on the activity of courts and legal scholars.

Another familiar and useful legal-theoretical discourse relates to the distinction between hard cases and easy cases or routine cases. My focus on change directs the attention in particular to hard cases or hard issues. For example, in cases that can be solved by the application of a clear and precise legislative rule, it should, with regard to the democratic legitimacy of the legislator, normally be routine to apply the enactment as prescribed. It is important to recall, however, that even though the emphasis here is on hard cases, there is no clear line between the hard and the easy ones. An easy case may be turned into a hard one, for example, if the easy solution appears to be societally strongly unfortunate or contradicting a general sense of justice. In legal scholarship, a forward-looking scholar may even direct particular attention to weak signals indicating possible starting points for new narratives on legal change in a seemingly stable environment – and thereby contribute to starting these narratives. The use of comparative materials, the movement of legal ideas across European borders, may also occasionally be used in order to legitimate the detour from an established domestic standpoint.

One should by no means read this as a proposal for an 'anything goes' attitude towards law. The rule of law is an important value that has to be safeguarded also in a dynamic conception of law. One finds several indications of this in my analysis of the elements of the metaphor of a small narrative on legal change. The idea of a narrative implies an acknowledgement that previous steps in the narrative somehow affect the opportunities of the next step. One could perceive this as a reasoning that is analogous to the well-known Dworkinian chain novel theory of law. In my conception, however, the focus is rather on the new opportunities that every step brings in than on the limitations that follow from past decisions. From both perspectives, one has to recognise that the existing legal material also creates borderlines that legal reasoning cannot step over without losing its recognition as legal reasoning in the legal community. Here I use the concept 'legally possible' to refer to these mostly relatively diffuse borderlines.

Both when discussing the place of such borderlines and when choosing the best decisions within the legally possible, traditional doctrines of legal sources and legal-systematic coherence reasoning offer only limited assistance. I am advocating another approach to ease the obvious worries concerning the rule of law. By adopting a way of legal reasoning that is as transparent as possible, one might at least counteract the arbitrariness that is the ultimate foe of the rule of law. This proposal is clearly normative. One can seldom find ideal complete openness regarding both authoritative and substantive arguments in actual contemporary practice, and not so often even in contemporary scholarship.

The dynamic perspective on fragmentation, learning and transparency also leads to a particular view on the Europeanisation of private law. On the one hand, uncertainty and fragmentation do not go together well with the now abandoned idea of a European civil code. On the other hand, optimal use of learning resources requires a broad openness towards experience from across the borders. The familiar juxtaposition of the promotion of a European civil code and 'legal nationalism' appears to be wrongly posed. Europeanisation in a flexible and fragmented legal world has to move along other paths.

Even though I am committed to the European path, for me this path does not mean a wholesale embracing of some kind of slowly creeping harmonisation. The ethos of the EU is a union 'united in diversity', which implies that differences and variations are not seen as bad as such. The understanding of the EU as a laboratory of legal ideas, promoting continuous experimental learning across its internal borders, requires an acknowledgement that diversity has a value. A homogeneous order offers no inspiration for change. Acknowledging the value of diversity, however, does not imply a negative stance in principle to European harmonisation, as it may be useful for many familiar reasons. Following the suggested maxim of transparent legal reasoning, it is up to the legal actor who wants to use the harmonisation argument to argue why harmonisation is worth striving for with regard to the issue at hand. A sole reference to harmonisation as a goal in itself is seldom enough.

The concept of learning also implies a particular perspective on the debate whether pieces of law can be successfully 'transplanted' into another legal order. Learning is an active process that requires intellectual input from the recipient. One should not understand the use of foreign experience as a passive borrowing or transposition, but as an active process in which the legal experience acquired in another Member State is assessed in relation to the legal and societal context in which one wants to make use of that experience. This implies a recognition of the importance of substantive reasoning in connection with a transplantation move, including an assessment of the values involved.

II. FINAL MESSAGE: THE MORAL RESPONSIBILITY OF ALL LEGAL ACTORS

In a complex world, the challenges are so complex that all societal actors need to contribute to the responses. As the big picture is blurred, even small steps related to small issues may be important. This goes for law as well. Legal actors have an increasing responsibility for making their contribution to societal development. This is not a plea, however, for extending the power of legal professionals. It is a plea that legal actors should use the power increased by the complexity as responsibly as possible.

The metaphor on small narratives on legal change pictures the involvement of many actors in the development of law. The narrative may start in some particular, perhaps somewhat odd case; scholars may comment on and conceptualise the learning of the case; and the narrative may end in an enactment by the legislator. This is just one simple example. The starting points and the combinations of actors can vary almost infinitely. Many actors participate in creating the legal paths along which they are walking. Few legal actors can continuously assume the position of a bystander who only follows the rules without having any impact on the development of the rules themselves.

One of the key messages of the work is, therefore, that scholars, courts and other legal actors all bear a moral responsibility for how the law develops in their hands. Even though many routine situations perhaps do not offer much leeway for new and creative solutions, routine does not always prevail. A legal actor will face situations in which the choice of way forward matters. The actor may choose between starting a new narrative on change or just looking backwards – and the latter alternative is also a decision that can be morally assessed. Not only the beginning but also the proceeding and possible ending of a narrative are affected by the activity of various legal actors. At every juncture of a narrative, one has to make choices for which one cannot avoid moral responsibility.

Even though the moral responsibility at the outset seems quite light in routine cases and much heavier in hard cases, the picture is not always so self-evident. Also in apparently easy cases, the legal actor has a moral responsibility to be awake to spot results that would contradict a general sense of justice and to ponder whether such results can be legally avoided by turning the case into a hard one.

I wish to underline that the moral responsibility also includes legal scholars. The way in which scholars conceptualise issues may have a strong impact on how the narratives proceed. In a way, scholars act as gatekeepers, recommending what new legal materials one should include in the main rule conceptuality and what one should deem to remain as merely unacknowledged minor exceptions. The role of scholars is also crucial with regard to the Europeanisation of law and the movement of legal ideas.

Europeanisation means an immense broadening of the legal knowledge that is available for a legal actor. Within the framework of intellectual and temporal resources – this directs the attention towards the scholars – a morally responsible actor should attempt to make use of what the European legal laboratory has produced. A responsibility for good solutions includes a responsibility to try to learn across the borders and to use that learning in transparent legal reasoning.

It is easy to claim that legal actors should bear a responsibility for the societal effects of their activity. More difficult is the assessment of how that responsibility is fulfilled. What is a socially and morally 'good' activity? In an era of pluralist ethics, there are few general yardsticks for the assessment. The moral responsibility of a legal actor must be determined by the choices that the actor makes in concrete situations, by the moral roads that the actor has chosen to walk in a particular context. Without pre-set criteria for determining the goodness of a solution, one has to be content with an opportunity to contextually discuss and criticise it. Maximal transparency of the reasoning is a way to invite such a discussion.

Even though one cannot define goodness, only discuss it, the storyline of the book is convincing only if one assumes that most people want to do 'good', whatever that means. This assumption is not completely unrealistic.[2] For legal actors who

[2] In line with the popular cult book on the hopeful history of humankind, Bregman (2020).

sincerely want to bear their moral responsibility, transparent legal reasoning offers a useful tool for self-reflection.

In the light of growing societal uncertainty, it is increasingly important that law professionals are aware of, and willing to bear, their moral responsibility. Climate change, loss of biodiversity, pandemics, refugee crises, poverty and other similar challenges as well as smaller local ones call for new solutions by many societal actors. As several examples in this book indicate, legal actors can do their share. The rapidly growing number of cases concerning climate change is today the most spectacular demonstration of how arguably the most crucial challenge of humankind can be addressed by legal activity. As I have tried to show, however, legal actors may also contribute to better solutions to much smaller and more mundane issues. Not all judges and other actors have the opportunity to become legal heroes,[3] but they can all act as morally responsible subjects when performing their duties.

To underline the increasing importance of legal activities relating to pressing societal needs, I have in particular discussed the emergence and growth of legal micro-politics as an instrument for pushing change. Some of the mentioned cases are elements of micro-political strategies. As such cases are often hard ones in which established doctrines are challenged by contextual substantive reasoning, they tend to bring the moral responsibility of all involved legal actors to the fore.

Both the rise of global challenges and the need for new legal solutions underline the opportunities for legal creativity within the European laboratory. Open-minded judges and scholars who want to make use of the accumulated European legal knowledge are better equipped to bear their moral responsibility. In addition, in my personal view, not only instrumental reasons favour the adoption of a European perspective. In the era of Brexit and other populist nationalism, the need to look and learn across the borders might be greater than before. It might even be part of the moral responsibility of a European lawyer to defend openness towards Europe.

Although the opportunities of future-looking legal activity are not confined to private law, several examples in this book show that much can be done within the framework of this field of law. Private law is not immune to issues of vital societal relevance. If it were, I would not have written this book.

[3] Graver (2024) uses case studies on the activities of a dozen of various legal 'heroes' to demonstrate the moral responsibility of judges in difficult situations.

Bibliography

Aalto, P, *Public Liability in European Union Law Transformed* (University of Turku, 2010).

Aarnio, A, *The Rational as Reasonable* (D Reidel, 1987).

—— *Essays on the Doctrinal Study of Law* (Springer, 2011).

Ackermann, T, 'Sektorielles EU-Recht und allgemeine Privatrechtssystematik' (2018) 26 *Zeitschrift für Europäisches Privatrecht* 741.

—— 'Uniform Rules as Guidelines for National Courts and Legislatures: The German Experience' in F de Elizalde (ed), *Uniform Rules for European Contract Law?* (Hart, 2018) 91–102 (2018a).

Acquis Group (Research Group on the Existing EC Private Law), *Principles of the Existing EC Contract Law (Acquis Principles)*, Contract I: Pre-contractual Obligations, Conclusion of Contract, Unfair Terms (Sellier, 2007).

Adams, J and Brownsword, R, *Understanding Contract Law* (Fontana Press, 1987).

Ajani, G and Ebers, M (eds), *Uniform Terminology for European Contract Law* (Nomos, 2005).

Albarian, A, 'The Use of Comparative Law before the French Cour de Cassation: The View from Academia' in M Andenas and D Fairgrieve (eds), *Courts and Comparative Law* (OUP, 2015) 483–94.

Alexy, R, 'Rechtsregeln und Rechtsprinzipien' (1985) *Archiv für Rechts- und Sozialphilosophie Beiheft* 25, 13.

—— *A Theory of Legal Argumentation* (Clarendon Press, 1989).

Alexy, R and Peczenik, A, 'The Concept of Coherence and Its Significance for Discursive Rationality' (1990), 3 *Ratio Juris* 130.

Alpa, G, 'European Community Resolutions and the Codification of "Private Law"' (2000) 8 *European Review of Private Law* 321.

—— 'The Meaning of "Natural Person" and the Impact of the Constitution for Europe on the Development of European Private Law' (2004) 10 *European Law Journal* 734.

—— 'Foreign Law in International Legal Practice' in G Canivet, M Andenas and D Fairgrieve (eds), *Comparative Law Before the Courts* (BIICL, 2004) 195–210 (2004a).

Alter, A, *Irresistible: The Rise of Addictive Technology and the Business of Keeping Us Hooked* (Penguin Press, 2017).

Amaya, A, *The Tapestry of Reason: An Inquiry into the Nature of Coherence and its Role in Legal Argument* (Hart, 2015).

Andenas, M and Fairgrieve, D, 'Introduction: Finding a Common Language for Open Legal Systems' in G Canivet, M Andenas and D Fairgrieve (eds), *Comparative Law Before the Courts* (BIICL, 2004) xxvii–xl.

—— (eds), *Courts and Comparative Law* (OUP, 2015).

—— 'Courts and Comparative Law: In Search of a Common Language for Open Legal Systems' in M Andenas and D Fairgrieve (eds), *Courts and Comparative Law* (OUP, 2015) 3–22 (2015a).

Andersson, H, *Ansvarsproblem i skadeståndsrätten* (Iustus Förlag, 2013).

—— 'Europeisering av svensk skadeståndsrätt och försvenskning av de europeiska källorna – EKMR som vitaliserande tillämpningsexempel' in *De lege, Årsbok 2015* (Iustus Förlag, 2016) 37–66.

Andreadakis, S, 'Regulatory competition or harmonisation: the dilemma, the alternatives and the prospect of reflexive harmonisation' in M Andenas and C Baasch Andersen (eds), *Theory and Practice of Harmonisation* (Edward Elgar, 2011) 52–64.

Arbour, M-E, 'The Volkswagen Scandal at the CJEU: Defeat Devices between the Conformity Guarantee and Environment Law' (2022) 13 *European Journal of Risk Regulation* 670.

Arnaud, A-J, *Pour une pensée juridique européenne* (Presses Universitaires de France, 1991).

Arrowsmith, S, *Civil Liability and Public Authorities* (Earlsgate Press, 1992).

Atiyah, PS, *The Rise and Fall of Freedom of Contract* (Clarendon Press, 1979).

Atiyah, PS and Summers, RS, *Form and Substance in Anglo-American Law* (Clarendon Press, 1987).

August, V and Osrecki, F (eds), *Der Transparenz-Imperativ: Normen – Praktiken – Strukturen* (Springer, 2019).

Aurejärvi, E, *Erään murhan anatomia: Suomalainen tupakkatuomio* (Werner Söderström, 2004).

Avbelj, M and Davies, G, 'Introduction' in G Davies and M Avbelj (eds), *Research Handbook on Legal Pluralism and EU Law* (Edward Elgar, 2018) 1–8.

Baasch Andersen, C, 'Applied uniformity of a uniform commercial law: ensuring functional harmonisation of uniform texts through a global jurisconsultorium of the CISG' in M Andenas and C Baasch Andersen (eds), *Theory and Practice of Harmonisation* (Edward Elgar, 2011) 30–51.

Bacharis, G and Osmola, S, 'Rethinking the Instrumentality of European Private Law' (2022) 30 *European Review of Private Law* 457.

Baldus, Ch and Müller-Graf, P-C (eds), *Die Generalklausel im Europäischen Privatrecht: Zur Leistungsfähigkeit der deutschen Wissenschaft aus romanischer Perspektive* (Sellier, 2006).

Baldwin, R, 'Introduction – Risk: The Legal Contribution' in R Baldwin (ed), *Law and Uncertainty* (Kluwer, 1997) 1–18.

Von Bar, C, *A Common European Law of Torts* (Centro di studi e ricerche di diritto comparato e straniero, Saggi, conferenze e seminari 19, 1996).

—— 'The Study Group on a European Civil Code' (2000) 136 *Tidskrift, utgiven av Juridiska Föreningen i Finland* 323.

Bar-Gill, O, Ben-Shahar, O and Marotta-Wurgler, F, 'The American Law Institute's Restatement of Consumer Contracts: Reporters' Introduction' (2019) 15 *European Review of Contract Law* 91.

Barker, K, Degeling, S, Fairweather, K and Grantham, R (eds), *Private Law and Power* (Hart, 2017).

Bartl, M, 'Internal Market Rationality, Private Law and the Direction of the Union: Resuscitating the Market as the Object of the Political' (2015) 21 *European Law Journal* 572.

Bartl, M and Leone, C, 'Minimum Harmonisation and Article 16 of the CFREU: Difficult Times Ahead for Social Legislation?' in H Collins (ed), *European Contract Law and the Charter of Fundamental Rights* (Intersentia, 2017) 113–24.

Basedow, J, 'Codification of Private Law in the European Union: the Making of a Hybrid' (2001) 9 *European Review of Private Law* 35.

—— 'The Court of Justice and Private Law: Vacillations, General Principles and the Architecture of the European Judiciary' (2010) 18 *European Review of Private Law* 443.

—— *EU Private Law: Anatomy of a Growing Legal Order* (Intersentia, 2021).

Bauman, Z, *Modernity and Ambivalence* (Polity Press, 1991).

—— *Intimations of Postmodernity* (Routledge, 1992).

—— *Postmodern Ethics* (Blackwell, 1993).

—— *Life in Fragments: Essays in Postmodern Morality* (Blackwell, 1995).

—— *Retrotopia* (Polity Press, 2017).

Beale, H, 'Finding the Remaining Traps Instead of Unifying Contract Law' in S Grundmann and J Stuyck (eds), *An Academic Green Paper on European Contract Law* (Kluwer Law International, 2002) 67–72.

—— 'The draft academic common frame of reference and the "toolbox"' in M Andenas and C Baasch Andersen (eds), *Theory and Practice of Harmonisation* (Edward Elgar, 2011) 115–28.

—— 'The Role for European Contract Law: Uniformity or Diversity?' in F de Elizalde (ed), *Uniform Rules for European Contract Law?* (Hart, 2018) 9–34.

Beale, H, Fauvarque-Cosson, B, Rutgers, J and Vogenauer, S, *Cases, Materials and Text on Contract Law*, 3rd edn (Hart, 2019).

Bechmann, G, 'Risiko als Schlüsselkategorie der Gesellschaftstheorie' (1991) 74 *Kritische Vierteljahresschrift für Gesetzgebung und Rechtswissenschaft* 212.

Beck, U, *Risikogesellschaft* (Suhrkamp, 1986).

—— 'The Reinvention of Politics: Towards a Theory of Reflexive Modernization' in U Beck, A Giddens and S Lash, *Reflexive Modernization* (Polity Press, 1994) 1–55.

—— 'Self-Dissolution and Self-Endangerment of Industrial Society: What Does This Mean?' in U Beck, A Giddens and S Lash, *Reflexive Modernization* (Polity Press, 1994) 174–83 (1994a).

—— *Weltrisikogesellschaft: Auf der Suche nach der verlorenen Sicherheit* (Suhrkamp, 2007).

—— *Das deutsche Europa: Neue Machtlandschaften im Zeichen der Krise* (Suhrkamp, 2012).

Beck, U, Giddens, A and Lash, S, *Reflexive Modernization* (Polity Press, 1994).

Beckers, A, *Enforcing Corporate Social Responsibility Codes* (Hart, 2015).

—— 'The Regulation of Market Communication and Market Behaviour: Corporate Social Responsibility and the Directives on Unfair Commercial Practices and Unfair Contract Terms' (2017) 54 *Common Market Law Review* 475.
—— 'A Societal private law' (2022) 1 *European Law Open* 380.
Beckers, A and Teubner, G, *Three Liability Regimes for Artificial Intelligence: Algorithmic Actants, Hybrids, Crowds* (Hart, 2021).
Beka, A, *The Active Role of Courts in Consumer Litigation* (Intersentia, 2018).
Bell, J, 'Sources of Law' (2018) 77 *Cambridge Law Journal* 40.
Bender, PM, 'Limits of Personalization of Default Rules' (2020) 16 *European Review of Contract Law* 366.
Bengoetxea, J, *The Legal Reasoning of the European Court of Justice* (Clarendon Press, 1993).
Ben-Shahar, O and Porat, A, 'Personalizing Negligence Law' (2016) 91 *New York University Law Review* 627.
—— *Personalized Law: Different Rules for Different People* (OUP, 2021).
Berger, KP, *The Creeping Codification of the Lex Mercatoria* (Kluwer Law International, 1999).
—— 'Harmonisation of European Contract Law: The Influence of Comparative Law' (2001) 50 *International and Comparative Law Quarterly* 877
—— 'Auf dem Weg zu einem europäischen Gemeinrecht der Methode' (2001) 9 *Zeitschrift für Europäisches Privatrecht* 4 (2001a).
—— *The Creeping Codification of the New Lex Mercatoria*, 2nd edn (Kluwer Law International, 2010).
Van Den Bergh, R and Visscher, L, 'The Principles of European Tort Law: The Right Path to Harmonization?' (2006) 14 *European Review of Private Law* 511.
Bergslid Salvesen, SM, 'Hensynet til koherens i den dynamiske tingsretten' (2021) 134 *Tidsskrift for Rettsvitenskap* 410.
Besson, S, 'From European Integration to European Integrity: Should European Law Speak with Just One Voice?' (2004) 10 *European Law Journal* 257.
—— 'Fundamental Rights and European Private Law' in M Bussani and F Werro (eds), *European Private Law*, Volume I (Stämpfli, 2009) 7–46.
Biard, A and Kramer, X, 'The EU Directive on Representative Actions for Consumers: a Milestone or Another Missed Opportunity?' (2019) 27 *Zeitschrift für Europäisches Privatrecht* 249.
Blandhol, S, *Nordisk rettspragmatisme* (Jurist-og Økonomforbundets forlag, 2008).
Blume, P, 'Changes in the Sources of Law in Information Society' (1999) 13 *International Review of Law, Computers & Technology* 325.
Bobek, M, *Comparative Reasoning in European Supreme Courts* (OUP, 2013).
Bogetoft, RA, 'Er en dom et bedre præjudikat, hvis den har flere citationer? – Om netværksanalyser baseret på citationstal' (2020) 133 *Tidsskrift for Rettsvitenskap* 117.
Bonell, MJ, *An International Restatement of Contract Law* (Transnational Juris Publications, 1994).
Boulanger, C, 'The Comparative Sociology of Legal Doctrine: Thoughts on a Research Program' (2020) 21 *German Law Journal* 1362.
Bourdieu, P, *Om televisionen* (Brutus Östlings Bokförlag, 1998).
Bregman, R, *Humankind: A hopeful history* (Bloomsbury, 2020).
Brems, E and Ouald-Chaib, S (eds), *Fragmentation and Integration in Human Rights Law: Users' Perspectives* (Edward Elgar, 2018).
Brownsword, R, 'The Philosophy of Welfarism and its Emergence in the Modern English Law of Contract' in R Brownsword, G Howells and T Wilhelmsson (eds), *Welfarism in Contract Law* (Dartmouth, 1994) 21–62.
—— 'Editorial Introduction' in R Brownsword, H-W Micklitz, L Niglia and S Weatherill (eds), *The Foundations of European Private Law* (Hart, 2011) 3–9.
—— 'After Brexit: Regulatory-instrumentalism, Coherentism and the English Law of Contract' (2018) 34 *Journal of Contract Law* 139.
Brownsword, R, Van Gestel, RAJ and Micklitz, H-W (eds), *Contract and Regulation* (Edward Elgar, 2017).
Brownsword, R, Hird, NJ and Howells, G (eds), *Good faith in Contract* (Ashgate, 1999).
Brownsword, R, Howells, G and Wilhelmsson, T (eds), *Welfarism in Contract Law* (Dartmouth, 1994).
Brownsword, R, Micklitz, H-W, Niglia, L and Weatherill, S (eds), *The Foundations of European Private Law* (Hart, 2011).

Brüggemeier, G, 'The Control of Corporate Conduct and Reduction of Uncertainty by Tort Law' in R Baldwin (ed), *Law and Uncertainty* (Kluwer, 1997) 57–74.
—— 'Haftungsrecht – eine transnationale Falljurisprudenz? Ein Beitrag zur Europäisierung des Privatrechts' in L Krämer, H Micklitz and K Tonner (eds), *Law and diffuse Interests in the European Legal Order* (Nomos, 1997) 657–80 (1997a).
—— *Prinzipien des Haftungsrechts* (Nomos, 1999).
—— 'Western Tort Law: A Jurisprudence of Injury' in M Bussani and F Werro (eds), *European Private Law* (Stämpfli, 2009) 293–334.
—— 'Risk and Strict Liability: The Distinct Examples of Germany, the United States, and Russia' (2013) 21 *European Review of Private Law* 923.
Bulterman, M and Wissels, C, 'Strategies developed by – and between – national governments to interact with the ECJ' in M Dawson, B de Witte and E Muir (eds), *Judicial Activism at the European Court of Justice* (Edward Elgar, 2013) 264–78.
Burgers, L, *Justitia, the People's Power and Mother Earth* (University of Amsterdam, UvA-DARE (Digital Academic Repository), 2020).
—— 'Should Judges Make Climate Change Law?' (2020) 9 *Transnational Environmental Law* 55 (2020a).
—— 'Friends of the Earth Netherlands versus Royal Dutch Shell: All companies must act against climate change', Blog post (29 May 2021), available at transformativeprivatelaw.com/friends-of-the-earth-netherlands-versus-royal-dutch-shell-all-companies-must-act-against-climate-change.
Burgers, L, Van Duin, Joanna and Mak, C, 'Judges in Utopia: The Transformative Role of the Judiciary in European Private Law' (2020) 28 *European Review of Private Law* 865.
Burgess, A, 'Flattering Consumption, Creating a Europe of the Consumer' (2001) 1 *Journal of Consumer Culture* 93.
Busch, C, 'Implementing Personalized Law: Personalized Disclosures in Consumer Law and Privacy Law' (2019) 86 *The University of Chicago Law Review* 309.
Busch, C and Schulte-Nölke, H (eds), *Fundamental Rights and Private Law: A Practical Tool for Judges* (Sellier, 2011).
Busch, D, 'The Principles of European Contract Law before the Supreme Court of the Netherlands – On the Influence of the PECL in Dutch Legal Practice' (2008) 16 *Zeitschrift für Europäisches Privatrecht* 549.
Büthe, T and Mattli, W, *The New Global Rulers: The Privatization of Regulation in the World Economy* (Princeton University Press, 2011).
Bydlinski, F, *System und Prinzipien des Privatrechts* (Springer, 1996).
Van Caenegem, RC, *Judges, Legislators and Professors: Chapters in European Legal History* (CUP, 1987).
Cafaggi, F, 'Private Regulation in European Private Law' in A Hartkamp, M Hesselink, E Hondius, C Mak and E du Perron (eds), *Towards a European Civil Code*, 4th edn (Kluwer Law International, 2011) 91–126.
—— 'On the transformations of European consumer enforcement law: judicial and administrative trialogues, instruments and effects' in F Cafaggi and S Law (eds), *Judicial Cooperation in European Private Law* (Edward Elgar, 2017) 223–61.
Cafaggi, F and Iamiceli, P, 'Uncertainty, Administrative Decision-Making and Judicial Review: The Courts' Perspectives' (2021) 12 *European Journal of Risk Regulation* 792.
Cafaggi, F and Law, S, 'Judicial dialogue in European private law: introductory remarks' in F Cafaggi and S Law (eds), *Judicial Cooperation in European Private Law* (Edward Elgar, 2017) 1–32.
Canaris, C-W, *Systemdenken und Systembegriff in der Jurisprudenz entwickelt am Beispiel des deutschen Privatrechts*, 2nd edn (Duncker & Humblot, 1983).
—— *Grundrechte und Privatrecht: eine Zwischenbilanz* (Walter de Gruyter, 1999).
Canivet, G, 'The Use of Comparative Law Before the French Private Law Courts' in G Canivet, M Andenas and D Fairgrieve (eds), *Comparative Law Before the Courts* (BIICL, 2004) 181–93.
—— 'The Practice of Comparative Law by the Supreme Courts: Brief Reflections on the Dialogue Between the Judges in French and European Experience' (2006) 80 *Tulane Law Review* 1377.
—— 'The Use of Comparative Law before the French Private Law Courts' in M Andenas and D Fairgrieve (eds), *Courts and Comparative Law* (OUP, 2015) 472–82.
Canivet, G, Andenas, M and Fairgrieve, D (eds), *Comparative Law before the Courts* (BIICL, 2004).

Cantero Gamito, M, 'The role of the EU in the transnational governance of standards, contracts and codes' in M Cantero Gamito and H-W Micklitz (eds), *The Role of the EU in Transnational Legal Ordering* (Edward Elgar, 2020) 2–25.

Cantero Gamito, M and Micklitz, H-W (eds), *The Role of the EU in Transnational Legal Ordering: Standards, Contracts and Codes* (Edward Elgar, 2020).

Caplovitz, D, *The poor pay more* (Free Press, 1968).

Caporaso, JA, 'The European Union and Forms of State: Westphalian, Regulatory or Post-Modern?' (1996) 34 *Journal of Common Market Studies* 29.

Caruso, D, 'The Missing View of the Cathedral: The Private Law Paradigm of European Legal Integration' (1997) 3 *European Law Journal* 3.

Carvalho, J, 'Law, language, and knowledge: Legal transplants from a cultural perspective' (2019) 20 *German Law Journal* 21.

Castells, M, *The Power of Identity* (Blackwell, 1997).

—— *End of the Millenium*, rev edn (Blackwell, 1999).

Casti, JL and Karlqvist, A (eds), *Complexity, language, and life: mathematical approaches* (Springer Science & Business Media, 2012).

Cherednychenko, OO, *Fundamental Rights, Contract Law and the Protection of the Weaker Party* (Sellier, 2007).

—— 'The EU Charter of Fundamental Rights and Consumer Credit' in H Collins (ed), *European Contract Law and the Charter of Fundamental Rights* (Intersentia, 2017) 139–66.

—— 'Rediscovering the public/private divide in EU private law' (2020) 26 *European Law Journal* 27.

Claes, M and De Visser, M, 'Are You Networked Yet? On Dialogues in European Judicial Networks' (2012) 8 *Utrecht Law Review* 100.

Clive, E, 'The Lasting Influence of the Lando Principles' in MJ Bonell, M-L Holle and P Arnt Nielsen (eds), *Liber Amicorum Ole Lando* (DJØF Publishing, 2012) 69–83.

Coen, D, 'Empirical and theoretical studies in EU lobbying' (2007) 14 *Journal of European Public Policy* 333.

Coen, D and Richardson, J (eds), *Lobbying the European Union: institutions, actors, and issues* (OUP, 2009).

Coendet, T, 'Of Judges and Jurisdictions: An Overture to Comparative Legal Reasoning in National Case Law' (2014:1) *Ancilla Iuris* 1.

Collins, H, 'Good Faith in European Contract Law' (1994) 14 *Oxford Journal of Legal Studies* 229.

—— 'The Voice of the Community in Private Law Discourse' (1997) 3 *European Law Journal* 407.

—— *Regulating Contracts* (OUP, 1999).

—— *The European Civil Code: The Way Forward* (CUP, 2008).

—— 'Governance implications for the European Union of the changing character of private law' in F Cafaggi and H Muir-Watt (eds), *Making European Private Law* (Edward Elgar, 2008) 269–86 (2008a).

—— 'Does "Fragmented Europeanisation" Require a European Civil Code?' (2009) 145 *Tidskrift utgiven av Juridiska Föreningen i Finland* 213.

—— 'The European Economic Constitution and the Constitutional Dimension of Private Law' (2009) 5 *European Review of Contract Law* 71 (2009a).

—— (ed), *European Contract Law and the Charter of Fundamental Rights* (Intersentia, 2017).

—— 'Building European Contract Law on Charter Rights' in H Collins (ed), *European Contract Law and the Charter of Fundamental Rights* (Intersentia, 2017) 1–32 (2017a).

—— 'The Revolutionary Trajectory of EU Contract Law towards Post-national Law' in S Worthington, A Robertson and G Virgo (eds), *Revolution and Evolution in Private Law* (Hart, 2018) 315–36.

Colombi Ciacchi, A, 'Judicial governance in private law through the application of fundamental rights' (2014) 1 *Austrian Law Journal* 120.

Colombi Ciachi, A, Brüggemeier, G and Comandé, G (eds), *Fundamental Rights and Private Law in the European Union*, Volumes 1 and 2 (CUP, 2010).

Comparato, G, *Nationalism and Private Law in Europe* (Hart, 2014).

Condon, R, 'From "the law of A and B" to productive learning at the interface of contract' in R Brownsword, RAJ van Gestel and H-W Micklitz (eds), *Contract and Regulation* (Edward Elgar, 2017) 171–97.

—— *Network Responsibility: European Tort Law and the Society of Networks* (CUP, 2022).

Conway, H and Stannard, J (eds), *The Emotional Dynamics of Law and Legal Discourse* (Hart, 2016).

Cotterrell, R and Del Mar, M (eds), *Authority in Transnational Legal Theory* (Edward Elgar, 2016).
COVID-19-Consumer Law Research Group, 'Consumer Law and Policy Relating to Change of Circumstances Due to the COVID-19 Pandemic' (2020) 43 *Journal of Consumer Policy* 437.
Craig, P, 'The Domestic Liability of Public Authorities in Damages: Lessons from the European Community?' in J Beatson and T Tridimas (eds), *New Directions in European Public Law* (Hart, 1998) 75–90.
Culver, K and Giudice, M, 'Claims to authority, legal systems, and dynamic social phenomena' in R Cotterrell and M del Mar (eds), *Authority in Transnational Legal Theory* (Edward Elgar, 2016) 49–74.
Cummings, SL and Eagly, IV, 'A critical reflection on law and organizing' (2001) 48 *UCLA Law Review* 443.
Curran, VG, 'On the Shoulders of Schlesinger: The Trento Common Core of European Private Law Project; (2003) 11 *European Review of Private Law* 66.
Curtin, D, 'Public accountability of transnational rule making: a view from the European Union and beyond' in M Faure and A van der Walt (eds), *Globalization and Private Law* (Edward Elgar, 2010) 32–54.
Dagan, H, 'Doctrinal Categories, Legal Realism, and the Rule of Law' (2015) 163 *University of Pennsylvania Law Review* 1889.
Dagan, H and Heller, M, *The Choice Theory of Contracts* (CUP, 2017).
Dalberg-Larsen, J, 'The Legal Profession in a Changing World' in T Wilhelmsson and S Hurri (eds), *From Dissonance to Sense: Welfare State Expectations, Privatisation and Private Law* (Ashgate, 1999) 99–114.
Damjanovic, D and De Witte, B, 'Welfare Integration through EU law: The Overall Picture in the Light of the Lisbon Treaty' *EUI Working Papers* LAW 2008/34.
Damm, R, 'Verbraucherrechtliche Sondergesetzgebung und Privatrechtssystem' (1978) 33 *Juristenzeitung* 173.
—— 'Risikosteuerung im Zivilrecht – Privatrecht und öffentliches Recht im Risikodiskurs' in W Hoffmann-Riem and E Schmidt-Assmann (eds), *Öffentliches Recht und Privatrecht als wechselseitige Auffangordnungen* (Nomos, 1996) 85–142.
Dannemann, G and Vogenauer, S (eds), *The Common European Sales Law in Context* (OUP, 2013).
Davies, G, 'Interpretative pluralism within EU law' in G Davies and M Avbelj (eds), *Research Handbook on Legal Pluralism and EU Law* (Edward Elgar, 2018) 323–34.
Davies, G and Avbelj, M (eds), *Research Handbook on Legal Pluralism and EU Law* (Edward Elgar, 2018).
Davis, DM and Klare, K, 'Critical legal realism in a nutshell' in E Christodoulis, R Dukes and M Goldoni (eds), *Research Handbook on Critical Legal Theory* (Edward Elgar, 2019) 27–43.
Dawson, M, De Witte, B and Muir, E (eds), *Judicial Activism at the European Court of Justice* (Edward Elgar, 2013).
DCFR, *Draft Common Frame of Reference, Principles, Definitions and Model Rules of European Private Law* Outline Edition, Prepared by the Study Group on a European Civil Code and the Research Group on EC Private Law (Acquis Group) (Sellier, 2009).
Delmas-Marty, M, *Towards a Truly Common Law: Europe as a laboratory for legal pluralism* (CUP, 2002).
—— 'Governing Globalisation through Law' (2020) 11 *European Journal of Risk Regulation* 195.
Demeyere, S and Sagaert, V (eds), *Contract and Property with an Environmental Perspective* (Intersentia, 2020).
Dickson, B (ed), *Judicial Activism in Common Law Supreme Courts* (OUP, 2007).
Dickson, J, 'Interpretation and Coherence in Legal Reasoning' in EN Zalta (ed), *The Stanford Encyclopedia of Philosophy* (Fall 2005 edn), available at plato.stanford.edu/archives/fall2005/entries/legal-reas-interpret.
Domurath, I, *Consumer Vulnerability and Welfare in Mortgage Contracts* (Hart, 2017).
Doublet, D and Bernt, JF, *Retten og vitenskapen*, 2nd edn (Alma Mater Forlag, 1993).
Douzinas, C, 'The responsibilities of the critic: law, politics and the Critical Legal Conference' in E Christodoulidis, R Dukes and M Goldoni (eds), *Research Handbook on Critical Legal Theory* (Edward Elgar, 2019) 223–37.
Downes, L and Nunes, P, *Big Bang Disruption: Business Survival in the Age of Constant Innovation* (Portfolio Penguin, 2014).
Drobnig, U, 'The Use of Comparative Law by Courts' in U Drobnig and S van Erp (eds), *The Use of Comparative Law by Courts* (Kluwer Law International, 1999) 3–21.
—— 'The Use of Foreign Law by German Courts' in U Drobnig and S van Erp (eds), *The Use of Comparative Law by Courts* (Kluwer Law International, 1999) 127–47 (1999a).

Drobnig, U and van Erp, Sjef (eds), *The Use of Comparative Law by Courts* (Kluwer Law International, 1999).
Durovic, M and Tridimas, T (eds), *New Directions in European Private Law* (Hart, 2021).
Dworkin, R, 'Hard Cases' (1975) 88 *Harvard Law Review* 1057.
—— *Taking Rights Seriously*, New corrected impression (Duckworth, 1978).
—— *Law's Empire* (Fontana Press, 1986).
Dyson, M (ed), *Regulating Risk through Private Law* (Intersentia, 2018).
Ebbesson, J, 'Transboundary corporate responsibility in environmental matters: fragments and foundations for a future framework' in G Winter (ed), *Multilevel Governance of Global Environmental Change* (CUP, 2006) 200–24.
—— 'Piercing the state veil in pursuit of environmental justice' in J Ebbesson, P Okowa and PN Okowa (eds), *Environmental Law and Justice in Context* (CUP, 2009) 270–93.
Eckes, Christina, 'A timid defence of legal formalism' in M Bartl and JC Lawrence (eds), *The Politics of European Legal Research* (Edward Elgar, 2022) 192–207.
Eckhoff, T and Sundby, NK, *Rettssystemer* (Tanum-Norli, 1976).
Edmond, G and Mercer, D, 'Experts and Expertise In Legal and Regulatory Settings' in G Edmond (ed), *Expertise in Regulation and Law* (Ashgate, 2004) 1–31.
Eftestøl-Wilhelmsson, E, *Fra etterprovisjon til avgangsvederlag* (Gyldendal, 2005).
—— *European Sustainable Carriage of Goods: The Role of Contract Law* (Routledge, 2016).
Eidenmüller, H, 'Collateral Damage: Brexit's Negative Effects on Regulatory Competition and Legal Innovation in Private Law' (2018) 26 *Zeitschrift für Europäisches Privatrecht* 868.
Eli Principles for the COVID-19 Crisis; published eg in (2020) 28 *Zeitschrift für Europäisches Privatrecht* 729.
de Elizalde, F, 'The potential of EU consumer law for automated enforcement' (2022) *European Journal of Consumer Law* 155.
Eller, KH, 'Comparative Genealogies of "Contract and Society"' (2020) 21 *German Law Journal* 1393.
Eller, KH and Salminen, J, 'Reimagining Contract in a World of Global Value Chains' (2020) 16 *European Review of Contract Law* 1.
Ellis, J, '"Social Nature": Political Economy, Science, and Law in the Anthropocene' in PF Kjaer (ed), *The Law of Political Economy* (CUP, 2020) 181–201.
Engelbrekt, AB, Moberg, A and Nergelius, J (eds), *Rule of Law in the EU* (Hart, 2021).
Englard, I, *The Philosophy of Tort Law* (Dartmouth, 1993).
Eräsaari, R, *Sosiaalivaltio ja sosiaalipolitiikan itseymmärrys* (*The Social State and the Self-Understanding of Social Policy*) (Sosiaalipoliittinen yhdistys, 1984).
Ericson, RV, 'Why Law is Like News' in D Nelken (ed), *Law as Communication* (Dartmouth, 1996) 195–230.
Ewald, F, *L'état providence* (Grasset, 1986).
—— 'Die Versicherungsgesellschaft' (1989) 22 *Kritische Justiz* 385.
von Eyben, B and Isager, H, *Lærebog i erstatningsret*, 8th edn (Jurist- og Økonomforbundets Forlag, 2015).
Fairfield, JA: *Owned: Property, Privacy, and the New Digital Serfdom* (CUP, 2017).
Fairgrieve, D, Feldschreiber, P, Howells, G and Pilgerstorfer, M, 'Products in a Pandemic: Liability for Medical Products and the Fight against COVID-19' (2020) 11 *European Journal of Risk Regulation* 565.
Fairgrieve, D and Howells, G, 'Collective Redress Procedures – European Debates' (2009) 58 *International and Comparative Law Quarterly* 379.
Fassiaux, S, 'Covid-19: The regulation of air passenger rights in the EU – how the need for reform unveils an erosion of the rule of law' (2021) *European Journal of Consumer Law* 21.
Fauvarque-Cosson, B, 'National Reforms: New Instruments Towards Converging Rules within Europe? The Example of the French Contract Law Reform (2016)' in F de Elizalde (ed), *Uniform Rules for European Contract Law?* (Hart, 2018) 103–14.
Fenwick, M, Siems, M and Wrbka, S (eds), *The Shifting Meaning of Legal Certainty in Comparative and Transnational Law* (Hart, 2017).
Ferguson, N, *The square and the tower: networks, hierarchies and the struggle for global power* (Penguin, 2017).
Ferreri, S, 'General Report: Complexity of Transnational Sources' (2012) 20 *European Review of Private Law* 3.
Flessner, A, 'Juristische Methode und europäisches Privatrecht' (2002) 57 *JuristenZeitung* 14.

Foucault, M, 'Un système fini face à une demande infinie' in B Brunhes, M Foucault, R Lenoir and P Rosanvallon (eds), *Sécurité sociale: l'enjeu* (Syros, 1983) 39–63.
Franck, J-U, *Europäisches Absatzrecht* (De Gruyter Recht, 2006).
Frank, J, *Law and the modern mind* (Transaction Publishers, 1963) (first published 1930).
Frankenberg, G, *Comparative Law as Critique* (Edward Elgar, 2016).
Freedland, M, 'Introduction: Comparative and International Law in the Courts' in G Canivet, M Andenas and D Fairgrieve (eds), *Comparative Law Before the Courts* (BIICL, 2004) xv–xxvi.
Friedman, DD, *Law's Order: What Economics Has to Do with Law and Why It Matters* (Princeton University Press, 2000).
Friedman, LM and Teubner, G, 'Legal Education and Legal Integration: European Hopes and American Experience' in M Cappelletti, M Seccombe and J Weiler (eds), *Integration Through Law, Vol 1, Book 3, Forces and Potential for a European Identity* (Walter de Gruyter, 1986) 345–80.
Friedman, M, 'A Positive Approach to Organized Consumer Action: The "Buycott" as an Alternative to the Boycott' (1996) 19 *Journal of Consumer Policy* 439.
—— *Consumer Boycotts* (Routledge, 1999).
Friedmann, D and Barak-Erez, D (eds), *Human Rights in Private Law* (Hart, 2001).
Fuglinszky, Á, 'Legal Transplants: Snapshots on the State of the Art and a Case Study from Central Europe – Post Transplantation-adjustment of Contractual Liability in the New Hungarian Civil Code' (2020) 16 *European Review of Contract Law* 267.
Fuller, LL, *The morality of law*, rev edn (Yale University Press, 1969).
Gabriel, Y and Lang, T, *The Unmanageable Consumer* (SAGE Publications, 1995).
Galanter, M, 'Why the "Haves" Come Out Ahead: Speculations on the Limits of Legal Change' (1974) 9 *Law & Society Review* 95.
Garber, S and Bower, AG, 'Newspaper coverage of automotive product liability verdicts' (1999) 33 *Law & Society Review* 93.
Gearey, A, *Poverty law and legal activism: lives that slide out of view* (Routledge, 2018).
Gelter, M and Siems, M, 'Network, Dialogue or One-Way Traffic? An Empirical Analysis of Cross-Citations Between Ten of Europe's Highest Courts' (2012) 8 *Utrecht Law Review* 88.
Germain, CM, 'Legal Information Management in a Global and Digital Age: Revolution and Tradition' (2007) 35 *International Journal of Legal Information* 134.
Gerstenberg, O, *Euroconstitutionalism and Its Discontents* (OUP, 2018).
van Gerven, W, 'A Common Framework of Reference *and* Teaching' (2004:1) 1 *European Journal of Legal Education* 1.
van Gerven, W, Lever, J and Larouche, P, *Cases, Materials and Text on National, Supranational and International Tort Law* (Hart, 2000).
Gessner, V, 'Globalization and Legal Certainty' in V Gessner and A Cem Budak (eds), *Emerging Legal Certainty: Empirical Studies on the Globalization of Law* (Ashgate, 1998) 427–50.
Giddens, A, *The Consequences of Modernity* (Polity Press, 1990).
—— 'Living in a Post-Traditional Society' in U Beck, A Giddens and S Lash, *Reflexive Modernization* (Polity Press, 1994) 56–109.
—— *Turbulent and mighty continent: What Future for Europe?* (John Wiley & Sons, 2013).
von Gierke, O, *Die soziale Aufgabe des Privatrechts* (Springer, 1889).
—— 'The Social Role of Private Law' (2018) 19 *German Law Journal* 1017.
Gilles, P, 'Zur neueren Verbraucherschutzgesetzgebung in ihrem Verhältnis zum klassischen Privatrecht' (1980) *Juristische Arbeitsblätter* 1.
Gilmore, G, *The Death of Contract* (Ohio State University Press, 1974).
Glendon, MA, *Rights Talk: The Impoverishment of Political Discourse* (The Free Press, 1991).
Glenn, HP, 'Comparative Legal Reasoning and the Courts: A View from the Americas' in G Canivet, M Andenas and D Fairgrieve (eds), *Comparative Law Before the Courts* (BIICL, 2004) 217–227.
Global Climate Litigation Report, 'Global Climate Litigation Report: 2020 Status Review' (26 January 2021), available at www.unep.org/resources/report/global-climate-litigation-report-2020-status-review.
Glouberman, S and Zimmerman, B, *Complicated and Complex Systems: What Would a Successful Reform Medicare Look Like?* Commission on the Future of Health Care in Canada, Discussion Paper No 8 (2002).

Godard, O, 'Social Decision-Making Under Conditions of Scientific Controversy, Expertise and the Precautionary Principle' in C Joerges, K-H Ladeur and E Vos (eds), *Integrating Scientific Expertise into Regulatory Decision-Making* (Nomos, 1997) 39–73.

Gomez, F, 'The empirical missing links in the Draft Common Frame of Reference' in H-W Micklitz and F Cafaggi (eds), *European Private Law after the Common Frame of Reference* (Edward Elgar, 2010) 101–22.

Gomez, F and Ganuza, J-J, 'The Economics of Private Law Harmonised Law-making: Mechanisms, Modes and Standards' in R Brownsword, H-W Micklitz, L Niglia and S Weatherill (eds), *The Foundations of European Private Law* (Hart, 2011) 115–37.

Gordley, J, 'The Future of European Contract Law on the Basis of Europe's Heritage' (2005) 1 *European Review of Contract Law* 163.

Goudkamp, J and Nolen, D (eds), *Scholars of Tort Law* (Hart, 2019).

Granger, M-PF, 'Francovich liability before national courts: 25 years on, has anything changed?' in P Giliker (ed), *Research Handbook on EU Tort Law* (Edward Elgar, 2017) 93–127.

Graver, HP, 'Juss, politikk og dommeraktivisme i en flytende europeisk rettsorden' in *Festskrift til Carl August Fleischer* (Universitetsforlaget, 2006) 203–15.

—— 'Fornuft og følelser – om klassisk retorikk som modell for moderne juridisk metode' (2007) 120 *Tidsskrift for Rettsvitenskap* 527.

—— 'Judging for Utopia: Climate Change and Judicial Action' (2020) 28 *European Review of Private Law* 885.

—— *Valiant Judges, Iniquitous Law: Thirteen Stories of Heroes of the Law* (Routledge, 2024).

Graziadei, M, 'Fostering a European legal identity through contract and consumer law' in C Twigg-Flesner (ed), *Research Handbook on EU Consumer and Contract Law* (Edward Elgar, 2016) 82–108.

Grundmann, S, 'The Optional European Code on the Basis of the *Acquis Communautaire* – Starting Point and Trends' (2004) 10 *European Law Journal* 698.

—— 'The Structure of the DCFR – Which Approach for Today's Contract Law?' (2008) 4 *European Review of Contract Law* 225.

—— 'The role of competition in the European codification process' in H-W Micklitz and F Cafaggi (eds), *European Private Law after the Common Frame of Reference* (Edward Elgar, 2010) 36–55.

Grundmann, S and Grochowski, M (eds), *European Contract Law and the Creation of Norms* (Intersentia, 2021).

Grundmann, S, Kerber, W and Weatherill, S (eds), *Party Autonomy and the Role of Information in the Internal Market* (Walter de Gruyter, 2001).

Grundmann, S and Mazeaud, D (eds), *General Clauses and Standards in European Contract Law* (Kluwer Law International, 2006).

Grundmann, S and Stuyck, J (eds), *An Academic Green Paper on European Contract Law* (Kluwer Law International, 2002).

Guerra, G, 'An Interdisciplinary Approach for Comparative Lawyers: Insights from the Fast-Moving Field of Law and Technology' (2018) 19 *German Law Journal* 579.

Günther, K, 'Legal pluralism or uniform concept of law? Globalisation as a problem of legal theory' (2008) 5 *NoFo – Journal of Extreme Legal Positivism* 5.

Haba, M, *The Case of State Liability: 20 Years after Francovich* (Springer Gabler, 2015).

Habermas, J, 'Die neue Unübersichtlichkeit' (1985) 39.431 *Merkur* 1.

—— *The crisis of the European Union: A response* (Polity Press, 2012).

Hacker, P, 'Personalizing EU Private Law: From Disclosures to Nudges and Mandates' (2017) 25 *European Review of Private Law* 651.

Hagstrøm, V and Stenvik, A, *Erstatningsrett* (Universitetsforlaget, 2015).

Hahn, A-C, 'The Harmonisation of European Private Law Systems and the Role of Comparative Law' (2002) 30 *International Journal of Legal Information* 265.

Hall, PA and Soskice, D (eds), *Varieties of capitalism: The institutional foundations of comparative advantage* (OUP, 2001).

Harris, B, 'Representing Homeless Families: Repeat Player Implementation Strategies' (1999) 33 *Law & Society Review* 911.

Hart, D, 'Sozialschutzbezogene Normbildungsprozesse bei Risikoentscheidungen im Vertragsrecht' (1991) 74 *Kritische Vierteljahresschrift für Gesetzgebung und Rechtswissenschaft* 363.

Hartkamp, AS, *Judicial Discretion under the New Civil Code of the Netherlands* (Roma, Centro di studi e ricerche di diritto comparato e straniero, Saggi, conference e seminari 4, 1992).
—— 'Comparative Law Before the Dutch Courts' in G Canivet, M Andenas and D Fairgrieve (eds), *Comparative Law Before the Courts* (BIICL, 2004) 229–33.
—— *European Law and National Private Law*, 2nd edn (Intersentia, 2016).
Hartkamp, A, Hesselink, M, Hondius, E, Mak, C and du Perron, E (eds), *Towards a European Civil Code*, 4th edn (Kluwer Law International, 2011).
Håstad, T, 'DCFR Rules in the Swedish Supreme Court' in T Håstad (ed), *The Nordic Contracts Act* (DJØF Publishing, 2015) 179–84.
Hedemann, JW, *Die Flucht in die Generalklauseln* (Mohr, 1933).
Heidelbach, J and Evald-Schelde, M, 'Retsevolution – hvad evolutionsbiologi og systemteori kan afslöre om vilkårene for retssystemets og retsnormernes udvikling' (2018) 131 *Tidsskrift for Rettsvitenskap* 382.
Heidemann, M, 'Methodology of Uniform Contract Law – The UNIDROIT Principles as a Source of Law' (2007) 18 *European Business Law Review* 709.
—— 'International commercial harmonisation and national resistance – the development and reform of transnational commercial law and its application within national legal culture' in M Andenas and C Baasch Andersen (eds), *Theory and Practice of Harmonisation* (Edward Elgar, 2011) 180–97.
Heirbaut, D and Storme, ME, 'The Belgian Legal Tradition: From a Long Quest for Legal Independence to a Longing for Dependence?' (2006) 14 *European Review of Private Law* 645.
Helin, M, *Lainoppi ja metafysiikka* (Summary: Legal dogmatics and metaphysics) (Suomalainen lakimiesyhdistys, 1988).
—— *Kieli oikeustodellisuuden rakentajana* (1998) 96 *Lakimies* 1027.
Helleringer, G and Purnhagen, K (eds), *Towards a European Legal Culture* (Nomos, 2014).
Hellner, J, *Skadeståndsrätt*, 5th edn (Juristförlaget, 1995).
Hemmo, M, *Sopimus ja delikti* (Kauppakaari, 1998).
Hesselink, MW, *The New European Legal Culture* (Kluwer, 2001).
—— *The New European Private Law: Essays on the Future of Private Law in Europe* (Kluwer Law International, 2002).
—— 'The Horizontal Effect of Social Rights in European Contract Law' (2003:1) *Europa e Diritto Privato* 1.
—— 'The Politics of a European Civil Code' in MW Hesselink (ed), *The Politics of a European Civil Code* (Kluwer Law International, 2006) 143–70.
—— *CFR & Social Justice* (Sellier, 2008).
—— 'A spontaneous order for Europe? Why Hayek's libertarianism is not the right way forward for European private law' in H-W Micklitz and F Cafaggi (eds), *European Private Law after the Common Frame of Reference* (Edward Elgar, 2010) 123–46.
—— 'If You Don't Like Our Principles We Have Others: On Core Values and Underlying Principles in European Private Law: A Critical Discussion of the New "Principles" Section in the Draft Common Frame of Reference' in R Brownsword, H-W Micklitz, L Niglia and S Weatherill (eds), *The Foundations of European Private Law* (Hart, 2011) 59–71.
—— 'Five political ideas of European contract law' (2011) 7 *European Review of Contract Law* 295 (2011a).
—— 'How Many Systems of Private Law are there in Europe? On plural legal sources, multiple identities and the unity of law' in L Niglia (ed), *Pluralism and European Private Law* (Hart, 2013) 199–247.
—— 'The New European Legal Culture – Ten Years On' in G Helleringer and K Purnhagen (eds), *Towards a European Legal Culture* (Nomos, 2014) 17–24.
—— 'Democratic contract law' (2015) 11 *European Review of Contract Law* 81.
—— 'The Justice Dimensions of the Relationship between Fundamental Rights and Private Law' (2016) 24 *European Review of Private Law* 425.
—— *Justifying Contract in Europe: Political Philosophies of European Contract Law* (OUP, 2021).
—— 'Reconstituting the Code of Capital: could a progressive European code of private law help us reduce inequality and regain democratic control?' (2022) 1 *European Law Open* 316.
Hirst, P, 'Challenges of Globalisation to the Nation State' (1997) 39 *Politiikka* 3.
van Hoecke, M, 'The Harmonisation of Private Law in Europe: Some Misunderstandings' in M van Hoecke and F Ost (eds), *The Harmonisation of European Private Law* (Hart, 2000) 1–20.
—— (ed), *Epistemology and Methodology of Comparative Law* (Hart, 2004).

van Hoecke, M and Ost, F, 'Legal doctrine in crisis: towards a European legal science' (1998) 18 *Legal Studies* 197.

van Hoecke, M and Warrington, M, 'Legal Cultures, Legal Paradigms and Legal Doctrine: Towards a New Model for Comparative Law' (1998) 47 *International and Comparative Law Quarterly* 495.

Höland, A, 'Leitbilder des europäischen Verbraucherrechts' in L Krämer, H-W Micklitz and K Tonner (eds), *Law and diffuse Interests in the European Legal Order* (Nomos, 1997) 195–219.

Holland, KM (ed), *Judicial Activism in Comparative Perspective* (St Martin's Press, 1991).

Hondius, E, 'From "Toolbox" to Academic Standard: The Current and Future Status of the Draft Common Frame of Reference' in R Brownsword, H-W Micklitz, L Niglia and S Weatherill (eds), *The Foundations of European Private Law* (Hart, 2011) 531–54.

Hondius, E, Santos Silva, M, Nicolussi, A, Coderch, PS, Wendehorst, C and Zoll, F (eds), *Coronavirus and the Law in Europe* (Intersentia, 2021).

Howells, G, 'Whose Responsibility to Plan for Future Changes in Circumstances – Debtor, Creditor or the State?' in T Wilhelmsson and S Hurri (eds), *From Dissonance to Sense: Welfare State Expectations, Privatisation and Private Law* (Ashgate, 1999) 437–59.

—— *The Tobacco Challenge* (Ashgate, 2011).

Howells, G, Micklitz, H-W and Wilhelmsson, T, *European Fair Trading Law* (Ashgate, 2006).

Howells, G, Twigg-Flesner, C and Wilhelmsson, T: *Rethinking EU Consumer Law* (Routledge, 2018).

Howells, G and Watson, J, 'Comparative Law in Consumer Litigation' in M Andenas and D Fairgrieve (eds), *Courts and Comparative Law* (OUP, 2015) 621–39.

Howells, G and Wilhelmsson, T, *EC Consumer Law* (Ashgate, 1997).

—— 'EC and US Approaches to Consumer Protection – Should the Gap Be Bridged?' (1997) 17 *Yearbook of European Law* (Clarendon Press, 1998) 207–67.

Huls, N, 'Critical Insurance Law' in T Wilhelmsson (ed), *Perspectives of Critical Contract Law* (Dartmouth, 1993) 149–68.

Husa, J, 'The Tip of the Iceberg or What Lies Beneath the Surface of Comparative Law' (2005) 12 *Maastricht Journal of European and Comparative Law* 73.

—— 'Emancipation or Deprivation for the European Legal Mind? The Contribution of the Legal Traditions Approach' (2006) 13 *Maastricht Journal of European and Comparative Law* 81.

—— *Interdisciplinary Comparative Law: Rubbing Shoulders with the Neighbours or Standing Alone in a Crowd* (Edward Elgar, 2022).

Hutchinson, AC, 'Life After Shopping: From Consumers to Citizens' in I Ramsay (ed), *Consumer Law in the Global Economy* (Ashgate, 1997) 25–46.

Hviid Nielsen, T, 'Risici – i teknologien, i samfundet og i hovederne' (1996) *Retfærd nr 73*, 61.

Hwang, S-P, 'Foreign Law, Democracy, and Constitutional Interpretation: A German-American Comparison' (2019) 20 *German Law Journal* 1119.

Jameson, F, *Postmodernism or, the cultural logic of late capitalism* (Verso, 1991).

Janaček, V, 'Digitalised Legal Information: Towards a New Publication Model' in C Öhman and D Watson (eds), *The 2018 Yearbook of the Digital Ethics Lab* (Springer, 2019) 149–65.

Jansen, N, 'Dogmatik, Erkenntnis und Theorie im europäischen Privatrecht' (2005) 13 *Zeitschrift für Europäisches Privatrecht* 750.

—— 'The authority of an academic "Draft Common Frame of Reference"' in H-W Micklitz and F Cafaggi (eds), *European Private Law after the Common Frame of Reference* (Edward Elgar, 2010) 147–72.

—— 'Dogmatising Non-legislative Codifications: Non-legislative Reference Texts in European Legal Discourse' in R Brownsword, H-W Micklitz, L Niglia and S Weatherill (eds), *The Foundations of European Private Law* (Hart, 2011) 31–57.

—— 'Informal authorities in European private law' in R Cotterrell and M Del Mar (eds), *Authority in Transnational Legal Theory* (Edward Elgar, 2016) 191–219.

Jansen, N and Zimmermann, R (eds), *Commentaries on European Contract Laws* (OUP, 2018).

Janssen, A and Schulze, R, 'Legal Cultures and Legal Transplants in Germany' (2011) 19 *European Review of Private Law* 225.

Janssen, A and Wahnschaffe, CJ, 'COVID-19 and international sale contracts: unprecedented grounds for exemption or business as usual?' (2020) 25 *Uniform Law Review* 466.

Jayme, E, *Multicultural Society and Private Law, German Experiences* (Roma, Centro di studi e ricerche di diritto comparato e straniero, Saggi, conferenze e seminari 33, 1999).

Jessup, PC, *Transnational Law* (Yale University Press, 1956).
Joerges, C, 'Der Schutz des Verbrauchers und die Einheit des Zivilrechts' (1983) 28 *Die Aktiengesellschaft* 57.
—— 'Zur Legitimität der Europäisierung des Privatrechts. Überlegungen zu einem Recht-Fertigungs-Recht für das Mehrebenensystem der EU' in C Joerges and G Teubner (eds), *Rechtsverfassungsrecht. Recht-Fertigung zwischen Privatrechtsdogmatik und Gesellschaftstheorie* (Nomos, 2003).
—— 'The Challenges of Europeanization in the Realm of Private Law: A Plea for a New Legal Discipline' (2004) 14 *Duke Journal of Comparative & International Law* 149.
Joerges, C and Kreuder-Sonnen, C, 'European Studies and the European Crisis: Legal and Political Science between Critique and Complacency' (2017) 23 *European Law Journal* 118.
Johnston, A, 'Spillovers from EU Law into National Law: (Un) Intended Consequences for Private Law Relationships' in D Leczykiewicz and S Weatherill (eds), *The Involvement of EU Law in Private Law Relationships* (Hart, 2013) 357–94.
—— 'Private Law and the role and influence of EU Law in the UK post-Brexit' (2022) 30 *Zeitschrift für Europäisches Privatrecht* 519.
Joint Response, 'Communication on European Contract Law, Joint Response of the Commission on European Contract Law and the Study Group on a European Civil Code, 30.09.01' (Osnabrück, 2002).
De Jong, ER, 'Tort Law and Judicial Risk Regulation: Bipolar and Multipolar Risk Reasoning in Light of Tort Law's Regulatory Effects' (2018) 9 *European Journal of Risk Regulation* 14.
Kadner Graziano, T, 'Die Zukunft der Zivilrechtskodifikation in Europa – Harmonisierung der alten Gesetzbücher oder Schaffung eines neuen? – Überlegungen anlässlich des 200. Jahrestags des französischen Code civil' (2005) 13 *Zeitschrift für Europäisches Privatrecht* 523.
—— 'Is it Legitimate and Beneficial for Judges to Compare?' in M Andenas and D Fairgrieve (eds), *Courts and Comparative Law* (OUP, 2015) 25–53.
Kahneman, D, Sibony, O and Sunstein, CR, *Noise: A Flaw in Human Judgment* (HarperCollinsPublishers, 2021).
Kangas, U, *Lesken oikeudellinen asema* (Summary: Legal Status of Widowed Persons) (Suomalainen lakimiesyhdistys, 1982).
Kas, B and Micklitz, H-W, 'Rechtsprechungsübersicht zum Europäischen Vertrags- und Deliktsrecht (2014-2018) – Teil I – II' (2018) *Europäisches Wirtschafts- und Steuerrecht* 181, 241.
Kästle-Lamparter, D, Jansen, N and Zimmermann, R (eds), *Juristische Kommentare: Ein internationaler Vergleich* (Mohr Siebeck, 2020).
Katz, DM, 'Quantitative Legal Prediction – or – How I Learned to Stop Worrying and Start Preparing for the Data-driven Future of the Legal Services Industry' (2013) 62 *Emory Law Journal* 909.
Kaupa, C, *The Pluralist Character of the European Economic Constitution* (Hart, 2016).
Kennedy, David, 'The Methods and Politics of Comparative Law' in M Bussani and U Mattei (eds), *The Common Core of European Private Law* (Kluwer Law International, 2003) 131–207.
Kennedy, Duncan, 'Form and substance in private law adjudication' (1976) 89 *Harvard Law Review* 1685.
—— *A Critique of Adjudication {fin de siècle}* (Harvard University Press, 1997).
—— 'Thoughts on Coherence, Social Values and National Tradition in Private Law' in MW Hesselink (ed), *The Politics of a European Civil Code* (Kluwer Law International, 2006) 9–31.
—— 'A Political Economy of Contemporary Legality' in PF Kjaer (ed), *The Law of Political Economy* (CUP, 2020) 89–124.
Kerber, W, 'European system of private laws: an economic perspective' in F Cafaggi and H Muir-Watt (eds), *Making European Private Law* (Edward Elgar, 2008) 64–97.
Keren-Paz, T, *Torts, Egalitarianism and Distributive Justice* (Routledge, 2018).
Kerikmäe, T and Särav, S, 'Paradigms for Automatization of Logic and Legal Reasoning' in D Krimphove and GM Lentner (eds), *Law and Logic, Contemporary Issues* (Duncker & Humblot, 2017) 205–22.
Kiesow, RM, *Kredite in der Risikogesellschaft* (Berliner Wissenschaftsverlag, 2005).
Kirchberger, C, 'The "i" in Legal Information Retrieval' in *Vem reglerar informationssamhället* (2010), available at ssrn.com/abstract=1957558.
Klauberg, T and Lebro, M, 'Dieselgate in Finland and Estonia: A Comparative Study with References to Germany' (2022) 158 *Tidskrift utgiven av Juridiska Föreningen i Finland* 277.
Kleineman, J, 'Ideell skada eller förmögenhetsförlust – nytt synsätt under framväxt?' (1995–96) 7 *Juridisk Tidskrift* 101.

Klüver, H, Braun, C and Beyers, J, 'Legislative lobbying in context: towards a conceptual framework of interest group lobbying in the European Union' (2015) 22 *Journal of European Public Policy* 447.

Koivisto, I, *The Transparency Paradox: Questioning an Ideal* (OUP, 2022).

Komárek, J, 'Reasoning with Previous Decisions: Beyond the Doctrine of Precedent' (2013) 61 *The American Journal of Comparative Law* 149.

Köndgen, J, *Selbstbindung ohne Vertrag* (Mohr, 1981).

Koopmans, T, 'Comparative Law and the Courts' (1996) 45 *International and Comparative Law Quarterly* 545.

Korkea-Aho, E, 'Legal Lobbying: The Evolving (But Hidden) Role of Lawyers and Law Firms in the EU Public Affairs Market' (2021) 22 *German Law Journal* 65.

Korkea-Aho, E and Leino-Sandberg, P (eds), *Law, Legal Expertise and EU Policy-Making* (CUP, 2022).

Korpiola, L and Poutanen, P, 'Digitaalinen riskiyhteiskunta ja korona' (2021) 137 *Maanpuolustus* 49.

Kortmann, J, 'The Tort Law Industry' (2009) 17 *European Review of Private Law* 789.

Kosonen, P, *European Integration: A Welfare State Perspective* (University of Helsinki Sociology of Law Series 8, 1994).

Koulu, R and Pakaslahti, H, 'Why We Need Legal Technology' in R Koulu and J Hakkarainen (eds), *Law and Digitalisation: Rethinking Legal Services* (Helsinki University Legal Tech Lab, 2018) 17–49.

Kramer, EA, 'Europäische Privatrechtsvereinheitlichung' (1988) 110 *Juristische Blätter* 477.

Krisch, N, 'Authority, solid and liquid, in postnational governance' in R Cotterrell and M Del Mar (eds), *Authority in Transnational Legal Theory* (Edward Elgar, 2016) 25–48.

Krommendijk, J, *National Courts and Preliminary References to the Court of Justice* (Edward Elgar, 2021).

Kukovec, D, 'Law and the Periphery' (2015) 21 *European Law Journal* 406.

Kumm, M, 'Who Is Afraid of the Total Constitution? Constitutional Rights as Principles and the Constitutionalization of Private Law' (2006) 7 *German Law Journal* 341.

Kyritsis, D, *Shared Authority: Courts and Legislatures in Legal Theory* (Hart, 2015).

Ladeur, K-H, 'Risikowissen und Risikoentscheidung' (1991) 74 *Kritische Vierteljahresschrift für Gesetzgebung und Rechtswissenschaft* 241.

—— 'The Future of Law – 'Serial Law'?', in P Kjaer (ed), *The Law of Political Economy* (CUP, 2020) 299–319.

Laffan, B, O'Donnell, R and Smith, M, *Europe's Experimental Union: Rethinking Integration* (Routledge, 2000).

Lando, O, 'Optional or Mandatory Europeanisation of Contract Law' (2000) 8 *European Review of Private Law* 59.

—— 'Some Features of the Law of Contract in the Third Millennium' (2000) 40 *Scandinavian Studies in Law* 343 (2000a).

—— 'The Structure and the Salient Features of the Principles of European Contract Law' (2001) 6 *Juridica International* 4.

—— 'On Legislative Style and Structure' (2006) 14 *European Review of Private Law* 475.

—— 'Can Europe Build Unity of Civil Law Whilst Respecting Diversity?' (2006:1) *Europa e Diritto Privato* 1 (2006a).

—— 'Culture and Contract Laws' (2007) 3 *European Review of Contract Law* 1.

Lando, O, Clive, E, Prüm, A and Zimmermann, R (eds), *Principles of European Contract Law, Part III*, Prepared by The Commission on European Contract Law (Kluwer Law International, 2003).

Lando, O and Beale, H (eds), *Principles of European Contract Law, Parts I and II*, Prepared by The Commission on European Contract Law (Kluwer Law International, 2000).

Lando, O, Holle, M-L, Håstad, T, Konow, B-E, Møgelvang-Hansen, P, Nystén-Haarala, S, Ólafsdóttir, Á and Zachariasson, L (eds), *Restatement of Nordic Contract Law* (Djøf Publishing, 2016).

Länsineva, P, *Perusoikeudet ja varallisuussuhteet* (Summary: System of Basic Rights and Property) (Suomalainen lakimiesyhdistys, 2002).

Leczykiewicz, D and Weatherill, S (eds), *The Involvement of EU Law in Private Law Relationships* (Hart, 2013).

—— (eds), *The Images of the Consumer in EU Law* (Hart, 2016).

van Leeuwen, B, *European Standardisation of Services and its Impact on Private Law* (Hart, 2017).

Legrand, P, 'European Legal Systems are not Converging' (1996) 45 *International and Comparative Law Quarterly* 52.

—— 'The Impossibility of "Legal Transplants"' (1997) 4 *Maastricht Journal of European and Comparative Law* 111.

—— 'Counterpoint: Law is also Culture' in F Ferrari (ed), *The Unification of International Commercial Law* (Nomos, 1998) 245–58.

Leino-Sandberg, P, *The Politics of Legal Expertise in EU Policy-Making* (CUP, 2021).

Lenaerts, K, 'Interlocking Legal Orders in the European Union and Comparative Law' (2003) 52 *International and Comparative Law Quarterly* 873.

—— 'The Rule of Law and the Coherence of the Judicial System of the European Union' (2007) 44 *Common Market Law Review* 1625.

—— 'The European Court of Justice and the Comparative Law Method' (2017) 25 *European Review of Private Law* 297.

—— 'New Horizons for the Rule of Law Within the EU' (2020) 21 *German Law Journal* 29.

Lenaerts, K and Gutman, K, 'The Comparative Law Method and the Court of Justice of the European Union: Interlocking Legal Orders Revisited' in M Andenas and D Fairgrieve (eds), *Courts and Comparative Law* (OUP, 2015) 141–76.

Lichtblau, K, 'Soziologie und Zeitdiagnose' in *Zwischen Klassik und Moderne* (Springer, 2017) 57–79.

Lidbom, C, 'Diskussion' in *Förhandlingarna vid det tjugosjätte nordiska juristmötet i Helsingfors den 24–26 augusti 1972* (Lokalstyrelsen för Finland, 1975) 53–59, 68–69.

Lindblom, PH, 'Processens funktioner – en resa i gränslandet' in *Festskrift till Stig Strömholm* (Iustus Förlag, 1997) 593–632.

—— *Sena uppsatser* (Norstedts Juridik, 2006).

—— *Progressive Procedure* (Iustus Förlag, 2017).

Lohse, EJ, 'The meaning of harmonisation in the context of European Union law – a process in need of definition' in M Andenas and C Baasch Andersen (eds), *Theory and Practice of Harmonisation* (Edward Elgar, 2011) 282–313.

López-Rodriguez, AM: *Lex Mercatoria and Harmonization of Contract Law in the EU* (DJØF Publishing, 2003).

Luckmann, T, 'The Privatization of Religion and Morality' in P Heelas, S Lash and P Morris (eds), *Detraditionalization* (Blackwell, 1996) 72–86.

Luhmann, Niklas, *Soziologie des Risikos* (Walter de Gruyter, 1991).

Lupo, N and Scaffardi, L (eds), *Comparative Law in Legislative Drafting* (Eleven International Publishing, 2014).

Lurger, B, *Vertragliche Solidarität* (Nomos, 1998).

—— *Grundfragen der Vereinheitlichung des Vertragsrechts in der Europäischen Union* (Springer, 2002).

—— 'The "Social" Side of Contract Law and the New Principle of Regard and Fairness' in A Hartkamp, M Hesselink, E Hondius. C Mak and E du Perron (eds), *Towards a European Civil Code*, 4th edn (Kluwer Law International, 2011) 353–86.

Macaulay, S, 'Elegant Models, Empirical Pictures and the Complexities of Contract' (1977) 11 *Law & Society Review* 507.

Madsen, MR, 'Transnational Fields: Elements of a Reflexive Sociology of the Internationalisation of Law' (2006) 29 *Retfærd* 3/114, 23.

Maduro, M, Tuori, K and Sankari, S (eds), *Transnational Law* (CUP, 2014).

Mak, C, 'De meerwaarde van grondrechten in het privaatrecht' (2004) 21 *Nederlands Tijdschrift voor Burgerlijk Recht* 124.

—— *Fundamental Rights in European Contract Law* (Wolters Kluwer, 2008).

—— 'Civil Courts as Constitutional Courts: Polity-building through private law in Europe' (2020) 28 *European Review of Private Law* 953.

Mak, E, *Judicial Decision-Making in a Globalised World* (Hart, 2013).

Mak, V, *Legal Pluralism in European Contract Law* (OUP, 2020).

Makkonen, K, *Zur Problematik der juridischen Entscheidung* (Turun yliopisto, 1965).

—— *Luentoja yleisestä oikeustieteestä* (Helsingin yliopiston Yleisen oikeustieteen laitoksen julkaisuja, 1998).

Markesinis, B and Fedtke, J, *Judicial Recourse to Foreign Law: A New Source of Inspiration?* (Taylor & Francis, 2006).

Markesinis, BS, 'Learning from Europe and Learning in Europe' in B Markesinis (ed), *The Gradual Convergence: Foreign Ideas, Foreign Influences, and English Law on the Eve of the 21st Century* (Clarendon Press, 1994) 1–32.

Maroney, TA, 'Emotions and the Discourse of Judging' in H Conway and J Stannard (eds), *The Emotional Dynamics of Law and Legal Discourse* (Hart, 2016) 261–86.

Martín-Casals, M, 'The Impact of the PETL on National Legislation and Case Law – A Survey' (2023)14 *Journal of European Tort Law* 4.

Mattei, U, 'Hard Minimal Code Now – A Critique of "Softness" and a Plea for Responsibility in the European Debate over Codification' in S Grundmann and J Stuyck (eds), *An Academic Green Paper on European Contract Law* (Kluwer Law International, 2002) 215–33.

Mattei, U and Di Robilant, A, 'The Art and Science of Critical Scholarship. Post-modernism and International Style in the Legal Architecture of Europe' (2002) 10 *European Review of Private Law* 29.

Mattei, U and Nicola, F, 'A "Social Dimension" in European Private Law? The Call for Setting a Progressive Agenda' (2007) 7 *Global Jurist* Iss 1 (Frontiers) Art 2, 1.

Mattei, U and Quarta, A, *The Turning Point in Private Law: Ecology, Technology and the Commons* (Edward Elgar, 2018).

Mattei, UA, Ruskola, T and Gidi, A, *Schlesinger's Comparative Law*, 7th edn (Foundation Press, 2009).

Mayer, B, 'Prompting Climate Change Mitigation through Litigation' (2023) 72 *International and Comparative Law Quarterly* 233.

McCann, M (ed), *Law and Social Movements* (Routledge, 2016).

McManus, JH, *Market-Driven Journalism: Let the Citizen Beware?* (SAGE Publications, 1994).

Medicus, D, '"Geld muss man haben". Unvermögen und Schuldnerverzug bei Geldmangel' (1988) 188 *Archiv für die civilistische Praxis* 489.

Menger, A, *Das Bürgerliche Recht und die besitzlosen Volksklassen* 3rd edn (H Laupp, 1904).

Michaels, R, 'Of Islands and the Ocean: The Two Rationalities of European Private Law' in R Brownsword, H-W Micklitz, L Niglia and S Weatherill (eds), *The Foundations of European Private Law* (Hart, 2011) 139–58.

Michaels, R and Jansen, N, 'Private Law Beyond the State? Europeanization, Globalization, Privatization?'(2006) 54 *The American Journal of Comparative Law* 843.

Micklitz, H-W (ed), *Rechtseinheit oder Rechtsvielfalt in Europa?* (Nomos, 1996).

—— *The Politics of Judicial Co-operation in the EU* (CUP, 2005).

—— (ed), *The Many Concepts of Social Justice in European Private Law* (Edward Elgar, 2011).

—— 'The (Un)-Systematics of (Private) Law as an Element of European Culture' in G Helleringer and K Purnhagen (eds), *Towards a European Legal Culture* (Nomos, 2014) 81–113.

—— (ed), *Constitutionalization of European Private Law* (OUP, 2014) (2014a).

—— 'Conclusions: Consumer over-indebtedness and consumer insolvency – from micro to macro' in H-W Micklitz and I Domurath (eds), *Consumer Debt and Social Exclusion in Europe* (Ashgate, 2015) 229–235.

—— 'Demokratie und Privatrecht. Thema, Theorien und Kontext, Diskussion' in S Grundmann, H-W Micklitz and M Renner (eds), *Privatrechtstheorie Band I* (Mohr Siebeck, 2015) 708–26 (2015a).

—— 'A European Advantage in Legal Scholarship?' in R van Gestel, H-W Micklitz and EL Rubin (eds), *Rethinking Legal Scholarship: A Transatlantic Dialogue* (CUP, 2017) 262–309.

—— *The Politics of Justice in European Private Law* (CUP, 2018).

—— (ed), *The Making of Consumer Law and Policy in Europe* (Hart, 2021).

—— 'What kind of private law for what kind of Europe? A rejoinder to Martijn Hesselink's "progressive code"' (2022) 1 *European Law Open* 402.

Micklitz, H-W and Cafaggi, F, 'Introduction' in H-W Micklitz and F Cafaggi (eds), *European Private Law after the Common Frame of Reference* (Edward Elgar, 2010) viii–xlvi.

Micklitz, H-W, Hondius, E, van Mierlo, T and Roethe, T (eds), *The fathers and mothers of consumer law in Europe: the foundational years 1950–1980* (European University Institute, 2019), available at cadmus.eui.eu/handle/1814/63766.

Micklitz, H-W and Kas, B, 'Overview of cases before the CJEU on European Consumer Contract Law (2008–2013) – Part I–II' (2014) 10 *European Review of Contract Law* 1, 189.

Micklitz, H-W, Palka, P and Panagis, Y, 'The Empire Strikes Back: Digital Control of Unfair Terms of Online Services' (2017) 40 *Journal of Consumer Policy* 367.

Micklitz, H-W and Radeideh, M, '*CLAB Europa* – The European Database on Unfair Terms in Consumer Contracts' (2005) 28 *Journal of Consumer Policy* 325.

Micklitz, H-W and Reich, N, 'The Court and Sleeping Beauty: The Revival of the Unfair Contract Terms Directive (UCTD)' (2014) 51 *Common Market Law Review* 771.

Micklitz, H-W, Sibony, A-L and Esposito, F, 'The bright and adventurous future of consumer law research' in H-W Micklitz, A-L Sibony and F Esposito (eds), *Research Methods in Consumer Law* (Edward Elgar, 2018) 1–36.

—— (eds), *Research Methods in Consumer Law* (Edward Elgar, 2018) (2018a).

Micklitz, H-W and Sieburgh, C, 'Primary EU Law and Private Law Concepts' in H-W Micklitz and C Sieburgh (eds), *Primary EU Law and Private Law Concepts* (Intersentia, 2017) 1–46.

Micklitz, H-W and Weatherill, S, 'Consumer Policy in the European Community: Before and After Maastricht' (1993) 16 *Journal of Consumer Policy* 285.

Mitchell, C, 'Network commercial relationships: what role for contract law?' in R Brownsword, RAJ van Gestel and H-W Micklitz (eds), *Contract and Regulation* (Edward Elgar, 2017) 198–234.

Möllers, TMJ, 'The Principle of Directive-Compliant Development of the Law and the *Contra Legem* Limit' (2020) 16 *European Review of Contract Law* 465.

Moore, SF, *Law as Process: An Anthropological Approach* (Routledge, 1978).

Moring, T and Himmelstein, H, *Politiikkaa riisuttuna* (Yleisradio, 1993).

Möslein, F, 'Legal innovation in European contract law: within and beyond the (Draft) Common Frame of Reference' in H-W Micklitz and F Cafaggi (eds), *European Private Law after the Common Frame of Reference* (Edward Elgar, 2010) 173–200.

Mossberg, O, *Avtalets räckvidd I* (Iustus Förlag, 2020).

Muir, E, Dawson, M and de Witte, B, 'Introduction: the European Court of Justice as a political actor' in M Dawson, B de Witte and E Muir (eds), *Judicial Activism at the European Court of Justice* (Edward Elgar, 2013) 1–10.

Muir Watt, H, 'Of Transcultural Borrowing, Hybrids, and the Complexity of Legal Knowledge: An Example of Comparative Law Before the French Courts' in G Canivet, M Andenas and D Fairgrieve (eds), *Comparative Law before the Courts* (BIICL, 2004) 33–48.

Mulder, J, *Social Legitimacy in the Internal Market* (Hart, 2018).

Nagy, CI, *Collective Actions in Europe* (SpringerOpen, 2019).

Nelken, D, 'Disclosing/Invoking Legal Culture: An Introduction' (1995) 4 *Social & Legal Studies* 435.

—— (ed), *Law as Communication* (Dartmouth, 1996).

Nicklisch, F, 'Risikosteuerung durch Haftung im deutschen und europäischen Technologie- und Umweltrecht' in F Graf von Westphalen and O Sandrock (eds), *Lebendiges Recht – Von den Sumerern bis zur Gegenwart* (Verlag Recht und Wirtschaft, 1995) 617–31.

Nicola, F and Davies, B (eds), *EU Law Stories: Contextual and Critical Histories of European Jurisprudence* (CUP, 2017).

Nicola, F and Tichadou, E, '*Océano Grupo*: A Transatlantic Victory for the Consumer and a Missed Opportunity for European Law' in F Nicola and B Davies (eds), *EU Law Stories: Contextual and Critical Histories of European Jurisprudence* (CUP, 2017) 369–90.

Nielsen, R, 'The Impact of Internationalization on the Nordic Doctrine of the Sources of Law' in B Dahl and R Nielsen (eds), *New Directions in Business Law Research* (GADJura, 1996) 9–23.

Niemi, J, 'Law and Crisis: Reflections on How Legal Problems Are Constructed and How They Can Be Studied' (2018) 41 *Retfærd* 3–4/160, 76.

Nieminen, A, *Towards a European Society? Integration and Regulation of Capitalism* (University of Helsinki, Department of Sociology, 2005).

Niglia, L, *The Transformation of Contract in Europe* (Kluwer Law International, 2003).

—— 'Taking Comparative Law Seriously – Europe's Private Law and the Poverty of Orthodoxy' (2006) 54 *The American Journal of Comparative Law* 401.

—— (ed), *Pluralism and European Private Law* (Hart, 2013).

—— *The Struggle for European Private Law: A Critique of Codification* (Hart, 2015).

Nogler, L and Reifner, U (eds), *Life Time Contracts: Social Long-term Contracts in Labour, Tenancy and Consumer Credit Law* (Eleven International Publishing, 2014).

Norros, O, 'Sopimusoikeudellisten periaatekokoelmien oikeuslähdearvo' (2007) 105 *Lakimies* 25.

Norton, JJ, Auerback, RM and Gaba, JM (eds), *Environmental liability for banks* (Lloyd's of London Press Ltd, 1995).

Odersky, W, 'Harmonisierende Auslegung und europäische Rechtskultur' (1994) 2 *Zeitschrift für Europäisches Privatrecht* 1.

Ogus, A, 'Risk Management and "Rational" Social Regulation' in R Baldwin (ed), *Law and Uncertainty* (Kluwer, 1997) 139–53.

O'Hara, L, *Konsistenz und Konsens: Die Anforderungen des Grundgesetzes an die Folgerichtigkeit der Gesetze* (Mohr Siebeck, 2018).
Örücü, E, 'Law as Transposition' (2002) 51 *International and Comparative Law Quarterly* 205.
Owen DG (ed), *Philosophical Foundations of Tort Law* (Clarendon Press, 1995).
Palmer Olsen, H and Esmark, M, 'Datalogisk retsforskning: Kan algoritmer finde juridisk centrale domme afsagt af EMD?' (2018) 41 *Retfærd* 1/160, 61.
Paunio, E, *Legal Certainty in Multilingual EU Law* (Ashgate, 2013).
Pavillon, C, 'Private Standards of Fairness in European Contract Law' (2014) 10 *European Review of Contract Law* 85.
Peczenik, A, 'The Structure of a Legal System' (1975) 6 *Rechtstheorie* 1.
—— *On Law and Reason* (Reidel, 1989).
—— *Vad är rätt?* (Fritzes, 1995).
Pistor, K, *The Code of Capital* (Princeton University Press, 2019).
Pollack, M, 'Learning from EU Law Stories, The European Court and Its Interlocutors Revisited' in F Nicola and B Davies (eds), *EU Law Stories: Contextual and Critical Histories of European Jurisprudence* (CUP, 2017) 577–602.
Poludniak-Gierz, K, 'Personalization of Information Duties Challenges for Big Data Approach' (2018) 26 *European Review of Private Law* 297.
Porat, A and Strahilevitz, LJ, 'Personalizing Default Rules and Disclosure with Big Data' (2014) 112 *Michigan Law Review* 1417.
Postema, GJ (ed), *Philosophy and the Law of Torts* (CUP, 2001).
Pöyhönen, J, *Sopimusoikeuden järjestelmä ja sopimusten sovittelu* (Suomalainen Lakimiesyhdistys, 1988).
—— 'Korvausmallit vahingonkorvausoikeudessa' (1999) 32 *Oikeustiede-Jurisprudentia* 297.
—— *Uusi varallisuusoikeus* (Kauppakaari, 2000).
Přibáň, J (ed), *Liquid Society and Its Law* (Ashgate, 2007).
Purnhagen, K, 'How to manage the Union's diversity: The regulation of New Plant Breeding Technologies in *Confédération paysanne and Others*' (2019) 56 *Common Market Law Review* 1379.
Radbruch, G, *Rechtsphilosophie*, 6th edn (Stuttgart, 1963).
Raes, K, 'Communicating Legal Identity: A Note on the Inevitable Counterfactuality of Legal Communication' in D Nelken (ed), *Law as Communication* (Dartmouth, 1996) 25–44.
Ramsay, I, 'Bankruptcy and Consumer Credit in the Declining Welfare State' in T Wilhelmsson and S Hurri (eds), *From Dissonance to Sense: Welfare State Expectations, Privatisation and Private Law* (Ashgate, 1999) 461–76.
Ranieri, F, 'Doctrine et jurisprudence étrangères dans le développement du droit civil allemand au 20ième siècle' (2006) 14 *European Review of Private Law* 685.
Rautenbach, C and du Plessis, L, 'In the Name of Comparative Constitutional Jurisprudence: The Consideration of German Precedents by South African Constitutional Court Judges' (2013) 14 *German Law Journal* 1539.
Raz, J, 'The Law's Own Virtue' (2019) 39 *Oxford Journal of Legal Studies* 1.
Rees, G and White, D, 'Judging Post-Controversy Expertise: Judicial Discretion and Scientific Marginalisation in the Courtroom' (2023) 32 *Science as Culture* 109.
Reese-Schäfer, W, 'Zeitdiagnose als wissenschaftliche Aufgabe' (1996) 6 *Berliner Journal für Soziologie* 377.
Rehder, B and van Elten, K, 'Legal Tech & Dieselgate Digitale Rechtsdienstleister als Akteure der strategischen Prozessführung' (2019) 39 *Zeitschrift für Rechtssoziologie* 64.
Reich, N, *Europäisches Verbraucherschutzrecht* (Nomos, 1993).
—— 'Union Citizenship – Metaphor or Source of Rights?' (2001) 7 *European Law Journal* 4.
—— 'Free Movement v. Social Rights in an Enlarged Union – the *Laval* and *Viking* Cases before the ECJ' (2008) 9 *German Law Journal* 125.
—— *General Principles of EU Civil Law* (Intersentia, 2014).
Reich, N, Micklitz, H-W, Rott, P and Tonner, K, *European Consumer Law*, 2nd edn (Intersentia, 2014).
Reich, R, *Saving Capitalism: For the Many, Not the Few* (Alfred Knoph, 2015).
Reifner, U, *Alternatives Wirtschaftsrecht am Beispiel der Verbraucherverschuldung* (Luchterhand, 1979).
Reifner, U and Volkmer, M, *Neue Formen der Verbraucherrechtsberatung* (Campus Verlag, 1988).

Remien, O, *Zwingendes Vertragsrecht und Grundfreiheiten des EG-Vertrages* (Mohr, 2003).
Renner, M, 'Menschenrechts- und umweltbezogene Unternehmensverantwortung zwischen Kapitalmarkt und Lieferkette' (2022) 30 *Zeitschrift für Europäisches Privatrecht* 782.
Requejo Isidro, M and Otero Crespo, M, 'Comparative Law before the Spanish Private Law Courts in the 21st Century' in M Andenas and D Fairgrieve (eds), *Courts and Comparative Law* (OUP, 2015) 552–68.
Riedl, K, 'The Work of the Lando-Commission from an Alternative Viewpoint' (2000) 8 *European Review of Private Law* 71.
—— *Vereinheitlichung des Privatrechts in Europa* (Nomos, 2002).
Riesenhuber, K, *System und Prinzipien des Europäischen Vertragsrechts* (de Gruyter, 2003).
—— (ed), *European Legal Methodology* (Intersentia, 2017).
—— 'Rechtsvergleichung als Methode der Rechtsfindung?' (2018) 218 *Archiv für die civilistische Praxis* 693.
Rifkin, J, *The European Dream* (Polity Press, 2004).
Ripstein, A, 'Private order and public justice: Kant and Rawls' (2006) 92 *Virginia Law Review* 1391.
Robertson, A and Goudkamp, J (eds), *Form and Substance in the Law of Obligations* (Hart, 2019).
Da Rocha, CJ, Pepino, FFM and Martins, RL (eds), *Legal responses to COVID-19 around the world* (OABESA Goiás /LexMagister, 2020).
Rorty, R, 'The Banality of Pragmatism and the Poetry of Justice' (1990) 63 *Southern California Law Review* 1810.
Rosa, H, *Social Acceleration: A New Theory of Modernity* (Columbia University Press, 2013).
—— *Unverfügbarkeit* (Residenz Verlag, 2018).
Ross, A, *Om ret og retfærdighed*, 2nd edn (Nyt Nordisk Forlag Arnold Busck, 1966).
Rott, P, 'Minimum harmonization for the completion of the internal market? The example of consumer sales law' (2003) 40 *Common Market Law Review* 1107.
Rubin, EL, 'From Coherence to Effectiveness: A Legal Methodology for a Modern World' in R van Gestel, H-W Micklitz and EL Rubin (eds), *Rethinking Legal Scholarship: A Transatlantic Dialogue* (CUP, 2017) 310–50.
Rühl, G, 'Behavioural analysis and comparative law: improving the empirical foundation for comparative legal research' in H-W Micklitz, A-L Sibony and F Esposito (eds), *Research Methods in Consumer Law* (Edward Elgar, 2018) 477–512.
Rühmkorf, A, *Corporate social responsibility, private law and global supply chains* (Edward Elgar, 2015).
Rutgers, J, 'The Right to Housing (Article 7 of the Charter) and Unfair Terms in General Conditions' in H Collins (ed), *European Contract Law and the Charter of Fundamental Rights* (Intersentia, 2017) 125–37.
Sabel, CF and Zeitlin, J (eds), *Experimentalist Governance in the European Union* (OUP, 2010).
Safjan, M and Düsterhaus, D, 'A Union of Effective Judicial Protection: Addressing a Multi-level Challenge through the Lens of Art 47 CFREU' (2014) 33 *Yearbook of European Law* 3.
Salminen, J, *From National Product Liability to Transnational Production Liability* (Turun yliopisto, 2017).
—— 'Tuotantovastuun käsite, metodit ja merkitys' (2018) 116 *Lakimies* 581.
Samuelsson, J, 'DCFR som svensk rättskälla?' in *De lege, Juridiska Fakulteten i Uppsala, Årsbok 2015* (Iustus Förlag, 2016) 197–227.
Sandgren, C, 'Vad gör juristen? Och hur? – del 1' (1999–2000) 10 *Juridisk Tidskrift* 591.
Sandvik, B, 'Miljöskadestånd – några utvecklingslinjer i miljöskaderätten' (1996–97) 8 *Juridisk Tidskrift* 394.
Sartor, G, 'Legislative Information and the Web' in G Sartor, M Palmirani, E Francesconi and M Angela Biasiotti (eds), *Legislative XML for the Semantic Web* (Springer, 2011) 11–20.
Scalia, A, 'Keynote Address: Foreign Legal Authority in the Federal Courts' (2004) 98 *Proceedings of the American Society of International Law Annual Meeting* 305.
Schäfer, B and Bankowski, Z, 'Mistaken Identities: The Integrative Force of Private Law' in M van Hoecke and F Ost (eds), *The Harmonisation of European Private Law* (Hart, 2000) 21–45.
—— 'Emerging Legal Orders. Formalism and the Theory of Legal Integration' (2003) 16 *Ratio Juris* 486.
Schiek, D, 'Contract Law, Discrimination and European Integration' in T Wilhelmsson and S Hurri (eds), *From Dissonance to Sense: Welfare State Expectations, Privatisation and Private Law* (Ashgate, 1999) 405–33.

—— *Differenzierte Gerechtigkeit* (Nomos, 2000).

—— 'Comparative law and European harmonisation – a match made in heaven or uneasy bedfellows?' in M Andenas and C Baasch Andersen (eds), *Theory and Practice of Harmonisation* (Edward Elgar, 2011) 425–49.

Schirmer, J-E, 'Nachhaltigkeit in den Privatrechten Europas' (2021) 29 *Zeitschrift für Europäisches Privatrecht* 35.

Schmid, CU, 'The Instrumentalist Conception of the *Acquis Communautaire* in Consumer Law and its Implications on a European Contract Code' in S Grundmann and M Schauer (eds), *The Architecture of European Codes and Contract Law* (Kluwer Law International, 2006) 255–69.

Schmidt-Kessel, M, 'Europäisches Vertragsrecht' in K Riesenhuber (ed), *Europäische Methodenlehre* (De Gruyter Recht, 2006) 309–29.

Schneider, UH, 'Europäische und internationale Harmonisierung des Bankvertragsrechts' (1991) 44 *Neue Juristische Wochenschrift* 1985.

Schulte-Nölke, H, 'From the *Acquis Communautaire* to the Common Frame of Reference – the Contribution of the Acquis Group to the DCFR' (2008) 14 *Juridica International* 27.

Schulze, R, 'Neues deutsches Schuldrecht und europäisches Vertragsrecht' in O Sandrock, B Grossfeld, C Luttermann, R Schulze and I Saenger (eds), *Rechtsvergleichung als zukunftsträchtige Aufgabe* (LIT Verlag, 2004) 77–101.

—— 'The New Challenges in Contract Law' in R Schulze (ed), *New Features in Contract Law* (Sellier, 2007) 3–21.

Schulze, R and Schulte-Nölke, H (eds), *Die Schuldrechtsreform vor dem Hintergrund des Gemeinschaftsrechts* (Mohr Siebeck, 2001).

Schulze, R and Wilhelmsson, T, 'From the Draft Common Frame of Reference towards European Contract Law Rules' (2008) 4 *European Review of Contract Law* 154.

Schulze, R and Zoll, F (eds), *The Law of Obligations in Europe: A New Wave of Codifications* (Sellier, 2013).

—— *European Contract Law*, 3rd edn (Nomos, 2021).

Schwab, K, *The fourth industrial revolution* (Crown Business, 2017).

Schweitzer, H, 'Digitale Plattformen als private Gesetzgeber: Ein Perspektivwechsel für die europäische "Plattform-Regulierung"' (2019) 27 *Zeitschrift für Europäisches Privatrecht* 1.

Seeliger, M and Sevignani, S (eds), *Ein neuer Strukturwandel der Öffentlichkeit?* Leviathan Sonderband 37/2021 (Nomos, 2021).

Sefton-Green, R, 'Social Justice and European Identity in European Contract Law' (2006) 2 *European Review of Contract Law* 275.

—— 'Sense and Sensibilities: The DCFR and the Preservation of Cultural and Linguistic Plurality' (2008) 4 *European Review of Contract Law* 281.

—— 'The DCFR: A Technical or Political Toolbox?' in A Somma (ed), *The Politics of the Draft Common Frame of Reference* (Wolters Kluwer, 2009) 39–50.

—— 'How far can we go when using the English language for private law in the EU?' (2012) 8 *European Review of Contract Law* 30.

Sein, K and Spindler, G, 'The New Directive on Contracts for Supply of Digital Content and Digital Services – Conformity Criteria, Remedies and Modifications – Part 2' (2019) 15 *European Review of Contract Law* 365.

Semmelmann, C, 'Legal Principles in EU Law as an Expression of a European Legal Culture between Unity and Diversity' in G Helleringer and K Purnhagen (eds), *Towards a European Legal Culture* (Nomos, 2014) 303–27.

Shapiro, M, 'The Frontiers of Science Doctrine: American Experiences with the Judicial Control of Science-Based Decision-Making' in C Joerges, K-H Ladeur and E Vos (eds), *Integrating Scientific Expertise into Regulatory Decision-Making* (Nomos, 1997) 325–42.

Sibony, A-L, 'Data and arguments: empirical research in consumer law' in H-W Micklitz, A-L Sibony and F Esposito (eds), *Research Methods in Consumer Law* (Edward Elgar, 2018) 165–215.

Sieburgh, C, 'A Method to Substantively Guide the Involvement of EU Law in Private Law Matters' (2013) 21 *European Review of Private Law* 1165.

Siisiäinen, M, 'Uusien ja vanhojen liikkeiden keinovalikoimat' in K Ilmonen and M Siisiäinen (eds), *Uudet ja vanhat liikkeet* (Vastapaino, 1998) 219–43.

Siliquini-Cinelli, L and Hutchison, A (eds), *More Constitutional Dimensions of Contract Law* (Springer International, 2019).
Simon, T, '"Grundrechtstotalitarismus" oder "Selbstbehauptung des Zivilrechts"?' (2004) 204 *Archiv für die civilistische Praxis* 264.
Sirena, P, 'Die Rolle wissenschaftlicher Entwürfe im europäischen Privatrecht' (2018) 26 *Zeitschrift für Europäisches Privatrecht* 838.
Sisula-Tulokas, L, 'Konventionstolkning och EU-domstolen' (2019–2020) *31 Juridisk Tidskrift* 49.
Skinner, Q, 'Meaning and Understanding in the History of Ideas' (1969) 8 *History and Theory* 3.
Slaughter, A-M, 'A Global Community of Courts' (2003) 44 *Harvard International Law Journal* 191.
Smits, J, *The Making of European Private Law: Toward a Ius Commune Europaeum as a Mixed Legal System* (Intersentia, 2002).
—— 'The Europeanisation of National Legal Systems: Some Consequences for Legal Thinking in Civil Law Countries' in M van Hoecke (ed), *Epistemology and Methodology of Comparative Law* (Hart, 2004) 229–45.
—— (ed), *The Need for a European Contract Law* (Europa Law Publishing, 2005).
—— 'European Private Law: A Plea for a Spontaneous Legal Order' in DM Curtin, JM Smits, A Klip and JA McCahery (eds), *European Integration and Law* (Intersentia, 2006) 55–107.
—— 'Democracy and (European) private law: a functional approach' in M Faure and A van der Walt (eds), *Globalization and Private Law* (Edward Elgar, 2010) 15–31.
—— 'Plurality of Sources in European Private Law, or: How to Live With Legal Diversity?' in R Brownsword, H-W Micklitz, L Niglia and S Weatherill (eds), *The Foundations of European Private Law* (Hart, 2011) 323–35.
—— 'Coherence and Fragmentation in the Law of Contract' in P Letto-Vanamo and J Smits (eds), *Coherence and Fragmentation in European Private Law* (Sellier, 2012) 9–23.
—— *The Mind and Method of the Legal Academic* (Edward Elgar, 2012) (2012a).
—— 'Comparative Law and its Influence on National Legal Systems' in M Reimann and R Zimmermann (eds), *The Oxford Handbook of Comparative Law*, 2nd edn (OUP, 2019) 502–23.
Smits, J and Letto-Vanamo, P, 'Introduction' in P Letto-Vanamo and J Smits (eds), *Coherence and Fragmentation in European Private Law* (Sellier, 2012) 1–8.
Snyder, S, *The Simple, the Complicated and the Complex: Educational Reform Through the Lens of Complexity Theory*, OECD Education Working Papers No 96 (OECD Publishing, 2013).
Solinas, M, *Legal Evolution and Hybridisation: The Law of Shares Transfer in England* (Intersentia, 2014).
Somers, S, *The European Convention on Human Rights as an Instrument of Tort Law* (Intersentia, 2018).
Soriano, LM, 'A Modest Notion of Coherence in Legal Reasoning. A Model for the European Court of Justice' (2003) 16 *Ratio Juris* 296.
de Sousa Santos, B, 'Three Metaphors for a New Conception of Law: The Frontier, the Baroque, and the South' (1995) 29 *Law & Society Review* 569.
de Sousa Santos, B and Rodrígues-Garavito, CA (eds), *Law and Globalization from Below: Towards a Cosmopolitan Legality* (CUP, 2005).
Spier, J, 'The rule of law and judicial activism: obstacles for shaping the law to meet the demands of a civilized society, particularly in relation to climate change?' in M Faure and A van der Walt (eds), *Globalization and Private Law* (Edward Elgar, 2010) 426–54.
Ståhlberg, P and Karhu, J, *Finsk skadeståndsrätt* (Talentum, 2014).
Stang, F, *Erstatningsansvar* (Aschehoug, 1919).
Stapleton, J, 'Private Law and Institutional Competition' (1999) 9 *Otago Law Review* 519.
Steele, J, 'Damage, Uncertainty, and Risk: Trends in Environmental Liability' in T Wilhelmsson and S Hurri (eds), *From Dissonance to Sense: Welfare State Expectations, Privatisation and Private Law* (Ashgate, 1999) 479–502.
—— *Risks and Legal Theory* (Hart, 2004).
—— 'Risk Revolutions in Private Law' in S Worthington, A Robertson and G Virgo (eds), *Revolution and Evolution in Private Law* (Hart, 2018) 75–97.
Stein, E and Castermans, AG, 'Urgenda v. the State of the Netherlands: The "Reflex Effect" – Climate Change, Human Rights, and the Expanding Definitions of the Duty of Care' (2017) 13 *McGill Journal of Sustainable Development Law* 303.

Lord Steyn, 'The XVIIth Congress of the International Academy of Comparative Law – The Challenge of Comparative Law' (2006) 14 *European Review of Private Law* 635.
Streeck, Wolfgang, 'How will capitalism end?' (2014) 87 *New Left Review* 35.
Stridbeck, U, *Från kontrakt till social rättighet: En analys av förhållandet mellan eldistributör och abonnent* (Lund University Press, 1992).
Study Group on Social Justice in European Private Law, 'Social Justice in European Contract Law: A Manifesto' (2004) 10 *European Law Journal* 653.
Stutterheim, RH, 'Consumer Law in the Year 1992 in Europe and the Netherlands: Law for the Consumer or Law for the Market?' in T Wilhelmsson (ed), *Perspectives of Critical Contract Law* (Dartmouth, 1993) 349–59.
Sunstein, CR, *Risk and Reason: Safety, Law and the Environment* (CUP, 2002).
Svendsen, GLH and Svendsen, GT, 'The Puzzle of the Scandinavian Welfare State and Social Trust' (2015) 3 *Issues in Social Science* 90.
Svetiev, Y, 'The EU's Private Law in the Regulated Sectors: Competitive Market Handmaiden or Institutional Platform?' (2016) 22 *European Law Journal* 659.
—— *Experimentalist Competition Law and the Regulation of Markets* (Hart, 2020).
Taekema, S, 'Beyond Common Sense: Philosophical Pragmatism's Relevance to Law' (2006) 29 *Retfærd* 4/115, 22.
—— 'Private Law as an Open Legal Order: Understanding Contract and Tort as Interactional Law' (2014) 43 *Netherlands Journal of Legal Philosophy* 140.
—— 'The Many Uses of Law: Interactional Law as a Bridge between Instrumentalism and Law's Values' in N Roughan and A Halpin (eds), *In Pursuit of Pluralist Jurisprudence* (CUP, 2017) 116–35.
Tagiuri, G, 'How EU law politicises markets and creates spaces for progressive coding' (2022) 1 *European Law Open* 390.
Taupitz, J, *Europäische Privatrechtsvereinheitlichung heute und morgen* (JCB Mohr, 1993).
Teubner, G, 'Legal Irritants: Good Faith in British Law or How Unifying Law Ends Up in New Divergences' (1998) 61 *Modern Law Review* 11.
Thompson, JB, 'Tradition and Self in a Mediated World' in P Heelas, S Lash and P Morris (eds), *Detraditionalization* (Blackwell Publishers, 1996) 89–108.
Tilmann, W, 'Das gewerbliche Rechtsschutz vor den Konturen eines europäischen Privatrechts' (1993) 42 *Gewerblicher Rechtsschutz und Urheberrecht, Internationaler Teil* 275.
Timmermans, C, 'Looking behind the scenes of judicial cooperation in preliminary procedures' in F Cafaggi and S Law (eds), *Judicial Cooperation in European Private Law* (Edward Elgar, 2017) 33–50.
Tjon Soei Len, LKL, 'Consumer protection, sexual services and vulnerability: Exploring social justice in European Contract Law' (2015) 11 *European Review of Contract Law* 127.
—— *Minimum Contract Justice* (Hart, 2017).
Tjong Tjin Tai, E and Teuben, K, 'European Precedent Law' (2008) 16 *European Review of Private Law* 827.
Tonner, K, 'Reiserecht und Umweltschultz' (1992) *Verbraucher und Recht* 13.
Tontti, J, 'European legal pluralism as a rebirth of IUS commune' (2001) *Retfærd* nr 94, 40.
Torpman, J and Jörgensen, F, 'Theoretical Developments on Legal Transplants' (2005) 91 *Archiv für Rechts- und Sozialphilosophie* 515.
La Torre, M, 'Legitimacy for a Supranational European Political Order – Derivative, Regulatory or Deliberative?' (2002) 15 *Ratio Juris* 63.
Trías, ER, 'The Modernisation of the Law of Obligations Using the Principles of European Contract Law' in F de Elizalde (ed), *Uniform Rules for European Contract Law?* (Hart, 2018) 83–90.
Tridimas, T, 'The ECJ and the National Courts: Dialogue, Cooperation, and Instability' in A Arnull and D Chalmers (eds), *The Oxford Handbook on European Union Law* (OUP, 2015) 403–30.
Tripkovic, B, 'Judicial Comparativism and Legal Positivism' (2014) 5 *Transnational Legal Theory* 285.
Tuori, K, 'Post-Modern Law?' in T Wilhelmsson and S Hurri (eds), *From Dissonance to Sense: Welfare State Expectations, Privatisation and Private Law* (Ashgate, 1999) 39–49.
—— *Critical Legal Positivism* (Ashgate, 2002).
—— 'Oikeudenalajaotus – strategista valtapeliä ja normatiivista argumentaatiota' (2004) 102 *Lakimies* 1196.
—— *Ratio and Voluntas: The Tension Between Reason and Will in Law* (Ashgate, 2011).

—— 'European Social Constitution: Between Solidarity and Access Justice' in K Purnhagen and P Rott (eds), *Varieties of European Economic Law and Regulation* (Springer, 2014) 371–400.

—— 'From pluralism to perspectivism' in G Davies and M Avbelj (eds), *Research Handbook on Legal Pluralism and EU Law* (Edward Elgar, 2018) 39–56.

—— *Properties of Law: Modern Law and After* (CUP, 2021).

Twigg-Flesner, C, 'The Potential of the COVID-19 Crisis to Cause Legal "Disruption" to Contracts and Contract Law' in E Hondius, M Santos Silva, A Nicolussi, P Salvador Coderch, C Wendehorst and F Zoll (eds), *Coronavirus and the Law in Europe* (Intersentia, 2021) 1091.

—— 'Who Knows what the Future Holds? The Fate of the EU's Acquis in English Contract Law' (2022/21) *Nederlands Tijdschrift voor Burgerlijk Recht* 160.

Twining, W, *Globalisation and Legal Theory* (CUP, 2000).

Uimonen, R, *Julkisuuspeli* (WSOY, 1992).

Unberath, H, 'Comparative Law in the German Courts' in G Canivet, M Andenas and D Fairgrieve (eds), *Comparative Law before the Courts* (BIICL, 2004) 307–16.

Unger, RM, 'The Critical Legal Studies Movement' (1983) 96 *Harvard Law Review* 561.

—— 'Legal Analysis as Institutional Imagination' (1996) 59 *Modern Law Review* 1.

Ussing, H, *Skyld og skade* (GEC Gad, 1914).

Vallejo, R, 'The Private Administrative Law of Technical Standardization' (2021) 40 *Yearbook of European Law* 172.

Varul, P, 'The Creation of New Estonian Private Law' (2008) 16 *European Review of Private Law* 95.

—— 'The Impact of Harmonisation of Private Law on the Reform of Civil Law in the New Member States' in R Brownsword, H-W Micklitz, L Niglia and S Weatherill (eds), *The Foundations of European Private Law* (Hart, 2011) 285–92.

Väyrynen, R, *Globalisaatiokritiikki ja kansalaisliikkeet* (Gaudeamus, 2001).

Vendrell Cervantes, C, 'The Application of the Principles of European Contract Law by Spanish Courts' (2008) 16 *Zeitschrift für Europäisches Privatrecht* 534.

Venice Commission, European Commission for Democracy through Law (Venice Commission), *Rule of Law Checklist* (Council of Europe, 2016).

Verbruggen, P, 'New Liabilities in Global Value Chains: An Introduction' (2022) 13 *European Journal of Risk Regulation* 541.

de Vilchez Moragues, P, *Climate in Court: Defining State Obligations on Global Warming Through Domestic Climate Litigation* (Edward Elgar, 2022).

Violini, L and Baraggia, A (eds), *The Fragmented Landscape of Fundamental Rights Protection in Europe* (Edward Elgar, 2018).

Vogenauer, S, 'Eine gemeineuropäische Methodenlehre des Rechts – Plädoyer und Programm' (2005) 13 *Zeitschrift für Europäisches Privatrecht* 234.

Vos, E, 'The European Court of Justice in the face of scientific uncertainty and complexity' in M Dawson, B de Witte and E Muir (eds), *Judicial Activism at the European Court of Justice* (Edward Elgar, 2013) 142–66.

Wadenström, R, *Stora och små europeiska historier: En avhandling om vårt postmoderna Europa* (Helsingin yliopiston filosofian laitoksen julkaisuja 3, 1998).

Wagner, G, 'Für einen Wettbewerb der Ideen im Europäischen Privatrecht!' (2003) 11 *Zeitschrift für Europäisches Privatrecht* 930.

—— Corona Law (2020) 28 *Zeitschrift für Europäisches Privatrecht* 531.

Waldron, J, 'Foreign Law and the Modern *Ius Gentium*' (2005) 119 *Harvard Law Review* 129.

Walker, N, *Intimations of Global Law* (CUP, 2015).

—— 'The Jurist in a Global Age' in R van Gestel, H-W Micklitz and EL Rubin (eds), *Rethinking Legal Scholarship: A Transatlantic Dialogue* (CUP, 2017) 84–111.

—— 'Law Unbounded?' in M Dahlberg (ed), *De lege: Law and Society, Contributions by the Honorary Doctors* (Iustus förlag, 2019) 359–72.

Ward, I, *A Critical Introduction to European Law* (Butterworths, 1996).

—— 'Europe in Search of "Meaning and Purpose"' in K Nuotio (ed), *Europe in Search of 'Meaning and Purpose'* (University of Helsinki, 2004) 1–19.

Watson, A, *Legal Transplants*, 2nd edn (University of Georgia Press, 1993).

—— 'Legal Transplants and European Private Law' Ius Commune Lectures on European Private Law 2 (Maastricht Institute for Transnational Legal Research, 2000).

Weatherill, S, 'Reflections on the EC's Competence to Develop a 'European Contract Law' (2005) 13 *European Review of Private Law* 405.
—— 'The "principles of civil law" as a basis for interpreting the legislative *acquis*' (2010) 6 *European Review of Contract Law* 74.
—— 'The Multi-level Structure of Private Law: Editorial Introduction' in R Brownsword, H-W Micklitz, L Niglia and S Weatherill (eds), *The Foundations of European Private Law* (Hart, 2011) 319–22.
—— 'Use and Abuse of the EU's Charter of Fundamental Rights: on the improper veneration of 'freedom of contract' (2014) 10 *European Review of Contract Law* 167.
—— *EU Consumer Law and Policy*, 2nd edn (Edward Elgar, 2013).
—— 'Is maximum harmonisation a myth? The story of Directive 2019/771 on contracts for the sale of goods' (2021) *European Journal of Consumer Law* 217.
Weiler, JHH, 'The European Circumstance and the Politics of Meaning: Not on Bread Alone Doth Man Liveth (Deut. 8:3; Mat 4:4)' (2020) 21 *German Law Journal* 96.
Weimer, M and de Ruijter, A (eds), *Regulating Risks in the European Union* (Hart, 2017).
Weinrib, EJ, *The Idea of Private Law* (OUP, 2012) (first published 1995).
Weller, M-P and Tran, M-L, 'Klimawandelklagen im Rechtsvergleich – *private enforcement* als weltweiter Trend?' (2021) 29 *Zeitschrift für Europäisches Privatrecht* 573.
Werro, F and Palmer, VV (eds), *The Boundaries of Strict Liability in European Tort Law* (Stämpfli, 2004).
Wetendorff Nørgaard, R, Nedergaard, P and Blom-Hansen, J, 'Lobbying in the EU Comitology System' (2014) 36 *Journal of European Integration* 491.
Wetterstein, P, 'A Proprietary or Possessory Interest: A Conditio Sine Qua Non for Claiming Damages for Environmental Impairment?' in P Wetterstein (ed), *Harm to the Environment* (Clarendon Press, 1997) 29–54.
Wexler, S, 'Practicing Law for Poor People' (1970) 79 *Yale Law Journal* 1049.
White, LE, 'Mobilization on the margins of the lawsuit: making space for clients to speak' (1987) 16 *New York University Review of Law & Social Change* 535.
Whitford, WC, 'The Function of Disclosure Regulation in Consumer Transactions' (1973) 68 *Wisconsin Law Review* 400.
Wieacker, F, *Industriegesellschaft und Privatrechtsordnung* (Athenäum Fischer Taschenbuch Verlag, 1974).
Wielsch, D, 'The Function of Fundamental Rights in EU Private Law – Perspectives for the Common European Sales Law' (2014) 10 *European Review of Contract Law* 365.
Wightman, J, 'Private Law and Public Interests' in T Wilhelmsson and S Hurri (eds), *From Dissonance to Sense: Welfare State Expectations, Privatisation and Private Law* (Ashgate, 1999) 253–76.
Wilhelmsson, T: *Critical Studies in Private Law: A Treatise on Need-Rational Principles in Modern Law* (Kluwer, 1992).
—— (ed), *Perspectives of Critical Contract Law* (Dartmouth, 1993).
—— *Social Contract Law and European Integration* (Dartmouth, 1995).
—— 'Jack-in-the-box theory of European Community law' in L Krämer, H-W Micklitz and K Tonner (eds), *Law and diffuse Interests in the European Legal Order* (Nomos, 1997) 177–94.
—— 'Consumer Law and the Environment: From Consumer to Citizen' (1998) 21 *Journal of Consumer Policy* 45.
—— *Senmodern ansvarsrätt: Privaträtt som redskap för mikropolitik* (Kauppakaari, 2001).
—— 'Europeiseringen av privaträtten: för ett fragmenterat utbyte av erfarenheter' (2001) 114 *Tidskrift for Rettsvitenskap* 1 (2001a).
—— 'Private Law in the EU: Harmonised or Fragmented Europeanisation?' (2002) 10 *European Review of Private Law* 77.
—— 'The Legal, the Cultural and the Political – Conclusions from Different Perspectives on Harmonisation of European Contract Law' (2002) 13 *European Business Law Review* 541 (2002a).
—— 'The Design of an Optional (Re)statement of European Contract Law – Real Life Instead of Dead Concepts' in S Grundmann and J Stuyck (eds), *An Academic Green Paper on European Contract Law* (Kluwer Law International, 2002) 353–72 (2002b).
—— 'Varieties of welfarism in European contract law' (2004) 10 *European Law Journal* 712.
—— 'Contract Law Enforcement of Provisions on Marketing: The Solution of the Consumer Sales Directive' in H Collins (ed), *The Forthcoming EC Directive on Unfair and Commercial Practices* (Kluwer Law International, 2004) 223–39 (2004a).

—— 'The Ethical Pluralism of Late Modern Europe and Codification of European Contract Law' in J Smits (ed), *The Need for a European Contract Law* (Europa Law Publishing, 2005) 121–52.
—— 'The Paradox of the Risk Society and the Fragmentation of Consumer Law' in I Ramsay, J Salloum, N Horrox and G Mowatt (eds), *Risk and Choice in Consumer Society* (Ant.N.Sakkoulas & Bruylant, 2007) 1–21.
—— 'The Contract Law *Acquis*: Towards More Coherence Through Generalisation?' in *4. Europäischer Juristentag, Sammelband* (MANZsche Verlags- und Universitätsbuchhandlung, 2008) 111–53.
—— 'Free Movement of Legal Sources: The Use of Foreign Sources in Private Law in Europe' in K Purnhagen and P Rott (eds), *Varieties of European Economic Law and Regulation* (Springer, 2014) 185–204.
—— 'Strict Liability for Dangerous Activities in Nordic Tort Law – an Adequate Answer to Late Modern Uncertainty?' (2019) 16 *Otago Law Review* 219.
—— 'The Emergence of Nordic Consumer Law and a Nordic Consumer Law Community and Its Impact on Nordic Legal Unity' in H-W Micklitz (ed), *The Making of Consumer Law and Policy in Europe* (Hart, 2021) 171–91.
Wilhelmsson, T and Hurri, S (eds), *From Dissonance to Sense: Welfare State Expectations, Privatisation and Private Law* (Ashgate, 1999).
Willett, C, 'Re-Theorising Consumer Law' (2018) 77 *Cambridge Law Journal* 179.
Williams, B, 'What Has Philosophy to Learn From Tort Law?' in DG Owen (ed), *Philosophical Foundations of Tort Law* (Clarendon Press, 1995) 487–97.
De Witte, B, Ott, A and Vos, E (eds), *Between Flexibility and Disintegration: The Trajectory of Differentiation in EU Law* (Edward Elgar, 2017).
Worthington, S, 'Revolution and Evolution in Private Law' in S Worthington, A Robertson and G Virgo (eds), *Revolution and Evolution in Private Law* (Hart, 2018) 3–9.
Worthington, S, Robertson, A and Virgo, G (eds), *Revolution and Evolution in Private Law* (Hart, 2018).
Wright, J, *Tort law and human rights* (Hart, 2001).
Yablon, CM, 'The Indeterminacy of the Law: Critical Legal Studies and the Problem of Legal Explanation' (1985) 6 *Cardozo Law Review* 917.
Zahle, H, 'The Polycentricity of the Law or the Importance of Legal Pluralism for Legal Dogmatics' in H Petersen and H Zahle (eds), *Legal Polycentricity* (Dartmouth, 1995) 185–99.
Zimmermann, R, 'Consumer Contract Law and General Contract Law: The German Experience' (2005) 58 *Current Legal Problems* 415.
Zumbansen, P and Saam, D, 'The ECJ, Volkswagen and European Corporate Law: Reshaping the European Varieties of Capitalism' (2007) 8 *German Law Journal* 1027.
Zweigert, K and Kötz, H, *Introduction to Comparative Law*, 3rd edn (Clarendon Press, 1998).

Index

www.ingramcontent.com/pod-product-compliance
Ingram Content Group UK Ltd.
Pitfield, Milton Keynes, MK11 3LW, UK
UKHW020845290926
15470UKWH00004B/1558

9 781509 977253